S0-BCS-140

The Idea Magazine For Teachers®

PRIMARY

2001–2002

YEARBOOK

Diane Badden, Managing Editor, *The Mailbox*® Magazine
Deborah G. Swider, Managing Editor, *The Mailbox*® Yearbook

The Education Center, Inc.
Greensboro, North Carolina

The Mailbox® 2001–2002 Primary Yearbook

Founding Editor in Chief: Margaret Michel
Managing Editor: Diane Badden
Assistant Managing Editor: Amy Erickson
Executive Director, Magazine Publishing: Katharine P. S. Brower
Editorial and Freelance Management: Karen A. Brudnak
Curriculum Director: Karen P. Shelton
Editorial Training: Irving P. Crump
Contributing Editors: Denine T. Carter, Kelli L. Gowdy
Copy Editors: Sylvan Allen, Karen Brewer Grossman, Karen L. Huffman, Amy Kirtley-Hill, Debbie Shoffner
Traffic Manager: Lisa K. Pitts
Staff Artists: Pam Crane, Nick Greenwood, Clevell Harris, Rebecca Saunders (SENIOR ARTISTS); Theresa Lewis Goode, Sheila Krill, Ivy L. Koonce, Clint Moore, Greg D. Rieves, Barry Slate, Stuart Smith, Donna K. Teal
Cover Artist: Lois Axeman
Typesetters: Lynette Dickerson, Mark Rainey
Editorial Assistants: Terrie Head, Hope Rodgers, Jan E. Witcher
Librarian: Dorothy C. McKinney

ISBN 1-56234-504-4
ISSN 1088-5544

Copyright ©2002 by The Education Center, Inc.

All rights reserved except as here noted. No part of this publication may be reproduced or transmitted by any means, electronic or mechanical, without written permission from the publisher. Please direct written inquiries to the address below. Permission is granted to the original purchaser to reproduce pages for individual classroom use only and not for resale or distribution. Reproduction for an entire school or school system is prohibited.

The Education Center®, *The Mailbox*®, *Teacher's Helper*®, *The Mailbox*® BOOKBAG®, *Learning*®, The Idea Magazine for Teachers®, and the mailbox/post/grass logo are registered trademarks of The Education Center, Inc. All brand or product names are trademarks or registered trademarks of their respective companies.

Printed in the United States of America.

The Education Center, Inc.
P.O. Box 9753
Greensboro, NC 27429-0753

Look for *The Mailbox*® 2002–2003 Primary Yearbook in the summer of 2003. The Education Center, Inc., is the publisher of *The Mailbox*®, *Teacher's Helper*®, *The Mailbox*® BOOKBAG®, and *Learning*® magazines, as well as other fine products. Look for these wherever quality teacher materials are sold, or call 1-800-714-7991.

Contents

Departments

Features

Language Arts Units

Literature Units

Math Units

Arts & Crafts

Arts & Crafts

"Thumb" Apples!

These apple trees are truly "thumb-thing" special! To begin, tear a tree trunk shape from brown paper and glue it on a 9" x 12" sheet of white construction paper. Use green tempera paint and a sponge to paint the tree's foliage. When the green paint is dry, pour a mixture of liquid soap and red tempera paint into a shallow pan. Use the paint to make a desired number of red thumbprint apples on and near the tree. Allow drying time. Then use crayons or markers to add colorful details and a background scene that would make Johnny Appleseed proud!

adapted from an idea by
Jane Manuel
Wellington, TX

Venus Flytrap

Incorporate this snappy project into a plant unit. Or use it in conjunction with *Judy Moody,* a delightful chapter book by Megan McDonald.

Materials for one project:
two 4" circles of green construction paper
two 4" circles of red construction paper
3" x 12" piece of green construction paper
4" x 7" piece of construction paper (Colors may vary.)
9" x 12" sheet of construction paper (Colors may vary.)
1" square of black tissue paper

flat wooden toothpicks
small white coffee filter
glue
scissors
crayons
clear tape

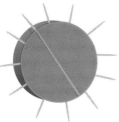

Steps:
1. Fold the four paper circles in half and then unfold each one.
2. Glue toothpicks around the edge of each green circle.
3. Glue a red circle atop each green circle, matching up the fold lines. Fold each resulting trap in half (keeping the red paper to the inside) and then set it aside to dry.
4. Trim the 4" x 7" paper to resemble a planter. Add desired decorations.
5. Cut one long stem and two shorter stems from the green paper.
6. Position the long stem between the shorter stems. Glue the stems and the planter on the 9" x 12" construction paper sheet.
7. Glue a trap to the top of each short stem. Wad up the black tissue paper square and glue it inside one trap.
8. Fold the coffee filter in half and then fold it in half again. Trim one inch from the open end. To form a flower, pinch the point and scrunch the sides of the filter. Tape the point to the top of the long stem. Gently open the blossom and glue the bottom edge of the bloom to the construction paper.

adapted from an idea by Stacy Confer
Jefferson Elementary, Emmaus, PA

Step 3

Open House Desk Topper

Extend a warm and "class-y" welcome to your open house guests! To make a desktop project, fold a 12-inch square of white construction paper in half diagonally and then fold the folded paper in half. Unfold the paper and position it so the fold lines form a *t*. Draw and color your school on the top half of the paper, making sure the school sits on the fold line. Next, cut the bottom half of the paper in half, using the fold line as a guide. Overlap the two pieces to form the bottom of the project. Use a pencil to lightly sketch a sidewalk leading away from the school. Then lay the project flat and color the sidewalk and desired landscaping. Reassemble the project and glue the overlapping pieces. On a 4" x 5" piece of white construction paper, illustrate yourself. Cut out the picture, leaving a tab (for gluing) at the bottom. Fold back the tab and glue it on the sidewalk. Welcome!

Jo Fryer—Gr. 1
Kildeer Countryside School
Long Grove, IL

Squirrel Sighting

In a nutshell, these bushy-tailed critters are simply too cute to pass up!

Materials for one project:
4" x 12" piece of gray construction paper
2" x 4" piece of gray construction paper
4" x 8" piece of gray construction paper
4" square of gray construction paper
construction paper scraps
4" leaf template
six 4" squares of construction paper in fall colors
glue
scissors
crayons

Steps:
1. **To make the body,** roll the 4" x 12" piece of gray paper into a cylinder and glue the overlapping edges together. Set aside to dry.
2. **For the head,** trim the four-inch square of gray paper into a desired shape and decorate. Keeping the seam at the back of the cylinder, glue the head to the front of the body.
3. **For the tail,** trim the 4" x 8" piece of gray paper into a desired shape. If desired, gently curl the tail before gluing it to the back of the body.
4. **For the feet,** fold in half the 2" x 4" piece of gray paper and cut out two matching feet. Add desired details and glue the feet to the body.
5. **For the bed of leaves,** trace the leaf template onto the remaining construction paper squares. Cut out. Arrange the leaves as desired and glue the overlapping surfaces. Glue the squirrel atop the leaves.

Rita Arnold—Gr. 1
Alden Hebron Grade School
Hebron, IL

Arts & Crafts

Fabulous Fall Foliage

Bring the fabulous foliage of fall indoors! Partially fill each of several shallow containers with a different fall color of tempera paint. Place a clean bottle brush in each container. To begin, tear a tree trunk shape from a 4" x 9" rectangle of brown paper and glue it on a 9" x 12" sheet of construction paper. Then use the paints and brushes to create colorful fall foliage. When the paint is dry, add crayon and marker details to complete the scene. Spectacular!

Catherine Della Torre—Gr. 1
Woodside School
River Vale, NJ

Frankenstein Look-Alikes

Students are sure to have a monstrously good time making and using these seasonal storage containers! *(Before you introduce the project, use a pointed instrument, such as an ice pick or the pointed end of a pair of scissors, to make two holes in each child's container for bolts.)*

Materials for one project:
18-oz. oatmeal container
    with lid
white tempera paint
green tempera paint
dishwashing liquid
paintbrush
2 hex head bolts with nuts
6" square of black felt
permanent black marker
construction paper scraps
scrap of silver gift wrap
    (or foil)
craft glue
scissors
rubber band

Step 3

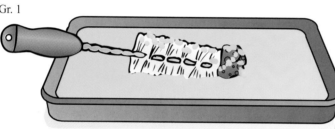

Steps:

1. **For the head,** mix white paint and green paint until a desired color is achieved. Add a squirt of dishwashing liquid (to keep dried paint from cracking). Then remove the container lid and paint the outside of the container. Set aside to dry.

2. **To attach the bolts,** poke a bolt through each teacher-made hole. Then reach inside the container and thread a nut onto each bolt, securing it in place.

3. **For the hair,** use the marker to trace the outline of the lid in the center of the felt. Draw a wavy hairline about ³⁄₄-inch outside the circle's perimeter. Cut the felt along the wavy outline. To attach the resulting hairpiece, snap the lid on the container. Spread craft glue on the felt inside the circle and run a trail of glue just outside the circle. Position the felt on the lid. Use the rubber band to hold the hair in place until the glue dries (see illustration).

4. **For the facial features,** cut two eyebrows from felt scraps, two eyes and a nose from construction paper, and a mouth from silver gift wrap. Use the marker to add details. Glue the cutouts in place.

5. **To use the container,** remove the lid and store sight-word cards or flash cards inside.

Cindi Zsittnik, Denia Phillips, and Sherry Shanks
Surrey School, Hagerstown, MD

Seasonal Suncatchers

Make your school windows the talk of the town! In October, adorn school windows with a glowing display of pumpkin personalities. When November arrives, replace the pumpkins with colorful cornucopias. Showcase a favorite decoration in December, and in January, roll out the snow pals!

Materials for one pumpkin suncatcher:
8" square blank paper
8" square clear Con-Tact® covering
masking tape
small tissue paper squares in desired colors

Steps:

1. On the blank paper, arrange tissue paper squares to create a desired pumpkin design.
2. Remove the backing from the Con-Tact covering. Keeping the sticky side up, lay the covering on your work surface and secure the corners with tape.
3. Transfer the tissue paper design to the clear covering. Then replace the backing and remove the tape.
4. To display the resulting suncatcher, remove the backing and adhere the project to the inside of a window.
5. To remove the project, simply peel it from the window. For transport home, either adhere the project to its original backing or mount it atop an eight-inch paper square.

Sarah Winther Shumaker—Gr. 1
Dover South Elementary School
Dover, OH

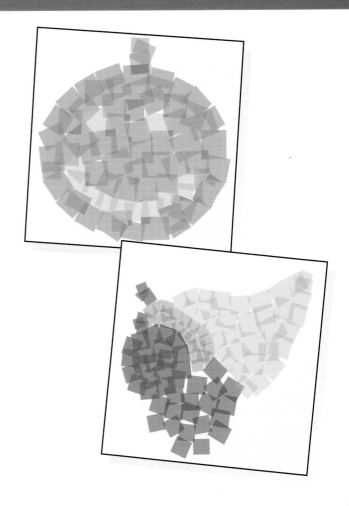

Stuffed Gobbler

This November, set aside time for each child to stuff and stitch a gobbler! To make a turkey-shaped template, enlarge the pattern from page 18 onto tagboard and cut out the resulting shape. To fashion a gobbler, trace the template two times on brown bulletin board paper. Cut out each shape. Align the cutouts and use a hole puncher to punch evenly spaced holes around the edges of the cutouts. Next, use yarn to lace through all but a few holes. Pack crumpled strips of newspaper or paper towels into the gobbler. When the bird is sufficiently stuffed, lace through the remaining holes and then tie and trim the yarn ends. Add construction paper details as desired. Now that's a stuffed bird!

Linda P. Lovelace—Gr. 1
Halifax, VA

9

Arts & Crafts

Festive Wreaths

Personalized wreaths make precious holiday gifts! To begin, glue a seven-inch circle of gold foil gift wrap in the center of a 14-inch cardboard pizza or cake round. Punch two holes side by side near the outer edge of the cardboard. Keeping the holes at the top of the circle, sketch a desired holiday design on the cardboard and program it for color. Fill in the design with tissue paper squares. To apply the tissue, wrap each square around the eraser end of a pencil, dip it in glue, and press it onto the cardboard. (This process takes several days.) Next, hot-glue a photo in the center of the foil. To ready the wreath for hanging, thread a length of colorful ribbon through the holes and securely tie the ribbon ends. Happy holidays!

Maureen Glennon—Gr. 1, Faller School, Ridgecrest, CA

Jolly Santa

Nestled among this Santa's whiskers is a hearty "ho ho ho!"

Materials for one project:

12" square of skin-toned paper
4" x 12" strip of red construction paper
1" x 12" strip of white construction paper
2¹/₂" x 8" strip of white construction paper
2" square of white paper
¹/₂" x 3" white construction paper strips for whiskers
construction paper scraps for eyes, nose, and mouth

scissors
glue
pencil

Steps:

1. **For the face,** cut a large heart shape from the skin-toned paper.
2. **For the hat,** trace the pointed end of the heart onto the red paper. Cut out the hat shape, align it atop the heart cutout, and glue. Glue the 1" x 12" strip of white paper to the bottom edge of the hat. Trim each end of the resulting hatband. Cut a hat ball from the two-inch white paper square. Glue it on the hat.
3. **For the facial features and mustache,** cut two eyes, a nose, and a mouth from the construction paper scraps. Fold the eight-inch strip of white paper in half to four inches. Draw half of a mustache shape on the paper as shown. Cut on the outline and unfold the cutout. Arrange the cutouts on the heart and glue in place.
4. **For the whiskers,** roll each of several ¹/₂" x 3" white paper strips around a pencil. Slide the rolled paper off the pencil and glue one end to Santa's face. Continue until a desired number of whiskers are in place.

Step 2

Step 3

Doris Hautala, Washington Elementary, Ely, MN

Nifty Nutcrackers

A lineup of these stately soldiers is a sight to see! Plan to drop a few wrapped candies and unshelled nuts inside each nutcracker before it's carried home for the holidays!

Materials for one project:
empty Pringles potato crisps can with lid
3" x 10" strip of blue construction paper
2" x 10" strip of black construction paper
1" x 10" strip of black construction paper
2" x 10" strip of skin-toned construction paper
2" x 10" strip of red construction paper
two 1" squares of skin-toned construction paper
two 1" x 2" pieces of red construction paper

2 wiggle eyes
1 pom-pom (for nose)
4 small buttons
construction paper scraps
sequins
black marker or crayon
scissors
craft glue

Steps:
1. Remove the lid from the can. Gather the ten-inch paper strips. Set the narrower black strip aside. Starting at the lower edge of the can, glue the remaining strips to the can in the following order: blue, red, skin-toned, black. Keep the seams aligned at what will become the back of the project.
2. Glue the narrow black strip around the lower edge of the can, atop the blue strip. Align the seam.
3. Cut a hand shape from each skin-toned paper square. Glue one hand to one end of each 1" x 2" piece of red construction paper. Glue the resulting arms to opposite sides of the container.
4. Add facial features, buttons, and other desired details. Snap on the lid and the nutcracker is ready to strut his stuff!

Denia Phillips, Sherry Shank and Cindi Zsittnik, Surrey School, Hagerstown, MD

Old-Fashioned Ornaments

These quaint ornaments, reminiscent of a simpler time, are sure to warm the hearts of your youngsters' loved ones! Cut a $\frac{1}{2}$" x $1\frac{1}{2}$" x 4' wooden board into two-inch blocks. (This yields 24 ornaments.) To make an ornament, use sandpaper to smooth away rough edges of one wooden block. Insert a small screw eye in the top of the block. *(Assist students with this step.)* Sketch a holiday shape on the front and back of the block. Use paint pens to color each sketch. Then thread a curled length of ribbon through the screw eye and securely tie the ribbon ends. The ornament is ready for display!

Sonya Franklin—Gr. 3
Springville Elementary School
Springville, AL

Arts & Crafts

Heartfelt Messages

There's a "tree-mendous" amount of love in this valentine greeting! Fold a 12" x 18" sheet of white construction paper in half. Next, cut a heart shape from each of 20 1½-inch squares of red, pink, or purple construction paper. Arrange the hearts on the front of the card in the shape of a tree. Glue the cutouts in place. Below the tree shape glue a brown paper trunk and a planter shape cut from paper. When the glue is dry, use crayons or markers to add foliage and a Valentine's Day greeting. Inside the card write a heartfelt message, add artwork, and sign your name. This handcrafted valentine greeting is sure to warm the heart of a loved one!

adapted from an idea by Mary Ann S. Jones
Clark Springs Elementary School
Richmond, VA

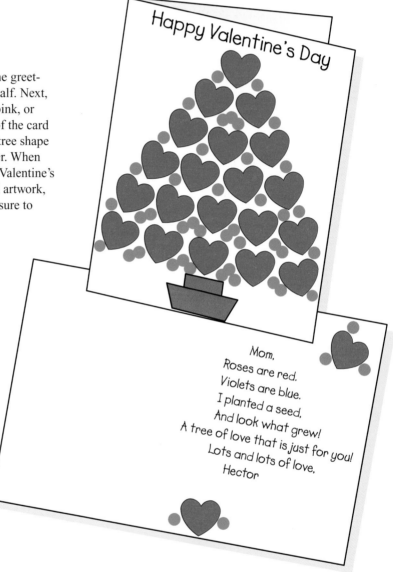

Happy Valentine's Day

Mom,
Roses are red.
Violets are blue.
I planted a seed.
And look what grew!
A tree of love that is just for you!
Lots and lots of love,
Hector

Abby

(pocket)

fold   9"

6"
diagonal cut

Holders With Heart

This striking yet simple-to-make valentine holder is hard to beat! To make the pocket, fold a 9" x 12" sheet of black construction paper in half (to 6" x 9"). Starting at the bottom corner, make a diagonal cut away from the fold to trim off the bottom two corners of the paper as shown. Unfold the pocket and align it atop the bottom half of a 12" x 18" sheet of black construction paper. Staple the two papers together along the sides and bottom of the pocket. Then trim away the bottom corners of the larger paper to match the pocket shape. Personalize a blank 3" x 5" card, glue the card on the pocket, and then decorate the holder to your heart's desire!

adapted from an idea by Debbie Lerner—Grs. 1–3
Red Bridge Elementary
Kansas City, MO

High-Flying Mosaics

Batten down the hatches! A gust of kite-making creativity is in the forecast! Trace a kite-shaped template on a 12" x 18" sheet of construction paper, and cut along the resulting outline. Draw lines on the cutout as shown. Next, glue one-inch construction paper squares atop the cutout to create a desired design. For best results, work outward from where the lines cross and carefully align the construction paper squares. When the glue dries, trim around the original kite shape. Next, hole-punch the bottom corner of the kite. Thread one end of a length of twine through the hole and securely fasten. Tie strips of colorful fabric or tissue paper to the kite string and the project is ready for display. Up, up, and away!

Jennifer Brahos
Mandan, ND

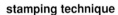

Green Pepper Prints

Your lads and lassies will smile upon this green pepper painting project! Plan to complete the project in two days.

On day one, cover a work surface with newspaper and pour a thin layer of green tempera paint into a shallow container. Cut away the top of a green pepper and then remove the insides from the pepper. Dip the cut end of the pepper into the paint and repeatedly press it onto white construction paper. Reload the pepper with paint as needed. Overlap the painted shapes as you cover the paper.

On day two, use green crayons in a variety of hues to color the unpainted areas of the paper. To display, mount the print on a slightly larger piece of colorful construction paper. Or trace a shamrock template on the back of the paper, cut along the resulting outline, and mount the cutout in a similar manner.

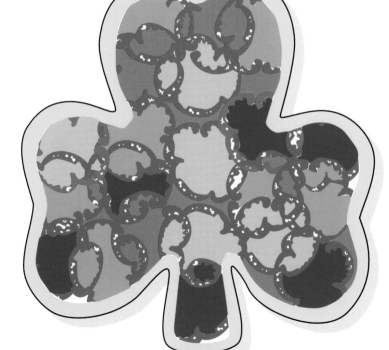

stamping technique

adapted from an idea by
Linda Masternak Justice
Kansas City, MO

13

Arts & Crafts

Soda-Bottle Blossoms

Paint a beautiful bouquet of springtime blossoms using the bottom of an individual-sized plastic soda bottle! To make a vase, fold a six-inch square of construction paper in half and trim as shown. Unfold the cutout and glue it near the lower edge of a vertically positioned 12" x 18" sheet of construction paper. Pour a thin layer of tempera paint into a shallow container. Dip the bottom of a plastic soda bottle into the paint and repeatedly press it onto the construction paper to make a desired number of blossoms. Reapply the paint on the bottle as needed. When the paint dries, use a circular sponge to paint the center of each blossom, or glue construction paper or pom-pom centers in place. Then use a green marker to draw stems. How nice!

Sonja Stoll
Summerfield Elementary School
Summerfield, KS

Quirky Quacker

Isn't this strange duck simply adorable? Sprout creativity (and grass!) with this grin-inducing project.

Materials for one project:

two 3 oz. paper cups
1" x 8" strip of construction paper
two 3" squares of construction paper
1" x 2" strip of yellow construction paper
2 small buttons (or wiggle eyes)
tempera paint

paintbrush
glue
scissors
grass seed
potting soil
water

Steps:

1. Turn over the paper cups and paint the sides and bottom of each one.
2. Use paint to add desired details to the 1" x 8" paper strip (arms) and the three-inch paper squares (feet).
3. When the paint is dry, glue the bottoms of the paper cups together, sandwiching the decorated paper strip between them.
4. Stack the decorated squares and trim, as shown, to make two triangular feet. Glue the top of each triangle inside the inverted cup.
5. Fold the yellow paper in half to a one-inch square. Trim as shown to make a bill. Glue the bill and button eyes to the top cup.
6. Fill the top cup with potting soil and plant grass seed in the soil. Lightly water the soil and keep the project in a sunny window until a tuft of green duck down sprouts! Now that's just ducky!

Step 4

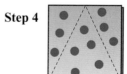

Step 5

Elizabeth Searls Almy
Greensboro, NC

Home, Tweet Home!

Even though these birdhouse windsocks are not ready for residents, they evoke plenty of fine-feathered thoughts!

Materials for one project:
6" x 18" strip of construction paper (for cylinder)
two 6" x 9" pieces of construction paper (for house)
four 1½" x 6" strips of construction paper (for house trim)
construction paper scraps
eight 16" strips of crepe paper
36" length of yarn
crayons or markers
hole puncher
scissors
glue

Steps:
1. Roll the 6" x 18" strip of paper into a cylinder and glue the overlapping edges together. Set aside to dry.
2. To make the house shapes, trim away the top two corners of each 6" x 9" piece of paper. Cut a scalloped border along one six-inch edge of each 1½" x 6" paper strip. Glue the resulting trim to the house cutouts as shown. Embellish the house shapes with desired decorations.
3. Glue one house shape atop the cylinder's seam and the other house shape directly opposite it, keeping the decorations to the outside.
4. Glue the crepe paper strips inside the lower rim of the project.
5. At the top of the cylinder, punch two holes directly opposite each other.
6. Thread each end of the yarn length through a different hole and securely tie.

Jill Putnam—Gr. 1
Wheelock Primary School
Fredonia, NY

Fabulous Foam Frame

In addition to being fun to make, this one-of-a-kind photo frame makes a precious gift! To make a frame, cut a piece of colorful craft foam that is slightly larger than the photo itself. For a vertical mount, use a pencil to trace along the top and bottom edges of the photo. For a horizontal mount, trace along the left and right edges. Then remove the picture and use scissors to cut a line that is parallel to and about ½-inch inside each pencil line. (See the diagram.) Turn the foam over and insert the photo into the resulting frame. Use glue, scissors, a hole puncher, and colorful scraps of craft foam to add desired decorations. Attach two strips of magnetic tape to the back of the project—one at the top and one at the bottom. Too cute!

Gina Reagan—Gr. 3
Summerfield Elementary
Summerfield, NC

15

Arts & Crafts

Beauteous Butterflies

Bring on the butterflies! Prepare individual containers of desired paint colors and provide a large paintbrush (or a sponge piece fastened to a clothespin) for each color. To make a fancy flier, fold in half a 12" x 18" sheet of white construction paper (to 9" x 12"). Unfold the paper. Working atop newspaper, place colorful dollops of paint on half of the paper. Then refold the paper, gently rub the top of the folded paper with an open palm, and unfold the paper. When the paint is dry, refold the paper and trace a butterfly wing template on it as shown. Cut along the resulting outline. Then unfold the paper and glue a construction paper body and bent pipe cleaner antennae in place. This one-of-a-kind flier is ready to spread its wings!

Georgia Hayes—Gr. 1
Christian Center Elementary
Sioux Falls, SD

Lunar Landing!

Celebrate man's first steps on the moon (taken July 20, 1969) with an out-of-this-world project! To make the lunar landscape, trace a large semicircle template onto a 12" x 18" sheet of black paper. Use a glue-soaked piece of sponge (attached to a clothespin handle) to apply a coat of glue to the semicircle. Evenly sprinkle oatmeal over the glue-covered semicircle and press the oatmeal in place. When the glue is dry, lift the project and gently tap off excess oatmeal. On drawing paper illustrate yourself, a traveling companion, a flag, and other desired decorations. Cut out the pictures. Glue the cutouts and a toothpick flagpole in place. Adorn the sky with foil stars and the project is ready to display!

Laura Kwiatkowski and Laurie Bushnell—Grs. K–1
Boardmanville Elementary, Olean, NY

Summertime Wreath

The possibilities for summertime wreaths are wide open! To make a wreath, choose a summer theme (patriotic, picnic, beach, etc.) and an item that relates to it. Next, cut the center from a white paper plate. Position the plate rim so that its outer edge faces downward. Sponge-paint the rim to reflect the chosen theme and set it aside to dry. Draw the theme-related item on the circle cutout (plate center) and cut it out. Trace the resulting template(s) multiple times on construction paper. Then cut out the shapes, add desired details with markers or crayons, and assemble as needed.

When the plate rim is dry, punch two side-by-side holes in the rim. Thread a length of yarn through the holes and tie the yarn ends. Then glue the prepared cutouts to the project.

Natalie Arnold—Gr. 1
Hammond Westside Primary
Hammond, LA

Bumblebee Bookmark

Have you heard the latest buzz? Bumblebee bookmarks are guaranteed to sweeten your students' enthusiasm for summertime reading!

Materials for one bookmark:

large yellow pom-pom
2 small black pom-poms
two 12" black pipe cleaners
3" length of black cloth-covered wire
(sold at craft stores by the spool)

craft stick
craft glue

Steps:
1. Glue the large yellow pom-pom near one end of the craft stick.
2. Glue the two black pom-pom eyes to the top of the yellow pom-pom.
3. Glue one end of a black pipe cleaner to the craft stick directly below the yellow pom-pom. Then carefully wrap the pipe cleaner around the yellow pom-pom, forming the bee's stripes.
4. Shape the remaining black pipe cleaner into a set of wings, keeping one end free. To attach the wings, fasten the free end of the pipe cleaner to a stripe at the back of the bee.
5. Shape the cloth-covered wire into a pair of antennae. Glue in place.

Step 4

Kay Baker—Gr. 1, Woodland Elementary School, Emporium, PA

Pattern

Use with "Stuffed Gobbler" on page 9.

©The Education Center, Inc. • *THE MAILBOX*® • *Primary* • Oct/Nov 2001

CLASSROOM DISPLAYS

Soar into the new school year with this eye-catching display! Have each child illustrate his likeness on drawing paper trimmed to resemble the window of a plane. Mount the projects on a large paper plane that's being piloted by you. Mount the plane, the title, and several cloud cutouts labeled with student-dictated goals for the new school year. Looks like the sky's the limit!

Ann Galster—Gr. 1, Ellicott Elementary, Colorado Springs, CO

Sprout self-confidence and camaraderie at this adorable garden! Mount the title and one colorful flower per child, plus a few extras for late enrollees. Have each child trace a template of a flower center onto skin-toned paper, cut out the circle, and then use construction paper, glue, and crayons to create her self-likeness. Showcase the projects as shown. Too sweet!

Misty Rios—Gr. 2, E. W. Ward Elementary, Downey, CA

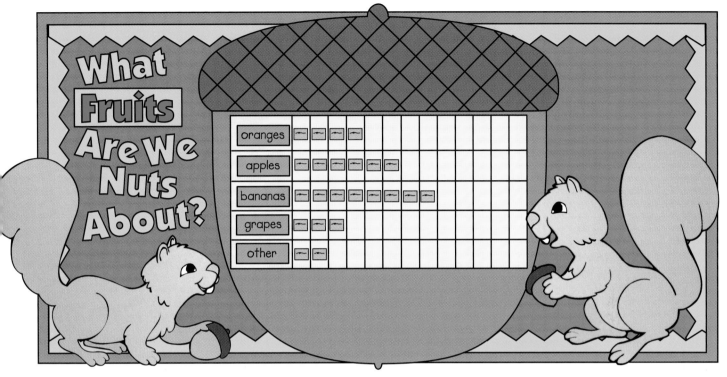

Students will be nuts about this interactive display! Mount a blank bar graph atop a large paper acorn. Display laminated cards, a title, and squirrel cutouts. Use a wipe-off pen to program the cards. After each child places a personalized sticky note on the graph, help the class interpret the results. Later, remove the notes, reprogram the cards, and invite students to complete another graphing activity!

Gillian C. Barclay-Smith, Columbia, SC

Here's a student-of-the-week display that begs to be noticed! Laminate a large bone cutout and a ready-to-program favorites chart. Display the laminated pieces with the title and artwork shown. Each week personalize the laminated pieces for the featured student and showcase photos, illustrations, and other mementos she has brought from home. Have her classmates describe (on copies of the booklet page from page 32) why they think she is Top Dog. Bind the pages between a personalized copy of the provided booklet cover (page 32) and blank construction paper, and then present the booklet to the Top Dog of the week!

Wendy Lunk—Gr. 2
B. Bernice Young School
Burlington Township, NJ

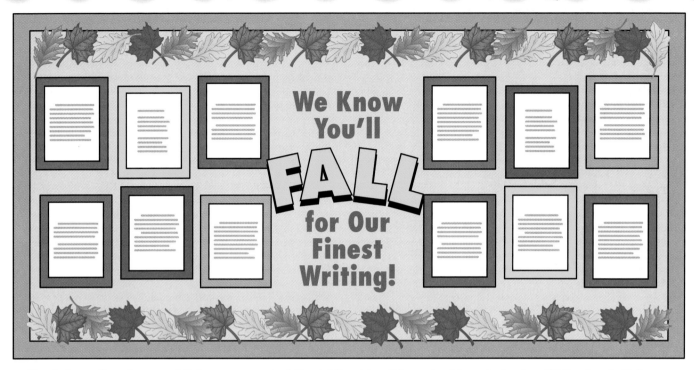

Here's the perfect place to publish your youngsters' finest fall writing. Mount the title and a border of fall-colored silk leaves. Ask each child to select a favorite piece of fall writing. Showcase the students' writing as shown. To keep the display current, invite students to replace their writing as frequently as desired. Spectacular!

Sara Truslow, Kling Elementary, Buena Vista, VA

Bubble, bubble, math's no trouble at this interactive display! To concoct a brew of word problem practice, each student writes and solves an original word problem. After her work is approved by you, she copies her problem on the front of a folded bubble cutout (see the illustration) and writes the answer inside. Post the bubbles, a title, artwork, and directions. Student interest in word problems is sure to bubble over!

adapted from an idea by
Carol Ann Perks—Grs. K–5 Gifted
Comstock Elementary, Miami, FL

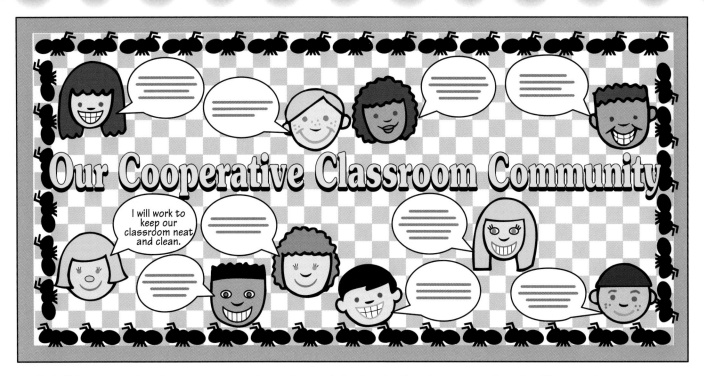

To build a cooperative classroom community, review ant behavior. Lead students to conclude that like ants, they too can accomplish great things by working together. Then have each child write how he'll contribute to the class community, trim around his writing to form a speech bubble, and create a self-portrait. Mount the projects on a checkered backdrop bordered with ant-shaped cutouts.

Kim Wachtel—Gr. 1, Sacandaga Elementary School, Scotia, NY

This Thanksgiving, serve a fine-feathered feast of main idea and supporting details! Display the title and a featherless turkey cutout on which you've written a main idea. Have each child write on provided paper a supporting detail for the main idea. Then have her mount her work on a colorful feather cutout. Display the feathers in a semicircle around the turkey body. Gobble, gobble!

Andrea Marsh—Gr. 3
Central Elementary School
Lafayette, TN

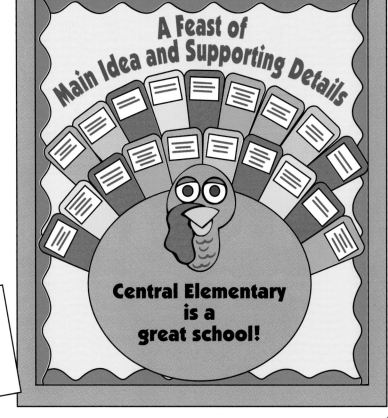

CLASSROOM DISPLAYS

Fashion eye-catching holiday greetings from paper chains! First, have students collaborate to make one or more paper chains of sufficient length to form each desired holiday symbol. Next, have them write personalized holiday messages on seasonal cutouts. Showcase the students' work with a title and other desired details. Happy holidays!

Kwanzaa involves looking back, looking forward, and having fun—and so does making this display! A child trims writing paper into the shape of a unity cup. On the cutout he describes an event from the past year of which he is most proud and writes a goal for the new year. He mounts his writing on a construction paper backdrop. Display the projects with a title and a paper-chain border.

Our thanks to the following teachers from Belmar Elementary School in Belmar, NJ, for inspiring the displays on this page: Kathleen Basaman, Katherine Bateman, Maureen Hartman, Meghan Mahoney, Deborah Manser, Patricia Monahan, Stefanie O'Donnell, and Maureen Swigon.

Paint a clear picture of winter using figurative language! Ask students to name things they do and do not like about winter. List their ideas on the board. Then, after a review of similes, have each child write and illustrate on drawing paper a simile that begins "Winter is…" Showcase the completed projects for all to see.

Rebecca Brudwick—Gr. 1, Hoover Elementary School, North Mankato, MN

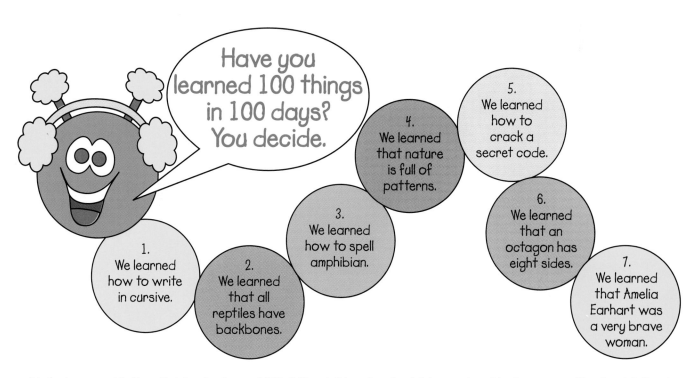

Students may not believe that they've learned 100 different things in school this year, but this clever caterpillar does! A few days before the 100th day of school, challenge students to recall 100 things they've learned. List their thoughts on chart paper. Then assign each child several entries from the list to copy onto numbered paper circles. Showcase the circles connected to a caterpillar head as shown. Impressive!

Skila Brown—Gr. 3, Cresset Christian Academy, Durham, NC

CLASSROOM DISPLAYS

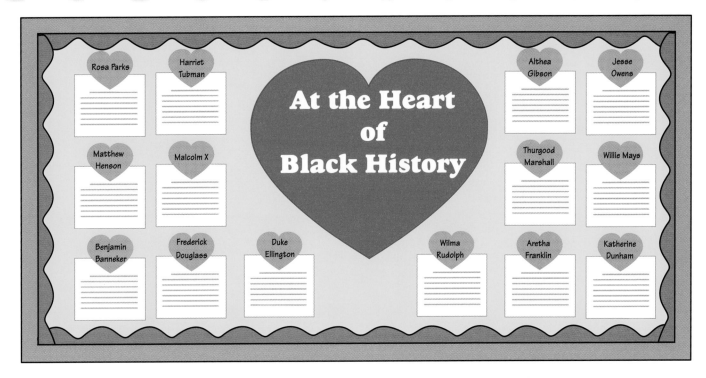

Get to the heart of Black History Month! Give each student a small paper heart labeled with the name of a famous Black American. Instruct her to learn about the person's contributions to black history and then describe them on provided paper. Showcase the student projects as shown. What a heartfelt activity!

Sharma Houston—Gr. 2, Pearsontown Elementary, Durham, NC

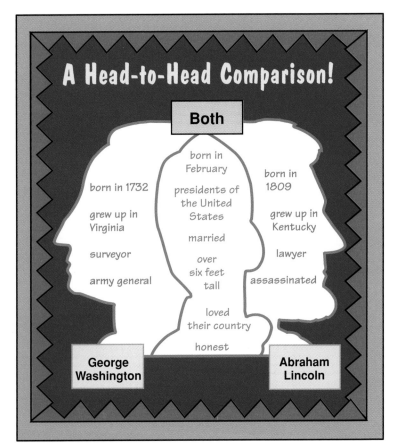

George and Abe take center stage at this patriotic display! Mount the title and an enlarged and labeled version of the Venn diagram from page 33. During a study of the two presidents, list facts that are learned in the corresponding areas of the diagram. If desired, have students list the facts on personal copies of page 33. Your youngsters' knowledge of George and Abe will be head and shoulders above the rest!

Lisa Strieker—Gr. 3
St. Paul Elementary School
Highland, IL

Our Kindness Rainbow

This display brilliantly demonstrates how simple acts of kindness can brighten each day! Mount the title. With help from your students, make a supply of hand cutouts in each of the six colors shown. When an act of kindness is observed or reported, note it on a cutout. Display the programmed cutouts so that a breathtaking rainbow unfolds!

Alexandra LeRose—Gr. 1, Sawgrass Elementary, Sunrise, FL

Mischievous leprechauns add charm to this interactive math display! Laminate a blank input card, output card, and rule card. Display the Irishmen, their machine, and a title as shown; then use a wipe-off marker to program the cards. Also provide a supply of answer sheets like the one shown. A child copies the rule on his paper and uses it to calculate the output numbers. To create a new activity, wipe off and then reprogram the laminated cards. No shenanigans here!

Ruth Heller—Gr. 3
Public School 156
Laurelton, NY

Name	Brad
Input	Output
3	6
5	8
7	10
1	4
6	
8	
2	
0	
4	
9	
Rule	+3

CLASSROOM DISPLAYS

We Must Give Our Earth a Hand!

Spotlight your students' ideas for protecting the environment! On a sheet of 4" x 5" blank paper, a child describes his thoughts for helping the earth (see "Timely Prompts" on page 106). Next, he colors a white construction paper copy of the pattern on page 34, cuts out the pattern, and staples his writing atop the cutout. Then he creates a self-portrait and attaches it to his project as shown. Happy Earth Day!

Belinda Taylor—Gr. 3, Rocky Creek Elementary, Lucedale, MS

Common Noun Challenge

Letter	Person	Place	Thing	
a	artist ancestor announcer	airport avenue	ant apricot almond	
b	baker boy	boulevard barnyard	bread bead	board book
c	caroler	canyon canal	cookie	
d	diver driver	desert den	dime diamond	
e	engineer electrician	earth	egg elephant	
f	firefighter friend fiddler	field foothill	firefly fire flamingo	
g	genius guard guide	grave gym	gerbil gift	
h	helper	hill habitat	ham hammer hamster	

Spread the word about common nouns! Post a title and a chart labeled with subheadings and alphabet letters like those shown. Have each child take a turn naming a different noun for you to write on the chart. Repeat the activity on each of several days. When several nouns are listed for each letter, collect common nouns for additional charts that continue (and complete) the alphabetical sequence. Display the charts in alphabetical order for a breathtaking look at common nouns!

Sally Wallace—Gr. 3
O'Neill Elementary
O'Neill, NE

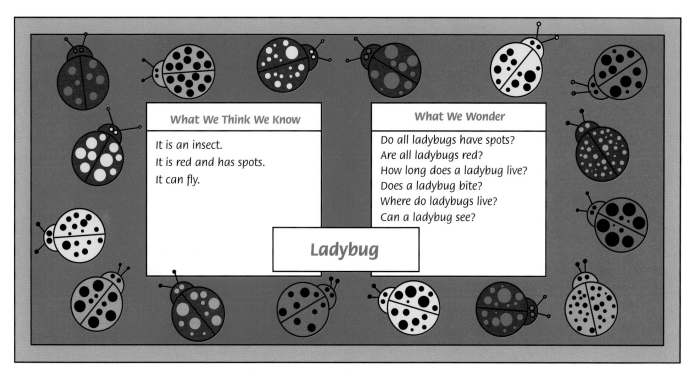

What We Think We Know

It is an insect.
It is red and has spots.
It can fly.

What We Wonder

Do all ladybugs have spots?
Are all ladybugs red?
How long does a ladybug live?
Does a ladybug bite?
Where do ladybugs live?
Can a ladybug see?

Ladybug

It's time to go buggy! To make a reusable display for bug studies, title two sheets of white poster board as shown. Laminate the posters and a blank nameplate. Mount the pieces. Next, use a wipe-off pen to write the name of the bug being studied on the nameplate and to record student-generated data on the posters. During the study, help students answer the questions they've posed and showcase bug-related projects at the display! *(See pages 283–286 for more ladybug-related activities.)*

adapted from an idea by Lisa Kelly, West Bloomfield, MI

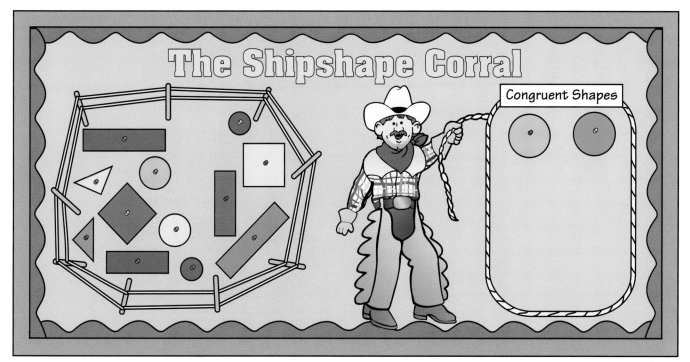

The Shipshape Corral

Congruent Shapes

Lasso geometry skills at this rootin'-tootin' display! Showcase a corral, a cowpoke and his lasso, and the title. To reinforce congruence, label the lasso as shown. Using pushpins, randomly display pairs of congruent shapes inside the corral. Every few days select volunteers to round up congruent pairs from the corral and display them inside the lasso. Vary the collection of cutouts as desired. To reinforce symmetry, retitle the lasso and stock the corral with a collection of cutouts that includes several symmetrical shapes. Yee-haw!

Here's a bulletin board that's a teacher's friend! Post the message shown and place a container of pushpins nearby. Ask each child to post at least one piece of work that represents her best efforts. Instruct students to update their work samples weekly to keep the display current. A highly motivating, child-centered bulletin board that's maintained by students—now that's a dream come true!

Linda Macke—Gr. 2, John F. Kennedy Elementary, Kettering, OH

Students have a whale of a time showing off their finest work at this versatile display. Post a whale cutout, a strip of scalloped bulletin board border, and a title that includes a laminated poster board rectangle. Use a wipe-off marker to label the poster board with a category, and then showcase youngsters' self-selected work in the shape of a spout. Reprogram the rectangle and update the display as desired.

Lydia Wagoner—Grs. 1–2, Providence School, Waynesboro, PA

These busy bees are buzzing with memories from the past school year! For each child, staple writing paper between two yellow construction paper squares. Trim each booklet to resemble a bee's body. A child describes a favorite memory inside his booklet. Next, he cuts a head, two wings, and two antennae from construction paper. Then he adds crayon details, attaches the cutouts, and titles his work. Showcase the projects as shown. Buzz, buzz!

adapted from an idea by Catherine Della Torre—Gr. 1, Woodside School, River Vale, NJ

Piece together a quilt of patriotism! On a nine-inch square of writing paper, a child describes a favorite patriotic pastime or responds to a writing prompt related to patriotism. He illustrates his writing on a nine-inch square of white construction paper. Staple each child's work together as shown, and then mount the projects on a bulletin board backed with blue paper. Embellish the display with white star cutouts and red crepe paper streamers. Hooray for the red, white, and blue!

Vicki Dabrowka, Clearwater, Florida

Booklet Cover and Page

Use with "Introducing..." on page 21.

No Bones About It!

_____
student

is our
TOP DOG
of the week!

_____
teacher

_____
date

©The Education Center, Inc. • *THE MAILBOX® • Primary •* Aug/Sept 2001

 ©The Education Center, Inc. • *THE MAILBOX® • Primary •* Aug/Sept 2001

A Head-to-Head Comparison

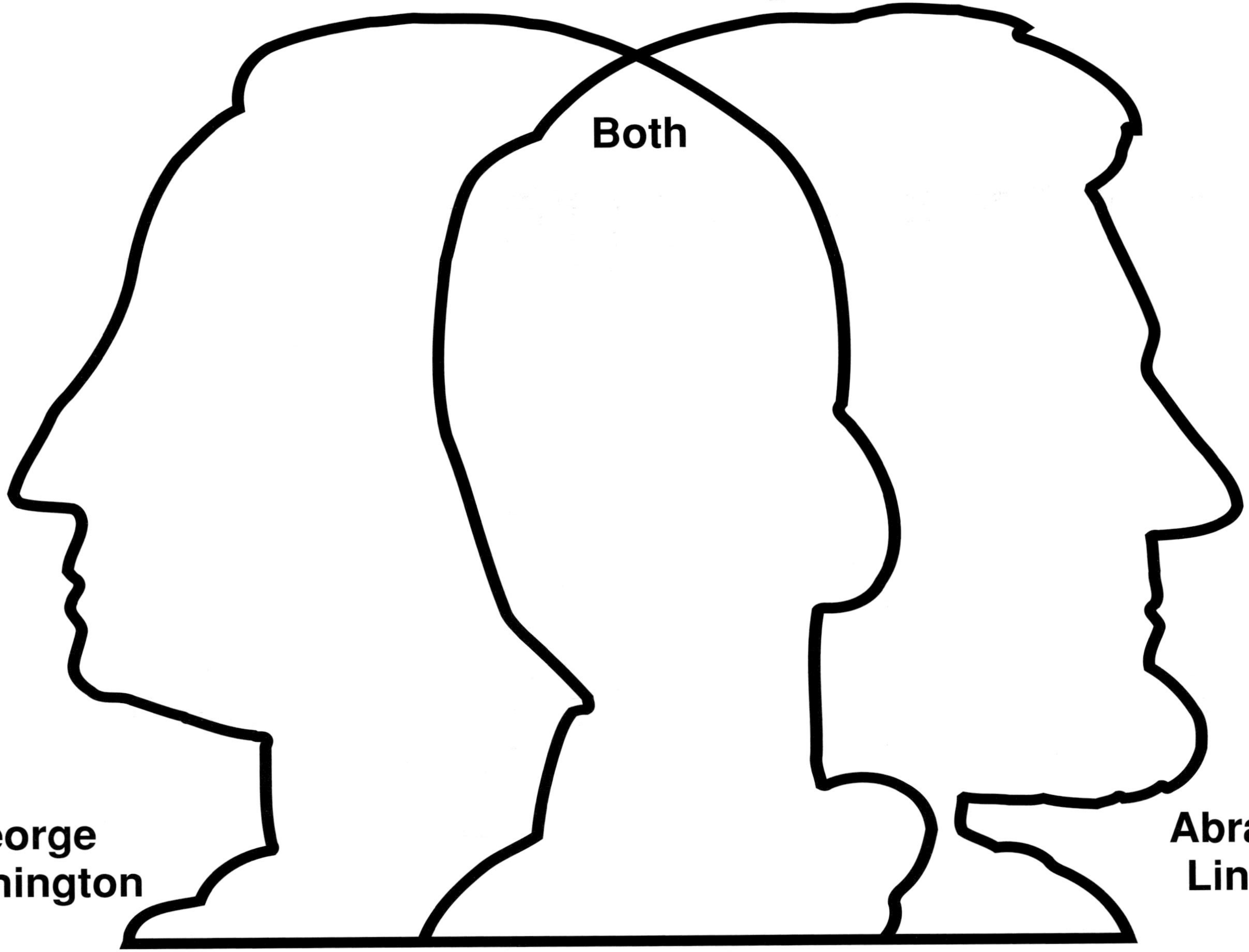

Both

**Abraham
Lincoln**

**George
Washington**

©The Education Center, Inc. • *THE MAILBOX®* • *Primary* • Feb/Mar 2002

Note to the teacher: Use with the classroom display on page 26.

Patterns

Use the earth pattern with "We Must Give Our Earth a Hand!" on page 28 and "Timely Prompts" on page 106.

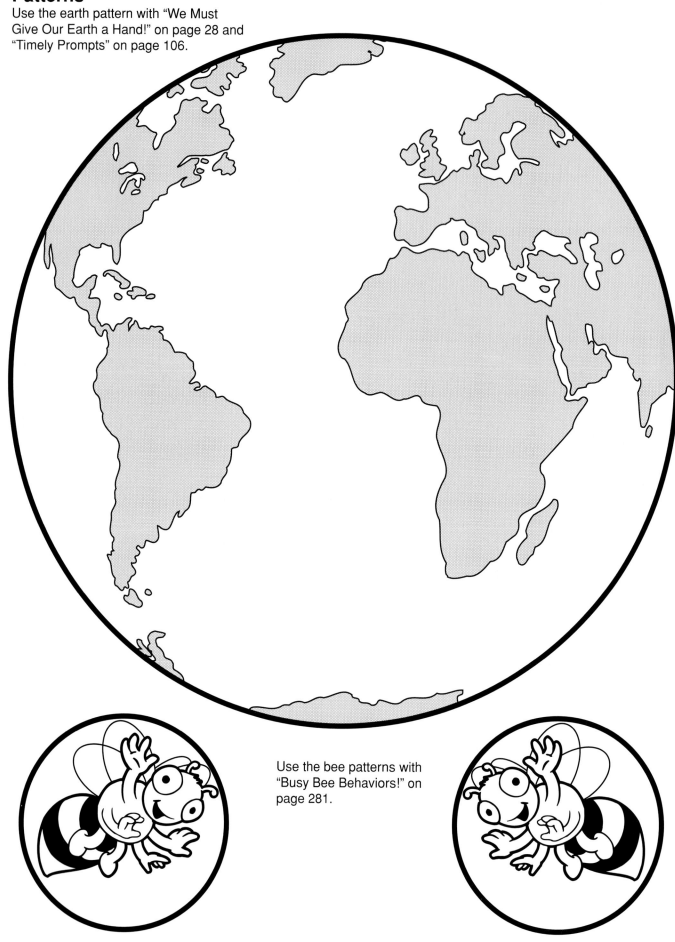

Use the bee patterns with "Busy Bee Behaviors!" on page 281.

©The Education Center, Inc. • *THE MAILBOX®* • *Primary* • April/May 2002

COMPREHENSION CROSSING

Comprehension Crossing

Making Reading Meaningful

Help With Homophones

When it comes to understanding **homophones,** this colorful critic is a growing resource! Cut several 12-inch circles from construction paper. Decorate one circle to resemble a caterpillar head and then mount it on a classroom wall. Keep the remaining circles handy. After introducing a homophone pair, write one word from the pair at the top of a circle cutout and the other word at the bottom of the cutout. Next, select two volunteers and give each one a 3" x 5" card. Have each child illustrate on her card the meaning of a different word from the pair. Mount the cards on the circle as shown and then connect the circle to the caterpillar. This adorable bug grows right along with your students' knowledge of homophones!

Lisa Crowell—Gr. 1, Elden Elementary, Baldswinville, NY

Word Investigations

Prompt students to use **context clues** to unlock the meanings of unknown words in text. Before students begin to independently read a new story, have each child divide a sheet of paper into three columns. Have him title the first column "Unknown Word," the second column "What I Think the Word Means," and the third column "What the Word Really Means." When a youngster encounters an unfamiliar word, he copies the word on his paper in the first column. In the second column he writes what he thinks the word means, based on clues from the story. Then he continues reading. Later, when all students have finished the reading assignment, revisit each unknown word. Confirm your students' accurate word hunches and, when needed, lead the class to a better understanding of a word. Have each student use the information to complete the third column on his paper.

Brenda Wilke—Gr. 3, West Park Academy, Chicago, IL

Growing Vocabularies

Literature connections give these **vocabulary** books special meaning! Give each student a booklet that has construction paper covers and 14 pages (seven sheets of white paper). The youngster draws a line across the center of each page except the last one. Working in alphabetical order, she labels half a page for each letter. After an independent reading session, the youngster chooses a new or significant word from her reading. She writes it on the appropriate page, adds the book title, and then writes a sentence with it. The story context clarifies how to use the word. Plus, it helps keep the meaning fresh in students' minds!

Kathleen McGowan—Grs. K–2 Special Education
Central Elementary
Union, MO

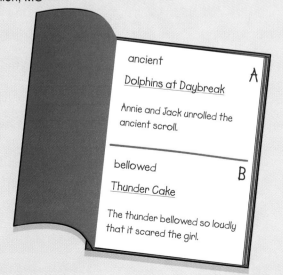

Comprehension Crossing

Making Reading Meaningful

Pumpkin Possibilities

Stretch students' imaginations and cultivate an understanding of **cause and effect** in the process! Program several paper strips with ordinary or outlandish pumpkin-themed outcomes (effects), such as the ones shown. Place the strips in a plastic pumpkin pail. Ask a volunteer to remove a strip from the pail and read it aloud. Allow time for each student to think about possible causes of the described outcome. Next, have each youngster quietly share his ideas with a neighboring classmate. Invite several students to tell the class the causes they brainstormed. Then repeat the process with each remaining outcome. A bumper crop of creative ideas is sure to result!

Rebecca Beal
Alpharetta, GA

The pumpkin fell off the porch.

My pumpkin turned purple!

Revealing Lineup

Uncover **story details** with this critical-thinking activity! Give each student a few sticky notes, a 6" x 9" piece of white paper, and a 1 1/2" x 6" colored paper strip. As the youngster reads one or more assigned chapters, he uses a sticky note to mark each page that has a word he thinks is especially important to the story. Next, he selects one word and writes it on the colored strip. He folds the white paper in half and glues the word at the bottom of the folded paper as shown. He adds a related illustration above the word. Then he unfolds the paper and writes inside why the word is significant.

If desired, tack a string along a classroom wall and showcase the projects along it. Then use the thought-provoking lineup to prompt discussion about the words and their connections to the story.

adapted from an idea by Kimberly Hofstetter
Bloomfield Hills, MI

Character Quilt

Here's an eye-catching **comparison and contrast** idea! Select three or more characters from a recently completed class read-aloud. Draw a square grid that has a column for each character and a row for each character trait you want students to investigate. Then label the columns and rows. Give each student a copy of the grid and a slightly larger wallpaper square. To complete the grid, a student decides which traits each character displayed and colors the corresponding grid square. Then she cuts out the grid, glues it on the wallpaper, and uses a crayon to draw stitch marks. Display the students' resulting patchwork squares so that they resemble a quilt. Ask the class to refer to the display to compare and contrast the characters. Encourage students to recall story details that support their observations. What a nifty way to piece together a character analysis!

Lisa Leonardi
Norfolk, MA

The word "runt" is important because that's how it all started. If Wilbur hadn't been a runt, Fern might never have met him!

blissful

Comprehension Crossing

Making Reading Meaningful

Eat Your Words?

Here's a partner activity that makes understanding **figurative language** as easy as pie! Read aloud *Amelia Bedelia* by Peggy Parish. With students' help, contrast the maid's literal interpretations with Mrs. Rogers's expectations. Pair students and then give each twosome a sheet of drawing paper. Assign each pair of students a food-related figurative expression such as the ones shown. Instruct the youngsters to write a sentence with the expression and illustrate how Amelia might interpret it. Have the students explain the figurative meaning of the sentence on the back of the paper. Bind students' completed work into a class book titled "Sentences That Take the Cake!" to create a grin-inducing addition to your classroom library.

Lisa Morris
LaGrange, GA

Figurative Expressions
apple of my eye
in a pickle
spill the beans
easy as pie
cry over spilled milk
cool as a cucumber
eat like a bird
top banana
sell like hotcakes
walk on eggs
butter someone up
in a jam
like two peas in a pod

Sentences That Take the Cake!

Connections Beyond Compare

When it comes to helping students **make connections,** this activity is beyond compare! Read aloud a selected nonfiction book about a hero or heroine. Prompt a class discussion to identify the person's heroic traits. Then ask students to brainstorm people they know personally or through books who have similar characteristics.

Next, give each student two half sheets of writing paper and a 12" x 18" sheet of white paper. On one piece of writing paper, have the youngster write about the heroic qualities of the person featured in the book. On the second piece, ask her to write about another hero or heroine who shares some of these characteristics. Then instruct her to position the unlined paper horizontally and divide it in half. Ask her to glue her writing, as shown, and illustrate her work. Invite each student to share her completed work with the class. No doubt the varied responses will deepen students' understanding of the word *heroic!*

adapted from an idea by Lisa Leonardi
Norfolk, MA

Newsworthy Details

Story elements are in the news with this handy graphic organizer! Before a student reads a story, give him a copy of the graphic organizer on page 41. Encourage him to consider each provided question as he reads. When the youngster finds an answer, he writes it in the appropriate space. To complete his paper, he responds to the "Editorial" question. Not only does this idea give him the scoop on story elements, but it also gives him a purpose for reading!

Colleen Dabney
Williamsburg-JCC Public Schools
Williamsburg, VA

WOMEN MUST VOTE!
Susan B. Anthony didn't think it was fair that women couldn't vote. She stood up for what she believed in and helped get voting rights changed. She was an important leader!

Rosa Parks stood up for her beliefs. She didn't think it was right that black people had to sit in the back of the bus. She was a leader for people who wanted blacks to be treated fairly.

Comprehension Crossing
Making Reading Meaningful

Books in Bloom

Watch **character analysis** skills blossom with this springtime display! At the completion of a chapter book, give each student a construction paper copy of page 42. The student writes the book title and the name of an assigned character in the provided spaces. He labels each petal with a different word or phrase that tells about the character. Next, he lightly colors the center of the flower. He cuts out the flower and then adds a stem and leaves that he has fashioned from construction paper. Invite each student to read his work to the class and explain how the words relate to the character. Then mount students' completed flowers along a classroom wall to create an eye-pleasing patch of posies!

adapted from an idea
by Susan Meisky
High Point, NC

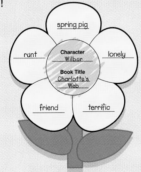

Vocabulary Stretcher

Set the stage for comprehension with **vocabulary** cards! Before students begin an assigned reading, select several key words from it. Draw and program a grid to make a card for each word. Give each student a copy of the grid and have her cut apart the cards. To assess students' prior knowledge, announce the definition of a selected word without revealing the word. Have each student silently guess the word and then hold up her corresponding card. Scan the raised cards for accuracy; then ask the students to put the cards down. Continue with the remaining words in a like manner.

To check her responses, have each student find the words as she reads and think about each word's context. When every student has finished reading, repeat the definition activity, verifying the correct answers. You can be sure stronger vocabularies will be in the cards!

Cortney Garland-Wesley—Gr. 2, South Range Elementary
Derry, NH

Postcards With Character

Here's a **literary response** activity that really delivers! Give each student a lined 5" x 8" index card. On the blank side of the card, the youngster illustrates an event from a book that he has read. Then he turns the card over and draws a line down the center of the lined side. On the left half of the card, he writes a message from one character to another about the illustrated event. On the right half, he writes the book title and illustrates a stamp. He hole-punches the top of the resulting postcard and attaches a loop of yarn. Tack each student's postcard to a titled bulletin board so that the card can be flipped to view either side. What a "send-sational" way to check comprehension!

Maxine Pincott—Gr. 3
Oliver Ellsworth School
Windsor, CT

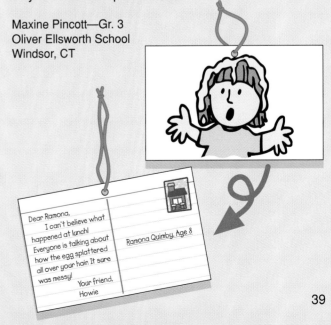

Dear Ramona,
I can't believe what happened at lunch! Everyone is talking about how the egg splattered all over your hair. It sure was messy!
Your friend,
Howie

Ramona Quimby, Age 8

Comprehension Crossing
Making Reading Meaningful

Believe It, or Not!

Distinguishing **real and make-believe** is in the cards! Read aloud a picture book that contains a blend of real and make-believe, such as Steven Kellogg's *The Mysterious Tadpole.* Ask students to recall events that could happen in real life. Then have them describe events that could not really happen and explain why. Next, give every child eight blank cards. Have each student describe and illustrate on individual cards two real and two make-believe story events. Then have him label two blank cards "real" and two blank cards "make-believe." Set aside time for student pairs to combine their cards and play a Concentration-type game. Keep a stock of blank cards on hand and encourage students to create game cards for a variety of books.

adapted from an idea by
Vicki Dabrowka
Clearwater, FL

By the Letter

Use this class project to review **story details** from any chapter book. To begin, challenge students to provide one or more story-related words that begin with the letter *a.* (Clarify that a word may or may not appear in the story.) Repeat the challenge for each alphabet letter. If no words are provided, skip the letter. Next, have each child choose a different story-related word and write its initial letter in the top right-hand corner of a sheet of provided paper. Then have each child write "[Letter] is for [selected word]..." followed by her explanation. Also have her illustrate her work.

For a fun finale, seat students in a circle so that their work is alphabetized and have them read their story details in alphabetical order. Bind the alphabetized papers into a class book titled "The ABCs of [the original book title]."

Vicki Dabrowka

A is for annoyed because that is how spelling makes Ramona feel!

A Mental Movie

Increase comprehension by coaching students to use **imagery.** Now and then read a picture book to the class without revealing the book's illustrations. Pause after the beginning, the middle, and the ending of the story. At each break, challenge students to make a mental image of what was just read. If desired, describe your mental image to the class and invite volunteers to add details. Or ask volunteers to share what they envision. To wrap up the activity, have each child divide a 6" x 18" strip of drawing paper into three sections, label the sections "beginning," "middle," and "ending," and describe and illustrate in each one the corresponding part of his mental movie. This showing of comprehension is sure to be a hit!

Cecelia Szeg—Reading Recovery
Slackwood Elementary School
Lawrenceville, NJ

Booksville News

_____ (date)

Booksville, USA

| Special Edition | 50¢ |

_____ summarized by _____
(book title)   (student)

Who is the story about?

_____

_____

_____

_____

Where does the story take place?

_____

_____

_____

When does the story happen?

_____

_____

What is the problem?

_____

_____

_____

How is the problem solved?

_____

_____

_____

Editorial
Is the setting important to this story? Why or why not?

_____

_____

_____

_____

Pattern

Use with "Books in Bloom" on page 39.

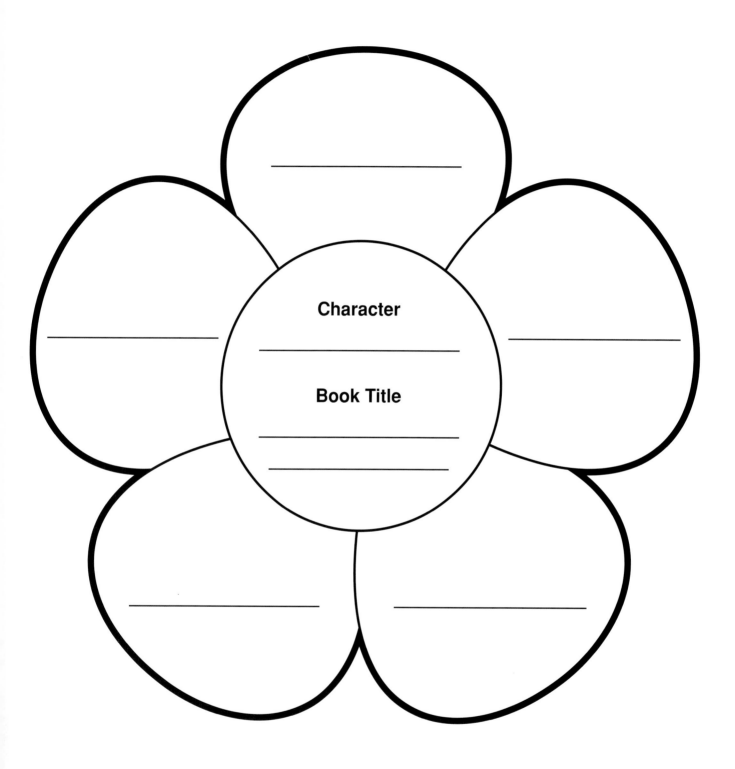

Character

Book Title

©The Education Center, Inc. • *THE MAILBOX*® • *Primary* • April/May 2002

LEARNING CENTERS

Learning Centers

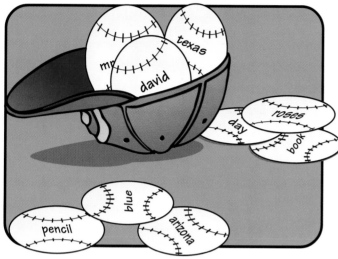

Sorting for Capitals

Warm up your youngsters' **capitalization skills!** Using all lowercase letters, program a supply of baseball cutouts (page 55) with words that need capital letters and words that do not. Laminate the cutouts for durability and then use a permanent marker to code the back of each baseball that needs a capital. Store the cutouts in a resealable plastic bag. Place the bag and an upside-down baseball cap at a center. A student sorts baseballs that need capital letters into the cap and those that do not into a discard pile. Then she flips both sets of cutouts to check her work.

Susan Brown
Palmyra Elementary School
Palmyra, VA

Picture This!

Review **initial sounds and letters** with this two-part center. Place scissors, Post-it® Brand notes, letter-size envelopes, pencils, and discarded magazines at a center. A student cuts out five magazine pictures. For each picture, he writes on a Post-it note the letter (or letters) that makes its initial sound and attaches the note to the picture. Then he slips his work inside a personalized envelope and submits it for your review.

The following week place glue, a booklet of construction paper pages labeled from "A" to "Z," each student's envelope, and a trash can at the center. A child glues each cutout on the corresponding booklet page and then discards the programmed note. Display the alphabetical resource in the class library for all to enjoy.

Stephanie L. Drone—Gr. 1
Coquina Elementary
Titusville, FL

By the Number

Put students in the swim with **number order!** Use the pattern on page 58 to make five fish in each of five different colors for a total of 25 fish. Program each color of fish with numbers for sequencing; then make an answer key. Laminate the fish and the key and then cut them out. Store each color of fish in a separate resealable plastic bag. Place the bags and the answer key at a center. A student sequences the fish in each school and then uses the answer key to check his work.

adapted from an idea by
Dawn Schroeder—Gr. 1
Kluckhohn Elementary
LeMars, IA

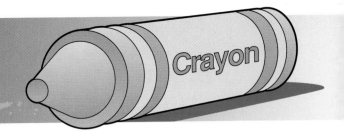

Spelling Station

Keep students in touch with **spelling** year-round! Ask each child to bring to school a personalized spiral notebook for use at the spelling station. Store a set of alphabet stamps at the center. Each week post a current list of spelling words and provide a colorful stamp pad. Every week a student takes his notebook to the center and on the first blank page carefully stamps the posted spelling words. The notebooks quickly become handy spelling references that can be used throughout the year to keep students' spelling sharp!

Pam Marks—Gr. 1
Bulluck Elementary
Rocky Mount, NC

"Apple-icious" Acrostics

Get to the core of **descriptive writing!** Cut a supply of 3" x 6" rectangles of red paper and 6" x 9" rectangles of white paper. Place the precut paper, scraps of green paper and brown paper, scissors, glue, a black crayon, and pencils at a center. A student uses the black crayon to write her name vertically down the left margin of a white paper rectangle. Then she writes a self-describing word or phrase that begins with each letter of her name. To make the apple project pictured, she trims around her resulting acrostic poem. Next, she trims two red rectangles to create the top and bottom apple portions. She glues her acrostic poem between the two cutouts, fashions a stem and leaf from scrap paper, and glues the cutouts in place. Now that's an "a-peel-ing" writing project!

Jane Manuel
Wellington, TX

Grins and a Grid

Provide practice with **ordered pairs** at this grin-inducing math center! On a sheet of poster board draw and label a grid. Laminate the poster board. Next, use rolled tape to attach individual photos of familiar faculty members at different points on the grid. Place the grid at a center along with paper and pencils. Also post a list of who is featured on the grid and provide an answer key. A student writes the name of each faculty member shown on the grid followed by the ordered pair that describes the person's grid location. Then he uses the answer key to check his work.

Ruthie Jamieson Titus—Gr. 3
Union Elementary
Poland, OH

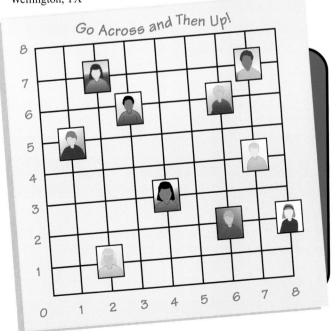

Learning Centers

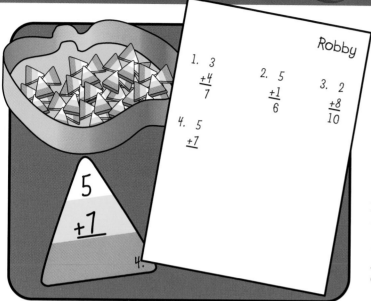

Candy Corn Calculations

Who knew practicing **basic math facts** could be so sweet? Number ten candy corn cutouts and program each one with a different math fact to solve. Laminate the cutouts for durability. Place the cutouts, a container of candy corn, a supply of blank paper, and pencils at a center. A student copies and answers each math fact on his paper. Then he uses the candy corn manipulatives to check his work. If desired, display on your desk a bowl of candy corn that you've bagged into individual portions. Invite each child who completes the center to take a sweet treat.

Shelley Courty—Gr. 2
Jefferson Elementary School
Carmi, IL

Sightly Jack-o'-Lanterns

Brighten **sight word practice** at this partner center! Use the patterns on page 56 to make an even number of orange jack-o'-lantern shapes and a matching number of yellow tachistoscope strips. Program each strip with sight words. Laminate the strips and patterns for durability. Cut out the shapes. Use an X-acto® knife to slit the dotted lines on each jack-o'-lantern and then insert a strip into each jack-o'-lantern as shown. Place the projects at a center. Partners take turns reading (and verifying) the sight words on different jack-o'-lanterns—when Partner 1 reads, Partner 2 verifies, and vice versa. Students' sight word vocabularies will be glowing!

Rebecca Beal
Alpharetta, GA

Ears and Eggs

Here's an "eggs-cellent" way to fine-tune **listening skills!** Ready two plastic eggs by placing the exact same item(s) in each egg. In a like manner, prepare five more egg pairs without duplicating the contents of any pair. Store the eggs in a basket. Place the basket and an empty 12-cup egg carton at a center. A student gently shakes the individual eggs, listening for identical sounds. When she finds two eggs with matching sounds, she stores the pair at one end of the egg carton. She continues in this manner, until the egg carton holds the six pairs of eggs. Then she carefully opens each egg pair to check her work.

Sarah Saia
Wilmington, NC

Cashing In

Money-counting skills are sure to profit at this partner center! Label the lids of an even number of empty film canisters with different money amounts. In a separate container place quarters, dimes, nickels, and pennies that can be used to make each money amount. Place the container of coins, the canisters, and a felt square at a center. Partner 1 selects a canister, places coins inside it that equal the programmed amount, and passes the canister to his partner. Partner 2 pours the coins onto the felt square and verifies the count. After the coins and empty canister are returned to their original locations, Partner 2 selects a different canister and the process is repeated. The partners continue in this manner until the coins in each canister have been counted and verified. Now that's a center you can take to the bank!

Nell Roberts—Gr. 1
The Covenant School
Charlottesville, VA

Can of Worms Directions
Arrange the worms to make six sentences that make sense.
Copy the sentences on your paper.
Add missing capital letters and punctuation.
Draw a brown line under each subject.
Draw a purple line under each predicate.

an earthworm

cannot see

the bird in the tree

is looking for a worm

earthworms

tunnel underground

Can of Worms

Subjects and predicates are the key to this can of worms! Begin with six sentences. Write the subject and predicate of each sentence on individual strips of tan paper. Laminate the paper strips for durability and then trim them into worm shapes. Store the cutouts in a clean and empty can without sharp edges. Place the can of worms, a direction card, writing paper, crayons, and pencils at a center. A student combines the subjects and predicates to make six sentences that make sense. As she copies the sentences on her paper, she capitalizes and punctuates them. Then she underlines each subject and predicate as outlined on the direction card. One thing is certain—students won't try to worm out of this center!

adapted from an idea by Susan Marie Stires—Gr. 3
Sam Houston Elementary
Wichita Falls, TX

Practicing Penmanship

At this center reinforcing **letter formation** is a breeze! Mount a variety of unused writing practice pages on 11" x 14" sheets of tagboard in fall colors. Laminate each project and then trim it into a leaf shape. Place the cutouts, wipe-off markers, moist towelettes, and a trash can at a center. Using a provided marker, a student practices his penmanship directly on each cutout. Then he wipes the cutouts clean before he leaves the center.

Lisa Vrana—Gr. 1
Schenck Elementary
San Antonio, TX

Learning Centers

Peppermint Sums

Take a sweet approach to **basic addition facts!** Use a candy pattern like the one shown to make six white construction paper candies and three red construction paper candies. Program every other section of each white candy with a different alphabet letter and math fact problem. Label the sections of the red candies with the corresponding answers. Cut out each white candy and each red candy section. Code the backs of the red cutouts for self-checking and then laminate the center pieces for durability. Store the cutouts in a holiday tin at a center. A student assembles the peppermint candies. To check her work, she flips the red candy sections. Yummy!

Kacie L. Farmer, Dale, IN

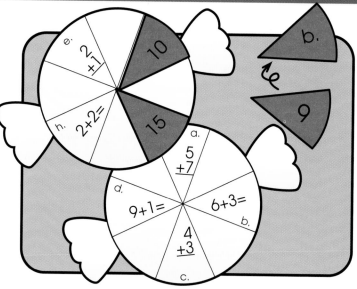

Silly Sentences

Sentence structure takes shape at this grin-inducing center! Use a colorful marker to write ten adjectives on individual cards. Use a second color of marker to write ten plural nouns on individual cards and a third color of marker to write ten plural verbs on individual cards. Store each set of cards in a separate labeled container. Place the cards, drawing paper, pencils, and crayons at a center. A student divides a sheet of paper into fourths as shown. He selects one card from each container. In an empty box on his paper, he writes the three words as a complete sentence and then illustrates his writing. In a like manner, he writes and illustrates three more silly sentences.

Sandy Scarborough—Gr. 2
Brennen Elementary
Columbia, SC

In a Few Words

Promote a variety of **writing skills** at this easy-to-maintain center! Stock a center with story paper, pencils, and crayons. Each week at the center display a different wordless picture book and instructions for a writing activity. A student reads the book and then completes the writing exercise.

Cheryl Watt—Gr. 1
Friendship Valley Elementary
Westminster, MD

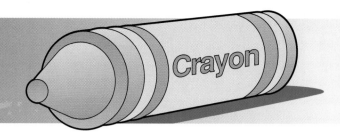

Cool Facts

This **fact and opinion** center is totally cool! Number 15 cards and write a different penguin fact on each one. Next, sequence the cards and label the lower right-hand corners so the hidden message "Penguins are cool!" is revealed. (See the illustration for clarity.) Label a second set of numbered cards with opinions about penguins. Code these cards with letters that do not appear in the hidden message. Then glue the cards in each numbered pair on opposite sides of a black construction paper card. Laminate the two-sided cards for durability and store them at a center. A student arranges the cards in numerical order, fact side up. If his work is accurate, the hidden message can be read.

Sheila Criqui-Kelley—Gr. 1, Lebo Elementary
Lebo, KS

Hurray for Arrays!

Modeling multiplication builds a solid understanding of the multiplication concept. Label a class supply of cards with different fact problems. Place the cards, cereal pieces, glue, crayons, and sturdy paper at a center. A student selects a fact card. Then she makes and labels an array that models the problem and reveals its answer.

Sally Wallace—Gr. 3, O'Neill Elementary, O'Neill, NE

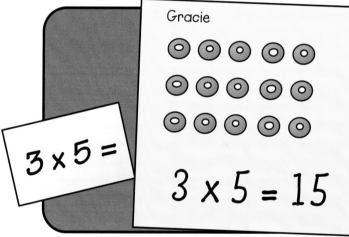

"Soup-er" Guide Words

Stir up extra **guide word practice!** First, prepare an answer key like the one shown. Next, label each of five plastic bowls with a different guide word pair (from the key) and program individual craft sticks with the entry words provided. Store the sticks in a container decorated to resemble a soup can. Place the container, the plastic bowls, and the answer key at a center. A student sorts the craft sticks into the appropriate bowls. Then he uses the answer key to check his work.

Erin Harp
Manchester, NH

Answer Key

apple–cereal
bananas   bean
berry   carrot
   celery

cheese–flour
cherry   cracker
doughnut   egg
       fish

frosting–lemon
gravy   ham
honey   jelly
       juice

lettuce–raisin
lobster   marshmallow
oatmeal   peanut
   radish

raspberry–yam
rice   salt
sausage   turkey
     wheat

Learning Centers

Broken Hearts

Computation is the key to mending these broken hearts! Cut out and number several construction paper hearts. Program each cutout with a different math sentence that is missing an addend, a subtrahend, a minuend, or a factor. Then prepare an answer key. Laminate the hearts and key for durability. Place the key in a gift bag. Use a different jigsaw-style cut on each heart to separate its problem and answer. Add the cutouts to the gift bag. Place the bag, pencils, and a supply of paper at a center. A student pieces together the puzzles, solves the math problems on her paper, and uses the answer key to check her work. The hearts are mended!

adapted from an idea by Sarah Saia, Wilmington, NC

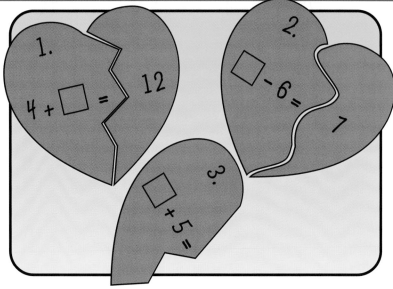

cotton ball		marble	
fluffy	soft	smooth	round
white	small	red	hard
		small	
sandpaper		popcorn	
thin	bumpy	salty	yummy
rough	scratchy	small	fresh
brown		crunchy	

The smooth, red marble rolled into my bag of small, crunchy popcorn.

"Sense-ational" Adjectives

Take a five-sense approach to **adjectives!** Display a cotton ball, a marble, and a piece of sandpaper at a center, and provide crayons, pencils, and blank paper. A student visually divides a sheet of paper into fourths and uses a crayon to title one box for each of the three objects on display. In the fourth box he names a favorite snack food. Below each noun he lists three to five adjectives that describe how the object looks, sounds, feels, smells, or might taste. (Caution students not to taste any of the objects.) Then, on the back of his paper, he writes and illustrates a descriptive sentence about one or more of the objects. Aren't adjectives awesome?

Josephine Flammer—Gr. 2, Brook Avenue School
Bay Shore, NY

Roll 100!

Strengthen **place value and addition** skills with a partner game! Place a die, paper, and pencils at a center. To begin, each player rolls the die and writes the number she rolls on her paper as a one or a ten. (For example, if a child rolls a three, she may record the roll as 3 or 30.) Then each player rolls the die again, records her number (as a one or ten), and adds it to her previous roll. Play continues in this manner until each child tallies seven rolls. The winner of the game is the player whose total score is closer to, but not over, 100. Roll on!

Jacki Itchkow—Gr. 3, Public School 165 Q, Flushing, NY

Rheanna

Rolls
1   10
2 + 40
     50
3 + 6
     56
4 + 4
     60

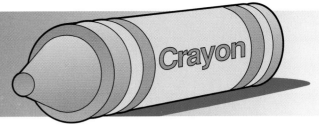

Tricky Plurals

Irregular plurals are in the cards! List several irregular plurals, each with its singular form. Place the list at a center along with blank cards, crayons, and pencils. A student initials five blank cards. On one side of each card he copies and illustrates a different singular noun from the list. On the other side of each card he copies and illustrates the plural form of the noun. Store the cards at the center.

For a follow-up activity, remove the list of plurals from the center. A twosome shuffles and stacks the cards. Partner 1 reads aloud the top card. If the word is singular, he provides the plural form of the word, and vice versa. Partner 2 flips the card to verify the answer. Then the card is placed on the bottom of the stack. Play alternates between the partners for as long as desired. Challenge capable students to spell the word forms they provide!

Sue Miller—Gr. 2, Helen H. Hansen Elementary, Stoughton, MA

Word List	
Singular	Plural
goose	geese
foot	feet
mouse	mice
die	dice
man	men
child	children
tooth	teeth
ox	oxen

teeth

J.C.

tooth

Food for Thought

At this center, students **identify food groups** for a scrumptious sorting activity. To prepare, cut an assortment of food pictures from discarded magazines. Glue the pictures on construction paper, laminate for durability, and cut out. Code the back of each cutout for the corresponding food group. Store the cutouts in a plastic basket. Place the basket at a center along with one card programmed for each of the six food groups. A student sorts the cutouts by food group and then flips the cutouts to check her work. Delicious!

Kimberly A. Minafo, Pomona, NY

Milk Group

Fruit Group

Vegetable Group

Meat Group

Fats and Sweets

Grain Group

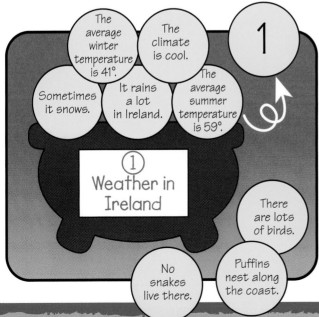

The average winter temperature is 41°.

The climate is cool.

Sometimes it snows.

It rains a lot in Ireland.

The average summer temperature is 59°.

1

① Weather in Ireland

There are lots of birds.

No snakes live there.

Puffins nest along the coast.

Pots of Gold

Create a wealth of **main idea and supporting details** practice! Cut out five paper coins for each of five paper pots. Number five blank cards, program each one with a main idea, and glue each one to a pot. Next, program each of the pot's coins with a detail that supports the main idea. Code the back of each coin with the number of the corresponding card. Laminate the pieces for durability and store the cutouts at a center. A student uses his knowledge of main ideas and supporting details to sort five coins into each pot. To check his work, he flips the coins. Golden!

Kathryn Wilson, Wilson Academy, Henderson, NC

Learning Centers

Coin Exchange

You can bank on **accurate coin exchanges** taking place at this partner center. Place a die and a container of imitation coins at a center. (For a game that concludes at 50¢, provide the following coins: ten pennies, three nickels, three dimes, three quarters, one half-dollar.) To play, partners take turns rolling the die. Each partner collects cents equal to the number he rolls. When a partner collects his coins, he evaluates his coin set. If he can exchange coins for a coin of greater value, he makes the trade. If a player overlooks a trade during his turn, his partner can point out the missed trade during his own turn and earn an extra roll of the die. The first player to collect 50¢ wins the game.

Anne M. Bosarge—Gr. 3
Lyman Elementary School
Richmond Hill, GA

Action Pack

This center is packed with opportunities for **using action verbs!** Stuff a backpack with props that suggest action, such as a jump rope, ball, spoon, ruler, book, and drinking cup. Place the backpack, half sheets of blank paper, crayons, and pencils at the center. A student selects a prop from the backpack and brainstorms actions associated with it. Then, on each side of a half sheet of paper, she writes and illustrates a different action sentence about the prop and uses a crayon to underline each action word she uses. When every child has completed the center, compile the students' work into a class booklet titled "Ready for Action!"

adapted from an idea by
Linda Masternak Justice
Kansas City, MO

Diane throws the ball as far as she can.

Take a Spin!

Capitalization of proper nouns drives this geography-themed center! Place a map, a spinner labeled with four familiar geography terms (see the illustration), blank paper, a ruler, crayons, and pencils at a center. A student divides a sheet of paper into four columns and writes at the top of each column a different term from the provided spinner. Next, he spins the spinner. On the map he finds an example of the term that he spun, writes its name in the corresponding column of his paper, and underlines each capital letter. Then he spins the spinner again and repeats the procedure. Ask each child to record ten or more spins on his paper. Now that's a low-cost way to travel the country and practice capitalizing proper nouns!

Julie Ivory—Gr. 1, Seton Catholic School, Davenport, IA

State	Capital City	Lake	River
			Yukon River
	Little Rock		Snake River
Kentucky			
Oregon			

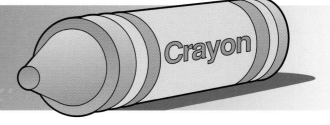

Strawberry Wishes

At this card-making center, students **write for a purpose.** Place copies of the poem from page 57 at a center along with 9" x 12" sheets of light-colored construction paper, half sheets of writing paper, a red stamp pad, crayons or markers, glue, scissors, and pencils. A student folds a sheet of construction paper in half (to 6" x 9"), cuts out a copy of the poem, glues the poem to the front of the card, and adds a desired greeting. Then, using her best penmanship, she writes on a half sheet of writing paper three or more wishes for the intended recipient of her card. She glues her writing inside the card, adds a closing, and signs her name. To embellish her work with strawberries, she uses the ink pad to make red thumbprints on the card and then adds details to the prints as shown. Very sweet!

Amy Climer—Gr. 3, Houston Elementary, Cincinnati, OH

Pronoun Replacements

Students link **pronouns** to nouns at this sentence-building center. Laminate a construction paper copy of the cards from page 57. Then cut out the cards and store them at a center along with writing paper, crayons, and pencils. A student sorts the cards by symbols, and then he arranges the cards in each set to make a complete sentence. When he writes each sentence on his paper, he replaces each pronoun with an appropriate noun or nouns. Very clever!

adapted from an idea by Cynthia Holcomb—Gr. 2
Irion County Elementary
Mertzon, TX

Scheduling Time

Here's a kid-pleasing activity that integrates **telling time and writing.** Place a clock stamp, a stamp pad, pencils, crayons, and a supply of blank paper at a center. A student titles her paper "A Perfect Saturday" and then stamps a column of clock faces down the left edge of the paper as shown. She programs the first clock to show the time she'll get out of bed. To the right of the clock she writes the matching analog time in crayon, and then she uses a pencil to describe what she plans to do at that time. She programs and labels the remaining clocks on her paper to show the activities she'd schedule for her perfect day. Display the completed schedules and plenty of time-related conversations will follow!

Stacie Stone Davis
Lima, NY

Learning Centers

Teapot Travels

This **creative-writing** center is the ticket to adventure! Place a teapot, story paper, pencils, and crayons at the center. Each week select a different travel destination and display resources at the center that describe and picture this place. A student gently rubs the teapot and pretends he is magically transported to the featured destination. Using the provided resources, he imagines himself having an adventure there. He rubs the teapot a second time for his return trip. Then he writes and illustrates a story about his adventure. Frequent fliers are frequent writers!

Theresa DeShong—Gr. 3
Nut Swamp School
Middletown, NJ

The Grand Canyon

My trip to the Grand Canyon was exciting! I rode a mule to the very bottom of the canyon. There is a big river there. I saw some people floating on a raft. My mule sure got tired carrying me back to the top of the canyon. I got a little scared, but we made it!

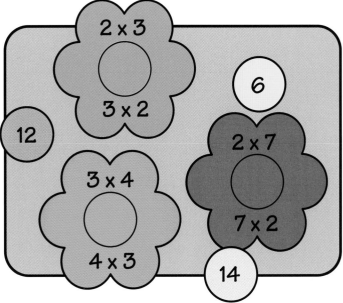

Basic Facts Blossoms

Create a colorful garden of **multiplication facts review.** Use the patterns on page 58 to make an equal number of construction paper flower blossoms and centers. Label each flower center with a different product. Then, for each flower center, program a blossom with one or two variations of its problem (see the illustration). Laminate the cutouts for durability and cut them out. For self-checking, code the back of each blossom with its corresponding product. Store the cutouts in a plastic bag at a center. A student matches each flower center to a flower blossom. Then she flips the blossoms to check her work.

Shannon D. Matthews—Gr. 2
Lake View Academy
Oklahoma City, OK

Plurals on the Side

A review of **spelling patterns** awaits students at this center. Label each of four library card pockets with a different spelling pattern for forming plurals. Glue the labeled pockets to the sides of an empty cube-shaped tissue box. Then program each of several tagboard strips with a singular word to which one of the spelling patterns applies. Store the strips inside the tissue box and place the box, blank paper, pencils, and crayons at a center. A student divides his paper into four sections and titles one section for each of the four spelling patterns. Then he sorts the word into the pockets by spelling pattern and writes the plural form of each one in the corresponding section of his paper. Plural spelling patterns are quickly squared away!

Lisa Strieker—Gr. 3, St. Paul Elementary, Highland, IL

Patterns

Use the baseballs with "Sorting for Capitals" on page 44.

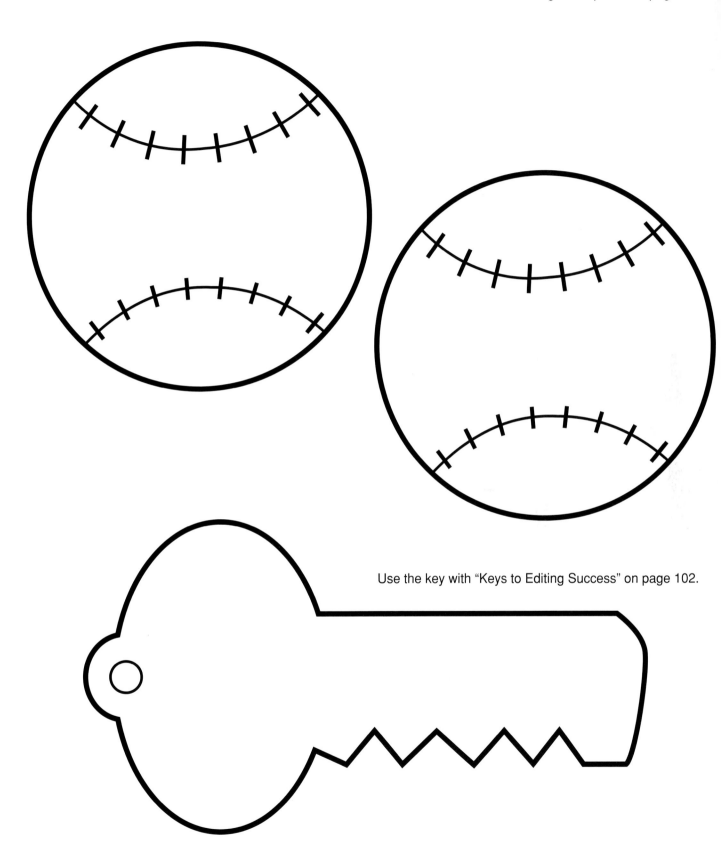

Use the key with "Keys to Editing Success" on page 102.

Patterns
Use with "Sightly Jack-o'-Lanterns" on page 46.

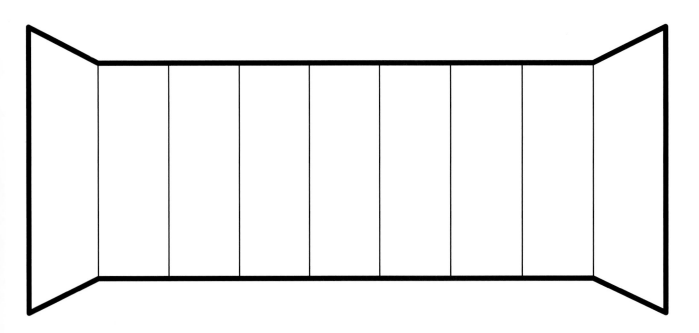

©The Education Center, Inc. • THE MAILBOX® • Primary • Oct/Nov 2001

Use the poem with "Strawberry Wishes" on page 53.

Sweet Wishes for You!

My wishes for you are so sweet.
I hope they knock you off your feet!
I wrote them carefully by hand
Because I am your biggest fan!

Use the cards with "Pronoun Replacements" on page 53.

She ■	waved ■	at ■	the ■	principal. ■
He ●	plays ●	soccer ●	after ●	school. ●
It ▲	fell ▲	on ▲	the ▲	floor. ▲
They ◆	talk ◆	on ◆	the ◆	phone. ◆
We ⬬	like ⬬	to ⬬	play ⬬	together. ⬬

Patterns

Use the flower blossom and center with "Basic Facts Blossoms" on page 54.

Use the fish with "By the Number" on page 44.

©The Education Center, Inc. • *THE MAILBOX® • Primary •* June/July 2002

Lifesavers: Management Tips for Teachers

LIFESAVERS...
management tips for teachers

Monthly Workmats

Protect desktops and strengthen calendar skills with monthly workmats! Each month have every child program a blank calendar grid for the current month and label it with family- and school-related events. Next, have him glue the calendar on a 12" x 18" sheet of construction paper, personalize the project, and add desired artwork. Laminate the completed mats. Ask students to work atop their mats when they use potentially messy supplies such as glue and paint. The end result is cleaner desktops and more calendar-related conversations!

Betty Klein—Gr. 1
Sheridan Road School
Fort Sill, OK

New Student Strategy

As you ready your classroom for the start of school, prepare for new student arrivals later in the year. Label each of several gallon-size plastic bags "New Student." Every time you label an item for individual students (such as a nametag, a lunch count stick, a cutout for the helper display, and a work folder), place an unlabeled item in each plastic bag. When a new student arrives, a smooth transition into her new classroom is in the bag!

Lu Brunnemer—Gr. 1
Eagle Creek Elementary
Indianapolis, IN

Show-and-Tell

You can't beat this five-day formula for show-and-tell. Divide students into five groups and name each group for a different weekday. Explain that each child may share with the class on his group's day. (Make special arrangements for school holidays.) Now that's an approach that's efficient and fair!

Anne E. South—Gr. 2, East Oro Public School
Orillia, Ontario, Canada

Ready to Begin

Here's an upbeat way to ready students for a new task. During September say, "One apple, two apples, three apples," adjusting the tempo of the phrase to allow sufficient time for students to ready themselves. Then snap your fingers twice, prompting a student response of "Johnny Appleseed!" Count pumpkins in October ("It's harvest time!"), Pilgrims in November ("We are thankful!"), and candles in December ("Happy holidays!"). Timely transitions are guaranteed!

Lynda Wiedenhaupt—Gr. 2, Oshkosh Christian School
Oshkosh, WI

Doable Documentation

Take a practical approach to documenting student behavior. Write each child's name on a Post-it® index flag. Attach each flag to a different page of a spiral notebook, leaving four blank pages between flags. Program each flagged page with family and medical information about the named student. Label each set of blank pages for the four quarters of the school year. To document student behavior, simply turn to the appropriate notebook page and then date and note your observation. Now that's doable!

Irene Thayer—Gr. 1, Odebolt-Arthur Community School
Odebolt, IA

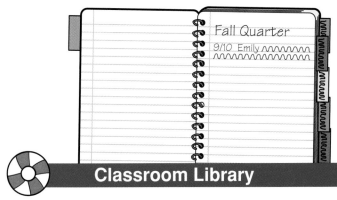

Classroom Library

Stick with this system and maintaining an orderly library will be as easy as *A, B, C!* Gather a supply of paint sticks (often free where paint is sold) and personalize one stick per student. Each time a student removes a book from the classroom library, she leaves her personalized paint stick in its place. She then removes the stick when she returns the book to its original location.

Linda Macke—Gr. 2, John F. Kennedy School
Kettering, OH

LIFESAVERS...
management tips for teachers

Organizing Correspondence

Keep parent correspondence at your fingertips! Label a tab divider for each child. Tape a 6" x 9" envelope to the back of each divider and then alphabetize the dividers and place them in a three-ring binder. Store correspondence in the envelope and log phone communications on the divider. Nifty!

Monnette Tyner—Gr. 3
Houston Elementary
Mineral Wells, TX

9/19 Positive call home.

10/15 Mother called about Amy's absence.

Chet
Amy
Bert
Brad

The Mailbox® Magazine

If you have difficulty recalling where you saw a specific idea in *The Mailbox* magazine, try this! Label individual cards with the topics, skills, and themes that you teach. Alphabetize the cards and store them in a file box. As you read through each issue of *The Mailbox*, note each idea you're eager to use on the corresponding card in your deck. The result is a customized card catalog of ideas from *The Mailbox*!

Abbie Andrews—Gr. 1
Wilkinson Elementary
Middleburg, FL

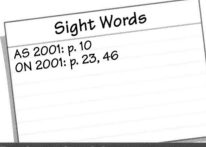

Sight Words

AS 2001: p. 10
ON 2001: p. 23, 46

Toeing the Line

Help the class form a straight line every time! Simply select a visible object that's located in the direction the students are heading and say, "Toes and nose toward [the object]!" The line quickly straightens!

Alyson Saieva—Gr. 2
Olita School
LaHabra, CA

Weekly Homework Bonus

Here's the ticket to completed student homework! Schedule a lunchtime video every Friday. Invite each child who successfully completes her homework for the week to view the video. If students routinely eat their lunches in the classroom, arrange for a parent volunteer to show the video in another food-friendly school location.

Ashley Rebman—Substitute Teacher
Durham, NC

See-Through Storage

Storing math manipulatives just got easier! Invite students to bring to school clean and empty plastic peanut butter jars with lids. Store math manipulatives inside the jars. Since the manipulatives are in plain sight, no labeling is required!

Sheila Criqui-Kelley—Gr. 1
Lebo Elementary
Lebo, KS

Thumbs-Up Behavior

Promote positive classroom behavior with this easy-to-maintain display! Mount the title "Thumbs Up for Good Behavior" and prepare a colorful supply of cutouts like the one shown. At the end of each day, quickly review the class's behavior. When it is satisfactory, add a cutout to the display. If an improvement is needed, provide a behavior pointer. When a predetermined number of cutouts are posted, reward the class with a special treat or privilege. Then remove the posted cutouts and repeat the positive plan!

Lee Rodrigue—Gr. 1
Vacherie Primary
Vacherie, LA

LIFESAVERS...
management tips for teachers

Reading in Progress

Who's reading and who's rereading? Use colorful bookmarks to find out! Give each child a laminated bookmark programmed like the one shown. A child displays the green side of his bookmark when he is reading an assignment for the first time. He displays the yellow side when he is rereading it. A quick glance and you know the status of each child's reading!

Reading in Progress!

Rereading in Progress!

Glenda Muccitelli—Gr. 3
Wright Elementary
Altoona, PA

Writing Workshop

This easy-to-make chart shows where each child is currently working in the writing process. Label a colorful tagboard strip for each writing stage, divide a sheet of poster board as shown, and then glue the stages on the poster board in sequential order. Laminate the finished chart and suspend it within students' reach. Each child maintains his own personalized clothespin. Now that's a clear picture of writing progress!

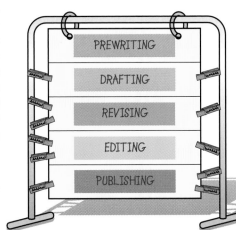

PREWRITING

DRAFTING

REVISING

EDITING

PUBLISHING

Jody Boyer—Gr. 2
Anderson Elementary
Plano, TX

Tidy Desks

Encourage neat and clean student desks with a small stuffed animal (or two)! Tell students that the animal's natural habitat is a clean and organized desk. Explain that each evening the critter will examine the inside and outside of every desk to find a clean home for the following school day. Invite the child whose desk is chosen to include the stuffed critter in his school activities for the day. Tidy desks will be all around!

Maya Kobashigawa—Gr. 3, Burton Valley Elementary
Lafayette, CA

Buckle Up!

Get students in the learning habit with a visualization technique! Ask each child to imagine her desk as a car (or spaceship or airplane) that takes exciting learning journeys. Suggest that the greatest learning occurs when a driver is buckled in with an imaginary seat belt. Each morning have students enact buckling up for the day's learning adventures. During the day, give buckle-up reminders to quicken transitions or refocus your youngsters' attention. Vroom!

Diana Cassidy—Gr. 3
Ascension Catholic School
Melbourne, FL

Pencil Pockets

These kid-appealing pencil holders are a teacher's dream come true! Collect pairs of outgrown or worn-out denim jeans. Cut out the back pockets along with the fabric to which the pockets are attached. Use a hot glue gun, Velcro, or double-sided tape to secure a pocket to each child's desktop. (If your pocket supply is limited, attach pockets to learning center tables, reading tables, and so on.) There you have it! Pencil holders that are durable, quiet, and impossible to lose!

Jeanne Brown—Gr. 3
Rochester Hills Christian School
Rochester Hills, MI

The Mailbox Companion™ Binder

Now that The Mailbox Companion™ provides you with even more of *The Mailbox*® magazine, take this step to stay organized! Place monthly divider tabs inside a large binder and label the outside of the binder for the current school year. Inside the binder store the online extenders and weekly seasonal offerings you print from the Web site. For easy access, keep the binder with your copies of the corresponding magazine issues. Wow! That's a beneficial binder!

Mary Morrison—Grs. K–4 Media Specialist
Watson Elementary School
Fairmont, WV

LIFESAVERS...
management tips for teachers

Wrist Reminders

Colorful wristbands are a great way to remind students and their families that book orders, field trip slips, and other pending paperwork are due! Type a brief reminder message on your computer, copy the message, and repeatedly paste it on the entire length of the page. Print the page onto sheets of neon-colored paper and then use a paper cutter to separate the messages. To fashion a reminder wristband, wrap a paper strip around a child's wrist and tape the ends.

Amy Matthews—Gr. 2
Rock Springs Elementary
Lawrenceville, GA

Book orders are due Friday, April 19!

Book orders are due Friday, April 19!

To a T!

Encourage smooth and speedy transitions with an oral phrase or a hand signal! Direct students to fold their hands and make eye contact with you when you form a *T* with your hands or say the phrase "T-time." Along with quick transitions, you'll promote class community!

Cheryl Chartrand—Gr. 3, Glenfield Elementary
Glenfield, NY

Student Book Boxes

Here's an easy way to provide students with appropriate books for independent reading. Ask each child to bring to school an empty cereal box. Remove the top and then trim the box as shown. After each student decorates her box, label it with her name. Store the boxes in an easily accessible area. In each child's box place books written at her independent-reading level. Each time a child is introduced to a book during guided reading, she places the new book in her box and removes a book she's read several times. Read on!

Cheryl Walker—Gr. 1
Westport School
Springfield, MO

Favorite Web Sites

Where's a perfect place to organize addresses of favorite educational Web sites? In an address book! List each site by topic. Then, below each Web address, jot a note about the site. Not only is the book easy to use, it's also easy to carry between home and school!

Sally Wallace—Gr. 3, O'Neill Elementary, O'Neill, NE

Recess Wheels

Springtime is a perfect time to set these wheels in motion! On the board write a student-generated list of appropriate recess activities. Next, visually divide two or three tagboard circles into equal sections and label the sections with activities from the list. Laminate the programmed circles for durability and then loosely secure a spinner in the center of each one. Store the resulting recess wheels in an area that is easy for students to access. A child who is looking for (or is in need of) an appropriate recess option spins a wheel on his way outdoors!

Cortney Ragsdale—Gr. 1
Terrace Elementary
Ankeny, IA

Sub Tub

Give your substitute teacher a helping hand! Label a lidded tub "Sub Tub." Inside the container store an explanation of your classroom procedures and discipline system, a weekly schedule, a seating chart, a folder of extra activities that are easy to implement, stickers and behavior awards for the students, change for the soft drink machine, and a nonperishable snack. Keep the tub in plain view, or tell a co-worker where it's stored. You'll rest easier knowing that your class will be well tended!

Amy Pierce
Pierce Private Day School
Irving, TX

LIFESAVERS...
management tips for teachers

Schoolwide Storage

Here's a space-saving tip for organizing and storing large quantities of donated items, such as egg cartons, juice cans, and film canisters. Request that shelving be put in an out-of-sight location that is easily accessible to teachers. On the shelves, place empty boxes, each clearly labeled with an item frequently needed for student projects. Then sort donations into the boxes. Solicit parent support to keep the storage area stocked and organized.

Janette Quarles—Speech Therapist Grs. K–2
Glenpool Public Schools
Glenpool, OK

Early Pickup

Reinforce time-telling skills with early-pickup reminders! Keep handy a supply of forms like the one shown. When a parent notifies you that he's picking up his child early from school, program a form with a time that's a few minutes earlier than the planned pickup time; then tape the note to the child's desk. When the parent arrives, the child is ready to go!

You may get ready at

Anne E. South—Gr. 2
East Oro Public School
Orillia, Ontario, Canada

Class Password

Attentive listening and eager cooperation are just two benefits of this top secret behavior plan! Declare a familiar word pairing, such as "bread and butter" or "spaghetti and meatballs," the class password. When you say the first word in the pairing, students immediately stop what they're doing, look at you, and say the second word. You can then communicate your message with your youngsters' full attention.

Virginia Toomey—Gr. 1
St. Rene Goupil School
Chicago, IL

Colorful Signals

Quietly monitor small-group noise levels with plastic cups. For each group, stack a yellow cup between a green and a red cup as shown. The green cup stays on top of a stack unless a group generates too much noise. If this happens, caution the group by moving its yellow cup to the top of its stack. Put the green cup back on top of the stack when the noise level becomes acceptable. Or temporarily place the red cup on top of the stack to signal a no-talk period. No doubt about it! These colorful cups are stacked for success!

Kathy Kleinhenz—Grs. 2–3
Menlo Park School
Huber Heights, OH

Dining In

Keep a lid on lunchroom behavior! Each Friday, invite every child who has shown positive lunchroom behavior that week to dine at the Classroom Cafe. Use placemats, soft music, and flowers to create the ambience of fine dining. Periodically surprise visiting patrons by serving them bite-size appetizers or desserts. Students work very hard to become regulars at this five-star diner.

Pam Stevens—Gr. 3
Lilburn Elementary
Lilburn, GA

Word Family File

Keep word family card sets organized and at your fingertips! Label a resealable freezer bag for each word family and hole-punch the bags for storage in a three-ring binder. Seal the corresponding set of cards inside each bag and then place the bags in a binder. When you need cards for a particular word family, you'll know right where to look!

adapted from an idea by
Sherri Smith—Gr. 1
John C. Calhoun Elementary
Calhoun Falls, SC

Math Mailbag

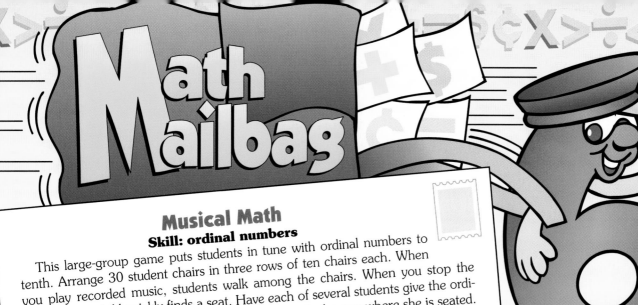

Math Mailbag

Musical Math
Skill: ordinal numbers

This large-group game puts students in tune with ordinal numbers to tenth. Arrange 30 student chairs in three rows of ten chairs each. When you play recorded music, students walk among the chairs. When you stop the music, every child quickly finds a seat. Have each of several students give the ordinal number that describes the position of her chair in the row where she is seated. Then restart the music. Continue play in this manner for as long as desired. For a fun finale, label ten craft sticks with ordinals through tenth. Stop the music and then randomly remove single sticks from the container. Announce each ordinal and direct the students in the corresponding chairs to exit the game. It's an exciting finish to an already great activity!

adapted from an idea by Marilyn Hilt—Grs. K–1, Lakeshore Road Elementary, Cicero, NY

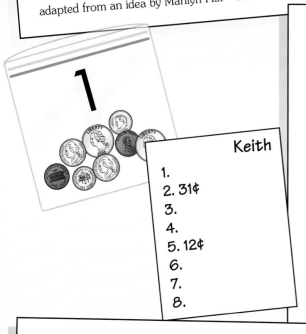

Keith

1.
2. 31¢
3.
4.
5. 12¢
6.
7.
8.

Money Bags
Skill: counting money

With this hands-on approach, students' money-counting skills are in the bag! Number a class set of resealable plastic bags. Place different combinations of toy coins in the bags and then make an answer key. For a large-group activity, have students number their papers to match the number of money bags and then give each child one bag. Each student counts the money in his bag and writes the total on his paper next to the bag's number. On a signal from you, each student hands his bag to a designated student and then counts the money in the bag he receives. Play continues in this manner until each child has counted the money in every bag. For a small-group activity, have each group member count the money in a different bag. Then have each group arrange its bags from least to greatest value. Or place the money bags in a math center. Whatever you decide, money-counting skills are sure to profit!

Peggy Bruno—Gr. 2, Squadron Line School, Simsbury, CT

Crack the Code
Skill: addition

Add a fun spin to addition practice! Cut out a 20-inch tagboard circle and a 16-inch tagboard circle. Use a brad to connect the two circles as shown. Write the letters of the alphabet around the outer rim. Write the numbers 1–9 on the inner rim, making sure the numbers align with the letters A through I. Then repeat the number series until every alphabet letter has a corresponding number. Post the resulting wheel in clear view of the class, along with a set of addition problems that have letters for addends. Each morning spin the wheel to determine the daily math code and challenge students to decode and solve the provided problems. Case solved!

Goldy Hirsch—Special Education Grs. 1–3, Beacon School, Brooklyn, NY

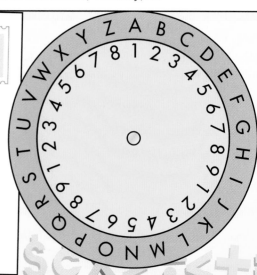

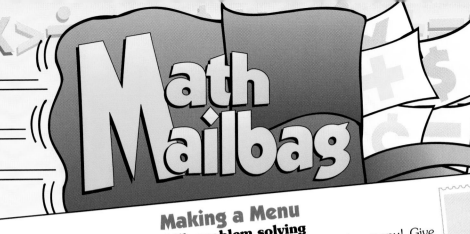

Math Mailbag

Making a Menu
Skill: problem solving

Try this appetizing approach to making a Thanksgiving menu! Give each child seven cards, each labeled with one of the following: turkey, dressing, mashed potatoes, green beans, carrots, beets, pumpkin pie. Challenge each child to use his cards to create six different dinner combinations that each include a meat, dressing, two different vegetables, and dessert. To increase the difficulty of the activity, give each child another meat (or dessert) card and challenge the class to find 12 different dinner combinations. Delicious!

Erin Harp—Gr. 2, Riddle Brook School, Bedford, NH

Home Deliveries
Skill: place value

This place-value activity just keeps on delivering! Program a class set of cards with different numbers appropriate for your students' place-value skills. Give each child a programmed card, a 9" x 12" sheet of construction paper, and a page of base ten block patterns. To make a house, a student cuts away the top two corners of her construction paper. Next, she cuts out base ten blocks to represent the number on her card. She glues the cutouts to her house shape. After she adds desired details to the front of the house, she flips the cutout over and on the back copies the number from her card. Last, she decorates the blank side of the card to resemble a postcard. Check each child's work for accuracy. Then collect the cards and cutouts and place them at a math center. To complete the center, a student delivers each postcard to its corresponding house. To check her work, she turns over the house cutouts.

Bonnie Baumgras—Grs. 3–5 Gifted and Talented, Kirk L. Adams Elementary Las Vegas, NV

Ring a Bell
Skill: computation

Keep computation skills sharp with this large-group game! Divide the class into two teams. Have the players from each team count off starting with 1. If the team counts are unequal, a player from the smaller team gets two numbers. Then have the players on each team arrange their chairs in a semicircle facing the opposing team. Display a call bell in the center of the circle. Each player needs a portable writing surface (like a book), paper, and a pencil. To play, state a math problem. Wait for each child to solve the problem on his paper. Then call out a player number. These two players stand up, place their supplies in their chairs, and advance to the call bell (without running). The player who rings the bell gives his answer. If it is correct, his team earns a point and the round is over. If his answer is incorrect, his opponent gives his answer in hopes of earning a point for his team. Then the players take their seats and another round begins. Continue play until one team earns a set number of points or time runs out.

Patricia Bittler—Gr. 3, Centerville Elementary School, Lancaster, PA

Math Mailbag

Fraction Match
Skill: identifying ¹/₂, ¹/₃, and ¹/₄

Students develop a keen eye for fractional parts during this fast-paced partner game. To make a set of game cards, a child cuts out the cards from a construction paper copy of page 71. Then he stores the cards in a resealable plastic bag. To play, students are in pairs. One partner deals his game cards, and the other partner sets his aside. After each player stacks his cards facedown, the players simultaneously turn over the top cards in their stacks. If the same fraction is illustrated on both cards, the player who is first to identify the appropriate fraction wins the pair. If the fractions don't match, the cards go in a discard pile, which can be shuffled and dealt as needed. The first player to make seven fraction matches wins the game.

adapted from an idea by Angela R. Thomas—Gr. 2, Seneca East-Republic Elementary, Republic, OH

$$2 \times 5 = 10 \qquad 4 \times 5 = 20$$
$$3 \times 5 = 15 \qquad 4 \times 5 = 20$$
$$5 \times 5 = 25 \qquad 8 \times 5 = 40$$

$$1 \times 5 = 5$$
$$3 \times 5 = 15$$
$$4 \times 5 = 20$$

High-Rolling Facts
Skill: multiplication facts

Use this partner activity to get students on a roll with multiplication facts! Each student pair needs a pair of dice, pencils, and paper. To begin, name a factor. Player 1 rolls the dice. On the paper she writes three multiplication problems based on her roll. To do this, she multiplies each number rolled by the designated factor. Then she adds the two rolled numbers and multiplies the resulting sum by the factor. After Player 2 verifies his partner's calculations, he takes a turn. The activity continues in a like manner until time runs out. Announce different factors as desired. Roll 'em!

Lori Lavender—Gr. 3, East Corinth Elementary, Corinth, MS

Gifts Galore
Skill: subtraction with regrouping

Sharpen subtraction skills as you reinforce the joy in giving. Provide a variety of advertising inserts and catalogs. Then designate an amount of money for each student to spend on holiday gifts for his family and friends. Also provide spending guidelines, such as a minimum number of purchases and how the purchases are to be listed and described on paper. Challenge each child to spend as much of his allotted money as possible without overspending. To extend the activity, have each child use a calculator to check his (or a partner's) calculations. Happy holidays!

Kelly Astrahan—Gr. 3, Einstein Elementary School, Hanover Park, IL

Person	Gift	Money
		$ 100.00
Mom	candle and holder	– 12.95
		$ 87.05
Josh	key ring	$ 87.05
		– 14.95
		$ 72.10
Kimmie	earrings	$ 72.10
		– 9.99
		$ 62.11
		$ 62.11
Cinder	cheeseburger squeak toy	

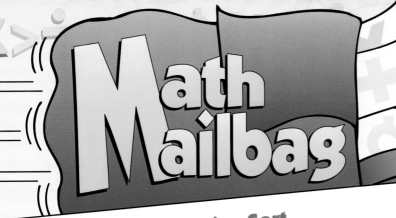

Math Mailbag

Valentine Sort
Skill: Collecting, displaying, and interpreting data

Sneak a little math into your Valentine's Day festivities! After students have opened their valentine cards, ask each child to sort his valentines into categories of his own choosing. Then ask each child to describe his sort. On the board list the attributes that are shared. Select four or five of these attributes and have students resort their valentines for each one. Record the outcome of each sort on the board. Next, give each student a blank graph on which to display the data that's been collected. Students can use their completed graphs to identify popular trends in valentine card purchases and solve assorted word problems.

Tami Wittich
Freedom Elementary
West Chester, OH

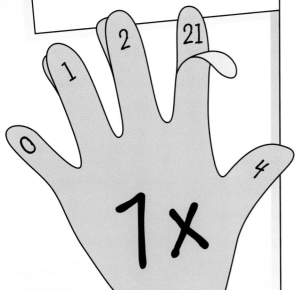

Helpful Hand
Skill: Basic facts

Provide individualized reinforcement of basic facts with this "hand-y" manipulative! To make a helpful hand, a student folds a 9" x 12" sheet of construction paper in half (to 6" x 9"). She traces her hand on the folded paper and cuts out the shape (cutting through both thicknesses). She glues the two cutouts together, leaving the fingertips unglued. When the glue is dry, she programs the front and back of her project with an addend, minuend, or factor of a fact table she finds challenging. On one side of the shape, she numbers the fingertips from 0 through 4. Then she carefully lifts each paper fingertip and writes the corresponding answer inside (see the illustration). Next, she flips the hand shape over, numbers the blank fingertips from 5 through 9, and writes the answers as previously described. Now that's a helpful hand!

Tiffany Giannicchi—Gr. 3
Allegany-Limestone Central School
Allegany, NY

What's the Chance?
Skill: Probability

Put a wee bit of an Irish spin on probability! Remind students that probability is the chance or likelihood that an event will happen. Also review the vocabulary terms *most likely, least likely,* and *equally likely.* Then give each student a copy of page 72 and a paper clip. Explain that Larry Leprechaun must give up the item that is spun the most times in 20 spins. Confirm that students know how to operate the spinner using their paper clips and pencils. Then have each child complete the activity as described. Very clever!

adapted from an idea by Linda Masternak Justice
Kansas City, MO

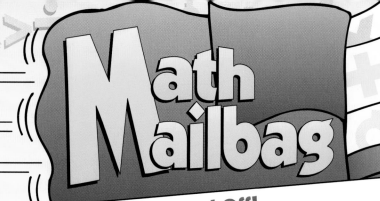

Math Mailbag

Round Off!

Skill: rounding numbers

Students get in step with rounding numbers during this large-group activity! Write each of the following 11 numbers on a half sheet of construction paper: 0, 10, 20, 30, 40, 50, 60, 70, 80, 90, 100. Have 11 students face the class and hold the numbers in numerical order. Next, announce a number between 0 and 100. The two students holding the numbers closest to the announced number step forward. (For example, if 24 is announced, the students holding 20 and 30 step forward.) Then the class determines to which ten to round. The child holding the chosen ten takes a bow before both students step back into line. Play continues as described for as long as desired.

Michelle Viera—Gr. 3, Public School 138, Bronx, NY

Multiply With Me!

A Personalized Approach

Skill: word problems

Give word problem practice a face-lift! For each child, make a booklet that consists of six half sheets of paper—five sheets precut with an identical circular opening followed by a sixth uncut sheet. A student tapes her photo to the uncut page so that her face shows through the openings. After she titles her booklet "[Math operation] With Me!" and decorates the cover, she turns to the first two-page spread. On the left-hand page she writes a word problem that stars herself in a desired role. She adds an illustration on the right-hand page. She repeats this technique on each of the next three spreads. On the last spread she provides an answer key. For daily word problem practice, have each child exchange booklets with a different classmate. A student solves the word problems on her math paper and then she uses the provided answer key to check her work. Before she returns the booklet to its owner, she signs the back cover.

Penny Blazer—Gr. 3, Spring Mills, PA

Mystery Messages

Skill: computation

For this large-group game, the key to cracking a mystery message is accurate computation! Laminate a set of alphabet cards and use a dry-erase marker to program the back of each card with a math problem to solve. Display the cards on the board in alphabetical order. Then draw a dash for each letter of a secret message and designate an area of the board for discarded letters. To begin play, ask one child to select a letter card, read aloud the problem on the back of the card, and then solve the problem on the board while his classmates solve it on their papers. Before the child presents his final answer, he consults with the class and, if necessary, recalculates. If his final answer is correct, write the chosen letter as it appears in the secret message (if it does), and discard the letter card. If his answer is incorrect, return the letter card to its original position. The child then chooses a classmate to take his place at the board, and the game continues as described until all letters in the message are earned. Store the letter cards for future games, reprogramming the problems as desired.

Kerry Robertshaw—Gr. 2, Mason Heights Elementary, Mason, OH

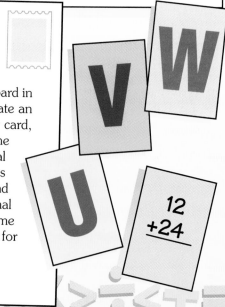

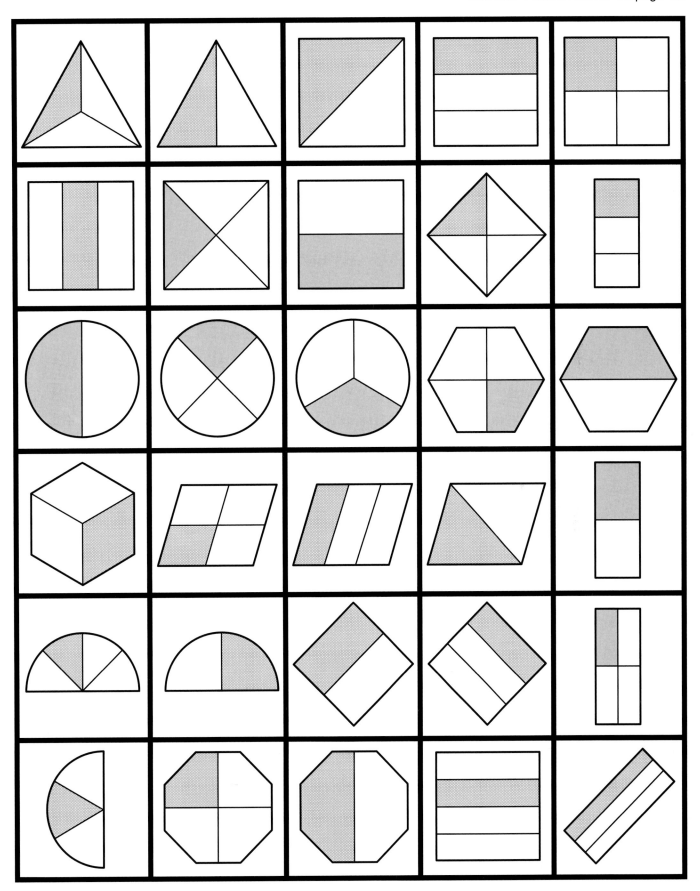

Spinning for Gold

Larry Leprechaun is counting on keeping his pot of gold!
Can you figure out why?

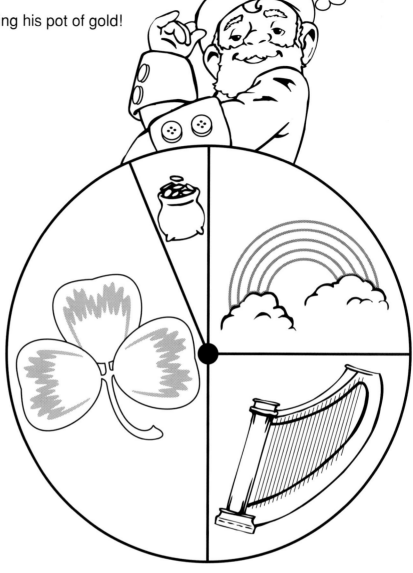

1. Predict which item the spinner is *most likely* to stop on in 20 spins.

2. Predict which item the spinner is *least likely* to stop on in 20 spins.

3. Predict which 2 items the spinner is *equally likely* to stop on in 20 spins.

4. Spin the spinner 20 times. For each spin, color 1 box on the graph.

5. Use your data to evaluate the 3 predictions you made. If a prediction was right, color the shamrock beside it.

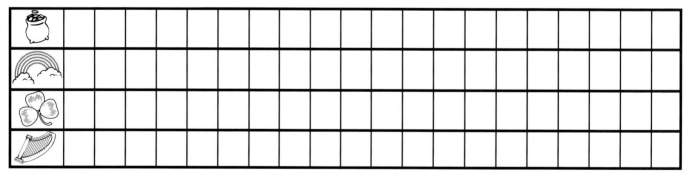

6. Explain why Larry will probably never need to give up his pot of gold. _____

_____

Bonus Box: On the back of this paper, draw and color a spinner that increases the odds that you will win Larry's gold. Try out your spinner!

©The Education Center, Inc. • *THE MAILBOX*® • *Primary* • Feb/Mar 2002 • Key p. 311

OUR READERS WRITE

Our Readers Write

A Word-Search Welcome

Here's a first-day activity that's sure to please! Prepare a word-search puzzle and a corresponding word bank that includes each child's name and your name. After students complete the activity, ask each child to introduce himself to the class and then reveal where in the puzzle his name is located. Send the papers home with students at the end of the day so they can share with their families the names of their new classmates and teacher!

Nell Roberts—Gr. 1, The Covenant School, Charlottesville, VA

Photo Gallery

Foster a spirit of schoolwide community with this quick-and-easy hallway display. Title a bulletin board "Our School Photo Gallery" and in the school office place a supply of photo caption forms similar to the one shown. Invite families to contribute photos and completed caption forms for the display. Encourage teachers and other school staff to do the same. The photo gallery is sure to be a real crowd pleaser!

Joanne Yantz and Debra Wilkins
Woodfern Elementary School
Neshanic, NJ

Family: _Green_
Event: _Michael, Dad, and Riot (the dog) had a great time at Smith Lake._

Me Bags

Build self-esteem and help students get to know each other better with this back-to-school activity! For each student, glue on the front of a paper bag a poem like the one shown. Have each child take his bag home and return it on a designated day with an item inside that represents something special about himself. Ask each child to share his item with the class and answer questions from his classmates.

Catherine Salvini—Multiage Grs. 1–2
Morningside Community School
Pittsfield, MA

Me

Please help me decide
What item goes inside.
Something about me
For all my friends to see.
What I like or do
That makes me special, too!

Wipe-Off Display

Now you can create a wipe-off bulletin board in a snap! From a fabric store, purchase clear vinyl to cover your display area. Create a desired bulletin board and then staple the clear vinyl atop it. Provide wipe-off markers for use at the display. Wipe away programming with a moist towelette and occasionally clean the vinyl with window cleaner.

Karen Bryan—Gr. 3
Buckeye Valley North Elementary
Radnor, OH

Toothy Plan

Make the loss of a tooth both exciting and educational! Cover an empty tissue box with colorful paper, leaving the opening. Decorate the box and a supply of empty film canisters with tooth stickers. Then store the canisters inside the decorated box. Display the box with a tooth-shaped writing journal. When a student loses a tooth, she puts the tooth in a canister for the trip home. Then, in the journal, she writes (or dictates for you to write) a few sentences about how she lost her tooth!

Sheila Criqui-Kelley—Gr. 1, Lebo Elementary, Lebo, KS

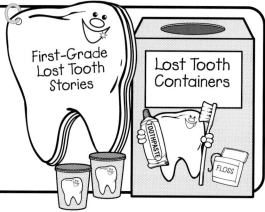

First-Grade Lost Tooth Stories

Lost Tooth Containers

Dandy Desktags

There's more than one use for student desktags! Keep these considerations in mind as you prepare desktags for the year:
- Select desktags with preprogrammed writing lines (or cut sentence strips into desired lengths). Each child's desktag doubles as a writing model for her name.
- Add a number to each desktag and then use the numbers to practice math skills such as number order, even and odd numbers, skip-counting, and basic facts.
- Color-code desktags with colorful dots and use the colors to form small groups.

Sister Maribeth Theis—Gr. 2
Mary of Lourdes Elementary
Little Falls, MN

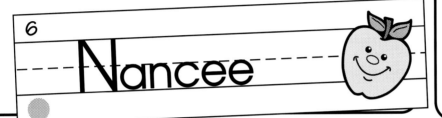

Class Scrapbook

Build writing skills throughout the year with this newsworthy activity! Routinely photograph your students engaged in events both inside and outside the classroom. When a roll of film is developed, give each child one snapshot. Pretending to be a reporter, the student writes the story behind the picture and then takes his story through the writing process. Publish each report and its corresponding photo in a class scrapbook. At the year's end, use the scrapbook to review the year. Then take the book apart and send each child home with his published pages.

Linda Stroik—Gr. 2
Bannach Elementary School
Stevens Point, WI

A Giving Tree

Harvest supplies for the new school year at this "tree-mendous" display! Cut out several construction paper leaves and label each cutout with a needed supply. Include both new purchases and recycled items. Display a tree cutout and use pieces of rolled tape to attach the leaves to the tree. A parent who wishes to donate a supply removes a leaf cutout from the tree and returns the cutout with her donation.

Betsy Ferrer—Grs. 1–2
Toll Gate Grammar School
Pennington, NJ

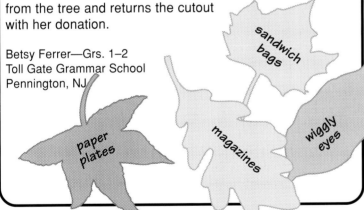

Practical Painting Smocks

Take this "cents-ible" approach to painting smocks! Invite each family to donate a box of kitchen garbage bags. To make a painting smock, cut a neck hole in the bottom of a bag and an armhole in each side seam. Toss used smocks in the trash or wipe them clean for reuse.

Melinda Casida—Grs. 2–3
Lincoln Elementary
Kingsburg, CA

Journal Newsletters

Weekly student-written newsletters are a perfect way to keep parents informed! Ask each family to provide a spiral notebook for this purpose. Every Friday, spend time with the class reviewing the past week. Also preview upcoming events of the next week. Then, in her notebook, each child writes a letter to her family in which she describes her accomplishments of the week and mentions upcoming events. Ask each family to write in the journal a response to the weekly letter. Students love the ongoing correspondence with their parents. And parents appreciate the chance to observe their children's progress from week to week.

Wendi Sumner—Gr. 3, Mill Plain Elementary, Vancouver, WA

Saying Thanks

Those who lend your class a helping hand are sure to appreciate this picture-perfect thank-you! Have a co-worker photograph you with your class and then use the developed photo to order a supply of photo greeting cards that bear a caption such as the one shown. Send the personalized card to thank a guest speaker, a field trip host, a parent volunteer, and so on. It's quick and easy for you, and it's a memorable keepsake for the recipient!

Julie Plowman—Gr. 1
Stuart-Menlo Elementary, Menlo, IA

Calendar Strips

This hands-on display gives students a clear picture of yesterday, today, and tomorrow. Each month enlist your students' help in programming one sentence strip for each day of the month. Use the sentence frame "Today is [day], [date]." Store the strips in sequential order. On a steel surface, display three pairs of magnetic clips along with partial sentence strips labeled "Yesterday was" and "Tomorrow will be." Every morning have two children update the display and then share the resulting information with the class.

Jane Miramontez—Gr. 2, Rising Star Elementary, Lenexa, KS

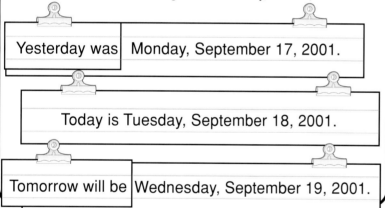

Yesterday was | Monday, September 17, 2001.

Today is Tuesday, September 18, 2001.

Tomorrow will be | Wednesday, September 19, 2001.

Topic Albums

Help students remember favorite activities from the year with this easy-to-manage approach. Ask parents and co-workers to donate the small albums that many photo centers distribute with developed pictures. At the end of a unit of study, give each child a 4" x 6" card. On the front of the card, a student writes the topic of study and describes her favorite activity from the unit. On the back of the card, she writes her name. Collect the cards and insert them into a class topic album or individual student albums. Memories are in place!

Michelle Biondo and Angela Renfro
Special Education
Gladden Elementary School
Belton, MO

Apples
I liked when we tasted different kinds of apples.

Back-to-School Science

Generate plenty of interest in the environment with this hands-on activity. During the first week of school, partially fill with dirt a large, plastic lidded bucket. (A 30-pound kitty litter container works well.) With help from your students, bury an assortment of items in the dirt, such as a piece of cardboard, a glass jar, a soda can, a Styrofoam® cup, a piece of newsprint, and a banana peel. List the buried items on paper, tape the list on the bucket, and secure the lid in place. Make plans to carefully dig through the mini landfill during the last week of school to discover which items decomposed and which did not!

Jerilyn Hogan—Gr. 2
Ballard Elementary School
Wilton, NY

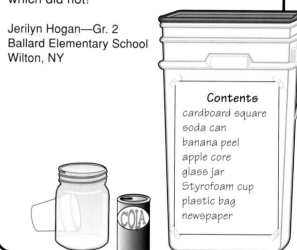

Contents
cardboard square
soda can
banana peel
apple core
glass jar
Styrofoam cup
plastic bag
newspaper

Months of the Year

Learning the months of the year and their sequence is at the root of this activity! Each month give every student a copy of a pattern similar to the one shown, along with a page that contains 12 petal patterns labeled with the months of the year. Each child cuts out the petals and glues them in order on the flower, starting with January (the first month) at the position "1." Then the student fills in the blanks in the flower's center. In no time, students' sequencing skills will be in full bloom!

Betsy Crosson—Gr. 1
Pleasant Elementary School
Tulare, CA

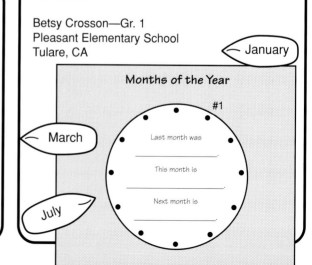

Months of the Year

January

March

July

#1

Last month was _____

This month is _____

Next month is _____

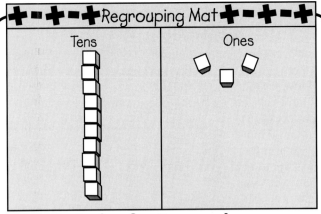

Recipe for Regrouping

Manipulatives and individual math mats are just what students need to cook up an understanding of regrouping. For each child, make and laminate a 12" x 18" construction paper math mat like the one shown. To solve a two-digit addition problem with regrouping, a student places manipulatives on her mat that equal the first addend. Next, she puts manipulatives on the mat that equal the second addend. Then she regroups the manipulatives (by converting ten ones to a ten) to find the sum of the two addends. To solve a two-digit subtraction problem with regrouping, a child places manipulatives on her mat that equal the larger number. Then she removes manipulatives from the mat that equal the smaller number. To do this she must first convert a ten to ten ones.

Brandi Russell—Gr. 2, Madison County Elementary School
Huntsville, AL

Sit 'n' Spell

The goal of this partner game is to sit and spell! Position a chair against a classroom wall. Each week post a different word list above the chair. To play, Player 1 sits in the chair and Player 2 stands, facing the chair. Player 2 reads a spelling word from the list for Player 1 to spell. If Player 1 spells the word correctly, he remains seated. If he misspells the word, he trades places with Player 2. Spelling practice continues in this manner until one player correctly spells every word on the list or time runs out.

Vicki Foote—Gr. 3, Thomas Edison School
Folsom, CA

Too Much Glue?

Keep a lid on glue usage! Dispense glue in plastic milk jug lids and give each child a cotton swab. Students quickly discover that a dab of glue will do. This means neater projects and less mess. Now that's an idea you'll stick with!

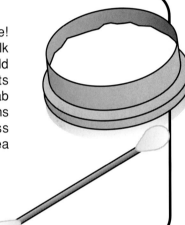

Marie Jacinto—Gr. 2
Decas School
Wareham, MA

Palatable Punctuation Practice

Students will get a "Kix®" out of ending punctuation practice when you take this tasty approach! Give each child a plastic sandwich bag of Kix cereal pieces. When a period is needed, a student glues a cereal piece in place. When a question mark or an exclamation mark is needed, he incorporates a cereal piece into the punctuation mark. Each time a child adds punctuation, he also eats one cereal piece from his bag. Delicious!

Ann Margaret Eddy—Gr. 1
Los Ranchos Elementary
San Luis Obispo, CA

Mood Meter

Use this nifty manipulative to zero in on how a child is feeling. Follow the steps shown to make a mood meter. At the beginning of a student conference, ask the child to turn the meter to show how she is feeling. Then have her use the meter again at the end of the meeting to indicate how she thinks the meeting went. Discuss the student's feelings before concluding the conference.

Making the mood meter:
1. Cut out two six-inch circles from tagboard. Laminate.
2. Stack and align the two circles. Poke a brad through the center of the circles to connect them.
3. Carefully cut out a section from the top circle as shown. Use a permanent marker to draw two eyes above the opening and a big smile in the opening.
4. Turn the top circle a quarter turn and draw a ⌣ in the opening.
5. Repeat Step 4 two more times. In each opening, draw a — or a ⌢.

adapted from an idea by William McGuire—Grs. K–4 P.E.
Cortland Elementary School, Cortland, IL

Pocket Answers

Add a creative twist to large-group skill review! Each child needs a paper pocket and a set of answer cards. To make the pocket, fold a 9" x 12" sheet of construction paper in half (to 6" x 9"). Next, fold up one inch at each open end as shown and staple the resulting pocket along each side, through all thicknesses. Answer cards (such as a "True" card and a "False" card or cards labeled with individual numbers) can be stored inside the pocket. During a skill review, a student tucks an answer card in the lip of her pocket and then raises the pocket. Awesome answer!

Brenda Scarbrough—Gr. 2
Fountain Lake Elementary
Hot Springs, AR

Paper Valances

Brighten a classroom window on a shoestring budget! To make a paper valance, cut a sheet of white bulletin board paper the width of the window. If the facing of the window is recessed, fold and staple (or hot-glue) the top of the paper to make a casing for a spring-type rod. Indicate the bottom of the valance by drawing a series of scallops. Cut along the outline and then paint a colorful design on the paper. When the paint dries, suspend the curtain or staple it in place.

Karen Parker—Art Teacher
Florence City Schools
Florence, AL

Word Problem PAL

When a student has a word problem to solve, suggest that she check her solution for a PAL. Explain that the letters in the acronym PAL stand for Problem, Answer, and Label—the three components of a word problem solution. If all three are present, then her solution is complete. Now that brings new meaning to a math buddy!

Cheryl Escritt—Gr. 3, Gibbon Elementary, Gibbon, NE

Book Hospital

Keep your collection of classroom library books in top condition! Display a container labeled "Book Hospital" and keep a roll of clear packing tape handy. Request that students place in the container any book from the classroom library that needs a repair before it is reshelved. It's amazing what a little TLC can do for a well-loved book!

Myrthala Fischer—Gr. 2
Francone School
Houston, TX

Daily Reflections

Conclude each school day on a positive note! Every week distribute student copies of a daily reflection chart like the one shown. At the end of each day have every child write on his chart what went well that day and a goal for improvement. Sign each student's chart and add a note, as desired. Ask each child to have his parent sign the chart and return it the following day. Parents are sure to appreciate the positive communications and, as an added bonus, you'll have detailed records for anecdotal notes.

Natalie Foster—Grs. 2–3, The Discovery School
Gambrills, MD

Daily Reflections by _Scott_			
For the Week of _January 14–18_			
What went well?	How can I improve?	Teacher	Parent
I did really well on my spelling pretest.	I will listen carefully to directions.	Great job on the pretest! Remember your math homework! Ms. Foster ☺	

Good or Service?

Make it your students' business to know whether local businesses sell goods or services! On the board, write a list of local businesses and enlist your students' help in labeling the businesses as providers of goods or services. Next, have each child design a 3" x 5" business card for a different business on the list. Collect the cards and erase the list from the board. Use the cards to quiz students on goods and services. It's business as usual!

Yvonne Callas—Gr. 2
Delaware Academy and
    Central School
Delhi, NY

Live Reports

Students will be eager to tune in to these country reports! Instruct each student to research a different aspect of a selected country's culture. Then have him prepare a presentation for a class newscast. Arrange to videotape the newscast and then select two volunteers to act as news anchors. Have the anchors invite each student reporter, in turn, to present his information. The show is bound to be a newsworthy hit, so plan to schedule a time for each student to take the videotape home to share with his family.

Kelley Smith, Union Hill School
Somerville, AL

Japan in the News
A Grade 3 Production

Memorable Lineup

Help students remember the usual order of the planets with this catchy tune. Point to each planet on an illustrated poster as you use the song to lead students from the sun to Pluto!

Amy Schneider—Gr. 1
Sacred Heart School
Topeka, KS

Solar System Song
(sung to the tune of "Twinkle, Twinkle, Little Star")

Mercury, Venus, Earth, and Mars—
These are planets among the stars.
Jupiter, Saturn, Uranus too,
Neptune, Pluto—now we're through.
Planets are in the Milky Way;
Try to name them all each day.

Perk for Parents

Here's a sweet way to thank students' parents for their support! For each note of appreciation, program a cutout with a candy-themed message and attach a wrapped treat. It's sure to bring a smile to the recipient's face!

Sharon Rankin, Aiken, SC

LIFESAVERS

Mrs. Hansen,
Thank you for helping with the field trip. You were a lifesaver!
Ms. Aiken

ALMOND JOY

Mr. and Mrs. Lewis,
It's a joy to work with parents like you! Thanks for making sure that Susan's homework is returned on time.
Ms. Aiken

Presidential Props

These Lincoln look-alikes can be made in a twinkling! A student glues a penny near the top of a vertically positioned jumbo craft stick. Then he uses a permanent marker and construction paper scraps to add clothing as shown. Invite each student to use his completed craft as a puppet and tell the class what he has learned about Honest Abe.

Christine Chiappone—Gr. 1
Rockwell School
Nedrow, NY

Banners by the Bunch

Colorful banners are an inexpensive alternative to poster board presentations. To make a banner about an assigned topic, a student cuts a length of bulletin board paper into a desired shape. She glues on information she has written about the topic and uses provided arts-and-crafts materials to embellish her work. Post students' banners on a hall wall to create an eye-catching (and informative!) display.

Amy Surman—Gr. 3, Franklin Elementary, Cape Girardeau, MO

Sunny Start

Bring a bit of sunshine into the classroom on a gloomy winter day! Before beginning the day's instruction, give each student a small serving of Sunny Delight drink. It's sure to chase the winter blues away!

Heather Fischer—Gr. 2, Prairie Heights Elementary, Dwight, KS

Reuse plastic bags and cardboard boxes.

Reduce by walking instead of riding.

Show you care! Do your share!

Recycle newspapers, cans, and glass.

The Three Rs

Put students in step with reusing, reducing, and recycling! On the board write a student-brainstormed list of different ways to practice each of the three Rs. Then have each student complete and illustrate a page similar to the one shown. Showcase your students' environmental enthusiasm for all to see!

Jill Hamilton Lutz—Gr. 1
Schoenecic Elementary, Stevens, PA

Noodle Nests

You can count on students sinking their teeth into this writing follow-up! After an oral reading of Bill Peet's *The Pinkish, Purplish, Bluish Egg*, serve each child an edible nest (see provided recipe) and ask her to write and illustrate a story about a unique creature that hatches from one of the eggs. Be sure to set aside time for interested authors to share their work with the class.

Shyrleen Back—Gr. 3, Donnelsville Elementary
Huber Heights, OH

Noodle Nests
(makes about 30 nests)

For one batch:
12 oz. bag chow mein noodles
3 tbsp. margarine
3 tbsp. creamy peanut butter

3 c. mini marshmallows
peanut M&M's candies (2 per nest)
muffin tins with paper liners

Directions:
1. Melt margarine over low heat. Gradually stir in peanut butter; then slowly add marshmallows. Stir until mixture is melted and smooth.
2. Remove mixture from heat. Add noodles and stir until noodles are coated.
3. Spoon mixture into paper-lined muffin tins.
4. Use back of spoon or fingertips (coated in butter) to shape nests.
5. When nests are cool, place two candies in each.

Writing Portfolios

Use a color-coded system for portfolios that clearly shows parents how a piece of writing progresses from start to finish. For example, have students use green paper for brainstorming or planning, yellow paper for first drafts, and white paper for final drafts. Now that's a bright idea!

Colleen Dabney
Williamsburg-JCC Public Schools
Williamsburg, VA

Page Number Values

Here's a quick and easy plan for providing extra place-value practice! Every time you announce a page number, use place-value terms to describe it. Page 37 becomes three tens and seven ones. Eight tens and four ones means page 84. It's a place-value prescription that really works!

Sue Weber—Gr. 2
Edson School, Kingston, NY

From Bean to Beanstalk

Add a kid-pleasing twist to your next bean-sprouting project! Read aloud a favorite version of *Jack and the Beanstalk.* Ask each child to illustrate Jack's house on one side of an 8" x 18" strip of tagboard, leaving about five inches of ground space. Laminate the projects; then securely staple an opened snack-size resealable bag to each one. Have each child partially fill his bag with moist potting soil, plant a presoaked lima bean (or two) in the soil, and seal the bag. Use clothespins to clip the projects to a chalkboard tray for easy access and viewing. When appropriate, open the bags so the plants that sprout can continue growing upward. Add water as needed. When a plant falls forward, help its owner secure it with a pipe cleaner stake (see illustration). Measuring these beanstalks is a must!

Karen Dufault—Gr. 2
Killdeer Public School
Killdeer, ND

Morning Message

Starting each day with a student-prepared message motivates the class to settle in quickly and provides a kid-pleasing forum for skill reinforcement. On a rotating basis, send each child home with an envelope containing a clean sheet of acetate, an overhead marker, and a request to pen the morning message for the following school day. Proofread each morning message before you project it for the class to read. Then ask each author to answer three message-related questions from the audience. What a great way to start the day!

Karole Matthews—Grs. 2–4, Riverside Elementary School
Monroe, MI

Good morning! Last night my soccer team won its game. I scored one goal. It was a head shot!

Dream Pets

What pets do your youngsters dream of having? Find out during National Pet Week, the first full week in May. Have each child illustrate, name, and describe her dream pet on provided paper. Then post the projects with the title "Dreaming About Pets."

Yvonne Lamb
Oshawa, Ontario, Canada

My Perfect Pet

If I could have any pet in the world I would choose a panda! It is so cute and cuddly. I would take very good care of it!

An Important Farewell

Let Margaret Wise Brown's *The Important Book* create the framework for a farewell writing activity. During an oral reading, emphasize the pattern that is established in the book. Next, ask each child to use the identified pattern to write about the important traits of a classmate (or student teacher) who is leaving. Bind the students' work into a class book that can be given as a heartwarming parting gift.

Diane Rinehard—Gr. 2, Beechgrove Elementary
Independence, KY

Randall
The important thing about Randall is his laugh.
He is very kind to others.
He likes to read.
He runs very fast!
He remembers a lot.
But the important thing about Randall is his laugh.

by Melissa

From Bill to Law

Help students begin to understand how a bill becomes a law! After an oral reading of *House Mouse, Senate Mouse* by Peter W. Barnes and Cheryl Shaw Barnes, assist the class in composing a bill that includes three reasons why it should become a law. Submit the bill to a fourth-grade class acting as the House. If the House approves the bill, ask a fifth-grade class acting as the Senate to vote on it. Pass an approved bill to the school principal to sign or veto. If at any time the bill is not approved, assist the class in rewriting the bill for resubmission. Whew! Making a law is hard work!

Kish L. Harris—Gr. 2
Capron Elementary, Capron, VA

Comprehension Clips

When a student takes this approach to completing a multiple-choice comprehension skill sheet, the proof is in the clippings! A child needs two copies of the skill sheet. He writes his name and marks his answers on one sheet. From the other sheet he cuts out proof that each answer he's marked is correct. Then he glues the cutouts below or beside the corresponding answers. Clip, clip!

Tammie Isbel—Gr. 3, Lott Elementary
Lott, TX

Desk Maneuvers

Purchase a stool on wheels and set in motion a series of timesaving strategies. During independent reading time, roll right up to a child's desk to complete a running record. During writing workshop, park yourself beside a child's desk for some one-on-one editing. A stool maneuvers easily, and it allows you to sit comfortably at a child's eye level. Shop the automotive section of your local department store for a stool that's padded and has space where assorted supplies such as a clipboard, a stopwatch, and highlighters can be stored. Roll on!

Sandy Preston—Gr. 2
Brockway Area Elementary School, Brockway, PA

A Perfect Fit!

You can anticipate plenty of smiles when this puzzle takes shape! Gather photos from the past school year and make a large poster board puzzle that has one puzzle piece per child. On the front of each piece, write a different child's name and glue a collage of photo cutouts that feature the child. Laminate the puzzle pieces and attach magnetic tape to the back of each one. Display the assembled puzzle for all to enjoy. On the last school day, give each child her puzzle piece—which makes a great refrigerator magnet—as a memento from the past year!

Antoinette McCoy—Gr. 1
Woodside Elementary, River Vale, NJ

Picture-Perfect Introductions

Wrap up the school year with a project that permits students to introduce themselves to their next teachers! Each child completes a half-page form similar to the one shown. She glues her completed form to the top half of a 9" x 12" sheet of construction paper. On the bottom half of the paper, she mounts a recent photograph of herself. Then she adds desired decorations. Place each child's project with her school records so that it will be passed along to her next teacher!

Lisa Patterson and Sharon Scialdone
Gr. 1, New Brighton Elementary School
New Brighton, PA

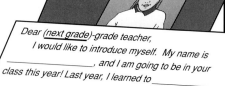

Dear (next grade)-grade teacher,
I would like to introduce myself. My name is
_____, and I am going to be in your
class this year! Last year, I learned to _____
_____.
My favorite subject was_____.
I was really good_____.
This year, I hope to learn_____
_____. See you soon
From,

A *Second Printing*

Your young authors will be pleased as punch with this publishing suggestion. Explain that for this year's final community service project you would like each child to republish a favorite story he has written. Tell students that the stories will be given to the children's ward at a local hospital. Provide the needed supplies and make arrangements for the books to be delivered. Your authors will be bursting with pride!

Cathy Rike—Gr. 1
Jefferson Elementary
Winston-Salem, NC

The Day Sofie

Math to Remember

Review math skills with a publishing project! On each of several days, have every student design a math page that reinforces an assigned skill and make an answer key for the page. Next, have each student organize her skill sheets and answer keys in an assigned order, staple the pages inside a 9" x 12" construction paper folder, and then title the folder "Math Review for You! Designed by [student's name]." Then place a strip of paper with each child's name in a container. Every student draws a name from the container and completes this classmate's book of math review. Awesome!

Suzanne Albaugh—Gr. 2
Wintersville Elementary
Wintersville, OH

Rock On!

This gem of a song helps students remember the three kinds of rocks!

Learning About Rocks
(sung to the tune of "The Mulberry Bush")
This is the way we learn about rocks,
Learn about rocks, learn about rocks.
This is the way we learn about rocks
And remember the three kinds.

One special kind is igneous rock,
Igneous rock, igneous rock.
One special kind is igneous rock.
It's melted rock that hardens.

Layered rock is another kind,
Another kind, another kind.
Layered rock is another kind.
Call it sedimentary.

And we can't forget the rocks that change,
The rocks that change, the rocks that change.
And we can't forget the rocks that change.
They're known as metamorphic.

This is the way we learn about rocks,
Learn about rocks, learn about rocks.
This is the way we learn about rocks
And remember the three kinds.

Barbara Marks—Gr. 3
St. John LaLande School, Blue Springs, MO

READING SKILLS ROUNDUP

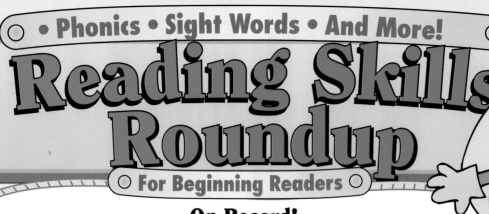

• Phonics • Sight Words • And More!
Reading Skills Roundup
For Beginning Readers

SIGHT WORDS

On Record!

Here's a handy way to keep parents informed about the growth of students' reading vocabularies! Divide a sheet of paper into 26 sections and then label them alphabetically. Give each youngster a copy of the sheet and have him staple it inside a personalized folder. When a student acquires a new sight word, instruct him to write it in the section that corresponds with the word's initial letter. Periodically make a copy of the sheet for the youngster to take home and share with his family. Not only will parents know exactly what words to reinforce, but you'll also have an on-going record of students' reading progress!

Linda Morgason—Grs. K–1, Baxter Elementary, Richmond, IN

SHORT VOWELS

Word Treats

Vowels are the key ingredients for this tempting activity! Tell students that the vowel in a three-letter word holds the consonants together, much like the filling holds a cookie sandwich together. To reinforce this point, give each student five paper circles to represent cookie filling and ten construction paper cookie cutouts. The youngster programs one filling cutout for each vowel: *a, e, i, o, u.* She labels five of the cookie cutouts *p* and five of them *t*. Next, the student sandwiches a filling cutout between two cookie cutouts to make a word. The student repeats the process with the remaining cutouts, rearranging them as necessary in order to make five words. She staples each resulting cookie sandwich together and then copies the words on a provided piece of paper. After each student reads her batch of words to a classmate, serve cookie sandwiches to celebrate your youngsters' reading success!

adapted from an idea by Jill Barney—Gr. 1, Jackson Christian Elementary, Jackson, MI

pet
put
tap
pit

-AP

Under Construction

Onsets and rimes are the trusty tools at this word-building center! Program a blank card for each of the following onsets: *b, c, cl, d, f, l, m, n, s, t, tr,* and *v.* Label a different-colored card with the rime (word family) *-ap.* Place the cards in a center along with an answer key and a supply of house cutouts lined and labeled like the one shown. A student places the rime card on a work surface and stacks the onset cards facedown. Next, he draws a card and places it beside the rime. He determines if the onset and rime form a real or nonsense word, writes the word in the appropriate column on the cutout, and then places the onset card in a discard pile. He uses the remaining onset cards to build and record words in a like manner. Then he uses the answer key to check his work.

adapted from an idea by Carol Constantine—Grs. K–6 Title 1, Leicester Central School, Leicester, VT

-ap

Real	Nonsense
cap	bap
nap	vap
clap	fap
trap	dap
tap	
sap	
lap	
map	

What's in a Name?

Give back-to-school introductions a phonics twist! Give each youngster one-half of a sentence strip and have her sign it. Ask each student, in turn, to read her strip aloud and then use a loop of tape to adhere it to the board. After every youngster has introduced herself in this manner, enlist students' help to group the names by initial letter. Then ask the class one or more of the provided questions to review phonics skills by name!

Linda Morgason—Grs. K–1
Baxter Elementary
Richmond, IN

Questions
Are there more names that begin with vowels or consonants?
Do any names have the initial and final letters in common?
What names begin with consonant digraphs? Blends?
For each initial letter, what names have the same number of syllables?

Digraph Display

ch-	sh-	th-
church	shop	this
chip	shell	thumb
	should	

Help students develop an ear for digraphs! Display a poster-sized chart divided into three columns labeled as shown. Give each student three blank cards and have him label one for each listed digraph. Announce the sound of a chosen digraph, and ask each student to hold up the corresponding card. Invite a volunteer who is holding the correct digraph to name a word that begins with it. Record the word on the poster. Repeat the process a desired number of times, randomly alternating the digraph sounds and challenging students to name words that are not already listed. Display the resulting lists for student reference, and encourage youngsters to add to them throughout the year!

adapted from an idea by Beverly Bippes—Gr. 2
Humphrey Public School, Humphrey, NE

Get Ted Ready!

Dress up reading practice with this "beary" colorful partner game! Program a 20-box grid with ten short *e* words and ten random words. Give each student pair a copy. Have one player in each twosome cut the boxes apart, shuffle the resulting cards, and then stack them facedown. Provide each youngster with a copy of page 95. Explain that the goal is to be the first player to color the bear and the four pieces of clothing (sweater, overalls, left shoe, and right shoe).

To play, a student draws a card and reads the word. If it has a short *e* sound, she colors the bear or one piece of clothing, then places the card in a discard pile. If the word does not have a short *e* sound, she discards the card and her turn is over. Play alternates until one player is declared the winner. (The students shuffle and restack the discarded cards as necessary.) Provide any needed time for youngsters to finish coloring their bears. Then invite each student to cut out her bear, mount it on construction paper, and write a sentence with at least one short *e* word. Now that's reading fun from head to toe!

Sara Harris—Gr. 3, West View Elementary, Knoxville, TN

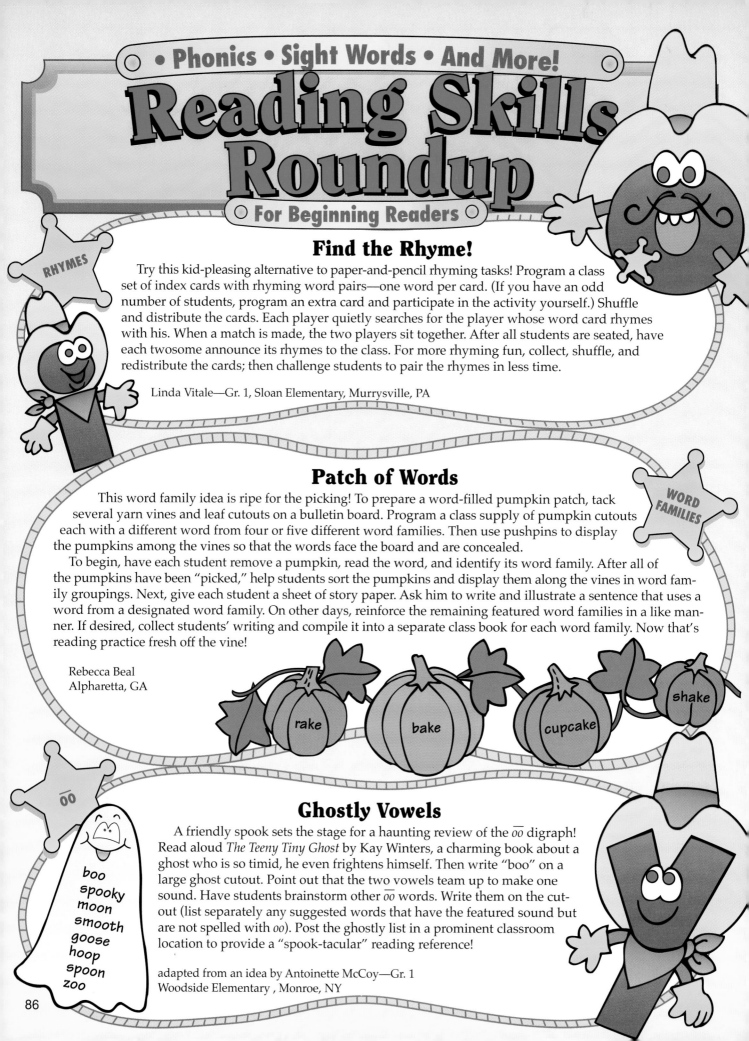

• Phonics • Sight Words • And More!

Reading Skills Roundup

For Beginning Readers

RHYMES

Find the Rhyme!

Try this kid-pleasing alternative to paper-and-pencil rhyming tasks! Program a class set of index cards with rhyming word pairs—one word per card. (If you have an odd number of students, program an extra card and participate in the activity yourself.) Shuffle and distribute the cards. Each player quietly searches for the player whose word card rhymes with his. When a match is made, the two players sit together. After all students are seated, have each twosome announce its rhymes to the class. For more rhyming fun, collect, shuffle, and redistribute the cards; then challenge students to pair the rhymes in less time.

Linda Vitale—Gr. 1, Sloan Elementary, Murrysville, PA

Patch of Words

WORD FAMILIES

This word family idea is ripe for the picking! To prepare a word-filled pumpkin patch, tack several yarn vines and leaf cutouts on a bulletin board. Program a class supply of pumpkin cutouts each with a different word from four or five different word families. Then use pushpins to display the pumpkins among the vines so that the words face the board and are concealed.

To begin, have each student remove a pumpkin, read the word, and identify its word family. After all of the pumpkins have been "picked," help students sort the pumpkins and display them along the vines in word family groupings. Next, give each student a sheet of story paper. Ask him to write and illustrate a sentence that uses a word from a designated word family. On other days, reinforce the remaining featured word families in a like manner. If desired, collect students' writing and compile it into a separate class book for each word family. Now that's reading practice fresh off the vine!

Rebecca Beal
Alpharetta, GA

rake   bake   cupcake   shake

ōō

Ghostly Vowels

A friendly spook sets the stage for a haunting review of the ōō digraph! Read aloud *The Teeny Tiny Ghost* by Kay Winters, a charming book about a ghost who is so timid, he even frightens himself. Then write "boo" on a large ghost cutout. Point out that the two vowels team up to make one sound. Have students brainstorm other ōō words. Write them on the cutout (list separately any suggested words that have the featured sound but are not spelled with *oo*). Post the ghostly list in a prominent classroom location to provide a "spook-tacular" reading reference!

boo
spooky
moon
smooth
goose
hoop
spoon
zoo

adapted from an idea by Antoinette McCoy—Gr. 1
Woodside Elementary , Monroe, NY

Sound Shake-Up

Here's a lively introduction to consonant digraphs! In advance, label a plastic opaque jar "Letter Shaker." To present a consonant digraph, cut two white cards and one colored card to fit inside the jar. Write the digraph on the colored card and each letter of the digraph on a white card. Secretly drop the colored card inside the jar. Use the white cards to review the sound that each letter makes. Then explain that these two letters can be combined to make a different sound. To demonstrate, sing the verse shown. Drop each letter card in the jar as noted and then remove the colored digraph card when the last line is sung. Students are sure to want an encore, so have them join in for a repeat performance!

Kathy Ader—Gr. 1
Kensington Parkwood Elementary
Kensington, MD

Sound Shake-Up for Ch
(sung to the tune of "The Hokey-Pokey")

You put a *c* in,   (Drop the *c* card in the jar.)
You put an *h* in;   (Drop the *h* card in the jar.)
You put them both in and you
    shake them all about.   (Shake the jar.)
You do the Hokey-Pokey and
    you mix them all around.   (Shake the jar as you turn in a circle.)
And /*ch*/ is what comes out!   (Remove the *ch* card from the jar.)

Memorable Words

Keep sight word practice at students' fingertips! Have each student sign a copy of the bookmark pattern on page 96 and cut it out. As sight words are introduced, instruct the youngster to write them on his bookmark and practice reading them independently. Periodically ask him to read his list aloud. Make a tally mark beside each word that he reads correctly. When the youngster masters a complete bookmark of words, invite him to take it home to read to his family. Impressive!

adapted from an idea by Cindy Schumacher—Gr. 1, Prairie Elementary, Cottonwood, ID

A Word Celebration

Wrap up students' recognition of *-ir* words! Program a copy of the guest list pattern (page 96) with *birthday* and other *-ir* words. Give each student a copy of the list. Suggest that *-ir* deserves birthday-style recognition since *birthday* and many other special words depend on it. In preparation, secretly assign a listed word to each student. Instruct each youngster to fold a 4" x 9" piece of construction paper in half and write her word inside. Have her refold the paper and decorate it to resemble a gift box. Then ask her to glue the project on provided paper and write a sentence that uses a blank in place of the assigned word.

To celebrate *-ir*, each student reads her sentence aloud. Her classmates try to identify the missing word, referring to their guest lists as needed. When appropriate, the youngster "opens" her gift to reveal (or confirm) the answer. After every gift is opened, serve decorated cupcakes to celebrate a job well done. If desired, display students' work on a bulletin board trimmed with streamers.

adapted from an idea by Stephanie Altman—Special Education K–3
Silverdale Elementary
Maysville, NC

stir

Mom needs to _____ the spaghetti so that it doesn't stick to the pot.

Reading Skills Roundup

For Beginning Readers

Word "Bone-anza"

Make no bones about it—this sight-word display is tailor-made for the 100th day of school! In advance, select 100 familiar sight words and program a separate dog bone cutout for each one. Place the cutouts in a clean dog dish. Set the dish near a bulletin board titled "Word 'Bone-anza.' "

To begin, read aloud *I'll Teach My Dog 100 Words* by Michael Frith. Suggest that learning to read 100 words is a huge accomplishment for anyone—canine or human! To illustrate this idea, invite a student to remove a bone cutout from the dish and read it aloud. Then attach the bone to the board. Continue with the remaining bones in a like manner, adding them to the display in rows of ten for easy counting. Not only will students have a pride-boosting reminder of their reading achievements, but you'll also have a ready-to-use list for quick sight-word reviews!

adapted from an idea by Beverly J. Velto—Gr. 2
Broadview Elementary, Weirton, WV

because

where

SIGHT WORDS

"Sound-sational" Vowel Game

Here's a partner activity that puts an entertaining spin on short vowels! Give each student one copy of pages 97 and 98, and a quart-size resealable plastic bag for game storage. Have the student color the patterns. Then direct her to cut out the cards, answer key, and spinner. To play, one student scrambles her cards and arranges them facedown. The other student puts her game materials aside. The first player uses a paper clip and pencil to spin. She announces the vowel sound on which the spinner lands and then turns over a card of her choice. If the card has the vowel sound indicated by the spinner (and verified by the key), she keeps it. If it does not, she turns the card facedown again. Play alternates in this manner until every card has been claimed by a player. The player with the greater number of cards wins. If the players have an equal number of cards, the game is declared a tie. Set aside additional game time on each of several days. Then have each youngster take her game home for more "sound-sational" learning fun.

Linda Morgason
Baxter Elementary, Richmond, IN

SHORT VOWELS

88

The Phonics Special

REVIEW

When it comes to a kid-pleasing phonics review, this idea hits the spot! Title a decorative poster as shown. Laminate the poster and display it in a prominent classroom location. Place a supply of scrap paper and an empty container nearby. Use a wipe-off marker to program the poster with a selected vowel, a digraph, or another word element. Throughout the day, encourage students to be on the lookout for words with the featured element. When a youngster spots a word, he writes it on a piece of scrap paper and deposits it in the container. At the end of the day, remove each piece of paper from the container and read it aloud. Write the words on the poster; then invite volunteers to underline the featured element in each one. To reinforce a different word element, simply wipe off the poster and advertise another great special!

Jennifer Gibson—Reading Recovery, Sedgefield Elementary, Greensboro, NC

The Phonics Special

tr

trip   trouble
traffic   treat
trick

train

Shake, Rattle, and Read!

WORD FAMILIES

Shake up word family practice with a partner center! Use a permanent marker to program each of 12 circle stickers with a different word family (rime). Glue each circle in a separate section of an empty egg carton. Drop a button in one section, close the carton, and place it at a center stocked with paper and pencils. To use the center, a twosome numbers a sheet of paper from 1 to 12.

Next, one student shakes the egg carton and then opens it. He reads the word family on which the button rests and says a word that includes it. The other student writes the word. Alternating roles, the youngsters continue the process until they have written 12 different words. What an "egg-cellent" way to connect reading and writing!

Beverly Bippes—Gr. 2
Humphrey Public School, Humphrey, NE

-ack -ing -est -ell ···· -ump
-ug -op -an -ake -ot -eat

Digraph Chain

CH

Link students' efforts to create a colossal digraph reference! Write a student-generated list of *ch* words on the chalkboard. Next, give each student nine 1" x 12" construction paper strips—five of one color and four of another. Have him write a different *ch* word in the middle of each of the five strips, referring to the class list as necessary. To make a chain, instruct the youngster to staple the ends of each programmed strip to make a ring and then use the remaining strips to link the rings as shown. Ask a volunteer to read his words aloud. Have each remaining student, in turn, read his chain and then use a provided paper strip to link it to the previous reader's chain. Display the resulting class chain to create a handy digraph reference. When it's time to replace the display, disconnect students' chains. Then encourage each youngster to take his chain home and read it to his family!

cheese
chair
chicken

Dawn Bartels—K–3 Special Education
Graham South Elementary, St. Paris, OH

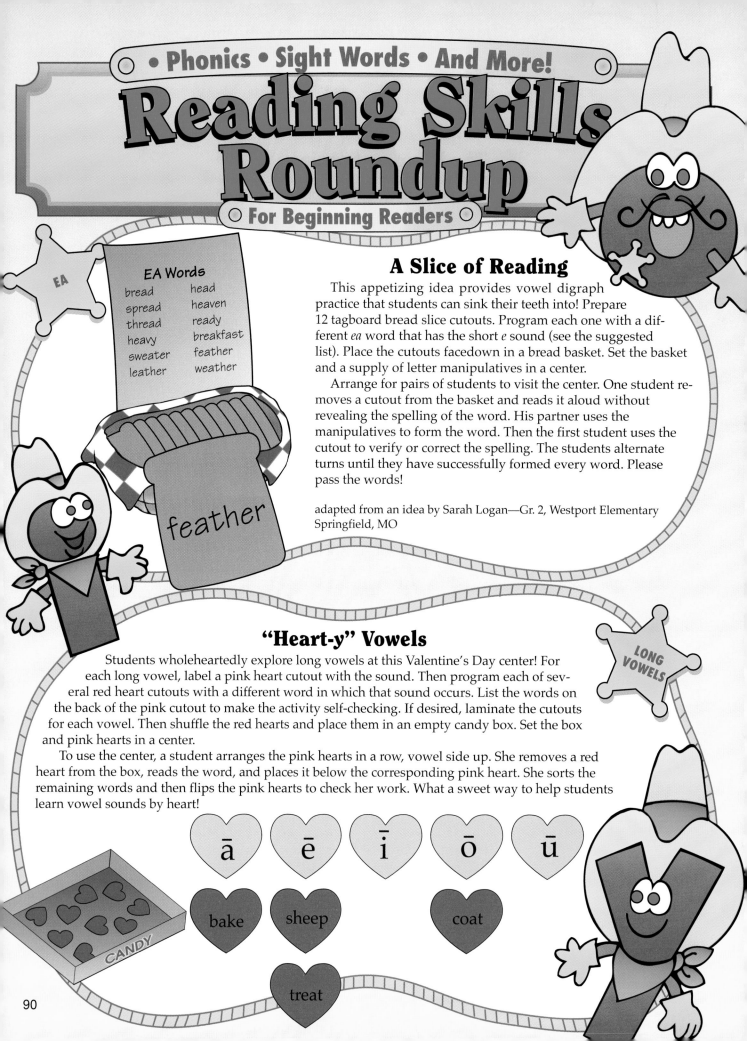

Reading Skills Roundup

• Phonics • Sight Words • And More!

For Beginning Readers

EA Words

bread	head
spread	heaven
thread	ready
heavy	breakfast
sweater	feather
leather	weather

EA

feather

A Slice of Reading

This appetizing idea provides vowel digraph practice that students can sink their teeth into! Prepare 12 tagboard bread slice cutouts. Program each one with a different *ea* word that has the short *e* sound (see the suggested list). Place the cutouts facedown in a bread basket. Set the basket and a supply of letter manipulatives in a center.

Arrange for pairs of students to visit the center. One student removes a cutout from the basket and reads it aloud without revealing the spelling of the word. His partner uses the manipulatives to form the word. Then the first student uses the cutout to verify or correct the spelling. The students alternate turns until they have successfully formed every word. Please pass the words!

adapted from an idea by Sarah Logan—Gr. 2, Westport Elementary
Springfield, MO

"Heart-y" Vowels

Students wholeheartedly explore long vowels at this Valentine's Day center! For each long vowel, label a pink heart cutout with the sound. Then program each of several red heart cutouts with a different word in which that sound occurs. List the words on the back of the pink cutout to make the activity self-checking. If desired, laminate the cutouts for each vowel. Then shuffle the red hearts and place them in an empty candy box. Set the box and pink hearts in a center.

To use the center, a student arranges the pink hearts in a row, vowel side up. She removes a red heart from the box, reads the word, and places it below the corresponding pink heart. She sorts the remaining words and then flips the pink hearts to check her work. What a sweet way to help students learn vowel sounds by heart!

LONG VOWELS

$\bar{a}$ $\bar{e}$ $\bar{i}$ $\bar{o}$ $\bar{u}$

bake sheep coat

treat

CANDY

90

Anybody Home?

Keep word building in the family! Make one copy of page 99 and write *ake* or *est* in the blank. Give each student a copy of the programmed sheet and a 9" x 12" sheet of white construction paper. The student colors the house as desired and then cuts it out along the bold outer lines. To prepare the door, he cuts along the right side and top and then folds back the resulting flap. The youngster glues the house onto the construction paper, being careful to keep the door open. Then he cuts apart the letter cards.

To identify words that are part of the featured word family (rime), he places each letter card, in turn, in the shaded box. If the letter and word family make a word, he writes the word in the doorway. If they do not, he writes the letter beside the house. After the youngster checks all possible words in this manner, he uses crayons to complete the scene with desired details. Now that's phonics fun—family-style!

Lisa Yun—Gr. 1, Public School 126M, New York, NY

Sight-Word Circles

WORD SORTS

Here's a quick and easy way to round up sight words! On a sheet of chart paper, list ten or more sight words. To sort the words, ask students to identify a phonics element that at least two of the words have in common, such as a particular vowel sound or number of syllables. Have a volunteer circle the corresponding words with a colorful marker. Repeat the process with different-colored markers until every word has been circled one time. For a kid-pleasing variation, color-code a different list of words as described and challenge students to identify your sorting method. Not only will students strengthen their reading vocabularies, but they'll also stretch their thinking skills!

Lu Brunnemer—Gr. 1, Eagle Creek Elementary
Indianapolis, IN

Digraph Celebration

CH

Add a festive flair to reading time with a *ch* party! To prepare, enlist students' help to decorate the classroom with paper <u>ch</u>ains. Reinforce the featured digraph with two or more of the ideas shown. Then conclude the celebration with refreshments such as pun<u>ch</u>, <u>ch</u>eese and crackers, or <u>ch</u>ocolate <u>ch</u>ip cookies. Three cheers for *ch*!

adapted from an idea by Rose Empey—Gr. 1
Green Acres School
Ogden, UT

CH Party Ideas

- Help the class write an original <u>ch</u>ant with several *ch* words.
- Have partners play a modified version of <u>ch</u>eckers that requires each player to say a *ch* word before taking a turn.
- Lead students in the <u>ch</u>a-<u>ch</u>a.
- On a prepared bulletin board, have students use <u>ch</u>alk to write *ch* words graffiti-style.
- Invite students to relax on bea<u>ch</u> blankets as you read a <u>ch</u>apter book aloud.

Reading Skills Roundup
For Beginning Readers

BLENDS

Tic-Tac-Trio

Students will be game for blends with this colorful version of tic-tac-toe! Prepare a sheet of tic-tac-toe grids. Program each grid space with a different word that has a blend. For each twosome, provide one copy of the prepared sheet and a different-colored crayon for each player. To take a turn, a player reads an unmarked word aloud and then underlines the blend to claim the grid space. Play alternates until one player claims a trio of words in a diagonal, horizontal, or vertical row and is declared the winner, or until every word has been claimed and the game is declared a tie. The players use the remaining grids for additional games. Now that's a winning strategy for reading practice!

adapted from an idea by Betty Silkunas
Lower Gwynedd Elementary
Ambler, PA

black	close	drain
slide	cracker	bright
fly	glow	frog

Sight Word Sort

Spring is a perfect time to size up students' sight word vocabularies! Divide the chalkboard into four columns and label them as shown. Stack a class supply of sight word cards (each with three or more letters) facedown near the chalkboard. Have each student, in turn, take the top card, read it aloud, and announce the number of letters in the word. Then help her use a loop of tape to place the card in the corresponding column. After all of the cards have been sorted in this manner, lead students in chorally reading the first word as they clap once for each syllable. Write the number of syllables beside the card. Continue in the same manner with the remaining words. For a "sound-sational" phonemic awareness variation, have students note the number of sounds in each word after they sort the cards as described.

Betty Silkunas

SIGHT WORDS

3 Letters		4 Letters		5 Letters		6 or More Letters	
can	1	soon	1	about	2	because	2
are	1	been	1	after	2	together	3
		goes		would	1	always	2
		said	1	laugh			

Count On Word Families!

Word family practice and a bit of luck make this partner game a winner! Prepare a spinner and number an eight-space grid as shown. Program each grid space with a different rime. Give each twosome a copy of a spinner, a paper clip, and 16 counters. Provide each student with a copy of the prepared grid.

To begin, one player spins. She uses a counter to mark a grid space that has the number indicated on the spinner. (If no unmarked space has the number, her turn is over.) She reads the rime aloud and names a word in the corresponding word family. Alternating turns, the players continue the game for an allotted amount of time or until one player marks all of her grid spaces. The player with the greater number of marked spaces wins!

adapted from an idea by Beverly Bippes—Gr. 2
Humphrey Public School, Humphrey, NE

WORD FAMILIES

1 -at	2 -ell	3 -ing	4 -ock
1 -ake	2 -ug	3 -ight	4 -ay

Digraph Shower

In this display idea, April showers don't bring May flowers—they bring a downpour of digraph practice! Mount a poster-size umbrella cutout on a bulletin board titled "Digraph Shower." Place a supply of raindrop cutouts and an empty container nearby. Throughout each of several days, encourage students to be on the lookout for words that have *sh*. After a youngster finds a word, he writes it on a raindrop and underlines the featured digraph. Then he signs the back of the raindrop and places it in the container. At the end of each day, remove each cutout, ask the owner to read it aloud, and then have him tack it to the board. Looks like rain!

Jan Robbins—Gr. 1, Fairview Elementary, Richmond, IN

SH

shine   dish

Classy Review Cube

Keep vowel skills on a roll! Cover an empty cube-shaped box with light-colored paper. Label each side of the box with a different vowel sound. Sit with students in a circle on the floor and then hand the prepared box to the student on your left. Have him gently toss the box and then announce the vowel sound that is displayed on the top. Ask him to state a word that has the corresponding sound. If he does not successfully name a word, invite a volunteer to name one. Then have the student who tossed the cube pass it to the student on his left. Have this student take a turn in the same manner, encouraging him and his classmates to avoid repeating previously named words. Continue around the circle until every youngster has had an opportunity to toss the box and name a word.

VOWELS

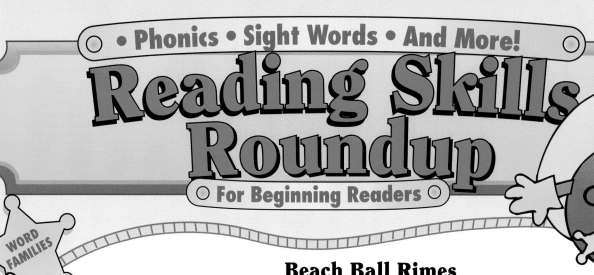

Reading Skills Roundup

WORD FAMILIES

Beach Ball Rimes

Bring summertime fun inside with a lively word family review! Use a permanent marker to divide a beach ball into several sections and then program each section with a different rime. Sit in a circle on the floor with your students. To begin, toss the ball to one student. The youngster identifies the rime in the section under her right thumb (or the closest rime if her thumb is on a line). She names a word that contains the rime and then tosses the ball back to you. If the student is unable to name a word, she passes the ball to the classmate on her right. If this student names a word for the rime, she tosses the ball to you. If she does not, she passes the ball to the right, and so on, until one youngster successfully names a word or the ball reaches you.

To continue, toss the ball to a different student. Repeat the process as described, challenging students to avoid repeating previously named words, until every youngster has taken at least one turn.

Susan Taffar—Gr. 2, Claysville School, Guntersville, AL

Roll, Name, and Write!

SHORT VOWELS

Here's a "die-namite" way to reinforce short-vowel skills! Give each student a copy of the die pattern on page 100. Ask him to color and cut out the pattern. Instruct him to fold the pattern on the thin lines and then use glue or tape to assemble the die. Next, pair students and give each twosome one sheet of paper. Have one student in each pair draw and label columns as shown. Explain that the goal is to write at least one word for each indicated vowel sound.

To begin, the first student rolls his die. If a picture is displayed on the top, he names it and identifies the corresponding vowel sound. With the help of his partner as necessary, he names a different word that contains the same sound and then writes it in the appropriate column. If the "Your Choice!" section is displayed on the top of the die, he names and writes a word for a short vowel of his choosing. The students alternate turns for an allotted amount of time; then they present their words for teacher approval. To keep students' vowel skills on a roll, suggest that each youngster take his die home and repeat the activity with a family member.

ă	ĕ	ĭ	ŏ	ŭ
mat	bell	pin		cup
map				duck

Linda Morgason
Baxter Elementary
Richmond, IN

Ted

Patterns

Use the bookmark with "Memorable Words" and the guest list with "A Word Celebration" on page 87.

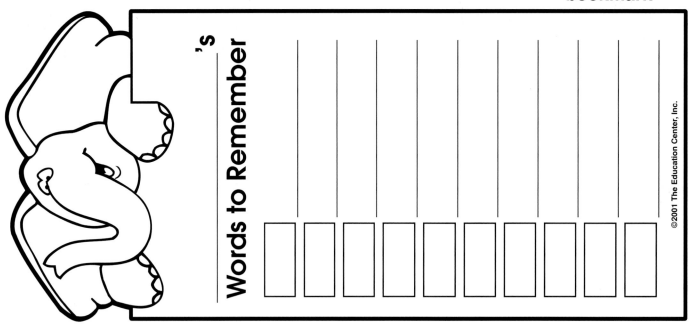

__'s
Words to Remember

©2001 The Education Center, Inc.

guest list

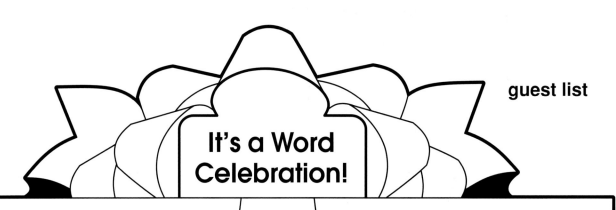

It's a Word Celebration!

Guests of Honor

1. _____
2. _____
3. _____
4. _____
5. _____
6. _____

7. _____
8. _____
9. _____
10. _____
11. _____
12. _____

©The Education Center, Inc. • *THE MAILBOX® • Primary •* Oct/Nov 2001

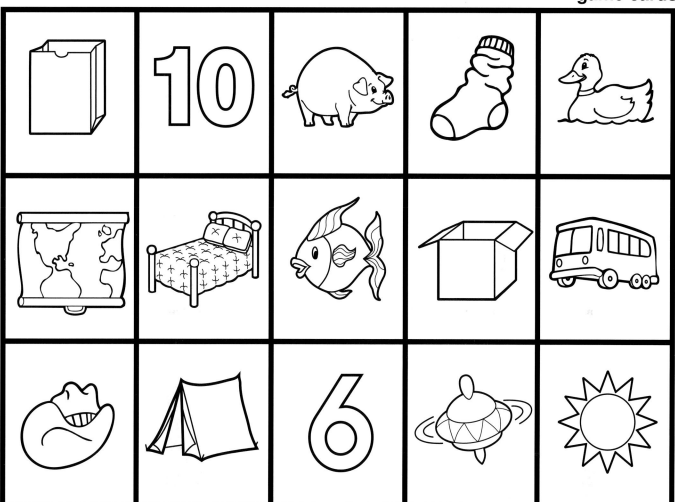

answer key

Patterns

Use the spinner with " 'Sound-sational' Vowel Game" on page 88.

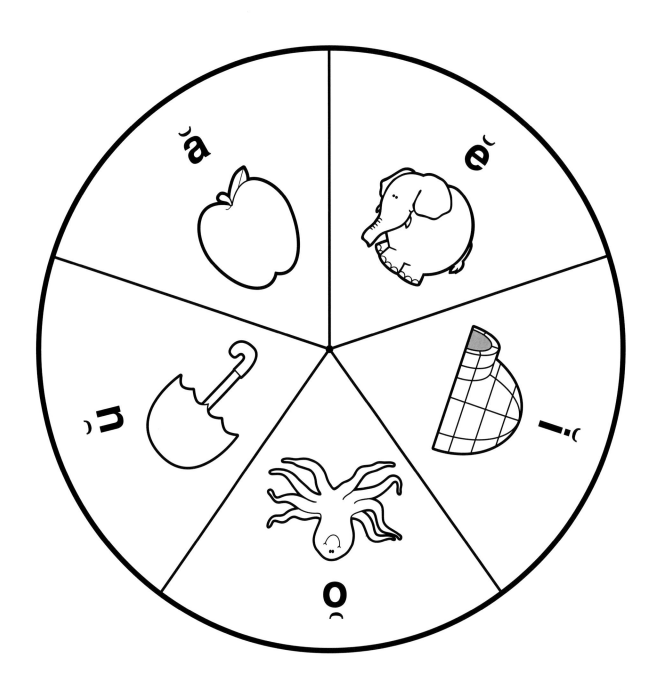

©The Education Center, Inc. • *THE MAILBOX*® • *Primary* • Dec/Jan 2001–2

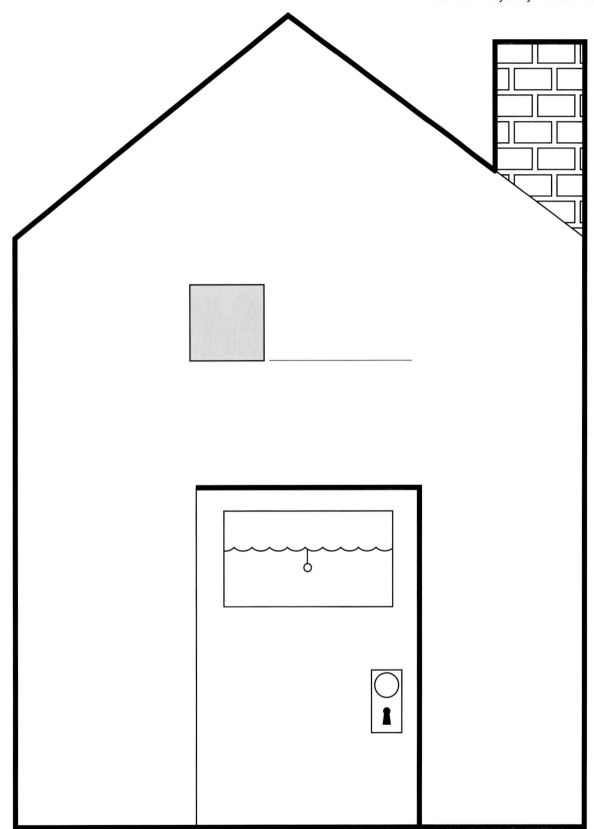

©The Education Center, Inc. • *THE MAILBOX*® • *Primary* • Feb/Mar 2002

b f m n r s t v w

Your Choice!

©The Education Center, Inc. • *THE MAILBOX® • Primary •* June/July 2002

WRITE ON!

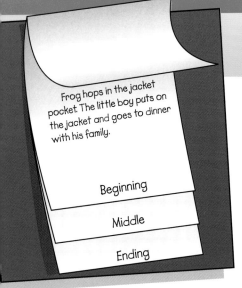

Frog hops in the jacket pocket. The little boy puts on the jacket and goes to dinner with his family.

Beginning

Middle

Ending

Write On!

From Beginning to Ending

Investigate **story organization** with a wordless picture book. Share with the class a book such as *Frog Goes to Dinner* by Mercer Mayer, *Pancakes for Breakfast* by Tomie dePaola, or *Sector 7* by David Wiesner. Encourage discussion about the story and lead students to identify the beginning, the middle, and the ending of the tale. Next, have each child stack two 6" x 18" strips of white construction paper, hold them vertically, and slide the top paper upward about one inch. Then have him fold the papers forward (creating four graduated layers) and staple near the fold. Instruct each child to write the title of the wordless book and "retold by [student's name]" on the front cover of his resulting booklet, and label the booklet pages "Beginning," "Middle," and "Ending." Then have him describe each part of the story on the corresponding booklet page.

Erin Hassen—Gr. 1, Red Oak Elementary, Oklahoma City, OK

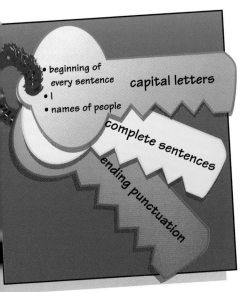

capital letters
- beginning of every sentence
- I
- names of people

complete sentences

ending punctuation

Keys to Editing Success

Unlock your youngsters' **editing skills** with one-of-a-kind keys! Program copies of the key pattern on page 55 with editing tips *(conventions)* appropriate for your young writers. Make a class supply of each pattern, copying each one on a different color of construction paper. Laminate the copies for durability and then cut out and hole-punch each one. To make a set of keys for each student, thread one key of every color onto a six-inch length of pipe cleaner and then twist the pipe cleaner ends to form a ring. Your youngsters' editing skills are sure to be enhanced!

Wendy Monaghan—Gr. 2, Veterans Memorial Elementary School, Brick, NJ

Spot
Sniffing the kitchen floor.
Chasing a furry squirrel.
Splashing in a puddle.
Nibbling on a sock.
That is Spot!
by Jasmine

Pooch Poetry

Emphasize **strong verb choice** during this canine-related activity. (National Dog Week is annually the last full week in September.) Write "running" on the board. Ask students to name other verbs that describe this action in a more interesting way (such as *galloping, racing,* and *dashing*). List their responses. Complete a similar activity with "eating." Lead students to conclude that strong verb choices make writing more interesting. Then have each child write a dog-related poem that names a dog (real or imaginary), describes four different actions of the dog, and concludes "That is [dog's name]!"

To publish his poem, a child copies his edited work on a 5" x 7" sheet of writing paper. Next, he folds a 12" x 18" strip of construction paper in half. He trims and decorates the folded paper to resemble a dog and then he glues his poem inside. Woof!

adapted from an idea by Linda Rudlaff, Mishawaka, IN

Write On!

Ideas and Tips for Teaching Students to Write!

In a Nutshell

This nutty idea is a memorable way to introduce the concept of **summarizing!** Display an acorn (or a picture of one). Tell students that the acorn gives a hint about what the expression "in a nutshell" means. Invite students to speculate about the meaning of the phrase. Then lead them to conclude that it means "in just a few words." Explain that when a person summarizes, he tells about main points very briefly, or in a nutshell. Next, give each student a sheet of writing paper and two 9" x 12" sheets of construction paper. Also provide access to a stapler and an acorn-shaped template that is approximately 7" x 9". The student uses the materials to make a one-page booklet like the one shown. He summarizes a favorite story inside the booklet. Then he titles and decorates the booklet cover. There you have it—summarizing in a nutshell!

Todd Helms—Gr. 2, Pinehurst Elementary, Pinehurst, NC

Creepy Couplets

Make writing time hauntingly fun with "spider-ific" **couplets!** To begin, post a student-generated list of Halloween words. Give each student a 3" x 5" index card and ask her to write a couplet (two lines of rhyming poetry) that includes one or more words from the list. Next, have each child make a construction paper spider. To do so, she glues a three-inch and an eight-inch circle together. She adds eight accordion-folded paper strips for legs, two wiggle eyes, and a construction paper mouth. Then she glues her couplet on her spider project. To showcase your students' work, tack a web of yarn on a bulletin board. Add the poetic arachnids and title the display "Creepy Couplets."

adapted from an idea by Rebecca Brudwick—Gr. 1, Hoover Elementary
North Mankato, MN

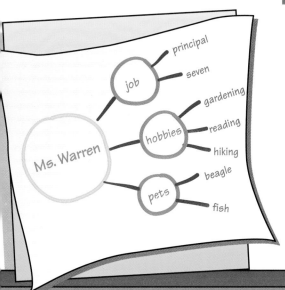

Take Note!

Introductions are in order with this **paragraph writing** activity! By student vote, select a school staff member whom the class would like to know better. Help students compile a list of interview questions; then arrange for the staff member to visit the class. Have volunteers interview the guest as the remaining students take notes. Conclude the interview with refreshments, such as cookies and punch.

After the guest's departure, enlist students' help to create a web that shows the information gathered (see the illustration). Point out that the web provides a handy reference of main ideas and details. Then ask each student to use the web to write two or more well-organized paragraphs. Not only will students improve their writing skills, but they will also become better acquainted with a staff member!

Ruthie Jamieson Titus—Gr. 3, Union Elementary, Poland, OH

Write On!

Ideas and Tips for Teaching Students to Write!

Timely Prompts

Pay tribute to Martin Luther King Jr. with thought-provoking **prompts.** Familiarize the class with Dr. King's role in history and how his memory is honored each January. Then ask each student to respond to one of the prompts below on provided paper. If desired, instruct each youngster to staple his completed writing inside a 9" x 12" construction paper folder. Then have him use a copy of the pattern on page 107, a length of yarn, and several construction paper leaves to embellish his folder as shown.

- Martin Luther King Jr. believed in solving disagreements without violence. Write about a time you solved a disagreement in a peaceful way.

- How might things be different in your school and neighborhood if Dr. King had not worked to change unfair laws?

- Dr. King once said, "Let freedom ring." What do you think he meant?

Calendar Stories

Spark **story ideas** with outdated calendars! Collect enough discarded calendars so that there is one monthly illustration per student plus a few extra. Cut apart the calendar pages. Have each student select a picture to use as a story prompt. (File the remaining pictures for future use, if desired.) To help brainstorm story ideas and details, ask each student to show his picture to the class. Invite his classmates to make "I wonder" statements about the picture. For example, a student might wonder what a pictured dog is thinking or what its name is. Have each youngster consider the comments as he writes a story. Then instruct him to mount his writing and the picture on a sheet of construction paper. When it comes to writing inspiration, this recycling idea is sure to be "write" on target!

Sheli Funderburk—Gr. 2, Grant School, East Wenatchee, WA

Bedtime Problems
My dog Lucky doesn't like to sleep downstairs. Last night he whined after I went to bed. I went downstairs to see if I could get him to stop. He looked so sad and lonely! I took Lucky to my room and made a bed for him in a box. Then we both fell right to sleep!

Story Strips

This picture-perfect lineup helps beginning writers create a story with a clear **beginning, middle, and end!** Divide students into groups of three. Give each group a four-section strip of perforated computer paper. Instruct the group members to verbally plan a story. Have the youngsters write and illustrate the title on the first section of the paper. Then ask each student to illustrate the beginning, middle, or end of the story on the appropriate section. Next, provide each youngster with a length of adding machine tape that is equal to the length of one story section. Have the youngster write a caption for his part of the story (or dictate a caption for an adult to write). Display each group's illustrated story and captions below the title "Story Lineup."

adapted from an idea by Jennifer Stinnett—Gr. 1, Arlington Elementary, Arlington, TN

day rise!

Susie thought everyone had forgotten her birthday.

Write On!

Ideas and Tips for Teaching Students to Write!

My Lucky Day
by John

I could not believe my eyes! Right in front of me was a big pot filled with gold. The leprechaun had told the truth! He said that if I would let him live with me, he would share the gold. I told him, "It's a deal!" I hope Mom doesn't mind!

Timely Prompts

Spark your youngsters' imaginations with a wee bit of Irish folklore and related writing **prompts!** According to legend, a leprechaun is only as big as a person's thumb, but he has a huge fortune. If a person catches a leprechaun, he can ask the tiny creature to lead the way to his pot of gold. After sharing this St. Patrick's Day information with students, distribute writing paper. Ask each student to respond to one of the prompts below. Then have him color a white construction paper copy of page 108, cut out the patterns, and glue them to his story as shown.

- Imagine that a leprechaun leads you to his pot of gold. Describe what happens next.
- What would your life be like if you were the same size as a leprechaun? Write a story to share your ideas.
- If you were a leprechaun, where would you hide your pot of gold? Tell about the hiding place and why you chose it. Then write clear directions to it.

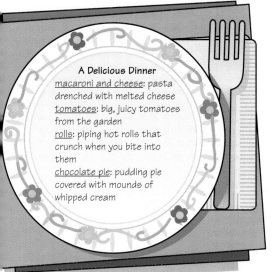

A Delicious Dinner
<u>macaroni and cheese</u>: pasta drenched with melted cheese
<u>tomatoes</u>: big, juicy tomatoes from the garden
<u>rolls</u>: piping hot rolls that crunch when you bite into them
<u>chocolate pie</u>: pudding pie covered with mounds of whipped cream

Food for Thought

Serve up **descriptive writing** practice for March, National Nutrition Month! Read aloud selected food descriptions from a variety of menus, pointing out particular words that create tempting visual images. Then give each student a six-inch circle that has been cut from a sheet of writing paper. The youngster lists the foods in a favorite meal. She writes a descriptive phrase for each one, modeling her work after the menu examples. She glues her writing on a dinner-sized paper plate and uses crayons to embellish the plate as desired. Then she mounts the plate, a plastic fork, and a paper napkin on a 12" x 18" sheet of construction paper. Showcase students' completed projects below the title "Delicious Descriptions."

adapted from an idea by Cynthia Mackel—Grs. 1–2, Rosemont Elementary, Baltimore, MD

March 21

Dear Principal,
Ms. Frizzle has awesome field trips. If some parents would go along, they could help watch the kids. That would make the trips really safe.
Students learn a lot on the field trips. They learn more by seeing things than by just reading about them.
I think Ms. Frizzle should take her students on more field trips.
Sincerely,
Alex

On the Road With Ms. Frizzle

Deliver a kid-pleasing **persuasive writing** experience with the help of the Friz! Read aloud one or more books from Joanna Cole's Magic School Bus series. Then ask students to suppose that the principal at Ms. Frizzle's school has refused to let her take any more field trips because he thinks they are dangerous. Ask each youngster to write a persuasive letter to try to change the principal's mind. Then have him decorate a small bus cutout to resemble the Magic School Bus and glue it on a sheet of construction paper with his letter. Display students' work on a bulletin board titled "Dear Principal."

Debbie Erickson—Grs. 2–3 Multiage, Waterloo Elementary, Waterloo, WI

Write On!

Ideas and Tips for Teaching Students to Write!

Earth Day at School

If I were a teacher, I would have my students help keep the playground clean. We would pick up the litter every Friday. We would plant flowers too. Then kids would really understand what it means to take care of the earth!

Timely Prompts

Promote environmental awareness with these Earth Day **writing prompts!** Ask students to share their thoughts about the importance of taking care of the earth. Guide them to understand that Earth's resources—air, water, and land—should be protected because people, plants, and animals depend on them. Then have each student respond to one of the prompts below on a 4" x 5" piece of blank paper. Use the directions on page 28 to display students' work!

- What can people do to take good care of the earth?
- Imagine that you are a teacher. Explain how you would teach your students about Earth Day.
- Some people say that every day should be Earth Day. What do you think they mean? Do you agree? Explain.

Swing Into Spring!

This April celebrate National Poetry Month (and spring!) with a picturesque **poetry writing** project! Have each student use the format shown to write a spring poem on a 3" x 5" lined index card. Then ask her to glue the card on a 3" x 5½" piece of construction paper. Instruct her to tape two lengths of yarn to the back of the paper—one near each top corner. To display her poem, the youngster paints a tree trunk and branch on a 12" x 18" sheet of construction paper as shown. She allows the paint to dry. Then she glues her poem and the yarn ends to her artwork to resemble a swing. She trims the yarn as needed and uses provided arts-and-crafts materials to complete the scene with desired details. Hurrah for spring!

What is spring?

Tiny pink blossoms,
Green buds on the trees,
And kickball in the park.

Julia

Phoebe Sharp—K–1 Special Education, Gillette School, Gillette, NJ

Predictable Plot

Enhance students' **story-organization** skills with the help of a predictable book! Read aloud *That's Good! That's Bad!* by Margery Cuyler. Next, divide students into small groups and have each group sit in a separate circle. Provide each group with a supply of story paper.

To begin a story similar to Cuyler's, one student in each group writes and completes the following sentence starter: "One day a mother and father gave a little boy a…" Then he reads his completed sentence to the group. The next student in the circle continues the story on another sheet of paper, ending with "Oh, that's good! No, that's bad!" He then reads his writing aloud. The students continue imitating Cuyler's story pattern until every student takes at least one turn and the allotted writing time ends. The students illustrate their work, sequence the resulting pages, and bind them between covers to make a book that isn't just good—it's great!

The neighbor's puppy loves to fetch sticks.

Oh, that's good!
No, that's bad!

adapted from an idea by Karen Cook—Grs. K–1, McDonough Primary School McDonough, GA

Patterns
Use with "Timely Prompts" on page 105.

©The Education Center, Inc. • THE MAILBOX® • Primary • Feb/Mar 2002

Language Arts
Units

Now Presenting...
Perfectly Proper Penmanship

Set the stage for handsome handwriting with this spiffy collection of ideas!

ideas contributed by Laura Mihalenko

First Things, First

What's the first step in using proper letter formation? Why, using proper posture, of course! Display the provided poem on a decorative chart. When it is time for a handwriting assignment, lead students in a choral reading of the poem. Encourage them to self-check for each of the criteria before they get to work. When proper handwriting posture becomes more routine for students, prompt them to read the poem silently before they begin a writing task. Ready, set, write!

Get Ready to Write!
Feet on the floor,
Chair pulled in.
Sit up straight.
Now let's begin!

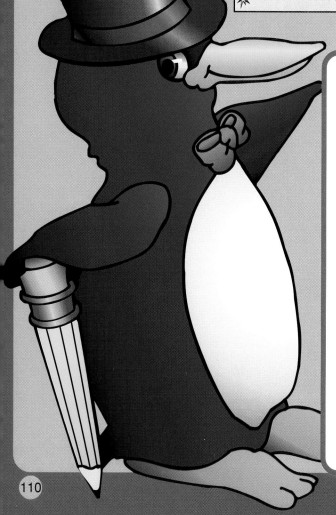

Penmanship Pal

This dapper little mascot provides beginning writers with a helpful reminder about spacing! Use a jumbo craft stick, two wiggle eyes, crayons, and glue to make a penguin character like the one shown. Display the completed penguin and introduce it to students as a penmanship pal. Explain that this mascot can help students spruce up their writing with eye-pleasing spacing. Demonstrate how to use the width of the mascot to determine the appropriate spacing between the words in a sentence. Then guide each student to make his own penmanship mascot with provided materials. Suggest that he store the completed mascot in a pencil box or another designated area for easy access. After the youngster becomes more proficient at spacing words, have him use the mascot as a visual reminder (rather than a physical guide) by stationing it beside his writing paper.

adapted from an idea by Cindy Schumacher—Gr. 1
Prairie Elementary
Cottonwood, ID

Hats Off to Handwriting!

Give letter-perfect assessment center stage! Post a class-created handwriting scale such as the one shown. Choose a letter to reinforce. Verbally describe its proper formation as you write the letter on a lined chalkboard. Invite students to share their observations about the letter's proper size, slant, and shape. Then give each student a sheet of writing paper. Ask her to brainstorm and write three nouns (adjectives, verbs) that begin with the featured letter, keeping the criteria for its formation in mind. Have the youngster use the displayed scale to rate each word and draw the corresponding number of hats beside it.

Next, invite each student to read her list aloud. Write the words on the board, avoiding duplications. Chorally read the resulting class list with students; then have each youngster use her best penmanship to copy three additional nouns. For a kid-pleasing conclusion, ask students to rate *your* handwriting. No doubt students will be eager to give this activity a repeat performance, so plan to use it to reinforce other letters as well!

Handwriting Scale

Perfectly proper

Not too shabby

Needs polishing

The Stylish Five

Count on stellar handwriting performances with this ongoing idea! Have each student personalize a folder. At the end of each grading period, distribute copies of the writing paper on page 112. Write the provided prompts on the board, inserting the appropriate month and season. Remind students that neat handwriting has five elements: good spacing, slant, size, shape, and smoothness. Each youngster uses his best penmanship to respond to a selected prompt. After he signs and dates his paper, he colors the illustrations. Then, on a copy of a self-assessment form similar to the one shown, the youngster colors the star for each element that he thinks is well demonstrated in his writing. He elaborates on his assessment in the provided space, staples the form to his writing, and tucks the papers inside his personalized folder. What a "star-ific" way to track students' handwriting progress!

adapted from an idea by Carolyn S. Kanoy
Winston-Salem, NC

Prompts
[Month] makes me think about…
[Month] is a great month because…
My favorite thing about [season] is…
This [season] I…

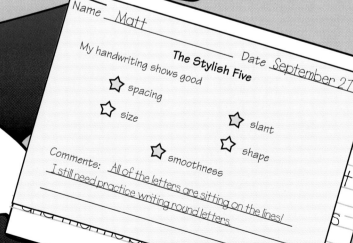

Name Matt   Date September 27

The Stylish Five

My handwriting shows good

☆ spacing

☆ size   ☆ slant

☆ smoothness   ☆ shape

Comments: All of the letters are sitting on the lines!
I still need practice writing round letters.

Name _____

Date _____

Writing Through the Year

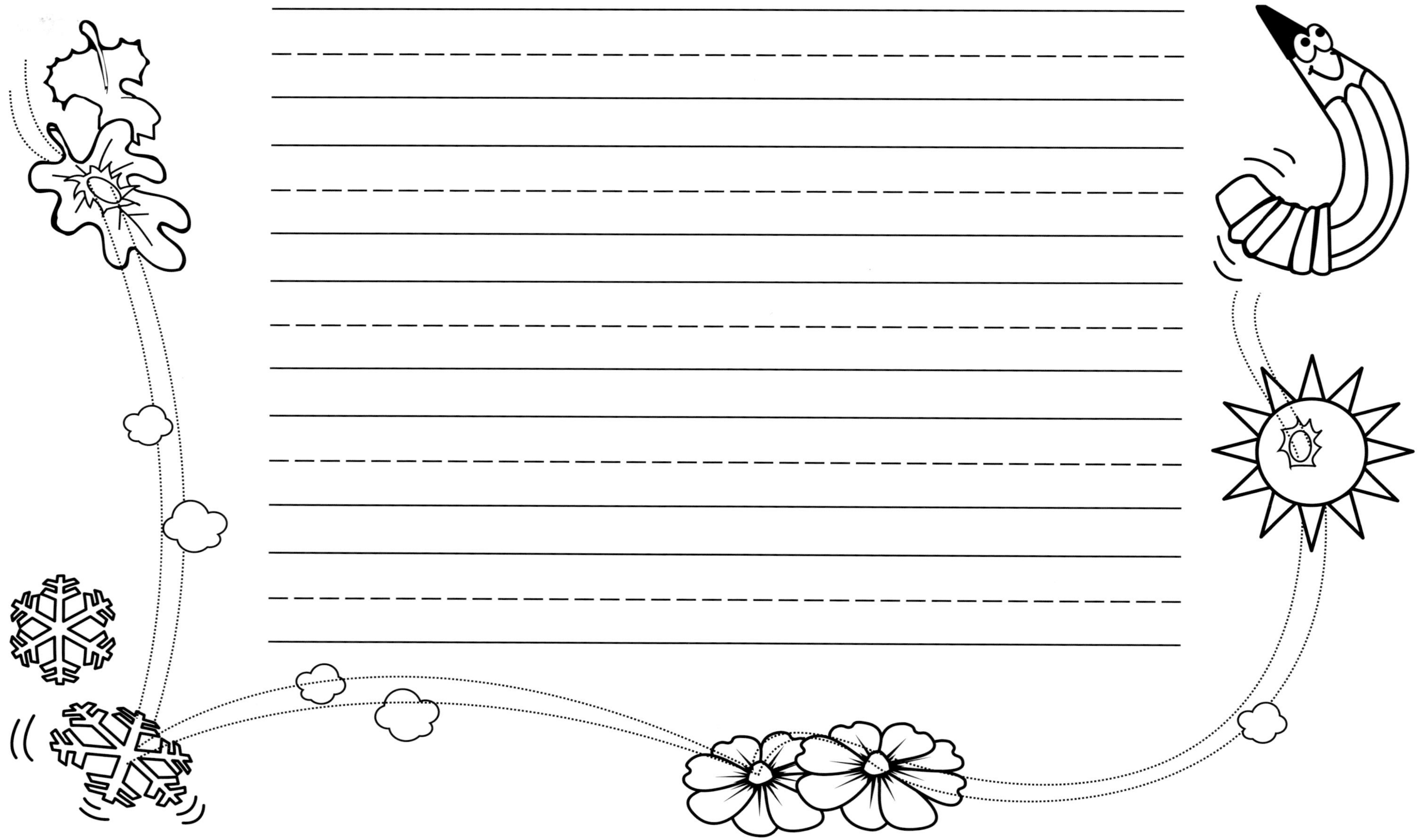

©The Education Center, Inc. · *THE MAILBOX*® · *Primary* · Aug/Sept 2001

Note to the teacher: Use with "The Stylish Five" on page 111.

Building a Classroom of Writers

Create a blueprint for writing success
with these easy-to-use contributor ideas!

Lay the Foundation

Choose from the suggestions on pages 113–115 to establish a class writing routine complete with helpful tools for your young authors!

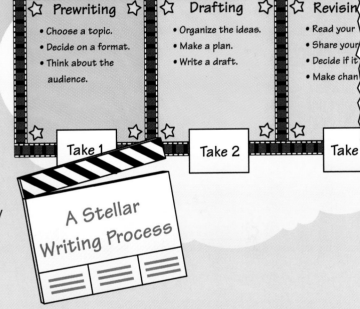

Prewriting
- Choose a topic.
- Decide on a format.
- Think about the audience.

Drafting
- Organize the ideas.
- Make a plan.
- Write a draft.

Revising
- Read your
- Share your
- Decide if it
- Make chan

Take 1   Take 2   Take

A Stellar Writing Process

Lights, Camera, Writing!

Give the writing process a starring role! Title a separate poster-sized sheet of paper for each stage of the writing process used in your classroom. Add brief explanations of the stages and then embellish the posters with star cutouts. Display the posters side by side in consecutive order. Then outline the posters with a filmlike border, and add "Take" labels and a titled director's board as shown. Explain to students that moviemaking involves many takes, with a director making decisions and changes at each stage in the process. Point out that many authors use a similar process when they write. Direct students' attention to the display and review the steps it outlines. Encourage youngsters to use the display as a writing guide. Student writing that earns rave reviews is sure to be the result!

Pam Sanderson—Gr. 2
Davis Drive Elementary
Apex, NC

"Soup-er" Writing

Set the stage for first-rate writing with this literature-based idea! Read aloud Marc Brown's *Arthur Writes a Story.* In this installment of the Arthur Adventure series, the beloved aardvark gains a new perspective about what makes a great story. At the conclusion of the book, prompt discussion about why Arthur's pet story is better received than his more outlandish tale. Next, display a jumbo kettle-shaped cutout labeled "'Soup-er' Writing." Have students brainstorm qualities of excellent writing, such as vivid details or a beginning that hooks readers. Record their ideas on the cutout. To encourage further exploration of these qualities, place an empty recipe box and a supply of blank recipe cards near the poster. When a youngster reads a book that exemplifies one of the listed qualities, have her describe on a card how the quality was shown, write the book title, and then deposit the card in the recipe box. On a designated day each week, share any newly deposited cards with students. Then post the cards around the cutout. Not only will students become better writers, but they'll also become more thoughtful readers, too!

Sonia Armstrong—Gr. 2, Thomas J. Lahey Elementary, Greenlawn, NY

At a Glance

It's a snap to manage a writers' workshop with these two colorful displays!

Pocket Chart: Write each student's name on a separate 1" x 3" card. Arrange the cards behind the clear plastic pockets of a store-bought pocket chart so that every name is visible. Designate a different color for each stage of the writing process and then cut a class supply of 3" x 3" cards for each color. Store the cards as shown, placing a labeled card in the front of each stack to make a color key. Instruct each student to tuck a blank card of the appropriate color behind his name to indicate where he is in the writing process.

Kathleen Gillin—Gr. 2, Cold Spring Elementary, Doylestown, PA

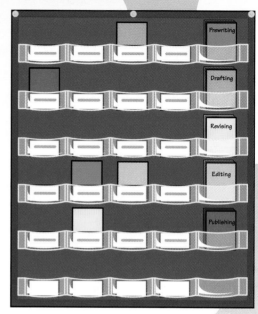

Clothespin Lineup: For each stage of the writing process, label a colorful 4¹/₂" x 12" poster board rectangle and laminate it for durability. Also prepare a poster board rectangle labeled "I'm Stuck!" to use when students want teacher guidance. Attach the top of each rectangle to the edge of a shelf or another accessible location that allows for clothespins to be clipped along the bottom of the rectangles. Have each youngster clip a personalized clothespin on the rectangle that reflects his current stage in the writing process.

Jennifer Boone—Gr. 3
Bethel Elementary School
Bethel, PA

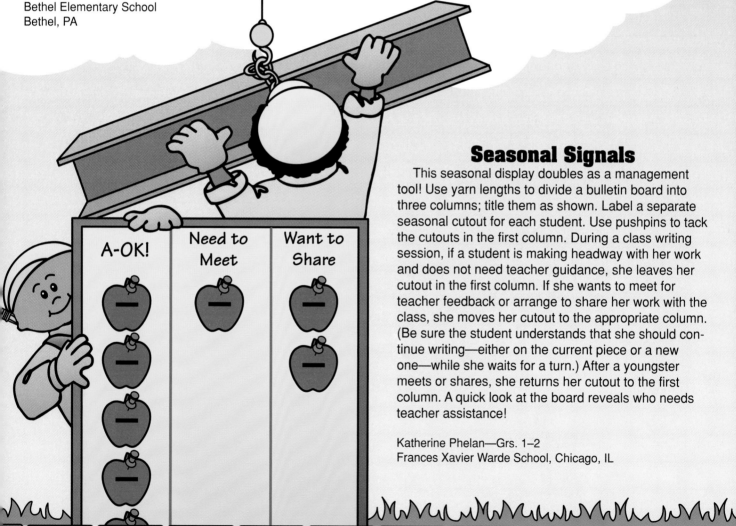

Seasonal Signals

This seasonal display doubles as a management tool! Use yarn lengths to divide a bulletin board into three columns; title them as shown. Label a separate seasonal cutout for each student. Use pushpins to tack the cutouts in the first column. During a class writing session, if a student is making headway with her work and does not need teacher guidance, she leaves her cutout in the first column. If she wants to meet for teacher feedback or arrange to share her work with the class, she moves her cutout to the appropriate column. (Be sure the student understands that she should continue writing—either on the current piece or a new one—while she waits for a turn.) After a youngster meets or shares, she returns her cutout to the first column. A quick look at the board reveals who needs teacher assistance!

Katherine Phelan—Grs. 1–2
Frances Xavier Warde School, Chicago, IL

Authors' Briefcases

It's easy for students to get down to the business of writing with these convenient carriers! To make an author's briefcase, attach loops of masking tape to the front of one pocket folder. Align a second pocket folder atop the taped folder and firmly press the two folders together. Open the resulting briefcase. Use clear tape to secure the outer edge of the joined folders as shown. Also tape tagboard handles inside the front and back covers of the briefcase. Then label the pockets to correspond with the class writing process. Have each youngster personalize his briefcase and then use it to store his work in progress. No more misplaced papers!

Cindy Schumacher—Gr. 1, Prairie Elementary, Cottonwood, ID

Joe's
Writing
Briefcase

Writer's Toolbox

How can your young authors maximize their writing time? By keeping the tools of the trade close at hand! Explain that every writer needs the right supplies to do his job. But because no two writers are exactly alike, the supplies they need vary. Write a student-generated list of possible writers' supplies on the board. Possibilities include sharpened pencils, lists of hard-to-spell words, and souvenirs that provide inspiration. Next, have each student create a toolbox in which to store his writing supplies. To do so, ask him to bring in a lidded shoebox (or a box similar in size). Provide a variety of arts-and-crafts materials and have the youngster use them to decorate his box. Then guide him in stocking it with helpful supplies. Have the student store the toolbox in a designated classroom area for easy access.

Karin Thompson, Easton, PA

Seeds for Stories

Students' writing is sure to blossom when they have a supply of personally chosen topics! Provide each student with a 4½" x 12" construction paper strip and several quarter sheets of blank paper. Direct the youngster to fold the strip in half. With the fold at the top, have her insert the stacked paper and then staple along the fold. Ask her to title the resulting notepad "[Name]'s Seeds for Stories." Encourage each student to keep a watchful eye for story topics wherever she goes. Have her jot down observations, questions, ideas—any notes that have the potential to grow into stories. When it's time to start a new piece of writing, she will have plenty of intriguing ideas to choose from!

adapted from an idea by Lona Burnett—Gr. 3
Ocean Breeze Elementary
Indian Harbour Beach, FL

new boy in our class

bird nest outside my window

Aunt Jane's surprise visit

Begin Construction

Help students shape their writing with the top-notch ideas on pages 116–117!

Writing With Purpose

Here's an idea that provides a powerful purpose for writing—an audience! Before your youngsters begin writing, ask each student to think of a person whom she would like to read her work. Suggest a parent, an older sibling, or an adult neighbor. Have each youngster complete her writing, using the established classroom routine to revise and edit it. Then provide her with a copy of a form similar to the one shown. The student completes the top portion of the form and staples it to her writing. She shares her work with the chosen reader at a mutually convenient time. The youngster returns her work and the completed form by a predetermined date. Then she stores the materials in a writing folder for a motivational reminder of an appreciative reader!

Pamela Cobler Packard, Campbell Court Elementary, Bassett, VA

September 20

Dear <u>Mr. Bartlett,</u>
    Here is a story that I wrote. It is called "The Perfect Weekend." I would love for you to read it! Please let me know what you think.

        Sincerely,
        Mindy

- - - - - - - - - - - - - - - -

Reader: <u>Mr. Bartlett</u>
Relationship to the author: <u>neighbor</u>

The thing I like most about the story is the surprise ending. I didn't expect it at all!

Decisions, Decisions!

Poems, letters, stories of every sort—writing can take countless formats! To investigate the possibilities, display a variety of written materials such as fiction books, pamphlets, and newspaper articles. Share them with students, explaining that each one represents a different writing format. Further explain that every author should use a writing format that is suitable for his readers and the information he wants to share. Next, post a sheet of chart paper titled "Writing Menu." Have students brainstorm writing formats; record their suggestions on the chart. Throughout the year, encourage your youngsters to consult the resulting writing reference for ideas (and inspiration!).

Paragraphs Beyond Compare

Comparing and contrasting is as easy as 1, 2, 3 with this paragraph plan! Draw a large two-circle Venn diagram on the chalkboard and label it with chosen topics. Enlist students' help to write information in each section of the diagram. Next, model on an overhead projector how to use the diagram to write three paragraphs. To do so, use the details that are unique to each topic in two separate paragraphs. Then use the details they have in common in a third paragraph. Provide time for students to practice using the same framework with self-selected topics. As they become more proficient, guide them to include opening and closing paragraphs in their work.

Josephine Flammer, Bay Shore, NY

A Story That Hits the Spot

This reproducible idea helps students cook up stories organized to perfection! Draw on the chalkboard a hamburger sandwich with lettuce. Lead students to identify the parts that hold it together (the top and bottom buns), the main part (the hamburger), and the special ingredient (the lettuce). Then challenge students to explain how a hamburger sandwich is like a story. After students share their ideas, give each youngster a copy of page 118. Use the sheet to clarify students' understanding of the analogy. Then have each youngster use the reproducible to plan a story about a topic of her choice. Provide time for her to later complete the story on provided paper. Now that's an idea made-to-order for young writers!

adapted from an idea by Goldy Hirsch—Special Education, Grs. 1–3
Beacon School, Brooklyn, NY

Story Strips

Put a comical spin on prewriting! To prepare, program a full sheet of paper with six blank comic strip frames. Copy the sheet to make a class supply plus a few extra. Clip selected comic strips from the newspaper. Read each strip aloud for students' listening enjoyment. Then ask students to verbally compare comic strips with fiction books. Lead them to conclude that both genres can be used to tell a story with a beginning, middle, and end. Comic strips show stories scene by scene, however, and do not provide much detail. Reread a previously shared comic strip, pausing after each frame for students to suggest details that could be incorporated if a longer version of the story were told. Next, give each youngster a copy of the prepared comic strip frames. Have him use the frames to block out an original story with sketches and notes, leaving any unneeded frames blank (provide additional copies as necessary). When it's time to further develop the story, the student will have a handy guide from start to finish!

Tara Kenyon
Medford, MA

Building a Classroom of Writers
Graphic organizer

A Story That Hits the Spot

The Beginning

The Juicy Middle

Special Details

The End

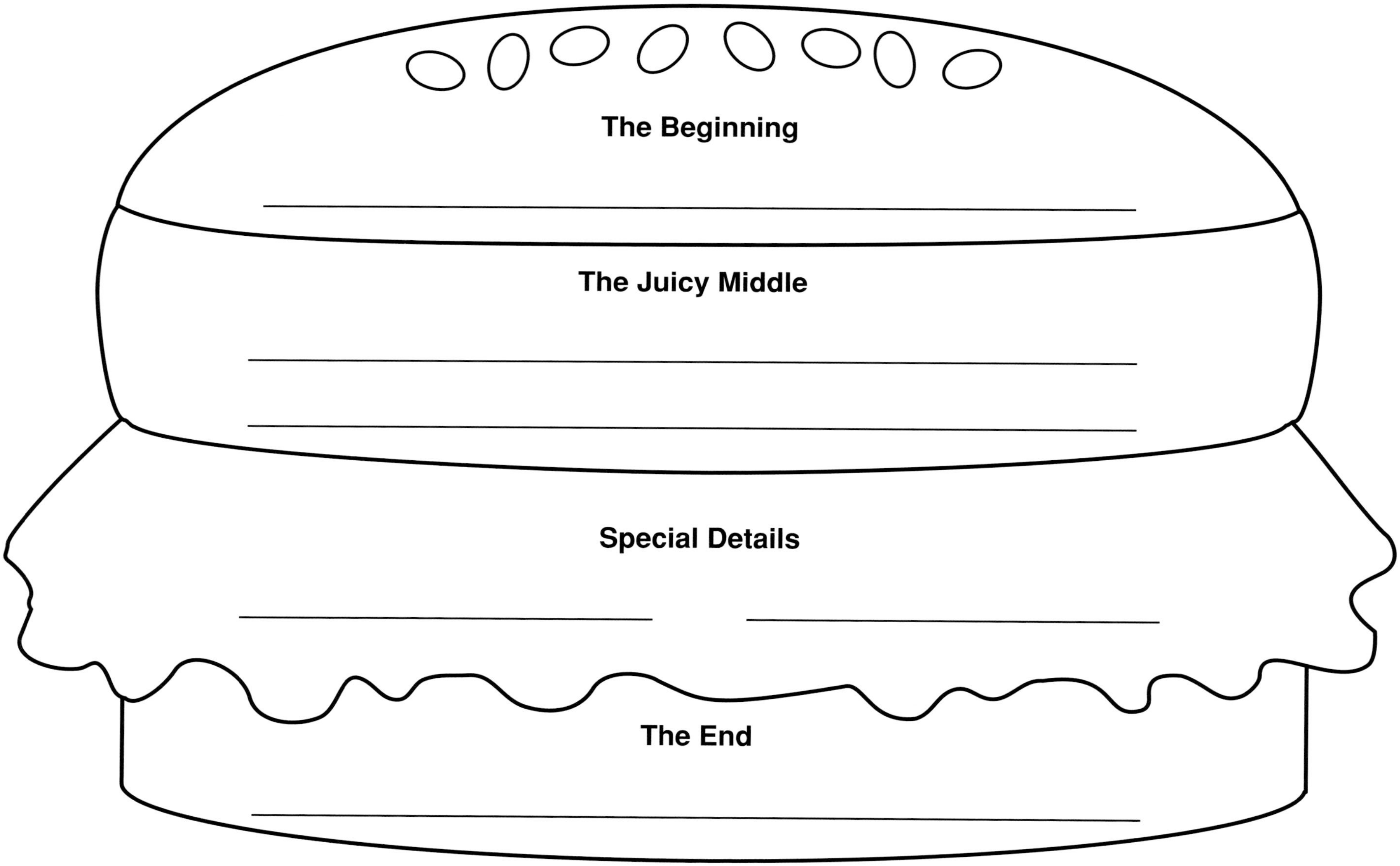

©The Education Center, Inc. • *THE MAILBOX®* • *Primary* • Aug/Sept 2001

Note to the teacher: Use with "A Story That Hits the Spot" on page 117.

Supersizing Comprehension

With Paul Bunyan and Pecos Bill

Use this colossal collection of kid-pleasing activities to supersize comprehension. After all, everything gets bigger when Paul Bunyan and Pecos Bill are involved!

ideas by Vicki Dabrowka—Gr. 2, Concord Hill School, Chevy Chase, MD

Heading Into Tall-Tale Territory

It's easy to trek into tall-tale territory with Paul and Pecos by your side, and that's no whopper! Simply find your favorite version of Paul Bunyan's tale and your favorite version of the story of Pecos Bill. Complete the "Before Reading" activity on this page and then set the stage for full-size fun by reading aloud each favorite tall tale strictly for your students' listening pleasure. Use the "During Reading" activities on pages 120 and 122 when you orally reread the tales. Then use the "After Reading" activities on pages 121 and 123 to conclude your tall-tale adventure. Now that's an itinerary that both Paul and Pecos would find impressive!

Before Reading

Nifty Knowledge
Activating prior knowledge

What does a *lumberjack* do? Who uses a *lasso*? What is an *ox*? Before introducing Paul, Pecos, and their respective stories, find out what students already know about select story-related vocabulary. To do this, write the following words on individual cards: *ox, rattlesnake, cowboy, lumberjack, ax, lasso, coyote, flapjack.* Display one word card at a time and ask students to verbalize what they know about the word's meaning. Then tape the card to the chalkboard. When all eight words are displayed, have each child divide a sheet of blank paper in half. Explain that there are many ways these words can relate to each other. Challenge each child to write on each half of his paper two words that are related in some way and then for each word pair write and/or illustrate his explanation. The end result is an intriguing glimpse of prior knowledge in use.

lasso—cowboy

ox—coyote

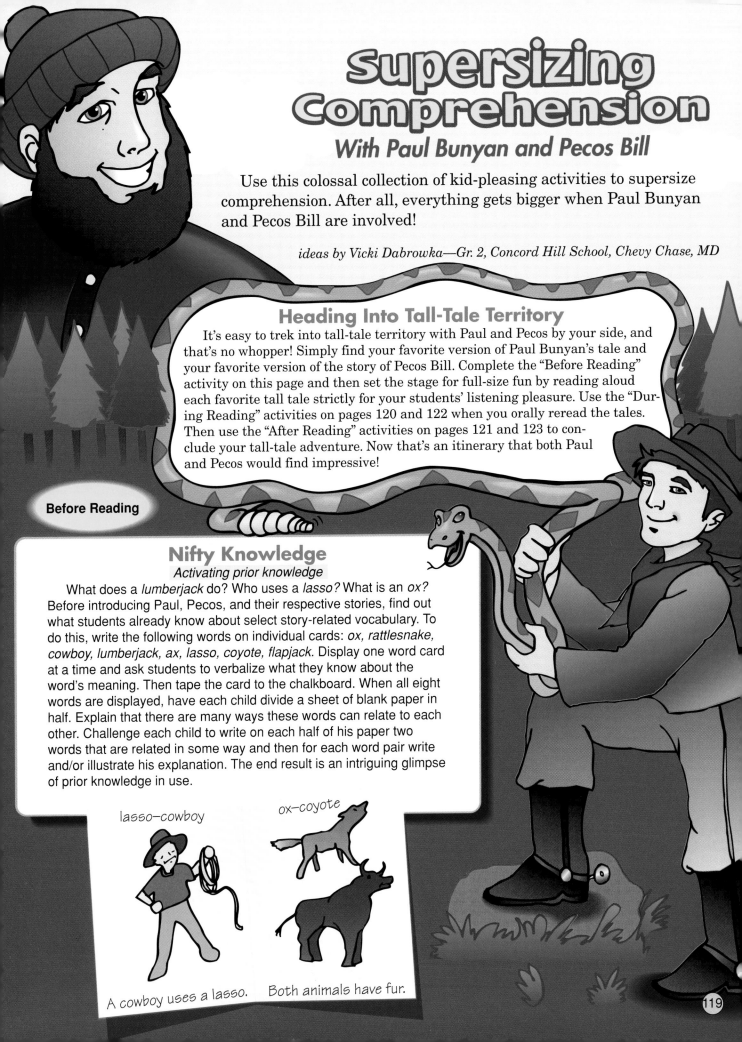

A cowboy uses a lasso.   Both animals have fur.

Picture This!
Creating mental images
It's not far-fetched to think that comprehension increases when story events are visualized. It really does! Try this comprehension strategy with students during a repeated oral reading of a Paul Bunyan (or Pecos Bill) story. To prepare, use a sticky note to flag each of several descriptive passages that clearly paint a picture. Then, during your oral reading, stop after each flagged passage and allow time for students to create mental images of what they just heard. Have volunteers describe the images they saw and explain for the class how the images helped them to better understand the story. For best results, model the process for students.

Stretching the Truth
Understanding hyperbole
Take students a step beyond identifying hyperbole and challenge them to understand its purpose. Reread for the class a story of Pecos Bill (or Paul Bunyan). Ask students to recall examples of extreme exaggeration. List the examples on the board. Then challenge students to find similarities between them. To do this, ask questions such as "Do you think the purpose of this hyperbole is to exaggerate the strength (bravery, intelligence, humor) of Pecos Bill?" Encourage plenty of discussion and accept all reasonable responses. Confirm that whichever purpose an author selects, the ultimate goal is to create an entertaining story. Then have each child try his hand at writing hyperbole by completing the student activity on page 122.

Character Cross-Examinations
Making comparisons
When it comes to character, students may be surprised to learn that they aren't all that different from Paul and Pecos! Post a length of bulletin board paper titled "Character Traits." After your first oral reading of each character's tale, list on the paper the positive traits students observed in the characters. After a repeated oral reading, write on the list any student-suggested additions. Next, have each child fold a sheet of tablet paper in half and then in half again. Have him unfold his paper, label and outline the four resulting columns as shown, and copy on his resulting chart a designated number of traits from the posted list. Then have him draw check marks on his chart to show who displays these special traits. When each child studies his completed chart, there's a good chance he'll discover that he shares plenty of positive character traits with Paul and Pecos!

Trait	Paul	Pecos	Me
brave	✓		
caring	✓	✓	
creative	✓	✓	
stubborn	✓	✓	✓
smart	✓	✓	
hardworking	✓	✓	✓
	✓	✓	✓
			✓

Larger-Than-Life Sighting
Making inferences

Tales about Paul and Pecos often include suggestions that the legendary heroes are still on the move. For a fun follow-up activity that reinforces inferencing, ask each child to write a news bulletin that announces a sighting of either Paul or Pecos. Ask each child to consider his chosen character's likes, dislikes, and habits before he determines the character's current whereabouts. Then have him write a brief news release that answers the following questions: Who? What? When? Where? How? Why? Over the course of several days, intermittently interrupt class work for individual students to share their newsworthy information. "Beep, beep, beep. Reporter Robbie McComb is standing by with a news bulletin about a surprise sighting of Pecos Bill."

Role Model Material?
Making and defending judgments

Are Paul Bunyan and Pecos Bill good role models? Let your students decide! To begin, write each character's name on the board. As students recall actions and behaviors of each tall-tale character, list the information under the corresponding name. Next, divide students into small groups. Challenge each group to evaluate the behaviors and actions listed for each character and discuss why each character is or is not a good role model for students. Then have students work individually to complete "A Tall-Tale Ruling" on page 123.

Introducing...
Showing an understanding of the tall-tale genre

Creating an original main character for a tall tale is a great way to assess a child's understanding of the tall-tale genre! In addition, this kid-pleasing wrap-up opens the door to numerous writing prompts!

Materials for one project:
copy of "Introducing…" from page 123
9" x 12" sheet of white construction paper
12" x 18" sheet of colored construction paper
1" pom-pom   pencil
crayons or markers   scissors
ruler   glue

Steps:
1. On the paper titled "Introducing…," write the name, height, and age of the character you are creating. Then write a paragraph about the character that includes information about the listed topics.
2. Illustrate the character on the white construction paper.
3. Fold the colored construction paper in half. Keeping the fold to the right, draw three edges of a door as shown below. Unfold the paper and cut along the outline.
4. Lay the paper flat so that the door and its frame are to the right. Glue the illustration on the left half of the paper and then glue the door frame atop the illustration.
5. Glue your written work on the inside of the door. Allow the glue to dry.
6. Close the door and glue the pom-pom door handle in place.

Lisa A. Waters—Gr. 2
St. Carthage School
Philadelphia, PA

Step 3

Name

Unbelievable!

Tall tales are full of exaggerations!
Write an unbelievable sentence about each tall-tale character.
Each character's name provides a purpose for exaggeration.

Bonus Box: On the back of this paper, write an exaggeration about a tall-tale version of yourself! Then illustrate your sentence.

Powerful Pete	Laughing Larry
Clever Clyde	Brave Bertha
Excitable Ethel	Serious Sam
Swift Sally	Thoughtful Theo
Brainy Betsy	Truthful Tammy

©The Education Center, Inc. • THE MAILBOX® • Primary • Oct/Nov 2001

Note to the teacher: Use with "Stretching the Truth" on page 120.

A Tall-Tale Ruling

Write your opinions.
Color the pictures.

Paul Bunyan

Pecos Bill

I think Paul Bunyan _____ a good role model
is/is not
for children. Two of my reasons are _____

_____

_____

_____

I think Pecos Bill _____ a good role model for
is/is not
children. Two of my reasons are _____

_____

_____

_____

©The Education Center, Inc. • THE MAILBOX® • Primary • Oct/Nov 2001

Introducing...

Name

Age

Height

- Family
- Hobbies

- Personality
- Talents

- Home
- Character

©The Education Center, Inc. • THE MAILBOX® • Primary • Oct/Nov 2001

Writing Tune-Up
Helping Students Revise Their Writing

Fuel your young authors' independence and steer them toward success with this collection of revision ideas and tips!

Tools of the Trade

Choose from the suggestions on pages 124 and 125 to outfit your students with handy writing tools, and shift the revision process into high gear!

Shop Talk

How do professional authors get their writing all spiffed up and ready to go? Author Eileen Christelow knows. She shares many of the answers in *What Do Authors Do?* Read the book aloud; then point out that the main characters use several different strategies to revise their writing. Display a sheet of chart paper that you have titled as shown. Ask students to recall the characters' strategies for improving their writing. List the responses on the poster. Invite students to make additional suggestions based on their own writing experiences, and add these ideas to the list. Then display the completed poster to provide a helpful reference of top-notch revision strategies.

What Authors Do When They Revise

- Cross out words.
- Read to other people and get feedback.
- Change words.
- Use carets to add details.
- Listen, watch, and think.
- Research to get more information.
- Change the order of things.

Golden Motivation

Add a golden touch to the writing process, and motivate even your most reluctant writers to revise their drafts! Label each half of a white shirt box, as shown, to make two paper trays. Stock the "Drafts" tray with white paper. Embellish the second tray with adhesive gold stars and stock it with yellow paper. Place the trays in an established classroom writing area. Have students use the white paper for first drafts and the yellow paper for revised drafts. If desired, prepare a third paper tray labeled "Fancy Finals" and stock it with decorative paper for publishing students' writing. Now that's a paper trail bound to inspire high-quality writing!

Linda Masternak Justice
Kansas City, MO

Awesome Author's Folder

There's no doubt about it—revising goes more smoothly when an author has all of her work neatly organized! To help your students organize their writing in progress, give each student two manila file folders that have different one-third cut tabs. The youngster places one folder inside the other and staples the folders together close to the outer fold. Next, she labels the tabs, as shown, and personalizes the front of the resulting multisection folder. Then she tapes a provided writing checklist or rubric inside the front cover. The student can easily refer to her brainstorming or a previous draft as she revises her writing. Plus, she can see the pride-boosting progression of her work!

adapted from an idea by Toni Rivard—Gr. 3, Somerset Elementary
Somerset, WI

Color-Coded Paragraphs

Brighten the revision process with highlighters! In advance, select two short paragraphs from a grade-appropriate science or social studies textbook. Copy them on a sheet of chart paper, trading one sentence in the first paragraph with one sentence in the second paragraph. If desired, insert an irrelevant sentence or two. To begin, remind students that every sentence in a paragraph should be about the same main idea. Also explain that paragraph organization is one thing that writers double-check.

To demonstrate an easy way to check paragraph organization, display the prepared writing and read it with the class. Then have students identify the main idea of the first paragraph. With students' help, use a highlighter to mark every supporting sentence. Use a different-colored marker to repeat the process with the second paragraph. Point out that the color coding reveals at a glance which sentences belong together and which, if any, sentences should be omitted in a final draft. Encourage students to use this colorful organization strategy with reports and other selected writing assignments.

E. Ashley Rebman—Gr. 2, The Christ School, Orlando, FL

Tune-Up Tip: Writing Models

Look no further than your classroom library for a source of stellar writing models! When a student notices a great story lead or a vivid description, have him mark the corresponding page with a sticky note. Periodically invite volunteers to share their findings with the class. Before long, your young writers will strive to imitate their favorite authors!

Repairs and Polishing

Use the ideas on pages 126 and 127 to help students patch their writing with missing details and enhance it with just the right words!

Colorful Words

Students take their writing to new heights with the help of this ongoing display! Select a word that students often overuse, such as *little, pretty,* or *said.* Write the word on a blank white card and glue it near the top of a colorful poster-sized balloon cutout. Challenge students to brainstorm or consult a thesaurus to identify words that have similar meanings but are more precise. Write the words on the balloon and attach a length of curling ribbon. Tack the balloon to a bulletin board titled "Colorful Words." Throughout the year, enlist students' help to add balloons for other words. When a student is looking for a substitute for an overused word, she'll have a bunch of colorful words to choose from!

Shelly Lanier, Lexington, NC

Author Interviews

Vague and confusing writing becomes a thing of the past with this revision strategy! Write the following sentences on the board: "Suzy played with her cat before school. It was fun." Read the sentences aloud; then remark that you wonder about some of the things that the author left out, such as how Suzy played with her cat, what the cat looks like, and what the cat's name is. Invite students to brainstorm questions for the author that could uncover these details and improve the story.

To follow up, pair students. In turn, each student reads to his partner a story that he has written. The partner asks questions to point out places in the story where additions, deletions, or clarifications might be made. The student author jots down the questions on provided paper and later considers them as he makes revisions. Clearer, more interesting writing will be the result!

Linda Masternak Justice
Kansas City, MO

Slinky Story

A favorite children's toy is just the ticket when it comes to helping young writers strengthen their story ideas! Hold a closed Slinky in your palm. Suggest that when the Slinky is closed and compact, it is not very interesting. Then slowly open the Slinky and point out that it becomes more intriguing as it is stretched out. Explain that a piece of writing is similar because important details "stretch out" the writing and make it more entertaining. Caution students that good authors carefully select the best words and details to give readers the full picture, rather than add words simply to make stories longer. When holding conferences with your students about their writing, remind youngsters to think Slinky!

Linda Rudlaff—Gr. 3, Nuner Elementary
South Bend, IN

What happened next?

Word Wonders

What a difference a word makes! Draw a T chart on the board and label the columns as shown. Nearby, write a sentence frame similar to the one shown. Then, in the appropriate columns, write student-generated adjectives and verbs that could be used in the sentence. Have students use various combinations of the listed words to create a number of different sentences, changing the verb tenses and adding words as needed to be grammatically correct. Discuss as a class how the word choices can dramatically change the meaning of the sentence. After this activity, students will look at their own word choices more critically!

Nancy Anderson, Troy, OH

adjectives	verbs
beautiful	dances
young	flies
injured	rests
magnificent	

The _____ butterfly _____ flower.

The magnificent butterfly danced by the flower.
The injured butterfly rests on the flower.

Take Three!

This simple idea helps young writers manage a key part of the revision process: word choice. Ask each student to silently read a draft of a story that she has written. Have her circle three words that she could replace to make the story clearer or more interesting. Next, pair students. In turn, each youngster shares her work with her partner and asks the partner to help brainstorm substitutions for the circled words. The youngster writes the suggestions on provided paper and tucks the notes in her writing folder for later reference. When it's time to make revisions, she'll have a clear-cut focus and plenty of helpful suggestions at her fingertips!

Linda Rudlaff—Gr. 3, Nuner Elementary, South Bend, IN

Get the Picture?

Drawing and writing are a perfect combination when it comes to revising story details! Give each student one sheet of drawing paper. At the bottom of the paper, have the youngster write "The dog ran." Then instruct him to illustrate the sentence. Invite each student to show the class his illustration. Next, ask students to share their observations about the variations among the illustrations. Lead them to conclude that many differences are due to the lack of specific information about the setting, the dog, and the dog's behavior. Revise the sentence with students' input so that it creates a clearer visual image.

To give students additional practice using words that create clear pictures, ask each youngster to take home a sheet of drawing paper and a draft of a story that he is writing. Have the student read his story to a family member and ask his listener to sketch the visual image it creates. Instruct the youngster to study the illustration to determine which story details need clarification and then revise his work accordingly.

Jan Robbins, Fairview Elementary School, Richmond, IN

Tune-Up Tip: Word Choice

Challenge your students to jot down new or nifty words that they spot in their reading. Set aside time each day for students to share their findings and write the words on a class poster. Watch writing vocabularies increase with each discovery!

Test Drive

Set students on the road to productive peer conferences and self-assessments with these ideas!

Writing Gems

Here's a gem of a writing checklist! Suggest to students that a piece of writing is like a diamond—it's a bit rough or plain at first, but with skillful work and a final polish, it can really shine! Distribute copies of the writing checklist on page 129 and review the questions with the class. Ask each student to store a copy of the checklist with his writing materials. Before he seeks feedback on a piece of writing, encourage him to complete the checklist and make any indicated revisions. Keep copies of the checklist on hand to help youngsters develop plenty of well-polished stories!

Kathleen Scavone, Middletown, CA

Expert Advice

Set the stage for peer conferences with this class activity! In advance, write a poorly developed story on an overhead transparency sheet. Tell students that every writer (even an adult!) benefits from feedback. Explain that the most helpful type of feedback points out strengths, as well as areas for improvement. Tell students that you have written a story and would like their input. Display the prepared story and read it aloud.

Next, invite youngsters to tell what they like about the story and why. Then encourage them to suggest improvements, such as adding details or using more specific words. List students' comments and suggestions on a sheet of chart paper. Later, consider students' advice as you revise the story. Share the new and improved version of the story with the class. You can be sure your young critics will be proud to have helped!

adapted from an idea by Elizabeth Searls Almy
Greensboro, NC

Ruler Rubric

How does your older students' writing measure up? Find out with this nifty rubric! Give each student a copy of the rubric on page 129. Discuss the listed criteria. Then, as a class, use the rubric to rate anonymous pieces of writing or selected passages from children's books. After students are familiar with the rubric, instruct each youngster to keep her copy in an accessible location. Have her use the rubric to size up her completed stories and keep track of her writing growth.

adapted from an idea by Elizabeth Searls Almy

Tune-Up Tip: Peer Conferences

Display a guide like the one shown to remind students how to confer with their classmates. Peer conferences will be letter-perfect! ●

Kathleen Scavone

The ABCs of Peer Conferences

A: Ask questions.

B: Be a good listener.

C: Comment thoughtfully.

Use the rubric with "Ruler Rubric" on page 128.

Ruler Rubric

1

The story
- leaves the reader with a lot of questions
- has some complete sentences
- has few details

2

The story
- has a lot of complete sentences
- creates a fuzzy picture
- has several details that are not needed

3

The story
- makes sense
- has complete sentences
- helps make a picture
- has a few details that are not needed

4

The story
- is easy to understand
- has complete sentences
- helps make a clear picture
- "hooks" the reader

©The Education Center, Inc.

Use the checklist with "Writing Gems" on page 128.

Name _____

Writing Gem Checklist

Did I...

☐ tell everything in the best order?

☐ use interesting details?

☐ take out details that are not important?

☐ use words that help make a clear picture?

☐ write complete sentences?

©The Education Center, Inc.

"What a Pair!"

Spotlighting Quotation Marks in Dialogue

What often has something to say and never shows up alone?
A quotation mark! Here's just what you need to get the word
out about using quotation marks in dialogue!

Daily Dialogue

Set the stage for a better understanding of dialogue!
Explain that dialogue is an oral or a written conversation
between two or more people. Ask students to think
about dialogue they've heard, engaged in, or read
within the last 24 hours. Then write a class-compiled
list of dialogue sources. Challenge each child to contribute a different source. Post the completed list and
encourage students to refer to it for dialogue-related
writing inspiration. Dialogue is everywhere!

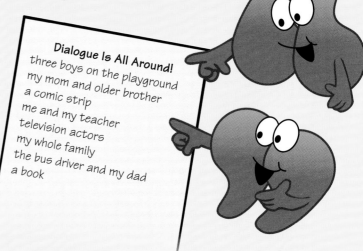

Dialogue Is All Around!
three boys on the playground
my mom and older brother
a comic strip
me and my teacher
television actors
my whole family
the bus driver and my dad
a book

Pairing Up

This partner activity sends students in search of written dialogue and quotation
marks! Every twosome needs paper, pencils, crayons, and a children's book that
provides examples of written dialogue. Working together, partners find three different examples of written dialogue in their book. Each student copies each example
on her paper and uses a crayon to circle each quotation mark. Then, for each example, she uses a crayon to underline the exact words that were spoken. Lead students to conclude that because quotation marks show where a speaker's words begin
and end, they always appear in pairs!

Karen D. Brown, Pleasant Lea Elementary, Lee's Summit, MO

"A-peeling" Punctuation

Try this fresh, large-group approach to adding quotation marks to written dialogue. Label
each of several different-colored tagboard strips with a different sentence of dialogue. Omit the
quotation marks. Cut each strip into two parts, separating the speaker's exact words from the
remainder of the sentence. You will also need four unpeeled bananas. Ask four students to
stand at the front of the classroom and face their classmates. Give two students two bananas each. Give the remaining two students a different section of the same tagboard
strip. Then challenge the foursome to use their props to display for the class a properly punctuated sentence of dialogue. Repeat the activity with different tagboard
strips and groupings of four students.
It's an activity students are
sure to go ape over!

Natalie Hughes-Tanner—Writing Specialist
Ermel Elementary, Houston, TX

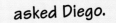

Where are my shoes?   asked Diego.

Something to Talk About

Here's a partner activity that earns rave reviews each time it's performed! Pair students and assign each twosome two characters from a familiar fairy tale or children's book. A pair selects a topic of conversation. Then each child portrays a different character as the twosome acts out a brief conversation between the characters (approximately three sentences of dialogue each). Then the students work together to write on paper the conversation they've performed, making sure to use quotation marks to set off each speaker's exact words. Edit each pair's project for spelling, capitalization, and punctuation.

Next, have each pair use its edited writing to make a chatter book that can be read and performed again and again. Give each pair one sentence strip for each sentence of dialogue, plus one. Each partner carefully copies each sentence of his character's dialogue onto a strip. Then he and his partner stack the strips in sequential order. On one side of the unused strip they write a desired title and on the other side they write their names. They place this strip on top of the stack and staple. Set aside time for each pair to perform the chatter book it created. Then place the books at a center to encourage additional readings and performances.

Natalie Hughes-Tanner—Writing Specialist
Ermel Elementary
Houston, TX

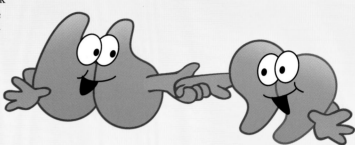

Look Who's Talking!

You'll have students grinning from ear to ear when you introduce this dialogue-writing activity. Give each child a copy of page 132. Ask her to cut out the four cartoon frames and sequence them to form a strip. Point out that in cartoons, speech bubbles convey dialogue. Next, read aloud the dialogue between the boy and his dog. As a class discuss how the cartoon pictures convey emotions and help a reader better understand the sequence of events. Then have each child choose a favorite frame. Ask her to write in sentence form, on provided paper, the dialogue in each speech bubble. Emphasize that the dog and boy need to be given names, that quotation marks must be inserted to set off each speaker's exact words, and that the first word of each quotation must be capitalized. (Include additional punctuation tips, if desired.) Also encourage her to convey emotion by carefully choosing sentence tags such as *whimpered* or *groaned* instead of *said*. Write on!

131

Cartoon Frames

Use with "Look Who's Talking!" on page 131.

©The Education Center, Inc. • THE MAILBOX® • Primary • April/May 2002

Lights, Camera, ACTION!
A Crowd–Pleasing Verb Unit

Put action verbs in the spotlight with these entertaining ideas, and count on glowing reviews from your young critics!

Skill: Understanding action verbs

Theme Song

Raise the curtain on your class verb study with this toe-tapping ditty! Copy the provided song on a sheet of chart paper and lead your youngsters through the lyrics. Periodically conduct additional song rehearsals to keep your youngsters' verb skills in tune!

Vicki Dabrowka—Gr. 2
Concord Hill School
Chevy Chase, MD

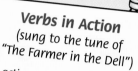

Verbs in Action
(sung to the tune of "The Farmer in the Dell")

All action words are verbs.
They make writing superb.
Heigh-ho, the derry-o,
All action words are verbs.

A verb tells what you do,
Like jump or swim or chew.
Heigh-ho, the derry-o,
A verb tells what you do.

Each sentence must have one—
The verb adds all the fun.
Heigh-ho, the derry-o,
Each sentence must have one.

Skill: Identifying action verbs

Playground
stand
run
jump
swing
toss
chase
talk
race

Casting Call

Send students on location to create a cast of verbs for future writing assignments! Give each student a booklet with construction paper covers and four white pages. Have her personalize the front cover as desired. On the chalkboard, write a student-generated list of at least four places youngsters frequently visit, such as the park, grocery store, and school cafeteria. Then instruct each youngster to label a booklet page for each of four chosen places.

Each day of your verb study, provide time for youngsters to enter in their booklets action verbs that correspond with observations in their selected sites. When it's time to complete a writing assignment, they'll have a variety of verb choices at their fingertips!

adapted from an idea by Kathy Dickerson—Gr. 3
Nolley Elementary, Akron, OH

Skill: Using action verbs

An Alphabet of Actions

Stretch students' vocabularies with action-packed storytelling! Read aloud *The A to Z Beastly Jamboree* by Robert Bender to provide inspiration. Then gather students in a circle. Explain that they will tell a silly story about a teacher who always does things in alphabetical order. To begin the story, say "Ms. Does-a-Lot <u>ate</u> breakfast." Ask the student seated on your left to repeat your statement and then use a verb that begins with *b* to add a sentence. Continue around the circle. Ask each child to repeat the statements already given and then add one of his own. Provide assistance as necessary. Now that's a story line sure to get rave reviews!

adapted from an idea by Erin Harp, Lewisville, NC

Speechless!

Skill: Understanding action verbs

Give your young actors starring roles in this verb game! Copy and cut out the word cards on page 137 to make a class supply. Place the cards in a container. Tell students that audiences can tell a lot about movie plots by carefully observing the actors, even if the movies are silent!

To illustrate this point, divide the class into two teams and designate a scorekeeper for each one. Have the teams arrange their chairs in two facing rows. To play, the first player on one team draws a card and reads the top word to himself. (If necessary, explain that the additional programming on each card is for a later activity.) Then he silently pantomimes the verb for his teammates. If they identify the verb within a designated amount of time, the team earns one point and the card is placed in a discard pile. If not, the student actor returns the card to the container and his turn is over. Play alternates between teams until every student has taken a turn. The team with the higher score wins. Students are sure to request a repeat performance!

adapted from an idea by Erin Harp, Lewisville, NC

Picture–Perfect Categories

Skill: Classifying words by related action verbs

Classification skills take center stage with this idea for older students! Secretly assign each student a different verb-related category like the ones shown. On a sheet of drawing paper, have her illustrate and label three things in her category. Ask her to sign the front of her paper and write the category on the back. Collect students' papers and number them. Tack each paper below the title "What Do They Have in Common?"

Set aside time on each of several days for students to write their guesses about their peers' categories on provided paper. Then have the owner of each displayed paper, in turn, read her three words aloud and invite her peers to share their guesses. Ask her to turn her illustration over to verify the correct answer.

Verb-Related Categories
Things that…
hop
melt
float
spin
shine
crunch

adapted from an idea by Linda Masternak Justice, Kansas City, MO

Silly Pairs

Skill: Determining subject-verb agreement

This agreeable subject-verb activity is bound to be a hit! Prepare two class sets of cards. Use a marker to program one set with singular and plural verbs. Use a different-colored marker to program the other set with singular and plural subjects. Place each set in a separate container. Give each student a blank index card. Have him write "Agree" on one side and "Disagree" on the other side.

To begin, ask a volunteer to remove one card from each container. Ask him to read the resulting subject-verb pair aloud. Instruct the remaining students to hold up their cards to indicate whether the subject and verb agree. Scan the raised cards for accuracy; then call on a student to share the correct answer. Have the volunteer place the subject and verb cards in discard piles. Continue in a like manner with the remaining students and cards.

Linda Masternak Justice

Skill: Identifying verb tenses

Verb Tense Shuffle

Simple choreography brings the concept of verb tenses to life! Have students stand in a row facing the front of the class. Announce an action verb (if desired, refer to a copy of page 137). If it is in the future tense, each student takes one step forward. If it is in the past tense, she takes one step backward, and if it is in the present tense, she hops in place once. Repeat the activity with a desired number of words. Now that's fancy footwork!

Toni Fink, Milwaukee Spanish Immersion School, Milwaukee, WI

Someday I will fly in a plane!

Skill: Using verb tenses

High–Flying Verbs

These colorful kites provide a fitting backdrop for verb-tense practice! To provide a captivating verb review, read aloud *Kites Sail High: A Book About Verbs* by Ruth Heller. Then assign each student a present-tense action verb. The youngster uses provided templates to make a diamond-shaped kite and three kite-tail bows from construction paper. He writes the assigned verb on one bow and the past and future forms of it on the remaining bows. On paper sized to fit the kite, he writes a sentence with each verb form and underlines the featured verbs. He glues the sentences to the kite and then uses tape and a length of narrow ribbon to assemble the kite as shown. Display students' work on a classroom wall to create an eye-catching verb reference.

Vicki Dabrowka—Gr. 2 , Concord Hill School, Chevy Chase, MD

The robin flies to its nest. My paper airplane flew across the room. Someday I will fly in a plane.

flies

flew

will fly

Skill: Identifying verb tenses

look
will look
looked

Now Showing!

It's a race to the movies with this partner verb game! Give each twosome one copy of pages 136 and 137, one paper clip to use with the spinner, and two small counters for game pieces. Have the youngsters cut apart the game cards and stack them facedown. Explain that the object of the game is to be the first player to reach either the movie that takes place in the past *(Dinosaur Days)* or the movie set in the future *(Space City)*.

To play, both players place their game pieces on the starred space. The first player draws a card and reads aloud the word at the top. The second student states the future and past tenses of the word. If she is correct, as verified by the cardholder, she spins and moves her game piece as indicated. If she is not correct, her turn is over. The first player places the card in a discard pile. The players alternate turns, following the gameboard directions as appropriate and reshuffling the cards as necessary. The first player to reach a movie wins!

Linda Masternak Justice, Kansas City, MO

Now Showing!

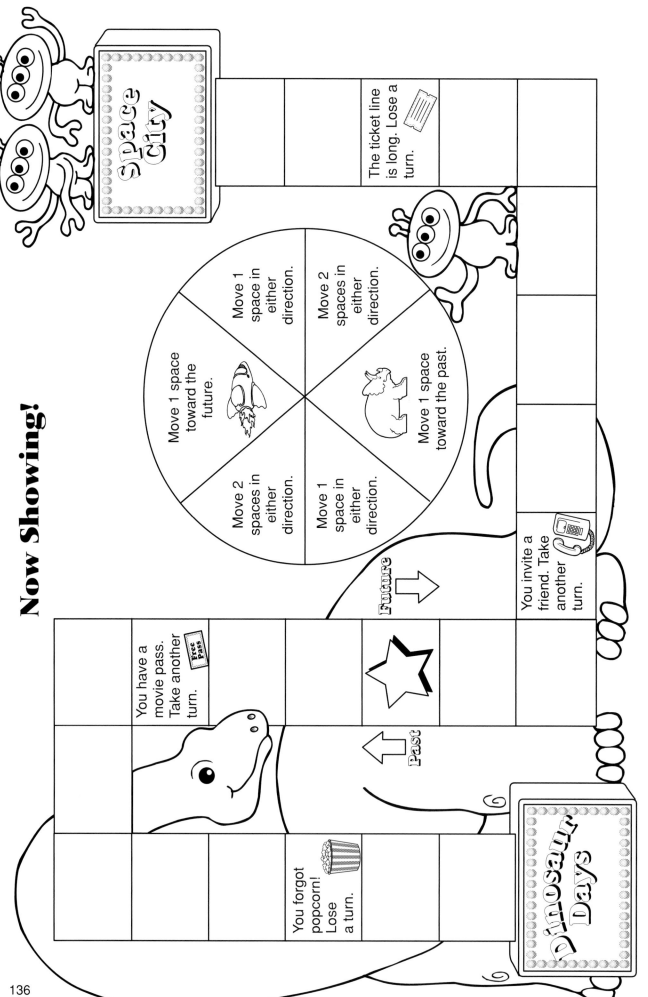

Space City

The ticket line is long. Lose a turn.

Move 1 space toward the future.

Move 1 space in either direction.

Move 2 spaces in either direction.

Move 2 spaces in either direction.

Move 1 space in either direction.

Move 1 space toward the past.

Future

Past

You invite a friend. Take another turn.

You have a movie pass. Take another turn.

Free Pass

You forgot popcorn! Lose a turn.

Dinosaur Days

©The Education Center, Inc. • *THE MAILBOX®* • *Primary* • Feb/Mar 2002

Note to the teacher: Use with "Now Showing!" on page 135.

Word Cards

Use with "Speechless!" on page 134 and "Now Showing!" on page 135.

eat will eat ate	**run** will run ran	**write** will write wrote	**fly** will fly flew
sing will sing sang	**build** will build built	**march** will march marched	**cry** will cry cried
catch will catch caught	**shake** will shake shook	**hop** will hop hopped	**pour** will pour poured
sweep will sweep swept	**blow** will blow blew	**climb** will climb climbed	**paint** will paint painted
hide will hide hid	**think** will think thought	**dance** will dance danced	**splash** will splash splashed
crawl will crawl crawled	**stretch** will stretch stretched	**sew** will sew sewed	**look** will look looked
pull will pull pulled	**buy** will buy bought	**listen** will listen listened	**read** will read read

Picture–Perfect Publishing
Showcasing Students' Writing

Your young authors have been brushing up their writing skills all year. Now it's time to share (and celebrate!) their finest work.

Add the Finishing Touches

Before your students unveil their writing, try the editing suggestions on this page and page 139. The ideas will paint a picture of the editing process and help students touch up their work!

How to Publish a Book

1. Brainstorm ideas.
2. Make a plan.
3. Research.
4. Write a draft.
5. Revise.
6. Edit. ✗
7. Plan the layout and illustrations. ✗
8. Design the book.
9. Check to make sure it's right.
10. Print the book.

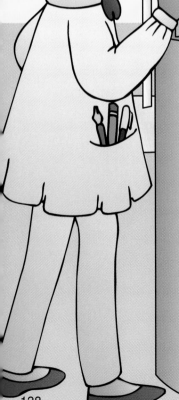

Conference Cards

Capture editing goals with this conference tip! During an editing conference with a student, identify one or two points for improvement. Write the corresponding goal(s) on a blank card. Tape the card to the student's desktop or the inside of his writing folder. No more forgotten goals!

Suzanne Helms—Gr. 2
LaBelle Elementary
Marietta, GA

Capitalize all proper nouns.

Exhibit Notes

The Big Picture

This literature-based idea brings the importance of editing and presentation into focus! Tell students that an author has valuable work to do after he composes and revises a piece of writing—he needs to prepare it for publication! Explain that publishing written work means sharing it with others. To provide a professional view of the process, read aloud *How a Book Is Published* by Bobbie Kalman. Then have students recall the main steps of publishing a book. List them on the chalkboard in sequential order. With students' input, draw a star beside each step that occurs after a writer composes and revises his work. What a great way to help students understand that putting words on paper is only one part of the process!

Marvelous Mini Lessons

What provides a handy source of kid-pleasing editing practice? Why, students' own writing, of course! At the beginning of a class writing time, model how to apply a selected grammar or mechanics skill. Then give each youngster a sentence strip. Have her study samples in her journal or portfolio to find a sentence to which the skill applies. Ask her to edit the sentence as needed based on the preceding mini lesson and then copy the correct version on the sentence strip. If the youngster does not find an appropriate sentence, have her write on the strip an original sentence that applies the skill. Instruct the student to underline the relevant part of the sentence. Then ask each student, in turn, to read her strip aloud and tack it to a bulletin board titled with the featured skill.

adapted from an idea by Nanette Avery—Gr. 1
Gordan Day School
Miami, FL

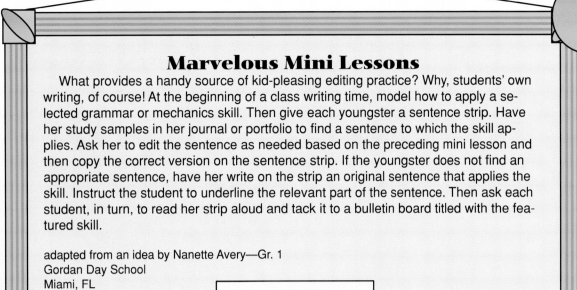

I live in <u>Miami</u>, <u>Florida</u>.

We went to <u>Michigan</u> to see my grandmother.

EDITING REMINDERS

Watch for noun-verb agreement.

Remember capitals.

Indent new paragraphs.

Take another look at the punctuation.

Edit for spelling.

Editing Guide

Steer your young editors in the "write" direction! Display the reminders shown above on a decorative poster or prepare individual student copies. The convenient reference will remind students exactly how to check their writing!

adapted from an idea by
Ruth L. Metzger—Gr. 1
North Elementary
Poland, OH

Spell and Check

Here's a positive way to help students take responsibility for editing their own spelling! Give each student a blank booklet that has 14 pages. Have her label half a page for each letter of the alphabet. Ask her to title her booklet "[Student's name]'s Spelling Dictionary." Place a supply of scrap paper in an easily accessible location for later use.

As a student edits her writing, ask her to watch for words that don't look right. Point out that if a word doesn't look right, there is a good chance that it is misspelled. When a student spots such a word, have her copy it on a piece of scrap paper and place the paper on the corner of her desk. To provide feedback, make a dot under each correct letter and then correctly write the word. Have the youngster make any needed corrections in her writing and then copy the correct spelling on the appropriate page of her dictionary for later reference. Not only will the youngster's spelling skills increase, but her independence in editing will grow as well!

Tanya Kirschman—Gr. 1
Fromberg Elementary
Fromberg, MT

Prepare for the Showing

Use the publishing ideas on this page to provide your students with appealing formats for framing their writing.

Hooked on Student–Written Books!

This quick-and-easy publishing suggestion doubles as a reading motivation idea! Ask a student volunteer to decorate two sheets of construction paper to make covers for a class anthology of student writing. Laminate the covers for durability. Staple students' writing between the covers; then hole-punch the top left-hand corner of the resulting book and attach a metal ring.

To create an inviting class book display, use the metal rings to hang published anthologies on cup hooks arranged within student reach along a classroom wall. Establish a sign-out system so that youngsters can borrow books overnight to share with their families. If desired, take each book apart at the end of the school year and invite each young author to keep the pages she contributed.

Sheila Criqui-Kelley—Gr. 1, Lebo Elementary, Lebo, KS

Our Field Trip
by
Ms. Christiansen's Class

Crafty Book Covers

Make durable student books with this creative idea! For each of two 10" x 12" pieces of craft foam, hole-punch the left-hand side to align with the holes of a clear top-loading sheet protector. To prepare the front cover, cut a 3" x 5" rectangle from one piece as shown. Write and illustrate a title page on a sheet of white paper so that the title is visible through the cover opening. Slide the completed title page and each sheet of student writing into a separate sheet protector. Use ribbon to bind the resulting pages between the covers.

Marie Christiansen—Gr. 2
Bushkill Elementary
Dingmans Ferry, PA

Writing on the Web

If you have a classroom Web site, this publishing idea is for you! Each month, post a sampling of students' writing on the Web site along with any desired graphics. Students' family members from both near and far can check out youngsters' latest writing accomplishments with just the click of a mouse!

Peggy Bruno—Gr. 2
Squadron Line School
Simsbury, CT

Honor and Celebrate!

Invite youngsters to share their writing masterpieces with the pride-boosting suggestions on pages 141–143.

Classy Authors' Party

Put student writing in the spotlight with weekly book celebrations! Plan an authors' party for the last day of each week. Establish a schedule so that each student has a turn to be one of several featured authors during a party. The week before a student's scheduled turn, have him summarize selected autobiographical information to make an "About the Author" page. Have him include the page at the end of the book that he publishes.

To honor the featured authors, position your teacher's chair in a central classroom location. Invite each author, in turn, to sit in the chair and read his book to the class. Allow time for the student audience to ask the author questions about his work and to provide positive feedback. Serve refreshments for students to enjoy as they ask the authors for their autographs.

Linda Rudlaff—Gr. 3, John F. Nuner Elementary, South Bend, IN

Literary Pajama Party

This authors' event gives new meaning to bedtime stories! On a designated day, invite each youngster to come to school with a stuffed animal and dressed in pajamas. (Gather a few stuffed animals to have on hand for students who do not bring any.) Arrange blankets in selected areas of the classroom. Pair students and ask each twosome to sit on a blanket. Then have each youngster read her published writing to her partner. After every student has shared her work, continue the special event with other book-related activities. Possibilities include watching a videotape of a favorite children's author (or a familiar book) or reading aloud books by professional authors as students enjoy a class snack. Sweet dreams of more publishing fun will be the result!

Shelly Waibel—Gr. 1, Tobyhanna Elementary, Pocono Pines, PA

Stories With Character

Raise the curtain on students' writing success! In advance, have each student select from his portfolio a story that he would like to share with his classmates. Ask him to come to school dressed as a chosen character in the story. Have him introduce the story to the class from the character's perspective and read it aloud. Then lead the student audience in a round of applause and encourage the author to take a well-deserved bow!

Diane DeBruin—Grs. 2–3
The Potter's House Christian School
Grand Rapids, MI

Author Buddies

Culminate a year's worth of buddy activities with a cross-grade-level authors' celebration! Meet with the teacher of your buddy class to set a date and determine a school location for the event, such as your classroom or a more open space such as the cafeteria. Make arrangements for refreshments and decorations. On the day of the event, instruct each pair of buddies to sit together. Ask each student, in turn, to read her published book(s) to her buddy. Invite the buddy to ask questions or make positive comments about the student's writing. Then serve the refreshments. The benefits of buddying up will be clear—writing models, admiring listeners, and twice the fun!

adapted from an idea by Carrie Geiger
Gainesville, FL

Circle Round

Round up author recognition with this management idea. Ask each youngster to select a piece of his writing that he would like to share. Divide the class in half and ask each student to hold his writing. Instruct the students in one half to form a circle. Have the students in the second half form a circle around the first one so that each youngster in one circle is facing a student in the other circle. (If you have an odd number of students, join the smaller circle.) Direct the students in each pair to softly read their writing to each other and then stand quietly.

When every student has shared his writing, signal the students in the outer circle to move clockwise by one person. Ask each student to share his writing with his new partner. Continue in a like manner for a desired period of time or until every youngster in one circle has read his work to every student in another.

Diane DeBruin—Grs. 2–3
The Potter's House Christian School
Grand Rapids, MI

Stories
Guaranteed
to Make You
Laugh

by
Ms. Chartrand's
Class

Authentic Audiences

Warm hearts with this writing project! By student vote, choose a community group or business, such as a local hospital or senior living center. Ask each student to write and edit an original story for the chosen audience. Help each student use a desired word-processing program to publish his story. Bind students' completed work into a class book and then arrange to present the book to the intended recipients. The experience is sure to be rewarding for the authors and readers alike!

Cheryl Chartrand—Gr. 3, Glenfield Elementary,
Glenfield, NY

Authors' Hall of Fame

Use this hall display to introduce guests to the young writers of an author celebration! To prepare, take an individual photo of each student and have it developed. Make a form similar to the one shown and copy it to make a class supply. Have each youngster complete a copy, glue his picture in the provided space, and then mount the form on a sheet of construction paper. Display students' resulting posters on a hall wall. Title the display "Our Authors' Hall of Fame" and embellish it with star cutouts. Three cheers for student authors!

adapted from an idea by
Diane DeBruin—Grs. 2–3
The Potter's House Christian School
Grand Rapids, MI

Publishing Parade

It's a parade! A parade of student books, that is! Send home invitations for an authors' party that you have planned. Have each youngster choose a book that she has published and would like to share with the party guests. After the guests are seated, ask the students to hold their books and form a line that starts at the front of the classroom and goes along the sides. Instruct the first student in line to step forward, show the guests her book, and briefly tell about it. Have her move to the end of the line; then ask the next student in line to step forward. Continue until every youngster has introduced her book. Then serve punch and cookies as the guests move about to look more closely at students' writing.

Heather Graley, Columbus, OH

Author: Sammy
Age: 8
My favorite book is <u>The Chocolate Touch</u>.

My best school memory is when <u>my team won the tug-of-war on Field Day.</u>

I get my writing ideas by <u>re___ other authors write ab___</u>

I like to write stories <u>___ laugh.</u>

How would you like me to sign this?

To Mom, Love, Eric!

Book-Signing Party

Students are sure to be fans of this writing celebration! To prepare, invite students' families to the event. Have each youngster write a brief synopsis of a book that he has written. Compile students' synopses into one list to make a handout. Make one copy for each expected guest plus a few extra for unexpected arrivals. Have each student wear a nametag and sit at a desk or table with his book and a provided pen. Give each guest a handout. Suggest that every guest visit each of several authors and listen to the author read his book. Then, for a keepsake of the event, have her ask him to autograph her handout near his synopsis. Now that's giving student authors star treatment!

adapted from an idea by Trish Draper—Gr. 1, Millarville Community School
Millarville, Alberta, Canada

Aflutter Over Retelling

Use these colorful suggestions to sharpen students' retelling skills, and watch comprehension soar!

ideas contributed by Rebecca Brudwick
Hoover Elementary, North Mankato, MN

Roll On!

Box up practice with important story elements! Cut six paper rectangles, each sized to fit a side of an empty cube-shaped tissue box. Label two rectangles for each of the following elements: characters, setting, and events. Glue each rectangle onto a different side of the box. At the completion of a class read-aloud, sit with students in a circle on the floor. Gently toss the prepared box and read aloud the word that is displayed on the top. Recall a detail that corresponds to this story element. Then pass the box to the student on your right. Ask the student to toss the box, read the word on top, and then name a detail that has not been shared. Continue around the circle until every student has taken a turn.

From the Beginning

Who better to summarize the stories in the well-known Arthur series than the beloved aardvark himself! To enhance understanding of these books by Marc Brown, give each student four 2" x 8½" strips of white paper. On one strip, the youngster writes the title of an Arthur book that she has read or enjoyed as a read-aloud. She labels another strip "Beginning" and writes one or two sentences to tell about this part of the book from Arthur's perspective. She repeats the process for the middle and end of the book on the remaining strips.

Next, give each student a 5" x 7" brown construction paper oval, a 9" x 12" sheet of construction paper, a black marker, and access to construction paper scraps. Guide the youngster to create a likeness of Arthur similar to the one shown. Then have her sequence her prepared strips and glue them on the construction paper sheet. Display students' completed work on a hall wall below the title "Arthur's Stories." Now that's a retelling activity with character!

Arthur's New Puppy

Beginning
I get a new puppy. His name is Pal.

Middle
Pal gets into all kinds of trouble.

End
I train Pal. I even teach him some tricks!

Winged Tales

Retelling skills take flight with this picture-perfect reproducible! Have each student review a completed independent-reading book to ensure that he is familiar with the main story elements. Next, give him a copy of the reproducible on page 146. Instruct him to write his name and the title of his chosen book. Ask him to illustrate each of four sequential story events in the corresponding circles and color the rest of the butterfly as desired. Then have each youngster use his completed illustrations to retell the story to a partner. To extend students' learning, ask each youngster to refer to his artwork as he creates a written retelling.

Puppet Pals

Simple, kid-pleasing plots make the Henry and Mudge books by Cynthia Rylant perfect for retelling, and student-made puppets provide just the right tool! To make a cutout of Henry, a student illustrates the character's face on a three-inch white construction paper circle. She cuts away two adjacent corners of a four-inch construction paper square to make a shirt, uses crayons to add desired details, and then glues the circle onto the shirt.

To make a cutout of Mudge, the youngster uses a four-inch tan construction paper square for the head. She fashions a snout, two eyes, and two ears from construction paper, as shown, and then glues them in place. She tapes a jumbo craft stick handle to the back of each cutout to make her puppets.

After each youngster completes her puppets, have her practice using them to retell her favorite Henry and Mudge story. When she is satisfied with her efforts, arrange for her to retell the story to a student in a lower grade. Then encourage her to take her puppets home and give a repeat performance for her family!

Tell Me About It!

Here's an assessment idea that will make students all smiles! Prepare a form similar to the one on this page and use it to make an overhead transparency. Display the transparency and prompt a class discussion about the retelling criteria shown. Next, ask students to consider these criteria as you retell a familiar story, deliberately making a few errors or omissions. Invite students to comment on your retelling and suggest how you might improve it. Then reflect on their remarks aloud as you mark the faces on the transparency to rate your retelling.

Periodically have each youngster complete a copy of a blank form to assess his own retelling skills. Not only will he develop an understanding of what is expected, but he will also gain a clear picture of his achievement!

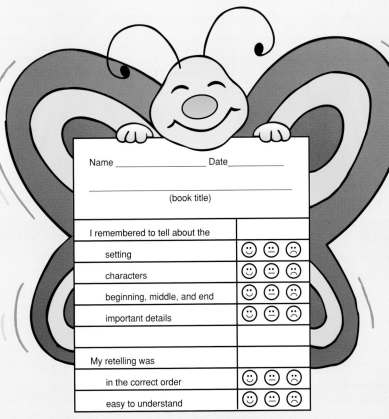

Name _____ Date_____

_____
(book title)

I remembered to tell about the	
setting	☺ ☺ ☹
characters	☺ ☺ ☹
beginning, middle, and end	☺ ☺ ☹
important details	☺ ☺ ☹
My retelling was	
in the correct order	☺ ☺ ☹
easy to understand	☺ ☺ ☹

_____
(book title)

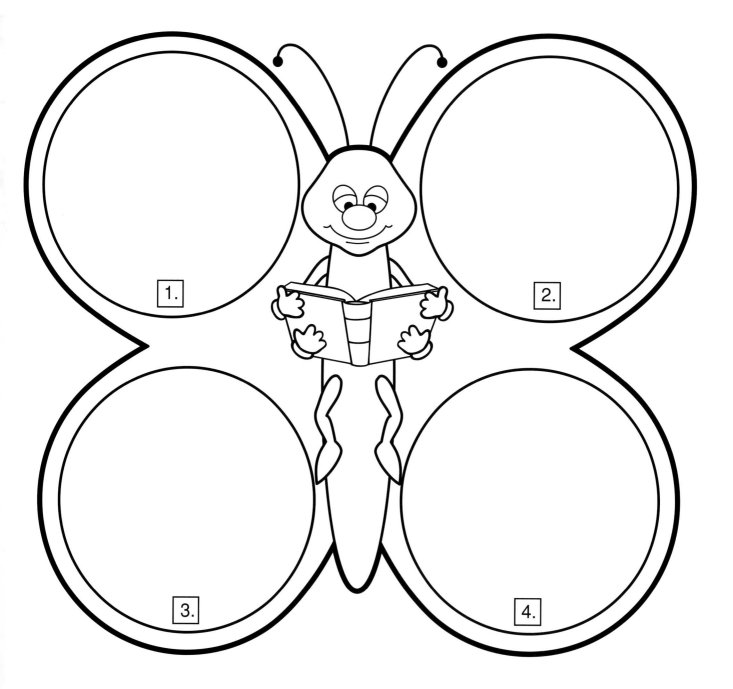

1.

2.

3.

4.

©The Education Center, Inc. • *THE MAILBOX®* • *Primary* • June/July 2002

146   **Note to the teacher:** Use with "Winged Tales" on page 145.

WELL, SHIVER ME WORDS!

A Treasure of Decoding Strategies

By Jove! Captain McWord and his crew have happened upon buried treasure more precious than gold! Expect a bounty of fun and good fortune as young pirates discover decoding strategies for reading on the high seas.

ideas by Starin Lewis, Kyrene School District, Tempe, AZ

Buried Treasure

Strategy: finding known words

Captain McWord's crew knows to be on the lookout for familiar words. After all, finding a familiar word in an unfamiliar one is like finding buried treasure! To practice this decoding strategy, have each child title a sheet of blank paper "[Student]'s Buried Treasure." On the board write "choppy." Have each child copy the word on his paper, find a familiar word in it *(hop or chop),* circle it with a crayon, and then use the word to decode the larger word. Next, ask a volunteer to state the word and use it in a pirate-related sentence. Showcase additional words that can be decoded in a similar manner (see "Lookout List" for suggestions) and repeat the described process with each one. Encourage students to use this gem of a decoding strategy over and over!

Lookout List

choppy	pirate
fortune	treasure
cannon	buckle
parrot	kidnap
captain	cutlass
booty	hideout

Theo's Buried Treasure

(cho)ppy

(boo)ty

(pirate)

Bags of Booty

Strategy: categorizing words

Yo, ho, ho! A wealth of knowledge about letters, sounds, and words is discovered when buccaneers sort this booty! Give each young pirate a resealable sandwich bag and a gold construction paper copy of some or all of the coins on page 150. To make his bag of booty, a child cuts out the coins, labels the back of each one with his initials or a symbol, and then stores the cutouts in the bag.

Provide time for investigating the booty. Direct students' attention to selected spelling patterns or phonic elements. Then warm up the buccaneers' sorting skills by identifying two sorting categories, such as words that have the short *a* sound as in *hat* and those that do not. When each student has his booty sorted, ask a volunteer to describe the outcome of his sort. Spend time discussing and solving any sorting discrepancies that arise among pirates.

Next, have students work individually or in pairs to sort the words into categories of their own choosing. Set aside time for the sorts to be described and explained. Or have each child describe his sort on paper. Pirates learn quickly that sorting booty develops a keen eye for decoding!

SHIPSHAPE DECODER

Strategy: recognizing word families

Reveal how word families foster decoding with a flag-raising activity! Make a construction paper copy of page 151 for each child and then use an X-acto knife to slit the dotted lines on each copy. A student colors the patterns and cuts them out along the bold lines. Then she inserts each strip into its matching set of slits as shown. She also divides a sheet of blank paper into fourths and labels each box for a different word family shown on the sail.

To use her manipulative, she adjusts the sail so a word family is shown in the opening. Then she slides the Jolly Roger flag until *d* appears. She slowly raises the flag. Each time she reads a word, she writes it on her paper in the corresponding box. When the flag is raised (no more letters appear), she adjusts the sail to display a different word family. Then she lowers the flag and repeats the process. Her flag-raising duties are complete after she's formed four sets of words. Next, on her paper, she underlines the like element in each box. Then she and a partner practice reading the words they made. It's smooth reading on the high seas when students use their word family wisdom!

SWASHBUCKLING SYLLABLES

Strategy: recognizing closed syllables

During this activity, buccaneers are reminded that syllables provide valuable decoding clues. Copy the syllabled words from Lists A and B onto individual cards. Divide students into six groups and give each group a word from List A. Explain that Captain McWord divided these words into syllables for easier decoding. Allow time for each group to decode its word and study the syllable pattern. Next, collect the word cards and display them in a pocket chart. Have each group read its word aloud for the class. Then have the class reread the words in unison. Discuss how each syllable is alike.

Repeat the activity using the List B word cards. Lead students to conclude that a syllable ending in a consonant generally contains a short-vowel sound. For a fun follow-up, on the board write individual words from List C. Allow time for each child to mentally divide each word into syllables and decode it. Then model the process for the class. Now that's a decoding strategy that's sure to come in handy!

List A
can•non
par•rot
dag•ger
ves•sel
bat•tle
bot•tom

List B
cap•tain
sil•ver
log•book
dan•ger
kid•nap
cut•lass

List C
absent
fossil
kitten
sunset
tidbit
traffic
velvet
inlet

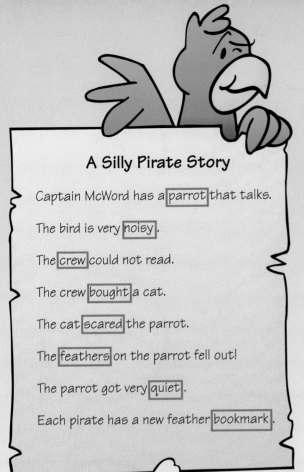

A Silly Pirate Story

Captain McWord has a parrot that talks.

The bird is very noisy.

The crew could not read.

The crew bought a cat.

The cat scared the parrot.

The feathers on the parrot fell out!

The parrot got very quiet.

Each pirate has a new feather bookmark.

X MARKS THE SPOT!

Strategy: using consonants and context

What's one reason Captain McWord's pirates are dandy decoders? They know how to search for clues! On chart paper (or the board) copy each sentence from "A Silly Pirate Story" at left. Cover each boxed word with two sticky notes. Trim the first sticky note to exactly cover the letter or letters that precede the first vowel. Trim the second sticky note to exactly cover the remainder of the word. To spotlight each hidden treasure, draw an X on the second sticky note in each pair.

To begin, read aloud (or have each child silently read) the first sentence as it is shown. Invite students to guess the covered word and explain the clues they used. List all guesses nearby. When several possibilities are listed, help students eliminate from the list guesses that appear less probable due to the part of speech or context of the sentence. Next, remove the first sticky note. Cross out each guess that does not begin with the uncovered letter(s) and record any additional student guesses. Finally, remove the second sticky note to learn if the buried treasure (missing word) has been identified.

Repeat the steps described for each remaining sentence. Your pirates are sure to agree that searching for clues is a seaworthy strategy!

PIRATE GUIDEBOOKS

Strategy: self-monitoring

These guidebooks really come in handy when a pirate fears he'll be shipwrecked by an unknown word! To make his guidebook, a pirate tightly crumples a 9" x 12" section of a brown paper bag and then flattens the paper. He repeats these two steps until his paper feels smooth and has a leatherlike appearance. Next, he folds the rectangle in half (to 6" x 9") and staples a supply of blank paper inside. Then he uses crayons or markers to personalize his guidebook cover.

Next, challenge students to recall the decoding strategies they explored with Captain McWord, along with others they use during independent reading. List the strategies on the board. Have each child title the first page in his book "Decoding Tips" and then list on the following pages strategies he can use to avoid becoming shipwrecked by an unknown word. To encourage students to use the decoding strategies, periodically ask students who are reading independently to complete a form like the one shown to the right. Pirates will be right on course for smooth reading!

Name Greg
Date June 5, 2001

I got stuck trying to read the word diamond.

I looked for a small word I could read. No luck. So I read the rest of the sentence. Then I guessed the word!

Coins

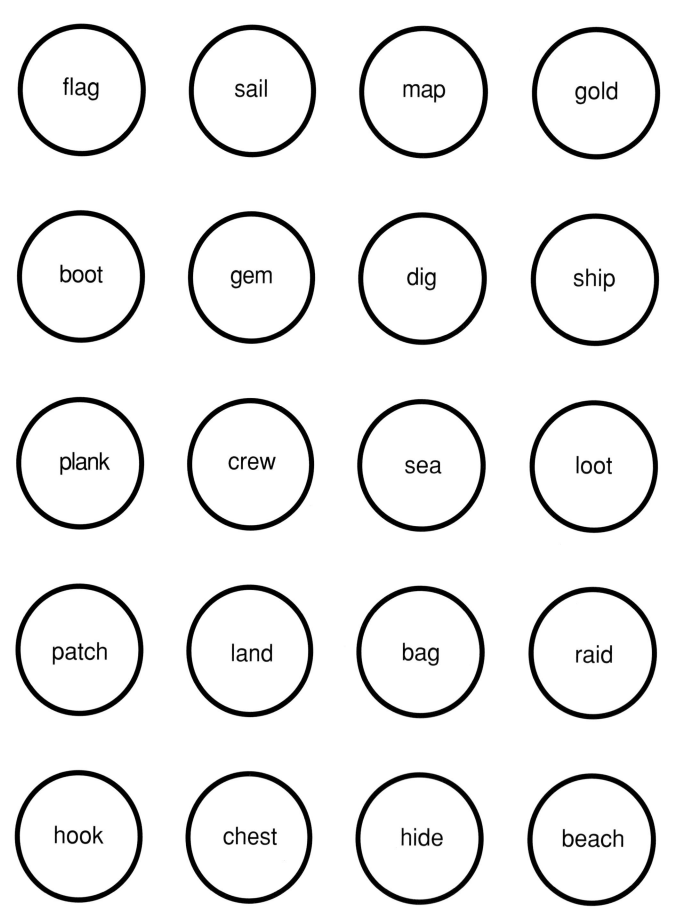

flag

sail

map

gold

boot

gem

dig

ship

plank

crew

sea

loot

patch

land

bag

raid

hook

chest

hide

beach

©The Education Center, Inc. • THE MAILBOX® • Primary • June/July 2002

Note to the teacher: Use with "Bags of Booty" on page 147.

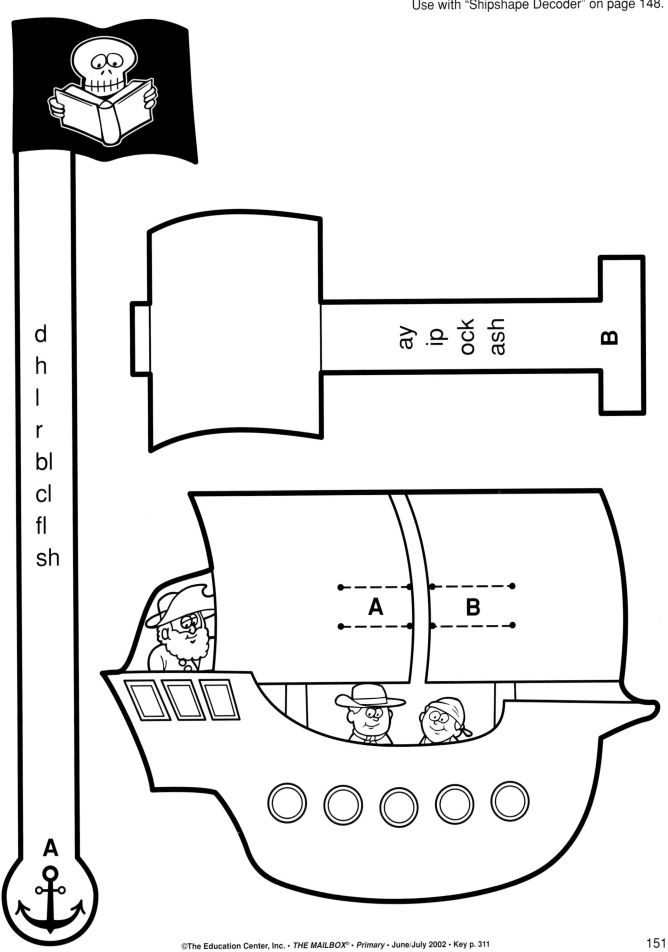

d
h
l
r
bl
cl
fl
sh

A

ay
ip
ock
ash

B

A   B

SENTENCE STAMPEDE

HOWDY, PARDNER! SADDLE UP YOUR BUCKAROOS FOR THIS BOOT-SCOOTIN' REVIEW OF SENTENCES!

ideas by Vicki Dabrowka

GROCERIES

SENTENCE SHOWDOWN

Skill: Complete and incomplete sentences

Corral your cowpokes for a sentence showdown! To prepare, program individual sentence strips with complete and incomplete sentences. Also have each student label a yellow tagboard star cutout "Deputy [student's name]." Gather students, making sure each deputy has her personalized badge. Display a prepared sentence strip, read it aloud, and pause. Then say "Deputies, cast your votes!" If a child believes the sentence is complete, she does nothing. If she believes the sentence is incomplete, she holds her badge high above her head. Follow up each vote by asking a volunteer to explain why the sentence is complete (incomplete). If a sentence is incomplete, have volunteers complete it in different ways. Continue the showdown in this manner until every sentence strip is judged or time runs out. To keep your cowpokes' skills sharp, schedule additional sentence showdowns!

Deputy Darlene

Deputy Darlene

FOUR-PART RODEO

Skill: Sentence types

Yee-haw! Wranglers team up to show off their sentence skills at this rip-roarin' rodeo. After a review of the four sentence types (statements, commands, questions, exclamations), divide students into four groups. Name each group for a different sentence type and teach each group a rodeo response. (See "Rodeo Responses" below.) To start the rodeo, announce a sentence. Allow time for each group to determine the sentence type. Then, on your signal, the group named for the type of sentence shared gives its rodeo response. Continue in this manner, making sure that each group receives equal opportunities to respond. For a post-rodeo challenge, write several sentences on the board, omitting ending punctuation. Ask each child to copy and punctuate the sentences and then label each one with its sentence type.

Rodeo Responses

Group	Response
Statements	We are wranglers.
Questions	What's up?
Command	Stop right there, pardner.
Exclamation	Yee-haw!

Barry Slate

SENTENCE PARDNERS

Skill: Subjects and predicates

Spur your buckaroos on to greater under-standing of subjects and predicates. Tape two sheets of different-colored chart paper to the board. Position the papers side by side, leaving about one inch between them. Title the paper to the left "Subjects" and the paper to the right "Predicates." As volunteers provide complete sentences, write the subject and predicate of each sentence on the papers. Lead students to conclude that a *subject* names whom or what a sentence is about, and a *predicate* tells what a subject is or does. This means that subjects and predicates are pardners in making complete sentences! For more practice with subjects and predicates, have each buckaroo complete a copy of "Cowpoke Chitchat" from page 154.

AVOIDING DISAGREEMENTS

Skill: Subject and verb agreement

Warn young cowpokes to steer clear of subject and verb disagreements! Post singular and plural present tense verbs (see provided list). On the board write the subjects "One cowpoke" and "Two cowpokes." Then give each child four blank 3" x 6" cards. Review that a singular subject needs a singular verb and a plural subject needs a plural verb. Then have each cowpoke copy the singular subject on a card and on another card write a predicate for the subject (using a verb from the posted list). Also have him copy the plural subject on a blank card and write on his remaining blank card a predicate for it.

Next, divide students into groups of three. Have each trio combine its predicate cards and display one set of subject cards. Challenge the team members to work together to create six different sentences with subject and verb agreement. Then have each trio trade predicate cards with another trio and repeat the activity. If desired, collect all predicate cards and place them at a center. Invite cowpokes to bring their subject cards to the center and form agreeable sentences!

RUSTLIN' UP RUN-ONS

Skill: Run-on sentences

There's no doubt about it. Run-on sentences start a stampede of confusion! Review with students that a run-on sentence contains two complete sentences. On the board write a run-on sentence. Then, under the guidance of your students, identify the two complete sentences. Repeat this activity two or three more times, using a different run-on sentence each time. Then give each wrangler a copy of "Chili and Biscuits" from page 154 and challenge him to rustle up the run-ons!

Present Tense Verbs

Plural	Singular
eat	eats
love	loves
beg	begs
build	builds
ride	rides
show	shows
find	finds
sing	sings
laugh	laughs
look	looks
watch	watches

153

Cowpoke Chitchat

What are the cowpokes saying?
To find out, pair each subject with a different predicate.
Write the sentences you make on another sheet of paper.

Subjects

Our campfire

A rattlesnake

That silly cowpoke

Charlie the cook

My old hat

The wind

Predicates

sings silly songs.

looks red at night.

eats marshmallows.

scares the cattle.

feels cold.

smells bad.

©The Education Center, Inc. • THE MAILBOX® • Primary • Aug/Sept 2001 • Key p. 311

Chili and Biscuits

Lasso each run-on sentence.
Then capitalize and punctuate every sentence.
You will have 13 sentences in all. Yee-haw!

1. charlie is the trail cook he likes to make chili and biscuits

2. his chili is hot it is made with hot peppers

3. his biscuits are soft and fluffy

4. everyone knows when charlie is cooking chili and biscuits

5. the yummy smell travels for miles

6. horses love the smell cowpokes love the smell

7. what is that smell could it be chili and biscuits

8. it's time to head back to camp charlie is cooking

©The Education Center, Inc. • THE MAILBOX® • Primary • Aug/Sept 2001 • Key p. 311

Note to the teacher: Use "Cowpoke Chitchat" with "Sentence Pardners" on page 153. Use "Chili and Biscuits" with "Rustlin' Up Run-Ons"
154   on page 153.

LITERATURE UNITS

The ABCs of Language Arts

ABC books aren't just for learning letters! From rhyming to comprehension, they provide loads of skill-boosting opportunities. Tap into the possibilities with these letter-perfect titles and language arts ideas!

ideas contributed by Sheryl Romasco

B is for Bobby and

ALLITERATION

Toot & Puddle: Puddle's ABC
Written and illustrated by Holly Hobbie
Learning to read and write is as easy as A, B, C when you have a friend like Puddle to help! A pleasing combination of narrative and alliterative text recounts how the lovable pig nurtures a pal's literacy skills.

When Puddle sets out to teach Otto how to write his own name, he turns to the trusty teaching tools of art, alliteration, and humor. In no time at all, Otto catches on and learns to write his friend's name, too! Use this get-acquainted activity to have students explore their classmates' names with a similar approach. To begin, revisit a selected page of alliterative text with students and ask what they notice. Lead them to conclude that each word has the same initial letter. Point out that the silly alliterative sentences and illustrations might have helped Otto remember the alphabet more easily.

Next, pair students. Give each student a piece of scrap paper and a sheet of drawing paper. With his partner's guidance, each student writes his partner's name on the scrap paper. He refers to the resulting spelling model as he writes "[Letter] is for [partner's name] and" near the top of the drawing paper. Then the youngster adds illustrations of people, places, and/or things that begin with the same letter as the name.

After each twosome completes its work, ask the student pair to stand at the front of the class. Have each youngster, in turn, use his poster to introduce his partner and present the spelling of his name. To conclude the activity, review the alliterative introductions by posing questions such as "Whose name begins with *B* like bear?" and challenging students to name each corresponding classmate. Now that's an idea sure to suit young readers and writers to a T!

The Accidental Zucchini: An Unexpected Alphabet

Written and illustrated by Max Grover
Expect the unexpected in this award-winning book! Vibrantly illustrated fork fences, ice-cream islands, and other surprising sights make this a grin-inducing favorite.

Creative thinking and alliteration go hand in hand with this entertaining follow-up! In advance, collect a variety of common items, such as a pencil and a spoon, so that there is at least one item for every student. Place the items in a large paper bag. Ask each student to remove an item from the bag without looking inside. Instruct her to imagine an unusual use or setting for the item that is modeled after the zany ideas depicted in *The Accidental Zucchini*. Give the youngster a 6" x 9" piece of white construction paper and have her place it on her desk horizontally. Ask the child to convey her idea in a two-word alliterative phrase near the bottom of the paper. Have her illustrate her work and then glue it on a 9" x 12" sheet of construction paper. Bind students' resulting pages into a class book titled "Unexpected!" to showcase their uncommon ideas about common items!

ruler roof

Cory combed cat

Cassie cuddled called

Alison's Zinnia

Written and illustrated by Anita Lobel
This circular tale takes readers from A to Z and back to A! Cleverly crafted alliteration describes how 26 girls tend to flowers for which they and their friends seem uniquely suited.

Plant the seeds for student-written alliteration with the predictable format of *Alison's Zinnia*! Draw four columns on the chalkboard. Label them to reflect the book's sentence structure (girl-verb-flower-girl). Revisit selected pages with the class and record the corresponding nouns and verbs in the correct columns. Point out that Lobel added words to this basic framework as necessary to construct complete sentences. Then have students try their hands at a simpler version. To do so, divide students into small groups. Give each group eight blank paper strips and a strip of paper bearing the name of a different animal. The students in the group use words that begin with the same letter as the animal to label half the strips with people's names and half of them with verbs. They arrange the strips in various name-verb-animal combinations and then select their favorite.

Next, invite a student from each group to read the chosen combination aloud, adding words as needed to make a complete sentence. Collect and store each group's entire set of strips in a separate envelope. Place the envelopes in a center to provide students with additional alliteration practice. To extend older students' learning, embark on a worldwide tour of the alphabet with Lobel's similarly formatted *Away From Home*.

157

Introduction Chant

J̲ my name is Julia.
How do you do?
I like swimming.
How about you?

From Anne to Zach
Written by Mary Jane Martin
Illustrated by Michael Grejniec

Meet Anne, Barry, and the rest of an alphabetical group of boys and girls in this charming book. The rhythmic introductions beg to be read aloud again and again!

Introductions are in order—alphabetical order, that is! In advance, copy the provided chant on a large sheet of chart paper, omitting the letter and words in the blanks. Read aloud *From Anne to Zach,* emphasizing the rhythm of the text. Invite students to join in during a second reading. Then, to facilitate students' own *A* to *Z* introductions, help students arrange themselves in a circle alphabetically by first name. Place the chant in an easily visible location and demonstrate how to orally complete it by inserting your name's initial letter, your name, and a favorite activity as you read the chant aloud. Have the student whose name is first in the alphabet follow suit. Continue around the circle in a like manner until everyone has taken a turn.

RHYMES

The Hullabaloo ABC
Written by Beverly Cleary
Illustrated by Ted Rand

Three exuberant children and a host of barnyard critters noisily greet the day. Clucks, clatters, and other image-provoking sounds bring the fun-filled farm scene to life.

It's rhyme time down on the farm! Show students the cover of *The Hullabaloo ABC,* and read the title aloud. Ask students to share their ideas about the meaning of the word *hullabaloo.* Encourage them to check their ideas by listening carefully as you read the book aloud. At the book's conclusion, check student's understanding of the word. Ask them to recall some of the noises that contributed to the hullabaloo. Then highlight selected noise words with a class game of Barnyard Rhymes.

To prepare, write each sound word listed on this page on a separate blank card. Stack the cards facedown. Give each student a copy of page 160 and 16 game markers. Have each child cut along the bold lines, randomly glue the game cards on the squares, and color the resulting gameboard to his liking. To begin play, draw the top card and read it aloud. Have each student mark the corresponding rhyming word on his board. Place the card in a discard pile; then continue play until one player marks four squares in a horizontal, vertical, or diagonal line and calls "Hullabaloo!" After verifying his responses, ask students to clear their boards. Invite the winner to be the word caller for the next "sound-sational" round.

Sound Words

thud
squeak
cock-a-doodle-doo
bray
quack
cluck
rumble
yell
thump
laugh
clatter
shout
toot
bang
hee-haw
ding-dong

Hullabaloo!

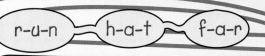

Word List
butterfly
riverbed
home run
hot dog
airline
nightmare
daydream
bathrobe
sunspots
rainbows
bulldozer
spelling bee
buttercup
cupcake
fruit fly

Sam won the spelling bee.

Word Play ABC

Written and illustrated by Heather Cahoon
What do you call a tree adorned with cooking pans? A pantry! Students are sure to enjoy this rib tickler that demonstrates that words don't always mean what they sound like!

Here's a comprehension-building activity bound to keep students in stitches! Read aloud the first two pages of *Word Play ABC* without showing students the illustrations. After allowing time for students to visualize what the words mean, reveal the illustrations. Invite youngsters to compare their "mind pictures" with the book's actual pictures. Continue with the remaining pages in a like manner. Next, reread the book for students' enjoyment. Then pair students and secretly assign each twosome a different noun from the provided list. Give the student pair a sheet of drawing paper and a sentence strip. The students illustrate a humorous interpretation of the noun. They also write an original sentence that uses the noun correctly, inserting a blank in place of the noun. Each twosome, in turn, displays its illustration and sentence. The youngsters challenge their classmates to use the two clues to determine the mystery noun. After it is correctly identified (or if their peers are stumped), the students write the noun in the blank.

Tomorrow's Alphabet

Written by George Shannon
Illustrated by Donald Crews
O is for acorn? T is for bread? Sure, when you look at the alphabet from Shannon's ingenious perspective! The unusual alphabetic pairings will undoubtedly intrigue older readers and prompt them to predict the author's reasoning.

Comprehension practice unfolds with this booklet project! Share Shannon's unique presentation of the ABCs by reading aloud *Tomorrow's Alphabet*. Then challenge youngsters to stretch their thinking by considering the alphabet from another unusual perspective—yesterday. To do so, assign each student a different letter of the alphabet and a 4½" x 12" white construction paper strip. Have the student fold the strip into three equal sections to make a booklet and then decorate the cover with the assigned letter. Instruct the youngster to use the illustrated format to describe how the letter fits in yesterday's alphabet. Then invite each youngster to share her booklet with the class, revealing the relationship between the letter and the item only after her peers have tried to guess it. For more letter-related brainteasers, be sure to check out *Q Is for Duck: An Alphabet Guessing Game* by Mary Elting and Michael Folsom.

P is for dog

because it is yesterday's puppy.

159

Patterns

Use with *The Hullabaloo ABC* on page 158.

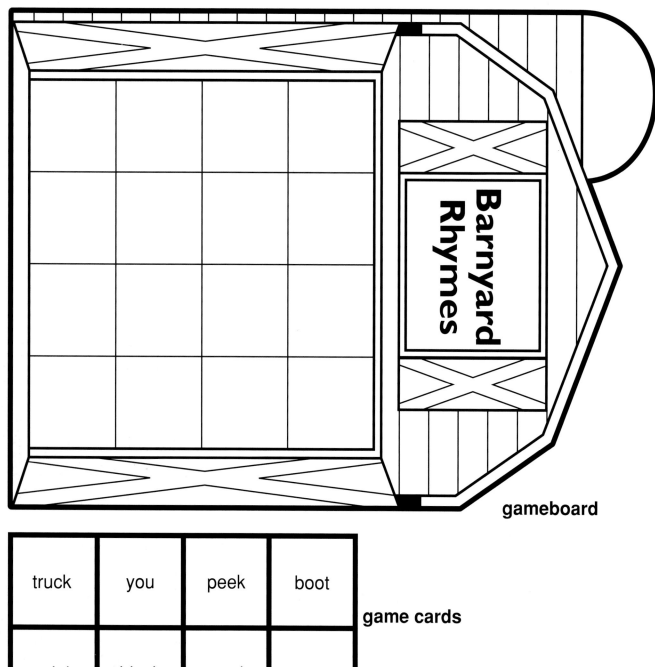

Barnyard Rhymes

gameboard

truck	you	peek	boot
neigh	black	mud	matter
long	giraffe	well	out
mumble	bump	sang	saw

game cards

©The Education Center, Inc. • *THE MAILBOX® • Primary •* Aug/Sept 2001 • Key p. 311

The Pick of the Literature Patch

Harvest bushels of reading enthusiasm with this crop of pumpkin-related books. Then cultivate a variety of essential skills with the kid-pleasing activities that follow!

ideas contributed by Vicki Dabrowka
Concord Hill School, Chevy Chase, MD

Pumpkin Circle: The Story of a Garden

Written by George Levenson
Photo-illustrated by Shmuel Thaler

A striking combination of photographs and rhythmic text depict the life cycle of pumpkins from slippery seeds, to ripe, golden treasures, and back to seeds. Tips for growing pumpkins are provided at the conclusion of this attractive selection.

Round up critical details with this circular sequencing activity! Show students the cover of *Pumpkin Circle*, and invite them to share their thoughts about why the text is arranged in a spiral. Encourage students to listen for details that support their ideas as you read the story aloud. At the end of the book, continue the discussion, leading students to conclude that the spiral represents the pumpkin's never-ending life cycle. Use the book's illustrations to guide the class in orally summarizing the cycle. Then, to help students' understanding take root, have each youngster complete a copy of page 164.

To extend the activity, give each student a sheet of writing paper and a 12" x 18" sheet of construction paper. Also provide a length of curling ribbon and a leaf cutout. The youngster cuts out his pumpkin. On the writing paper he writes a sentence for each picture in the life cycle sequence. Next, he folds the construction paper in half. Then he glues his writing inside the resulting folder, and his pumpkin, the leaf, and a curling ribbon vine on the outside of the folder. His own picture-perfect pumpkin circle is the result!

Related Reading

Carve out more information about how pumpkins grow with *The Pumpkin Book* by Gail Gibbons. This fact-filled book provides a bountiful crop of planting, harvesting, and decorating details!

Pumpkin Café

pumpkin muffin	30¢
pumpkin crunch pie	40¢
nutty pumpkin ice cream	45¢
chocolate pumpkin pudding	39¢
frosty pumpkin shake	75¢

Mitch buys one muffin every day. How much does he spend on muffins in one week?

Too Many Pumpkins

Written by Linda White
Illustrated by Megan Lloyd

Rebecca Estelle's intense dislike of pumpkins prompts her to avoid them at all costs. So when countless pumpkins sprout in her yard, she's determined to take action. Readers of all ages will be pleased with Rebecca Estelle's ingenious (and satisfying!) solution.

This unique menu idea serves up tempting problem-solving practice! At the book's conclusion, ask students to imagine that Rebecca Estelle transforms her next crop of pumpkins into treats for a Pumpkin Café. With student input, write and price a list of pumpkin goodies on a decorative poster. Then give each student a half sheet of paper and a pumpkin cutout. On the paper, have the youngster write and solve a menu-related math problem. Instruct him to copy the teacher-approved problem on one side of the cutout and the solution on the other side. After each youngster signs his work, collect the pumpkins. For daily math practice, post two or more randomly selected problems. Allow time for students to solve them independently. Invite volunteers to share their answers and problem-solving methods. Then ask the authors of the problems to reveal the correct solutions. Repeat the process on the following days until every student's problem has been solved by the class. If desired, place the menu and a supply of teacher-programmed pumpkins in a center for more mouthwatering math reinforcement.

Patty will <u>harvest</u> the pumpkins in the fall.

H   harvest   h

Patty's Pumpkin Patch

Written and illustrated by Teri Sloat

As Patty tirelessly tends her pumpkin patch, numerous animals busily explore it. Jaunty rhyming text describes Patty's gardening efforts, and an alphabetical sequence of illustrations introduces the bustling critters.

Whether she's planning, planting, or harvesting, Patty is almost always at work in the pumpkin patch! To explore her many garden tasks, have students recall the action words in the story. Write the words on a jumbo pumpkin-shaped cutout. Challenge students to brainstorm other gardening-related verbs. Add words to the cutout until you have at least one verb per child. Then use the words to create a class garden of verbs. To do so, assign each student a different verb from the list. Give her a 5" x 7" piece of white paper, a half sheet of 9" x 12" construction paper, and a 1½" x 18" brown paper strip. Have the student use the format shown to feature her word on the white paper. Next, instruct her to glue the provided materials together to resemble an oversized seed packet. Staple students' completed packets on a bulletin board titled "Plant the Seeds for Growing Vocabularies!" Then embellish the display with crumpled tissue paper soil and colorful construction paper flowers.

The Great Pumpkin Switch

Written by Megan McDonald
Illustrated by Ted Lewin

Grampa recalls a memorable childhood mishap that involves two boys, a giant pumpkin, and an evidence-eating pig. Watercolor illustrations lend a nostalgic feel to the entertaining tale.

Transport students back in time with Grampa's storytelling! To set the stage for active listening, display the book cover. Encourage students to tell what they conclude about the story from the cover. If necessary, help students recognize the details that indicate the story takes place a long time ago—during the 1920s. As you read the book aloud, have students watch and listen for clues to determine how that era compares with today.

At the conclusion of the book, draw two large pumpkins on the chalkboard to make a Venn diagram. Label them "Then" and "Now." To complete the diagram, prompt students to recall a number of story details. If a detail from Grampa's childhood could be true today, write it in the inner section of the diagram. Children riding bikes and taking piano lessons are details that fit this description. If a detail applies primarily to the past (making apple butter outside, for example), write it in the "Then" section and challenge students to identify the comparable contemporary information for the "Now" section.

When the diagram is complete, analyze it as a class. Then ask students to think about how Grampa's story might change if it took place this year. Have each student pen a story titled "The Great Setting Switch" to share her ideas. Afterward, divide students into small groups to read aloud their contemporary tales. Students are sure to agree—whether it's 1920 or 2001, a pumpkin as big as a washtub makes for a great story!

Prizewinning Pumpkin Tips #1

Tip 1: Be patient. Pumpkins take a long time to grow.

Pumpkin Fiesta

Written by Caryn Yacowitz
Illustrated by Joe Cepeda

There's nothing that Foolish Fernando won't do to win the coveted pumpkin crown. Nothing except put in an honest day's work, that is! Fernando's misguided efforts and the lesson he learns are humorously described in this Mexican fable.

Foolish Fernando and Old Juana are as different as two people can be! Have students brainstorm the traits of each character and identify the supporting story details. Then point out that Juana's traits contribute to her success, while Fernando's traits result in his loss of the crown. Next, remind students that Fernando has a change of heart at the end of the story and decides to follow Juana's advice to the letter. To help Fernando keep track of Juana's pumpkin-growing tips, give each student a 4 ½" x 6" construction paper booklet that has four white pages. The student uses construction paper scraps to decorate the cover with an award-winning pumpkin and titles the booklet as shown. Then he writes a pumpkin-growing tip on each booklet page. Juana would be proud!

Round and Round!

Color.
Cut along the dotted lines.
Glue the pictures in the correct order.

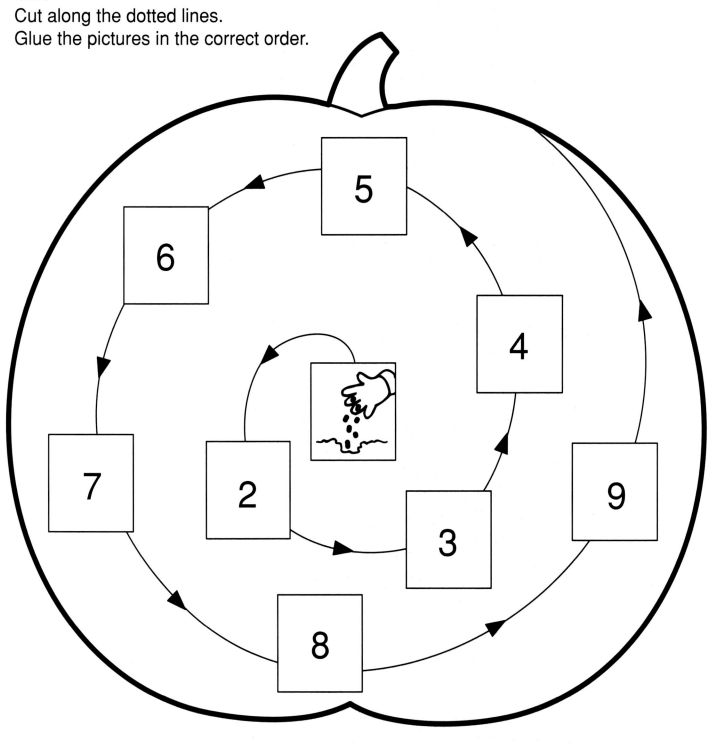

©The Education Center, Inc. • THE MAILBOX® • Primary • Oct/Nov 2001

Note to the teacher: Use with *Pumpkin Circle: The Story of a Garden* on page 161.

The Hundred Penny Box

by Sharon Bell Mathis

Courage, conflict, and compassion become inter-twined in this poignant Newbery Honor book. Young Michael's love for his great-great-aunt Dew and her ragged box of pennies drives him to question his mother's judgment. Why can't his mother understand that Aunt Dew, who is 100 years old, needs her old things and the memories that they hold?

ideas contributed by Julie Douglas, Florissant, MO, and Kristin Lane—Grs. 3–4 Reading, Dolvin Elementary, Roswell, GA

A Treasured Box

Both Aunt Dew and Michael treasure the "cracked-up" wooden box and its 100 pennies. Discuss with the class why ordinary pennies mean so much to the two characters. When students are clear that the value of the pennies is the memories that they hold, challenge each child to iden-tify an object he keeps for this reason. Then have each youngster spotlight his special object inside a handcrafted box. To make his box, a student folds up the bottom five inches of a vertically positioned 9" x 12" sheet of drawing paper, creating a flap. Next, he folds down the top of the paper so that it slightly over-laps the flap. After he trims away the top two corners of the paper, he decorates the outside of the box. Inside the box he illustrates an object he treasures and explains why it is special to him. Encourage students to share their com-pleted projects with the class.

My shells are special to me. They remind me of the summer when I was five years old. That summer my family spent a whole week at the beach!

The Counting Game

Michael enjoys counting Aunt Dew's pennies and listening to her reminisce about the years the coins represent. Ask students to explain how Michael's life is enriched by Aunt Dew's memories. To encourage youngsters to spend more time with older family mem-bers and friends, periodically invite them to share with the class some stories they've been told about the past. Then have each child write a thank-you letter to the senior whose tale she found especially captivating.

1994	1995	1996	1997	1998	1999	2000	2001	2002
I was born in New Mexico.	My grandpa came to live with us.	I made a tiny clay pot.	We moved to Ohio.					

Memory Timelines

How is a memory timeline like Aunt Dew's box of pennies? Each paper penny on the timeline represents a different year in a child's life! To prepare for the project, ask each child to chronologically list on paper the years of her life to date. Then have her take the list home and, with the help of a parent or guardian, write one memorable event from each year. Set a date for the completed lists to be returned to school.

To make a memory timeline, a student folds in half a 3" x 18" strip of light-colored construction paper. She folds the folded paper in half two more times, and then she unfolds the paper to reveal eight boxes. Next, she cuts out one paper penny for each year of her life. Working from left to right, she glues each penny near the top of a different box, and then she cuts away any blank boxes. (If a child needs to create an additional box or two, she glues an extension to the right end of her project.) After she draws a line the length of her paper, she labels the line with dates and memories. Then she folds forward the first section of her timeline, titles the blank surface "My Memory Timeline by [student's name]," and accordion-folds her completed project.

Character Coins

Use this "cent-sational" project to explore character development. First, ask students to identify personality traits of the story characters. On the board list the traits of each character below his or her name. Invite students to explain how these traits influenced their feelings about the characters. Next, have each child showcase his favorite story character on a large paper coin. To make his coin, a student traces a six-inch circle template onto drawing paper and cuts along the resulting outline. Near the center of the cutout he illustrates and names the character. Then he writes three traits of the character along the top rim of the cutout. Along the bottom rim he describes a favorite action of the character.

To extend the activity, have students post their completed coins on a class graph titled "Our Favorite Story Characters."

Worthy Reflections

Here's a penny-related writing activity that's packed with possibilities! On the board write "a penny for your thoughts." Also give each child one penny. Find out if anyone is familiar with the idiom on the board. Lead students to conclude that the phrase is an invitation to share one's thoughts. Then ask each child to share her thoughts in writing about one of the provided prompts. Last, have each child tape her penny to her completed work!

Story-Related Writing Prompts

- If you could give advice to one story character, who would it be? What would you tell this character?
- What is the most important thing you learned from this story? Why is it so important?
- Would you recommend this story to a friend? Why or why not?

100 Cents

Aunt Dew had 100 pennies in her box.
Fill in the blanks to make each coin set equal 100 cents.

a. ___ quarters	**k.** ___ dimes
b. ___ nickels	**l.** ___ half-dollars
c. ___ dimes ___2___ quarters	**m.** ___ dimes ___1___ half-dollar
d. _50_ pennies ___ nickels	**n.** ___ pennies ___5___ nickels
e. _4_ nickels ___ dimes	**o.** _12_ nickels ___ dimes
f. ___ pennies ___7___ dimes	**p.** ___ pennies ___2___ dimes
g. _50_ pennies ___ quarters	**q.** ___ nickels ___1___ quarter
h. ___ pennies ___1___ half-dollar	**r.** _10_ nickels ___ dimes
i. ___ nickels ___3___ quarters	**s.** ___ pennies _15_ nickels
j. _10_ nickels ___ half-dollar	**t.** ___ quarters ___1___ half-dollar

Bonus Box: On the back of this paper, write two different ways you can make 100 cents. Each time use three different kinds of coins.

©The Education Center, Inc. • THE MAILBOX® • Primary • Dec/Jan 2001–2 • Key p. 311

Note to the teacher: Use this activity upon completion of the book.

Name _____

168

A Special Love

Decide which character each sentence describes.
Use the code to color the quilt block.

Color Code

Michael = blue
Aunt Dew = yellow
Ruth = pink

Bonus Box: On the back of this paper, write two things you know about Michael's father, John.

I like to count Aunt Dew's pennies.	My son thinks I don't understand Aunt Dew.	I look exactly like my father.	I want Aunt Dew to start a new life in her new home.
I no longer live in my own house.	My past is important to me.	I like to move to the music.	I am 100 years old.
I think Aunt Dew does not like me.	I play music for Aunt Dew.	I threw away some of Aunt Dew's things.	I hid some of Aunt Dew's things in the closet.

©The Education Center, Inc. • *THE MAILBOX®* • Primary • Dec/Jan 2001–2 • Key p. 311

Note to the teacher: Use this activity upon completion of the book.

A Whirlwind
of Fact and Fiction
Tornado-Related Books and Activities

This just in: Tornadoes have been sighted in several fiction and informational books! Explore the stories of these fascinating storms with the tornado tales and follow-up ideas on pages 169–171. Then stay tuned and extend students' learning with the fact-filled selections on page 172.

ideas by Laura Wagner, Raleigh, NC

The Bravest of Us All
Written by Marsha Diane Arnold
Illustrated by Brad Sneed

From angry bulls to powerful tornadoes, nothing seems to frighten ten-year-old Velma Jean! That is, until one fateful day during the year that Cowskin Creek goes dry. Folksy language and watercolor illustrations bring this enlightening and heartwarming tale of bravery to life.

The contrast between the behavior of Velma Jean and her little sister raises an interesting question: What does it mean to be brave? Before sharing *The Bravest of Us All*, ask students to respond to this question. Then ask them to give it further consideration as you read the book aloud. At the conclusion of the story, invite students to recall details to support or revise their earlier responses. Lead students to realize that Velma Jean is fearless and daring when she accomplishes feats such as breaking in the colt or swimming in the horse tank, and it is not until she faces her fear of the storm cellar that she demonstrates true bravery.

To reinforce the concept of bravery, give each student a 9" x 12" sheet of white construction paper. The youngster folds the paper in half to 6" x 9" and then in half again. Next, she unfolds it once and cuts the crease in the top layer to the fold line. On the resulting left flap, she illustrates either Velma Jean or Ruby Jane. Then she lifts the flap and briefly describes how the chosen character demonstrates bravery. On the right half of her project, she illustrates and describes a time when she or someone she knows was brave. Display students' completed projects on a bulletin board titled "What Is Bravery?" Students are sure to see bravery in a whole new light!

I was brave when I went to the fair. I rode a Ferris wheel. I had never been on one before. I was really afraid at first. After a while, I got used to it. It was cool!

169

The Storm

Written by Marc Harshman
Illustrated by Mark Mohr

Rising wind. A green-yellow tint to the sky. Jonathan knows these are signs of an impending twister. Hurrying to beat the storm, he rushes out to the barn in his wheelchair to tend to the animals. Jonathan's fast thinking and courageous behavior reveal a side of him often overlooked by his classmates.

Jonathan would surely agree that in the unlikely case someone is caught in a tornado, it pays to know what to do. His familiarity with storm safety helps him and the horses escape the tornado unharmed. His courage, perseverance, and sense of responsibility also play a role. To explore how Jonathan's actions reflect these three character traits, give each student one 9" x 12" sheet of red construction paper and three half sheets of white paper. The youngster folds the red paper in half and then cuts away two corners as shown. Next, he staples the white paper between the resulting covers and trims the pages. For each trait, he labels a page and describes Jonathan's corresponding behavior. Then the student titles his booklet and adds details to the front cover to resemble a barn.

Jonathan in The Storm

I'm lucky that my cousins live next door. I get to play with them a lot!

One Lucky Girl

Written by George Ella Lyon
Illustrated by Irene Trivas

Amazing! That's how one neighbor describes Hawkeye's baby sister when she is discovered safe (and sound asleep!) after a devastating tornado. This true story captures one family's joy as they realize that despite the loss of their home, they still have what they treasure most—each other.

Tornadoes are among the strongest storms, but they are no match when it comes to the power of a family's love! Revisit with students the pages where Hawkeye first spots his sister and the family is reunited with her. Point out that the change in color scheme helps convey the family's intense joy as they celebrate the fortune they have in each other.

Next, give each student a seven-inch gray construction paper circle and a 5" x 8" blank card. Have her fold the card in half to 4" x 5". On one side, the student writes "I'm lucky that" and completes the sentence to tell one family- or friend-related reason that she is fortunate. On the other side, the youngster illustrates the sentence. To incorporate the card into a tornado mobile, the student starts at the edge of the provided circle and cuts in a spiral fashion to the center. Help the youngster use string and a hole puncher to assemble the mobile as shown. Then suspend the completed projects to create an eye-catching reminder of students' loved ones.

Twister

Written by Darleen Bailey Beard
Illustrated by Nancy Carpenter

One glorious sunny day, a tornado suddenly interrupts Lucille and Natt's playtime. The storm causes great damage, but the siblings assume a positive outlook once they are assured that their loved ones are safe. Striking illustrations complement this powerful portrayal of resiliency in the wake of Mother Nature's fury.

Boasting hailstone rings and riches, Lucille and Natt happily imagine that they're royalty—not two youngsters who just survived a tornado. Ask students to share their ideas about why the siblings are so content in the aftermath of the storm. Help them realize that the characters value each other far more than material possessions. Next, have students brainstorm happy times with their own families and friends when they felt as blessed as royalty. Then have each youngster showcase a favorite memory on a royal banner.

To do so, each student describes the memory on a half sheet of writing paper and illustrates it on a 4" x 6" piece of white paper. Next, he folds one end of a 12" x 18" sheet of construction paper to create a 1½-inch flap. He tucks a 1" x 16" construction paper strip in the fold and glues the flap closed. He turns his project over to conceal the flap and glues a 1½-inch circle on each end of the strip. The student makes a zigzag cut along the bottom edge of the resulting banner. Then he glues on his illustration and writing. Display students' royal memories on a hall wall for everyone to enjoy.

I remember when Mom, Olivia, and I camped on the island. It was awesome! We picked the perfect spot for our tent. After we got everything set up, we made s'mores. We told ghost stories. Then we went to bed. It was neat to sleep outside!

Tornado

Written by Betsy Byars
Illustrated by Doron Ben-Ami

A caring farmhand with a knack for storytelling quells a family's fear as they nervously wait out a twister. Each of his entertaining stories about his dog, Tornado, is related in a brief, illustrated chapter.

Pete's stories entrance his young listeners, helping them put their fears of the stormy weather aside. Ask students to identify characteristics that make Pete a good storyteller. Then write a student-generated list of storytelling tips on a sheet of chart paper. To put the suggestions to the test, invite students to brainstorm ideas for other stories that Pete might tell about Tornado. Divide students into groups and provide a flashlight for each group. Dim the lights and have each storyteller, in turn, hold a flashlight as he tells his listeners an original Tornado tale.

Storytelling Tips
- Look at your audience.
- Speak slowly and clearly.
- Speak with expression.
- Use hand gestures.
- Use facial expressions.

Read On!

Now that your students understand some of the far-reaching effects of tornadoes, there's no doubt they want to know more! Choose from the following read-alouds and activities to help your young meteorologists investigate twisters.

Tornado Titles

Tornadoes (Read About Series) by Anna Claybourne *Captioned photo illustrations and a detailed table of contents make this information-packed book a valuable resource.*

Twisters! by Kate Hayden *A riveting fictionalized account of a twister opens this easy-to-read compilation of scientific information and amazing facts.*

Wild Weather: Tornadoes! by Lorraine Jean Hopping *This installment of the Hello Reader! series describes how tornadoes are studied and concludes with a handy list of safety tips.*

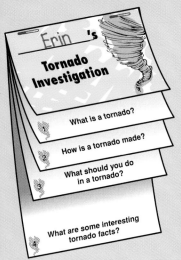

Storm Savvy

Help students get the scoop on tornadoes! Give each student a copy of the booklet pages and cover on page 173; then instruct the youngster to cut apart, sequence, and staple them together as shown. Have her sign and color the booklet cover. Throughout your tornado study, remind each student to be on the lookout for the information she needs for her booklet. Have her write it on the appropriate pages during time set aside for that purpose. After the youngster completes her booklet, encourage her to take it home and share the whirlwind of information with her family.

Ever Wonder?

Focus your class tornado investigation with this idea, and student interest is sure to stay high! Display a sheet of chart paper titled "Facts" and a sheet titled "Questions." Have students brainstorm facts about tornadoes, recalling what they learned from the picture books shared earlier and what they already know. Write the information on the appropriate poster. Next, ask students what they would like to know about tornadoes. Write their ideas in question form on the corresponding poster. After each read-aloud session, enlist students' help to add any newly acquired information to the fact list and make a check mark beside each answered question. Write additional questions as they arise. Count on students to learn up a storm!

Word Windstorm

This stormy word sort is predicted to boost comprehension skills! Post a list of tornado-related words from a featured book or another resource. Ask students to listen for the words as you share the chosen selection. Then lead a class discussion to clarify the words' meanings. Next, pair students and have the students in each twosome program a provided card for each word. Instruct them to sort the cards by a method of their choice. Ask them to tell the class how they sorted the cards and why. Now that's a vocabulary idea with a critical-thinking twist!

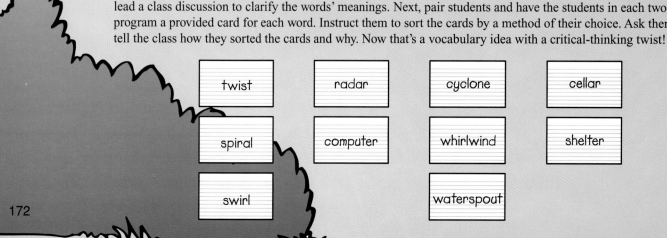

twist | radar | cyclone | cellar

spiral | computer | whirlwind | shelter

swirl | | waterspout

_____'s

Tornado Investigation

©2002 The Education Center, Inc.

A tornado starts when cold and warm air meet in a storm. The

_____ air twists up.

It stretches into a _____ cloud. Then it spins faster and faster.

How is a tornado made?

2

A tornado is a very strong windstorm. It is sometimes called a

_____

or a _____.

What is a tornado?

1

_____

_____

_____

_____

_____

What should you do in a tornado?

3

_____

_____

_____

_____

_____

_____

_____

_____

What are some interesting tornado facts?

4

Celebrate Reading With Dr. Seuss!

With their zany illustrations and tongue-twisting rhymes, Dr. Seuss books have been inspiring young readers for years. So what better way to recognize this author-illustrator's birthday than with a reading celebration? From here to there, you won't find stronger reading motivation anywhere!

Theodor Geisel, who used the pen name Dr. Seuss, was born on March 2, 1904. Read Across America Day—a national campaign to promote reading—is held on his birthday.

Imagination Stretcher

There's no doubt about it—Dr. Seuss's vivid imagination helped make his books unique. Where else would readers encounter a three-moon night or a long-tailed *zong*? Introduce students to these and other figments of Dr. Seuss's imagination with an oral reading of *Oh, the Thinks You Can Think!* Then, to spark your youngsters' own creativity, give each student a large piece of colorful paper, a sentence strip, and access to assorted arts-and-crafts materials. The student uses the entire piece of paper to draw an outline of an imaginary critter. He cuts along the outline and completes the critter with desired details. On the sentence strip, he writes a rhyming name for the critter and signs his name. Post students' labeled work on a hall wall below the title "Oh, the Thinks We Think!"

Rhyme Reference

What did Dr. Seuss do when he couldn't think of a rhyming word? He made one up! To provide a clear example of his silly rhymes, read aloud *There's a Wocket in My Pocket!* Revisit selected pages and ask students to distinguish between the real and nonsense words.

Next, give each student a blank card that you have programmed with a different rhyming pair—one real word and one nonsense word. Also provide a 12" x 18" sheet of white paper and a piece of scrap paper. The youngster places the large paper on her desk vertically and draws the outline of a large Dr. Seuss-style hat. She colors stripes on the hat, as shown, and writes the word pair on the hat brim. On the scrap paper, the student writes real or nonsense words that rhyme with the two assigned words. Then she copies the teacher-approved words on the white hat stripes and cuts out the hat. Display students' completed hats in a prominent classroom location to create a rhyme reference that would make Dr. Seuss proud!

wall   tall   mall
basketball small

ball   call   fall
baseball   stall

zall   hall

"Cat-chy" Poems

No Dr. Seuss celebration would be complete without *The Cat in the Hat*! To prepare for a poetic follow-up to this well-known book, ask each student to bring in a picture of a cat from a magazine, calendar, or similar source. (Be sure to have a few extras on hand for students who do not have one.) Share the book with students; then ask each youngster to imagine that she has a hat-wearing cat for a pet. On a sheet of writing paper, the student writes a rhyming poem about the special feline. She glues her poem and cat picture on a 12" x 18" sheet of paper. She uses crayons and provided paper scraps to fashion a red-and-white-striped hat for the cat and then glues it in place. What a "purr-fect" way to strengthen rhyming skills!

Cindy Calnen
Valley Road School
Clark, NJ

My Funny Cat
I have a cat
Who wears a hat.
She looks a little silly,
But she never gets chilly!
by Julia

What a Sight!

A seven-hump Wump, a serving of cherry-topped schlopp, and a book-reading parrot. Where can you find these unusual things? Why, in a Dr. Seuss book, of course! Advertise these and other unusual sights with this ongoing display, and watch reading motivation soar! Title a bulletin board "And to Think That We Saw…" Place a supply of construction paper, markers, scissors, and glue nearby. When a student completes a Dr. Seuss book, instruct her to make a construction paper sign and have her label it with an unusual sight in the book and the book's title. Staple the youngster's sign to the prepared board. Encourage students to check out the display when they're deciding what Dr. Seuss book to read next. Their peers' recommendations are bound to point them in the direction of memorable reading adventures!

tweetle beetles in Fox in Socks

the Fuddnuddler Brothers in Oh Say Can You Say?

Hats Off to Books!

Dr. Seuss makes an important point in *I Can Read With My Eyes Shut!*: "The more that you read, the more things you will know. The more that you learn, the more places you'll go." After reading the book to students, use this quote to prompt a class discussion about the importance of reading. Then, to further encourage your students' reading efforts, give each youngster a copy of the reading log on page 177. Each time he completes an independent-reading book, he writes the date and title. Then he colors the hats to reflect how much he liked the book, with one hat being the lowest rating and three hats being the highest. As the student's list of completed books grows, he won't want to keep his pride-boosting accomplishments under his hat!

Beyond Green Eggs

Count on students to develop an appetite for writing with this class book project! In advance, divide a sheet of white paper in half and program the lower half for students to complete as shown. Make one copy for every two students. To begin, read aloud *Green Eggs and Ham.* Then ask students to brainstorm other foods that the main character might be reluctant to try. Write their suggestions on the chalkboard. Next, pair students and assign each twosome a different food. Give each pair a copy of the prepared sheet. Have the youngsters complete the sentences to reflect how the character might feel about their assigned food and then add an illustration. After each twosome glues its work on a sheet of construction paper, bind students' resulting pages into a class book titled "Beyond Green Eggs."

Meredith Sudman
Cincinnati Country Day
Cincinnati, OH

I do not like green <u>liverwurst</u>.

I would not eat it <u>on a log</u>.
I would not eat it <u>with a dog</u>.
I would not eat it <u>in a school</u>.
I would not eat it <u>near a mule</u>!

Happy Birthday, Dr. Seuss!

Wrap up your Dr. Seuss celebration with this festive idea! Complete a copy of the invitation on page 177 with the appropriate information. Then duplicate the invitation to make a class supply and give one to each student to share with his family. Post a sign labeled "Reading Fun From Here to There" in the hall to direct visitors to your classroom. Decorate the classroom with balloons and streamers and set out a variety of Dr. Seuss books. Position a table for refreshments in an easy-to-access area. On the table, arrange punch, the directions for Seuss Sweets, and all necessary ingredients and supplies.

Encourage each guest to read with one or more students in a selected classroom area. Arrange for each person to visit the refreshment table and prepare a cupcake snack. If desired, conclude the event by leading students in a choral reading of the class book created in "Beyond Green Eggs" on this page. Happy birthday, Dr. Seuss!

Sheila Krill

Seuss Sweets

For one cupcake decoration:
sugar wafer
spoonful of white frosting
access to a tube of
    red decorator gel
frosted cupcake
napkin
plastic knife

Directions:
1. Place the sugar wafer on a napkin and cut it in half.
2. Frost the top of one wafer piece.
3. Carefully cut the second wafer piece in half lengthwise.
4. Use frosting to attach the large piece to a small piece, forming a hat shape as shown. (Discard the extra piece of wafer.)
5. Frost the hat brim and use the decorator gel to add stripes.
6. Place the hat on a frosted cupcake.

Use the reading log with "Hats Off to Books!" on page 175.

Name _____

Hats Off to Books!

Date	Title	Rating
		🎩 🎩 🎩
		🎩 🎩 🎩
		🎩 🎩 🎩
		🎩 🎩 🎩
		🎩 🎩 🎩

©2002 The Education Center, Inc.

Use the invitation with "Happy Birthday, Dr. Seuss!" on page 176.

You're invited to a birthday party in honor of

Dr. Seuss!

Date _____

Place _____

Time _____

Hosted by _____

If possible, please bring a Dr. Seuss book to read with students.

©2002 The Education Center, Inc.

Shark Lady
True Adventures of Eugenie Clark

Written by Ann McGovern
Illustrated by Ruth Chew

Swim and turn, swim and turn—the mysterious shark glides back and forth right before young Eugenie's eyes. No matter how many times Eugenie visits the aquarium, she always finds herself mesmerized by the movements of the biggest fish there. "Someday I'll swim with sharks," she thinks. Students are sure to be inspired by this captivating biography of Eugenie Clark and her journey to become a world-famous scientist.

ideas contributed by Tara Kenyon—Gr. 3, Ambrose School, Winchester, MA

Who Is Shark Lady?

Skill: setting a purpose for reading

To create a wave of excitement about this biography, write the title *Shark Lady* on the board. Invite students to speculate whether or not this is a real lady, and if so, what she might do. Next, show students the book cover. Reveal that they are about to read a true story about a young girl whose fascination with sharks and other marine life motivates her to become a scientist.

Ask students to brainstorm questions they have about the book's main character. Number and list the questions on a length of blue bulletin board paper that you've titled "A Sea of Questions." Scallop the top edge of the paper, if desired; then post the list for easy reference. Store a supply of shark patterns nearby. When the answer to a question is discovered, have a volunteer write the number of the question and its answer on a shark pattern, cut out the pattern, and tape it on the blue paper. At the completion of the story, encourage students to further investigate any questions that remain unanswered.

A Sea of Questions

1. When was Shark Lady born?

2. Has Shark Lady ever been bitten by a shark?

3. How many sharks has Shark Lady touched?

4. Where does Shark Lady live?

5. What is Shark Lady's favorite shark?

6. Does Shark Lady have any kids?

New York and Beyond

Skill: mapping the story setting

When her story begins, Eugenie is nine years old and living in New York City with her mother and grandmother. Her adventures will take her to several different locations around the world, including the South Sea Islands, Japan, Mexico, and Israel. Bring clarity to Eugenie's travels by recording them on a world map. To do this, keep yarn, scissors, masking tape, and a supply of small cutouts near the map. Number a cutout "1" and tape it near New York City on the map. In the fourth chapter when Eugenie travels to California, number a second cutout "2," display it near the California coastline, and connect the two posted cutouts with a length of yarn. In a like manner, continue posting Eugenie's travels on the map. Periodically ask a volunteer to refer to the map as she recaps for the class what has been learned about Eugenie's life story.

Word Explorations

Skill: sorting words by meaning

Promote a better understanding of story-related vocabulary with word explorations. On chart paper keep a running list of self-selected and student-suggested words. Have each child record the words on individual word cards and store them in a resealable sandwich bag inside his desk. Periodically write words from the list on the board. Have students remove the same words from their word collections. Request students' help in defining each word and recalling how it relates to the story of Eugenie Clark. Next, provide sorting guidelines or challenge students to sort the words by the shared meanings they discover. Invite students to describe how they have sorted the words and why. Encourage plenty of discussion. Then have the students store their word collections for future word explorations!

Dreams Come True

Skill: identifying character traits

As a young girl, Eugenie dreams of walking on the ocean floor, swimming with the sharks, and being a teacher. At the conclusion of the book, remind students of Eugenie's childhood dreams. Help them identify character traits that help Eugenie realize her dreams. Then have each child complete a copy of "Diving With Shark Lady" on page 180. Dreams really can come true!

Shark Sleuths

Skill: using reference materials

Throughout the story students learn about sharks through Eugenie's experiences and discoveries. Recall some shark types named in the story, such as hammerhead, lemon, nurse, and tiger. Then reveal that there are about 360 types of sharks swimming in oceans of the world!

Challenge your youngsters to become shark sleuths! Provide numerous shark-related books and give each child a graphic organizer which to record her research. A student uses her research to write a report on $8\frac{1}{2}$" x 11" paper. Next, she folds in half a 9" x 12" sheet of blue paper. Keeping the fold at the bottom, she trims the top edges of the paper to resemble water and then unfolds the paper. She trims a 4" x 6" rectangle of gray paper to resemble a shark fin. She glues the fin to the top of the blue paper, staples the top of her report to the blue paper so that the bottom of the fin is covered, and refolds the project, keeping her report to the inside. Expect numerous shark sightings when sleuths read their reports to the class!

Angel Shark

Name _____

180

Diving With Shark Lady

Eugenie Clark's character traits help her dreams come true.
Label each fish with one of her traits.
On the lines give proof of this trait from the story.

Bonus Box: On the back of this paper, write one dream you have for your future. Then name a character trait you have and describe how this trait could help you make your dream come true!

©The Education Center, Inc. • *THE MAILBOX*® • *Primary* • June/July 2002

Note to the teacher: Use at the completion of the story with "Dreams Come True" on page 179.

McBroom the Rainmaker

Written by Sid Fleischman
Illustrated by Amy Wummer

Hens that lay fried eggs. Cows that give powdered milk. There's no doubt about it—the Big Drought is on its way! Shifty Heck Jones capitalizes on the dry spell by peddling rusty nails that he claims make rain. But Josh McBroom is onto the scoundrel's weaselly ways and hatches a rainmaking scheme to break the drought himself. Told with down-home language and far-fetched exaggerations, this tall tale is guaranteed to leave your students in stitches!

ideas contributed by Julie Douglas, Florissant, MO

The Big Drought

Skill: Setting a purpose for reading

Before your students begin reading about McBroom and his one-acre farm, plant the seeds for understanding with this class activity. Title a sheet of chart paper "Drought." Divide the paper into two columns and label them as shown. Confirm that students know what *drought* means. Then explain that the book students will read tells about a farmer's experiences during a drought. Invite students to brainstorm words that they expect to find in the story and have them explain their reasoning. List the words in the first column of the chart.

Next, show students the book cover and read the title aloud. Tell them that the story events are extraordinary, and, as a result, some words that they wouldn't normally associate with a drought are important to the plot. Copy onto the chart the words shown in the second column. Then give each student a five-page construction paper booklet. For each word in the second column, have him label a separate page and write how he thinks the word relates to the drought. As he reads the book, encourage him to check his predictions. When he discovers a word's actual relationship to the dry spell, he adds the information to the appropriate booklet page (or writes a sentence that confirms his prediction). It all makes perfect sense now!

Drought	
Words We Expect	Words to Look For
dry	mosquitoes
wilt	nails
hot	swindle
steamy	cuckoo
thirsty	onions

Math With McBroom

Skill: Solving word problems

Tall tales are packed with exaggerations and unbelievable claims, and this one is no exception! Use math journals to help students measure up the outlandish story details. Have each youngster use a provided umbrella template to make a journal with construction paper covers and six white pages. At the end of each chapter, write a story-based word problem on the chalkboard. Have each student copy and solve the problem on a blank journal page. Announce the correct answer and then invite volunteers to tell the class how they reached their solutions.

Math With McBroom by Alice

Homegrown Hyperbole Clocks
Skill: Understanding and writing hyperboles

McBroom declares that he isn't one for telling lies, but as readers quickly discover, the farmer has an unquestionable flair for stretching the truth! At the conclusion of chapter 1, tell students that the author used hyperboles to add humor to the story. Read aloud several examples from the chapter, including the descriptions of vines and vegetables that McBroom and his family use to keep time. Lead students to realize that a hyperbole is a figure of speech that is an outrageous exaggeration.

To make a timely crop of hyperboles, give each student a blank 3" x 5" card, a 6" x 9" piece of construction paper, and a five-inch white paper circle. The youngster writes an original weather-related hyperbole on the card. Next, she makes a clockface on the circle and indicates a desired time. She vertically positions the construction paper and glues the clockface near one end and her hyperbole near the other. Then she rounds the top two corners and uses a marker to add any desired details. Display students' work on a bulletin board titled "Time for Hyperboles." Add yarn vines and leaf cutouts to embellish the unique patch of exaggerations.

It was so hot the tires on the school bus melted.

Flim-Flam and Fiddle-Faddle
Skill: Giving a persuasive presentation

Nails that make rain? It sounds ridiculous, but Heck Jones manages to convince a number of neighbors that a bunch of rusty nails is the answer to the dry spell. At the end of chapter 2, ask students to share their ideas about how the shifty peddler persuades folks to purchase the nails. Then pair students. Give each twosome a large sheet of drawing paper and a common object such as a stone, a length of string, or a spool of thread. Explain that the students in each twosome will present to the class a commercial that advertises their object as a rainmaker. Provide time for the partners to prepare persuasive dialogue that makes their claim and a poster that promotes their merchandise. For added fun, encourage students to try using folksy language similar to McBroom's speech patterns. Arrange for each student pair to display its poster and present its commercial. Look out, Heck Jones! You've got some competition!

Super Deluxe Rainmaker
Worth Millions!
Secret formula guaranteed to help crops grow in seconds!
Used by farmers everywhere
Just $9.95

Shower of Similes
Skill: Writing similes

In chapter 4, McBroom finally finds some rain! The topsoil in his wagon soaks up the rain like a sponge and the McBrooms get wet as fish! To investigate image-evoking similes such as these, write on the chalkboard "The first raindrops spattered as large as quarters." Circle the words *raindrops* and *quarters*. Tell students that the sentence is an example of a *simile*—a comparison of two unlike things that uses *like* or *as*. Invite youngsters to modify the displayed simile by brainstorming substitutions for the word *quarters*.

Next, give each youngster a raindrop cutout made from a full sheet of writing paper. Have him incorporate one or more similes into a brief description of a real or fictional setting. Ask him to glue his writing on a 9" x 12" sheet of blue construction paper. Then direct him to trim the construction paper, leaving a narrow border around his raindrop. Use a hole puncher and string to suspend each student's completed raindrop from the ceiling. Now that's a rain shower sure to please young writers!

An Awesome Beach

There is a really neat beach close to my house. The sand sparkles like gold in the sunshine. The waves roar like lions. The water looks pretty, but it is as cold as ice!

Evan

Y'all Come Back Now!
Skill: Recalling story details

With sights such as floating watermelons and gigantic skeeters, McBroom's farm would definitely be a memorable class trip destination! At the conclusion of the book, ask students to imagine that they went on a field trip to McBroom's farm. Then give each youngster a sheet of writing paper. Have her pen a first-person account of the imagined trip, being sure to include story details to describe two or more things that she "saw." Instruct her to glue her writing on a large sheet of white paper and illustrate it as desired to make a scrapbook page. Bind students' pages into a class scrapbook titled "Our Trip to McBroom's Farm."

Today we went on a class trip to a really strange farm. Anything that is planted there grows very fast. Vines grow an inch a second. Blossoms sprout in minutes. I saw onions grow as big as pumpkins right before my eyes! I will never forget my trip to McBroom's farm!
Samantha

More McBroom!

By now, your students have undoubtedly sprouted a keen interest in McBroom. Cultivate their reading motivation with these and other Fleischman books about the one-of-a-kind farmer!

McBroom's Ghost
McBroom Tells a Lie
McBroom Tells the Truth

Name _____

What Did He Say?

Read McBroom's statements below.
For each one, write the letter that shows another way to say it.
(Hint: You will not use two of the lettered sentences.)

a. It was very hot the next day.

b. We grow a lot of vegetables.

c. They cried a lot.

d. The mosquitoes could be very annoying.

e. The soil was very dry.

f. What a lot of noise!

g. The mosquitoes were getting cranky.

h. The children had a lot of fun playing in the rain.

i. That's nonsense!

j. I don't like to lie.

___ 1. "Their eyes began to flow like sprinkling cans."

___ 2. "…the varmints were getting downright ornery."

___ 3. "Fiddle-faddle…!"

___ 4. "Why, I'd as soon grab a skunk by the tail as tell a falsehood."

___ 5. "And my, didn't the young'uns frolic in that cloudburst!"

___ 6. "…mercy, what a racket!"

___ 7. "The bloodsucking rapscallions could be mighty pesky."

___ 8. "My, wasn't the next morning a scorcher!"

Bonus Box: On the back of this sheet, write the two lettered sentences that you did not use. Rewrite each one like McBroom might say it.

©The Education Center, Inc. • *THE MAILBOX*® • *Primary* • April/May 2002 • Key p. 311

Note to the teacher: Use this activity at the completion of the book.

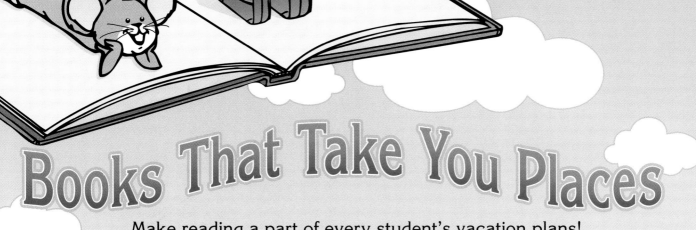

Books That Take You Places

Make reading a part of every student's vacation plans! Whether students travel or stay home this summer, great books are just the ticket for exciting adventures. Begin a fun-filled literary tour with the following selections and activities. Then use the reproducible on page 190 to set your youngsters on the road to summertime reading!

ideas contributed by Leslie Wilmes, Marion, IL, and Randee Zimmerman—Gr. 2, Massapequa Public Schools, Massapequa, NY

Edward and the Pirates
Written and illustrated by David McPhail

Edward loves to read! In fact, he enjoys books so much that he often imagines that stories come to life! One night Edward dreams that the pirates from one story appear and angrily demand his book. But Edward resolutely refuses to part with it and calmly resolves the seemingly perilous turn of events with the help of two familiar-looking characters.

Edward doesn't find the pirates' treasure, but he does discover something much more precious—the magic of reading! At the story's conclusion, begin this ongoing project to encourage students to treasure books. Have each youngster vertically position a 9" x 12" sheet of brown construction paper on a work surface. Instruct her to fold up the bottom approximately 4¹/₂ inches and then staple each side to make a pocket. Ask her to fold down the top and label it "[Student's name]'s Reading Treasures." Then have her use provided arts-and-crafts materials to decorate her project so that it resembles a treasure chest.

At the completion of each book in this unit, give each student a blank card. On one side, have her write the title, the author, and a sentence or two about the location she "visited" by reading the book. On the other side, have her illustrate the location. Encourage her to store each completed card inside her treasure chest. As her bounty of book-related treasure grows, so will her enthusiasm for reading!

The Raft by Jim LaMarche

It's awesome in the woods where Nicky's grandmother lives! You can see raccoons, foxes, and lots of other animals there.

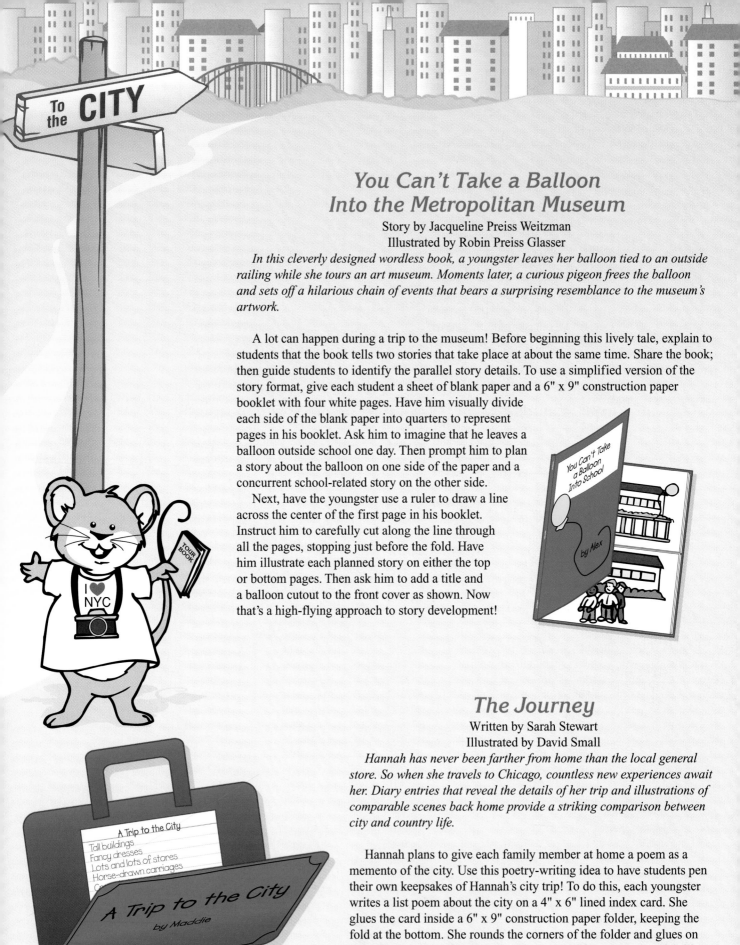

You Can't Take a Balloon Into the Metropolitan Museum

Story by Jacqueline Preiss Weitzman
Illustrated by Robin Preiss Glasser

In this cleverly designed wordless book, a youngster leaves her balloon tied to an outside railing while she tours an art museum. Moments later, a curious pigeon frees the balloon and sets off a hilarious chain of events that bears a surprising resemblance to the museum's artwork.

A lot can happen during a trip to the museum! Before beginning this lively tale, explain to students that the book tells two stories that take place at about the same time. Share the book; then guide students to identify the parallel story details. To use a simplified version of the story format, give each student a sheet of blank paper and a 6" x 9" construction paper booklet with four white pages. Have him visually divide each side of the blank paper into quarters to represent pages in his booklet. Ask him to imagine that he leaves a balloon outside school one day. Then prompt him to plan a story about the balloon on one side of the paper and a concurrent school-related story on the other side.

Next, have the youngster use a ruler to draw a line across the center of the first page in his booklet. Instruct him to carefully cut along the line through all the pages, stopping just before the fold. Have him illustrate each planned story on either the top or bottom pages. Then ask him to add a title and a balloon cutout to the front cover as shown. Now that's a high-flying approach to story development!

The Journey

Written by Sarah Stewart
Illustrated by David Small

Hannah has never been farther from home than the local general store. So when she travels to Chicago, countless new experiences await her. Diary entries that reveal the details of her trip and illustrations of comparable scenes back home provide a striking comparison between city and country life.

Hannah plans to give each family member at home a poem as a memento of the city. Use this poetry-writing idea to have students pen their own keepsakes of Hannah's city trip! To do this, each youngster writes a list poem about the city on a 4" x 6" lined index card. She glues the card inside a 6" x 9" construction paper folder, keeping the fold at the bottom. She rounds the corners of the folder and glues on a handle fashioned from construction paper. Then she writes the title of her poem on the outside of the resulting suitcase. What a wonderful trip!

The Raft

Written and illustrated by Jim LaMarche

Nicky dreads spending the summer with his grandmother. After all, she doesn't have a TV, and there are no kids near her home. Nicky's feelings change, though, as he discovers the enchantment of the river and how special his grandmother really is.

Much to his surprise, Nicky's summer turns out to be very memorable! Help students make connections with this vacation story by encouraging them to reflect on some of their own cherished memories. Give each student a 5" x 8" index card, six jumbo craft sticks, and three Popsicle sticks. The student folds the card in half lengthwise. Then, keeping the fold at the top, he briefly describes on one side of the card a special time with one or more older relatives or friends. Next, he arranges the six craft sticks side by side. He glues a Popsicle stick diagonally across the middle of the project and one each across the top and bottom of it. After the glue dries, he turns the resulting raft over. Then he uses a fine-tipped permanent marker to illustrate his description on the raft.

To display students' work, cover a low table with blue paper. Place each youngster's raft on the table and open his card slightly to stand his description beside the raft.

> I had fun when I visited my uncle and aunt at their cabin in Maine. We swam every day and went for boat rides. We toasted marshmallows at night. I loved riding the tire swing!
> Shawn

Three Days on a River in a Red Canoe

Written and illustrated by Vera B. Williams

A child gives a firsthand account of a family canoe trip from start to finish. The straightforward text and labeled illustrations provide an informative (and entertaining!) look at the ins and outs of camping.

The main character seems to enjoy her camping adventure—bad weather and all! But camping isn't for everyone. To investigate your students' opinions about this vacation choice, make a T chart on the chalkboard. Label one column with a happy face and one column with a sad face. As students recall positive details and perceived drawbacks of the trip, write the information in the appropriate columns. Then distribute writing paper. Instruct each youngster to write whether she thinks spending three days on a river in a canoe would be a fun vacation activity. Have her support her opinion with three reasons, referring to the class chart as necessary.

To showcase her thoughts, ask the youngster to pen a title for her writing on a provided canoe cutout and then glue the cutout at the top of her paper. Staple students' work to a bulletin board titled "Vacation Fun?" Then embellish the display with student-made construction paper trees and forest critters.

☺	☹
cooking outside	expensive supplies
fishing	mosquitoes
moose	storms
sleeping in a tent	no real showers
telling stories at night	a long drive

Grandma Summer

Written and illustrated by Harley Jessup

Ben's stay at a summer beach house provides him with many exciting firsts. And when he makes a fascinating discovery much like his dad did years ago, it provides a precious link to the past!

Glistening sand, smooth stones, and icy cold waves—the beach offers all sorts of wonderful treasures! Point out that Ben's time at the beach cannot be summed up just by telling what he did. A more complete picture of his vacation would also reveal what he saw, heard, and experienced in other ways.

To investigate these details, divide students into small groups and give each group a sheet of paper. Have each group list several story details that they think best tell about the vacation from Ben's perspective, being sure to include details that relate to each of the senses. Then ask one student from each group to read his group's list to the class and explain the reasoning for each chosen detail. To highlight the multisensory nature of the beach vacation, invite the remaining students to identify the senses that relate to selected details. Students are sure to agree—the beach is a "sense-ational" vacation spot!

Ben's Beach Vacation

gravel road
old beach house
crashing waves
storm
picture of Dad
shiny stones
fishing float
ice-cream cone

An Island Scrapbook: Dawn to Dusk on a Barrier Island

Written and illustrated by Virginia Wright-Frierson

An artist and her daughter explore a North Carolina island from morning to night. Detailed illustrations portray the twosome's notes and sketches, making this award-winner a kid-pleasing source of information.

Amy and her mother discover that the island is home to a wide variety of animals and plants! To heighten students' awareness of this diversity, draw a four-column chart on the chalkboard. Label one column for each of the following island habitats: dunes and shore, salt marsh, maritime forest, and pond. Reread the book, pausing after every few pages to have students name details that characterize the corresponding habitat(s). Write the information in the appropriate columns. Point out that it is important to protect all of the habitats because different animals and plants depend on each of them.

Next, assign a group of students to each listed habitat. (For large classes, assign the same habitat to more than one group.) Give each group a poster-sized sheet of white paper. Set aside a time for each group to use the book, provided arts-and-crafts materials, and the class-created chart to create a labeled poster of its habitat. Display the completed posters side by side on a hall wall to create a picturesque reminder of environmental diversity.

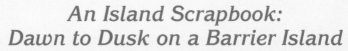

Dunes and Shore

pelicans
grasses
sand dollar
driftwood
snowy egret

Dolphins at Daybreak

Written by Mary Pope Osborne
Illustrated by Sal Murdocca

Jack and Annie are on another unbelievable journey! This time the Magic Tree House takes them to a coral reef where they search for the answer to the first of four mysterious riddles.

Shore up comprehension skills with an ocean-related center inspired by Morgan's riddle! Divide students into small groups (up to 12) and give each group a half sheet of writing paper. Secretly assign a different listed topic to each group. Ask the students in each group to write a riddle for their topic, referring to a copy of the book as necessary. Number students' completed riddles as you collect them.

Next, list the riddle numbers and the corresponding topics on a sheet of paper and then place the resulting answer key in a labeled envelope. Attach a jumbled list of the assigned topics to the front of a 9" x 12" envelope and store the riddles inside. Set the prepared envelopes in a center stocked with paper and pencils. To use the center, a student removes the riddles from the envelope and reads each one, in turn. He writes each riddle number on a sheet of paper, selects the corresponding answer from the provided list, and then writes the answer beside the correct number on his paper. He uses the answer key to check his work.

1. dolphin
2.
3.
4.
5.
6.
7.

1.

I'm gray and plain.
At first, Annie thought I was
    the answer to the riddle.
I look like I'm smiling.
What am I?

Riddle Topics

seagulls
mini sub
coral
starfish
jellyfish
sea horse
stingray
giant clam
dolphin
octopus
hammerhead shark
oysters

The Wild Whale Watch

Written by Eva Moore
Illustrated by John Speirs

In this chapter book from the Magic School Bus series, Wanda is convinced that the whale watch Ms. Frizzle has planned won't be an ordinary field trip. A magical transformation, a bit of suspense, and a close-up view of ocean life prove her right!

Research and summary skills make this project a whale of a success! In advance, prepare a chart similar to the one shown and copy it to make a class supply. Tell students that each of them will make a brochure for Captain Gil's whale watch business. Guide students to recall the types of whales featured in the book and list them on the chalkboard. Then give each youngster an 8½" x 14" sheet of paper and a copy of the chart.

Next, have each student write the names of three selected whales on her chart. The student completes the chart with information from the book and provided grade-appropriate resources. Then she folds the blank paper in thirds to create a brochure. She illustrates and writes a title on the cover. She unfolds the brochure and, on each of the three panels revealed, summarizes her information about the chosen whales. She turns the open brochure over and writes general information about whales on the remaining blank panels. She adds illustrations as desired to complete her project. Captain Gil would be proud!

	Whale 1	Whale 2	Whale 3
Type of Whale			
Toothed or Baleen?			
Food			
Habitat			
Other Interesting Facts			

Summertime Book Travels

Date	Title	Author	Setting

CITY

**You Can't Take
a Balloon Into
the National Gallery**
by Jacqueline Preiss Weitzman

City

The Gardener
by Sarah Stewart

COUNTRY

Canoe Days
by Gary Paulsen

BEACH

Clams All Year
by Maryann
Cocca-Leffler

ADVENTURES

Books 10, 11, and 12 in the
Magic Tree House series
by Mary Pope Osborne

**Ghost Town
at Sundown**

Lions at Lunchtime

**Polar Bears
Past Bedtime**

©The Education Center, Inc. • THE MAILBOX® • Primary • June/July 2002

Note to the teacher: Give each student a copy of this form to use as a summer reading log. Explain that if students enjoyed the books featured in this unit, they might also like the titles shown. Encourage them to look for these and other books in their local libraries.

MATH UNITS

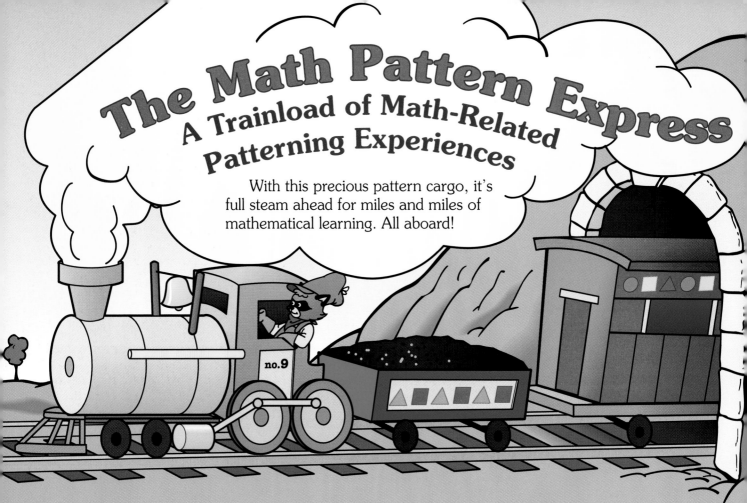

The Math Pattern Express
A Trainload of Math-Related Patterning Experiences

With this precious pattern cargo, it's full steam ahead for miles and miles of mathematical learning. All aboard!

Engineers in Training

Warm up your youngsters' patterning skills with a verbal response activity. On the board list words that describe train noises, such as *choo, toot, chug,* and *woo.* Then select words from the list and use them to create a simple verbal pattern like *choo, choo, toot.* Repeat the pattern several times, inviting students to join in when they recognize the pattern. Practice a variety of verbal patterns in this way. When your young engineers are on track, challenge them to add body motions to the patterns! *Choo, woo, chug, chug, chug...*

Individual Trains

Every engineer needs a train! In fact, several of the activities in this collection can't be completed without one! Give each child a white construction paper copy of page 194 and a resealable plastic bag. To make his train, a student personalizes and colors the train engine, uses the code to color the symbols on the boxcars, and cuts out the patterns on the bold lines. Then he stores his cutouts inside the resealable plastic bag for later use.

Unloading Nonpatterns

At this train station, blowing the whistle on nonpatterned loads is just part of an engineer's job! Have each child place her train cutouts from "Individual Trains" atop her desk. Then specify a color (or symbol) and instruct each student to connect a matching boxcar to her engine. Continue in this manner until four boxcars are added. Ask students to examine the resulting load and then give a thumbs-up for a patterned load or a thumbs-down for a nonpatterned load. After a volunteer explains why the load is patterned or nonpatterned, have students unload the boxcars and prepare for a new load. Continue in this manner for as long as desired, adjusting the number of boxcars per load and the complexity of each pattern or nonpattern to match your students' capabilities.

Picking Up Patterns

It's full steam ahead when students pair up to make and extend patterns! First have each child initial the backs of his cutouts from "Individual Trains." Then pair students. Partner 1 connects two boxcars to his engine cutout. Partner 2 repeats the established pattern by adding two of his own boxcars to the load. The partners, in turn, continue extending the pattern until their supply of appropriate cars runs out. Together the partners confirm that the pattern is complete and then each partner retrieves his boxcars. Partner 2 begins a new patterning activity by connecting two boxcars to his engine. Have student pairs continue making and extending patterns for as long as desired. To increase the challenge, instruct student pairs to extend each initial pattern to three or four boxcars.

Undercover Cargo

Identifying the pattern is the key to cracking the case of the undercover cargo! Using her cutouts from "Individual Trains," have each child form the following train: engine, red car, green car, triangle car, square car, circle car, blue car, square car, green car. Challenge each child to identify the train's pattern *(red, green, blue or square, circle, triangle)* and group the boxcars accordingly. If students are having difficulty, suggest that they look to find where the pattern begins repeating. Present several more cargo challenges—varying between two-, three-, four-, and five-car repeating cargo patterns. When you wrap up, invite students to pair up with a partner during free time and use their cutouts to create additional concealed cargo patterns!

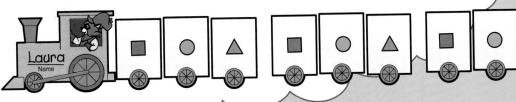

Boxcar Confusion

Patterning skills come in handy at a mixed-up train yard! To prove your point, have each child use his engine and boxcar cutouts (from "Individual Trains") to form the following train: engine, red car, blue car, green car, red car, blue car, green car, green car, blue car, red car. Explain that because two boxcars on the train have been accidentally switched, this train has lost its pattern. Suggest that students find the switched boxcars by first identifying the train's repeating pattern. When the switched boxcars are found, give students another boxcar mystery to solve.

For additional practice, have each child use his cutouts to make a train with a repeating pattern and then switch two boxcars on his train. Pair students and have each child solve his partner's boxcar mystery. Use "Cargo Switcheroo!" on page 195 to further reinforce your students' patterning skills.

Staying on Track

Daily practice is the ticket to keeping your engineers' patterning skills on track! For easy management, have each child record his patterning practice in an engineer's log. Give each child a copy of the engine pattern on page 194 to personalize and color. Then have him cut out the pattern and glue it onto the front cover of a booklet of blank pages. Each day provide a pattern with a corresponding task for students to complete in their logs. Choo, choo!

2, 2, 4, 3, 3, 6, 4, 4, 8

Patterns

Use with the activities on pages 192 and 193.

Color code: △ = blue □ = red ○ = green

©The Education Center, Inc. • *THE MAILBOX* • *Primary* • Aug/Sept 2001

Name _____

Cargo Switcheroo!

On each track two pieces of cargo are switched.
Find the repeating pattern and then circle the switched cargo.
Cut out the new cargo below and glue it in place.

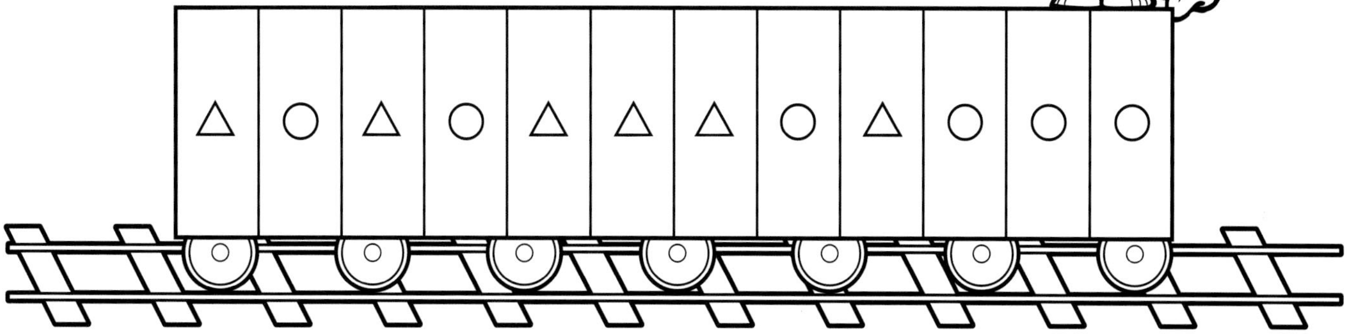

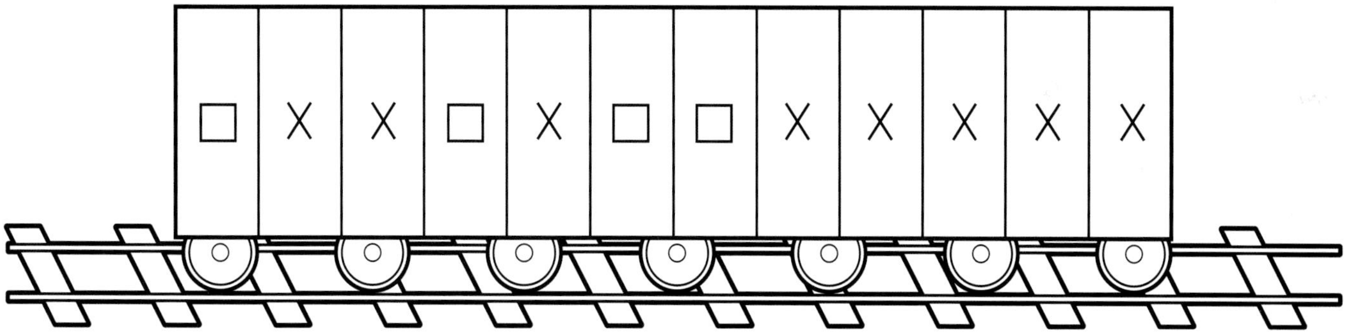

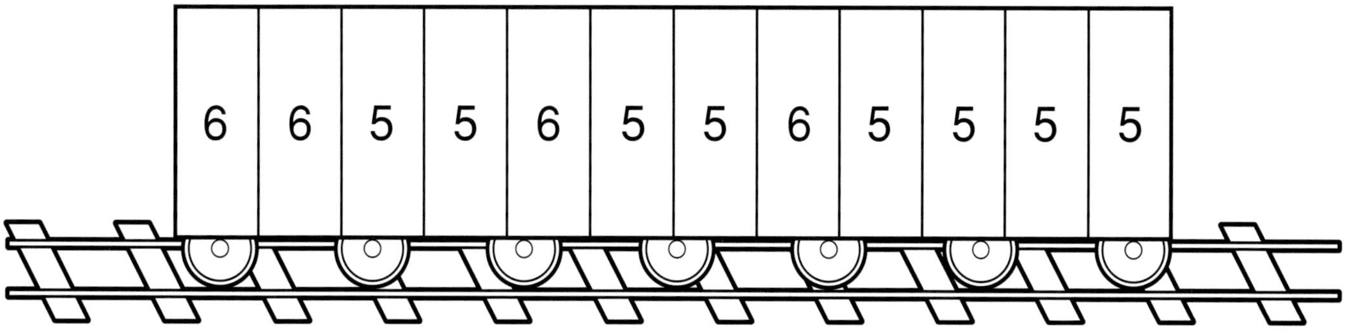

The Math Pattern Express
Analyzing patterns

Track 1: △ ○ △ ○ △ △ △ ○ △ ○ ○ ○

Track 2: □ ✕ ✕ □ ✕ □ □ ✕ ✕ ✕ ✕ ✕

Track 3: A C Z A C Z A Z C A C Z

Track 4: 6 6 5 5 6 5 5 6 5 5 5 5

©The Education Center, Inc. • THE MAILBOX • Primary • Aug/Sept 2001 • Key p. 311

Train Cargo

○	✕	Z	5
◁	□	C	6

Bonus Box: Color the cargo on each track without changing its pattern.

Note to the teacher: Use with "Boxcar Confusion" on page 193.

195

Numbers All Around!

Unearth a treasure trove of number sense with this "dino-mite" collection of easy-to-use activities!

ideas contributed by Kish Harris—Gr. 2, Southampton Academy, Courtland, VA

Extraordinary Excavation

Excavate extraordinary **number awareness** with this number-gathering activity. Give every student a construction paper copy of "Numbers About Me!" from page 198. Ask each child to color and personalize the booklet cover and then fold it in half. Staple a stack of 3" x 4½" blank paper inside each youngster's folded cover. Then challenge each child to unearth numbers that describe herself. Intrigue the class with an example like "The numbers one, two, three, and four describe me. I have one nose, two thumbs, three names (first, middle, and last), and four pets." Have each child list in her booklet the numbers she unearths about herself along with a brief explanation of each. After a few days of number excavating, invite students to share a few of their findings. No doubt they'll conclude that numbers are an important part of their lives.

Roles of a Number
tells how many
tells location
tells order
measures

Discovering Purpose

This homework challenge leads students to consider the **purpose of numbers**. Give each student a copy of "Tracking Down Numbers" from page 198. Ask each child to list different objects in his home where actual numbers are found. Examples include a telephone, TV remote, cookbook, clock, and so on. When students return their homework, compile their findings on the board. Next, tell students that numbers serve different purposes. Display the information from "Roles of a Number" on this page and discuss each role that is listed. Then assign a different symbol to each role, and, with your students' help, use the resulting code to label each number location on the class list. Wouldn't life be confusing without numbers?

Sizing Up Numbers

Students get a real sense of **number value** during this large-group game. In advance, label 20 large tagboard cards with the numerals 0–9 (two cards for each number) and make student copies of the gameboard on page 199. (For a three-digit number game, make a copy of the gameboard, blacken the "Thousands" columns on your copy, and then use it to make student copies.)

To play, each student needs a gameboard and a crayon. Shuffle the game cards and stack them facedown. Challenge each student to make in the first blank row of his gameboard the largest (or smallest) number he can. Then draw a game card, say the corresponding numeral, and display the card for student reference. Wait for students to write the numeral on their gameboards before drawing another card. When six digits are recorded, ask volunteers to say the different numbers they made. Write each number on the board. When the largest possible number is identified, instruct any child who wrote that number on his gameboard to also draw two tally marks in his point box. Then shuffle the cards and begin another round of play. Play until time runs out or a predetermined number of points has been scored by one or more students.

Barbara Caywood—Gr. 3, Partridge Grade School, Partridge, KS

Number Crunching

Daily number crunching is a "dino-mite" way to strengthen students' understanding of **number relationships**. Every day write four different numbers on the board and give each child a copy of "Number Crunching" from page 199. Have each student copy the numbers on her paper (in the provided circles) and complete the number-crunching activities. Set aside time for youngsters to check their work as a class. Or have students compare their work with partners or with members of a small group. Crunch, crunch, crunch.

What's Hatching?

Crack open an investigation of the **suitability of numbers**! Explain to students that some numbers are just right for some situations, but not right for others. For example, the number 12 could be how many feet deep a swimming pool is, but could not be the number of ears on an elephant. Or the number 10 could be the number of ounces in a milk shake, but could not be the age of a school bus driver. To get students thinking about the suitability of numbers, divide the class into small groups and assign each group a different number. Challenge the members of each group to think of situations in which the number does (and does not) make sense. Then have each group use the "could be, but could not be" format to prepare two different responses for sharing with the class. After each group has shared its statements, have students work independently to complete "What's Hatching?" on page 200.

Numbers About Me!

by

_____

©2001 The Education Center, Inc.

Name _____

Tracking Down Numbers

I found numbers on these objects:

_____

_____

_____

_____

_____

_____

_____

_____

_____

_____

©2001 The Education Center, Inc.

Note to the teacher: Use "Numbers About Me!" with "Extraordinary Excavation" on page 196. Use "Tracking Down Numbers" with "Discovering Purpose" on page 196.

Number Crunching

Write a different number in each circle.
Use the numbers to complete the activities below.

◯	Write the numbers from smallest to largest.	Write 1 number 3 different ways.	Write each odd number.
◯			
◯	Mentally add 5 to each number. Write the sums.\n\n_____ _____\n\n_____ _____	Complete the number sentences.\n\n_____ > _____\n\n_____ < _____	Write each even number.
◯			

©The Education Center, Inc. • THE MAILBOX® • Primary • Oct/Nov 2001

Sizing Up Numbers

Point Box

THOUSANDS			ONES											
HUNDREDS	TENS	ONES	HUNDREDS	TENS	ONES									

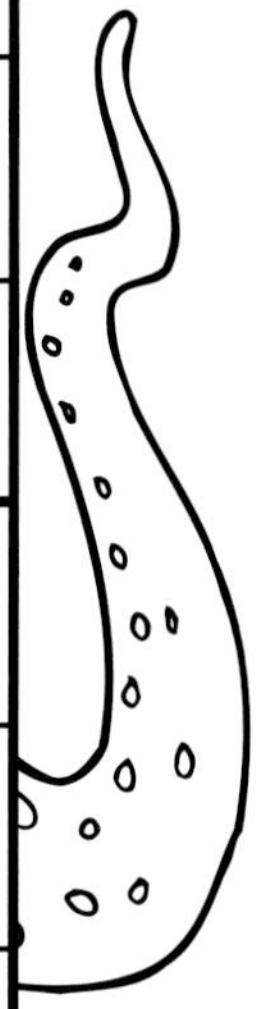

©The Education Center, Inc. • THE MAILBOX® • Primary • Oct/Nov 2001

Name_____

What's Hatching?

Decide what the number on each egg could and could not be.
Use the code to color the egg.

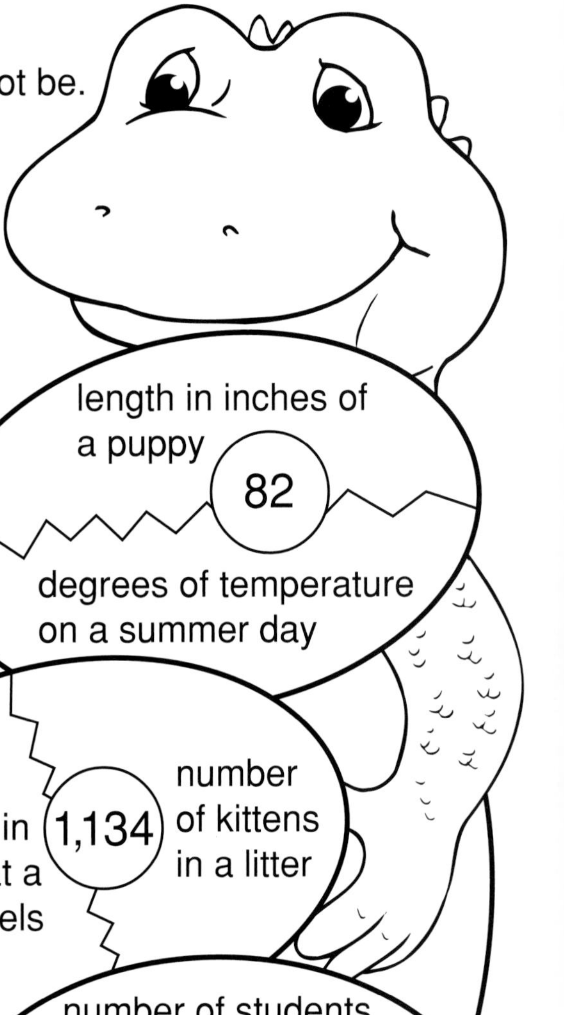

number of people in a family

6

age at which a person drives a car

number of cookies in a cookie jar

20

miles per hour at which a jet flies

length in inches of a puppy

82

degrees of temperature on a summer day

age of a school teacher

151

number of pennies in a piggy bank

the distance in miles that a train travels

1,134

number of kittens in a litter

minutes needed to eat a hamburger

10,753

dollars needed to buy a new car

gallons of water in a swimming pool

4

number of legs on a table

number of students in a classroom

263

number of pages in a book

number of times the sun sets each day

1

number of hairs on a horse

year the safety pin was invented

1849

year the computer was invented

Color Code

could be   = pink
could not be = blue

Bonus Box: Oops! One egg rolled away! On the back of this paper, draw a large egg and number it 12. On one half of the egg, write a phrase about the number that could be true. On the other egg half, write a phrase about the number that could not be true. Use the code to color the egg.

©The Education Center, Inc. • THE MAILBOX® • Primary • Oct/Nov 2001 • Key p. 312

Basic Facts Checkup

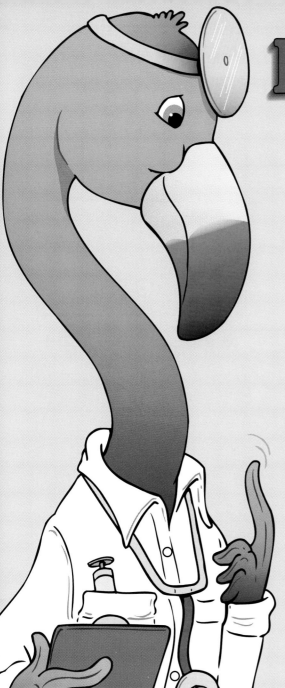

Take the pulse of your youngsters' basic facts knowledge with these patient-pleasing games and activities.

Come On Over!

To strengthen basic facts, try this large-group treatment! Divide students into two equal teams. Have each team stand in a straight line that faces the opposing team. The first child in each line steps forward and high-fives the opposing player. Then both players turn to face you. Flash a basic fact card. The child who responds first with the correct answer moves to the end of his team line, taking his opponent with him. The two students who are now first in line step forward, high-five each other, and turn to face you. Continue play as described until every child has taken a turn. To determine the winning team, have each team count off. The team with more players wins the round.

Renee Kerstetter
Selinsgrove Intermediate School
Selinsgrove, PA

Basic Facts Rx

Prescribe an assortment of basic facts practice using the reproducible on page 203. Make a copy of the page and then program each rectangle with a basic fact challenge, such as "List four different addition facts that have a sum of 11" or "List five different subtraction facts that have a difference of 6." It's the perfect medicine for reinforcing basic facts!

adapted from an idea by
Kelli Higgins
P. L. Bolin Elementary School
East Peoria, IL

Pop-Up Prescription

Here's a math warm-up that keeps mathematicians nimble! Choose a few fact answers such as 9, 10, 11, and 12. Program a class set of blank cards with the answers—one answer per card. Give each child a card to hold. Next, show the class a flash card that corresponds to an answer card. If the answer is on a child's card, she pops up (stands) and shows you her card. Quickly scan the answer cards displayed and ask a child who holds the correct answer to state it for the class. Then direct the students to sit down. Resume play by displaying another flash card. Continue play in the manner described for several minutes. Set a peppy pace for the game and your patients will not only be popping up and down—they'll be smiling, too!

Linda Rudlaff, John F. Nuner Elementary School
South Bend, IN

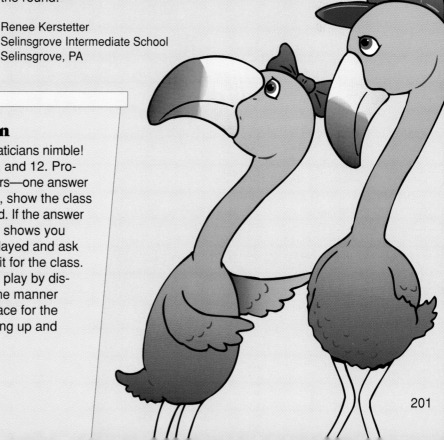

Computation Station

A daily dose of computation promotes a healthy understanding of basic facts! Prepare several cards for each digit from 0 through 9. Hole-punch the top of each card. Next, title a bulletin board "Computation Station" and ready the board with pushpins and construction paper details so that when digit cards are displayed, basic fact problems are formed (see the illustration). Each morning have a different set of digits on display and ask students to solve the problems in their math journals. Use a variety of methods to check the daily math task, including self-checking, peer checking, and teacher checking.

Linda Rudlaff

Take a Chair!

This variation of Musical Chairs keeps students in step with basic facts! Arrange student chairs back-to-back and in a straight line, making sure you have two less chairs than players. Students march around the chairs while music is playing. When the music stops, every student attempts to sit in a different chair. Show a flash card to the two students left standing. The child who is first to provide the correct answer remains in the game. The other child removes a chair from the playing area and sits in it. If two students simultaneously provide the correct answer, both remain in the game. Continue play as described. When the fifth player leaves the game, invite all five students to reenter the game (with their chairs). Continue play for as long as desired.

adapted from an idea by Janet Click
Ethridge Elementary
The Colony, TX

Tennis Ball Drill

If the doctor orders students to have a ball with basic facts, follow these steps. Label a tennis ball for each number from 0 through 9. Store the programmed balls in a bucket. Gather students in a circle on the floor. For a review of addition facts, state an addend. Roll the balls one at a time to different students. A student who receives a ball states the number on the ball and the declared addend as an addition fact. She solves the fact and then rolls the ball back. When all the balls have been rolled out and returned, select a different addend and continue the game as described. As students become familiar with the game, increase the speed at which it is played.

To review basic subtraction facts, provide a minuend of nine or larger. A student who receives a ball states the corresponding subtraction problem (the minuend minus the numeral on the ball), solves it, and returns the ball.

Elizabeth Roberts
Manor Elementary
Levittown, PA

Doctor's Orders!

Follow each order from the doctor.

1.	2.

3.	4.	5.

©The Education Center, Inc. • THE MAILBOX® • Primary • April/May 2002

Note to the teacher: Use with "Basic Facts Rx" on page 201.

Once Upon a Time...

An Enchanting Collection of Time-Telling Activities

With favorite fairy-tale characters by your side, spin a tale
of time-telling practice that has a delightfully happy ending!

contributions by Bonnie Baumgras, Las Vegas, NV

Knock! Knock!

Skill: matching digital and analog times

Open a door to continued practice matching digital and analog
times! Make a construction paper copy of page 206 for each child.
Laminate the copies and use an X-acto knife to slit the dotted lines
on each copy. Give each child a page of prepared patterns, a brad, and
access to clear tape. A student cuts out the clock hands and then cuts
along the bold lines. To assemble the manipulative, she pokes the
brad through the dot on the short clock hand, the long clock hand,
and the clock face (in that order); and then she fastens the brad. Next,
she inserts strip A into its matching set of slits, overlaps the ends of
the strip, and secures them with tape. She repeats this step with strips
B and C.

To use her manipulative, she adjusts the strips and the clock hands
so that the same time appears on both. Every day, pose different
fairy-tale scenarios (see provided samples) and have students show
the corresponding times on their clock manipulatives.

Candi DeFran, East River Elementary, Grosse Ile, MI

Please return at...

9 : 1 5

Sample scenarios:
Mama Bear poured porridge at 3:30.
Goldilocks ate Baby Bear's porridge at 4:14.
Papa Bear took a nap at 6:00.

Name _____ Once Upon a Time... Telling time

Time to Climb!

Bonus Box: Choose a time from this page. On the back of this paper, write a sentence that tells what the giant is doing at this exact time. Include the time in your sentence.

Time to Climb!

Skill: telling time

Fe! Fi! Fo! Fum! Keep page 207 handy, and
your youngsters' time-telling skills are sure to
keep growing and growing and growing! For
each time-telling review, make a copy of the
page and then program the copy to reinforce a
desired time-telling skill (such as time to the
half hour or time to the quarter hour) by drawing clock hands or by writing digital times on
the lines. Provide oral student directions or
program the cloud with one of the following:
"Write the time on the lines below each clock"
or "Draw hands on each clock to show the time
that is given." Now that's golden assessment!

A Day in the Life
Skill: understanding A.M. and P.M.

Add a fairy-tale twist to a review of A.M. and P.M. times! On the board write a student-generated list of fairy-tale characters. Have each child copy a name from the board onto his paper and then list eight activities the character might do at different times during a day: four before noon and four after noon. Next, have each student fold a 6" x 18" strip of light-colored construction paper in half (to 6" x 9"). Have him title the resulting front cover "A Day in the Life of [character's name]" and add a desired cover illustration. Also give each child two copies of the clock cards from page 208 (for a total of eight cards).

To make a timeline of his character's day, a student unfolds his paper. He uses a crayon to trace over the fold line and to label the left half of the paper "A.M." and the right half "P.M." Next, he completes a clock card for each activity by programming the clock with the time the activity will be completed, writing the corresponding digital time in the box, and describing the activity on the lines. Then he cuts out the completed cards and glues them in chronological order on the appropriate halves of his paper. Be sure to set aside time for students to share their projects with the class.

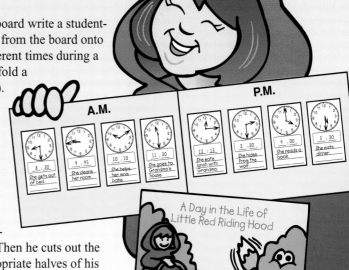

A Quarter Past 12
Skill: fractional measurements of time

Cinderella can lend students a hand learning fractional measurements of time! For each child make a construction paper copy of the clock and clock hand patterns from page 208. Laminate the copies for durability and then give each student a brad and a set of patterns. Have each child cut out the clock hands and then cut along the bold lines. To assemble her clock, she pokes the brad through the dot on the short clock hand, the long clock hand, and the clock face (in that order); and then she fastens the brad.

Ask students to explain the significance of the quarters. Lead them to conclude that each quarter (or one-fourth) of the clock face is labeled with a quarter. Then have each child position the hands on his clock to show a series of times that include *quarter past, quarter to,* and *half past* (explaining that two quarters equal a half). Have students keep the clocks handy for additional time-telling practice that includes fractional measurements of time.

Michele Repass—Gr. 2, Hugh Mercer Elementary, Fredericksburg, VA

Wolf Whereabouts
Skill: elapsed time

Monitoring the actions of the big bad wolf is definitely a task for student pairs! Each child needs her clock manipulative from "A Quarter Past 12" (or something similar). To begin, pose the following problem: "The big bad wolf got up at 7:30 (or half past seven). He had practiced huffing and puffing for 20 minutes when the phone rang. What time did the phone ring?" Challenge each twosome to use one or both of its clocks to solve the problem. Then invite students to share how they determined that the phone rang at 7:50. Continue posing a variety of problems for students to solve. If desired, have each pair record its answers on paper. See "That Wolf!" for some problems to get you started.

Pam Crane

That Wolf!

The big bad wolf sees a little pig leave its house at 3:10. He sees the same pig return at 3:45. How long has the pig been gone?

At 8:30 the big bad wolf will meet a little pig at the apple orchard. If it takes the wolf 25 minutes to get to the orchard, what time must he leave to arrive at the orchard on time?

The three little pigs invite the big bad wolf to have lunch with them at 11:45. The wolf arrives seven minutes early. What time does the wolf arrive?

Patterns
Use with "Knock! Knock!" on page 204.

Please return at...

A : B C

A		
12		
11	B	C
10	5	9
9	4	8
8	3	7
7	2	6
6	1	5
5	0	4
4		3
3		2
2		1
1		0

©The Education Center, Inc. • *THE MAILBOX® • Primary •* Feb/Mar 2002

Name _____

Time to Climb!

____:____   ____:____   ____:____   ____:____

____:____   ____:____   ____:____   ____:____

____:____   ____:____

Bonus Box: Choose a time from this page. On the back of this paper, write a sentence that tells what the giant is doing at this exact time. Include the time in your sentence.

©The Education Center, Inc. • THE MAILBOX® • Primary • Feb/Mar 2002

Note to the teacher: Use with "Time to Climb!" on page 204.

Clock Cards and Patterns

Use the clock cards with "A Day in the Life" on page 205.

Use the patterns with "A Quarter Past 12" on page 205.

 ©The Education Center, Inc. • THE MAILBOX® • Primary • Feb/Mar 2002

Knights of the Rounding Table

Step back into medieval days to strengthen students' skills in rounding numbers. Your young pages will soon be rounding numbers with royal success!

A Royal Tip

Remembering when to round to the greater ten becomes perfectly clear with a visual image! Ask each child to picture himself boarding a medieval-themed roller coaster at point zero. As his dragon-shaped car slowly inches up a steep hill, he chugs past the numbers one, two, three, and four. But when he reaches number five at the tippy top of the hill, his car suddenly zooms down the other side of the hill and stops at the number ten! With this visual image in mind, students are sure to remember that the number five means zoom ahead to the next ten!

Elizabeth Roberts—Gr. 2, Manor Elementary School, Levittown, PA

Conquer the Castle!

This partner game is packed with opportunities to round numbers to the nearest ten. To make his game, a child colors a copy of page 210. Next, he cuts along the dotted line, sets the castle gameboard aside, and cuts out the game pieces. Provide a quart-size resealable plastic bag for game storage.

Pair students and have each player stack his game pieces facedown. Explain that the object of the game is for a player to be first to reach the top of his castle. Each player begins play at the ground level of his castle. To take a turn, both players simultaneously draw their top game pieces. Each player rounds the number on his game piece to the nearest ten. If this number appears on the ground level of his castle, he covers it with his game piece. If not, he places the piece in a personal discard pile (which is later shuffled and reused). After both players play their game pieces, the two players take another turn by together drawing their top game pieces. When a player covers two spaces on the ground level of his castle, his play proceeds to the next castle level. Play continues in this manner until one player covers two spaces at each level of his castle and then covers the winning space at the top of his castle. Now that's a game that's sure to be played again and again!

Janet Ranieri—Gr. 3, Lowell Elementary, Rock Springs, WY

The Rounding Table

Here's a manipulative that gives students a leg up on rounding to the nearest hundred! Give each child a copy of "The Rounding Table" from page 211 and a business-size envelope (for storage). Have each child color the artwork and cut along the dotted lines.

To use his table, a child determines the two hundreds between which the number he is rounding falls and places the matching cutout in the provided spaces. If the number he is rounding has less than five tens, he rounds to the lesser hundred. If it has five tens or more, he rounds to the greater hundred. After a bit of practice, dub your students knights of the rounding table and have them complete "Nifty Number Shields" from page 211.

Game Pieces

5	75	18	3	61
24	93	87	77	25
22	59	13	65	84
41	44	27	1	52
48	31	82	7	67
88	17	4	73	47
39	55	94	14	35

Conquer the Castle!

You did it! 10

60 — 70 — 80 Advance to next level. Go up secret passage. 40 — 80 Visit dragon. Miss two turns. 90

20 — 30 — 50

70 — 80 Fall through trap door. Miss one turn. 40 — 90 — 10

30 — 10 — 50 — 60

20 — 0 — Enter here.

©The Education Center, Inc. • THE MAILBOX® • Primary • Oct/Nov 2001

Note to the teacher: Use with "Conquer the Castle!" on page 209.

Nifty Number Shields

Round each number to the nearest hundred.
Write your answer on the line.
Use the code to color each shield.

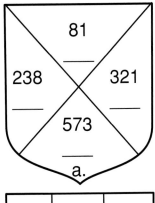

81
238 ___ 321
___ ___
573
___
a.

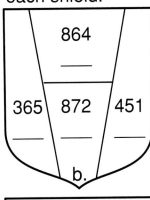

864
___
365 | 872 | 451
___
b.

54   719
___   ___
677   44
___   ___
c.

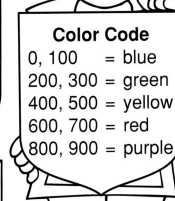

Color Code
0, 100   = blue
200, 300 = green
400, 500 = yellow
600, 700 = red
800, 900 = purple

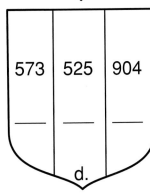

573 | 525 | 904
___ | ___ | ___
d.

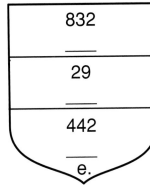

832
___
29
___
442
___
e.

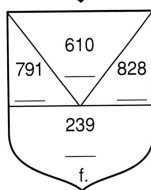

610
791   ___   828
___
239
___
f.

Bonus Box: How is rounding to the nearest hundred like rounding to the nearest ten? Write your answer on the back of this paper.

©The Education Center, Inc. • THE MAILBOX® • Primary • Oct/Nov 2001 • Key p. 312

The Rounding Table

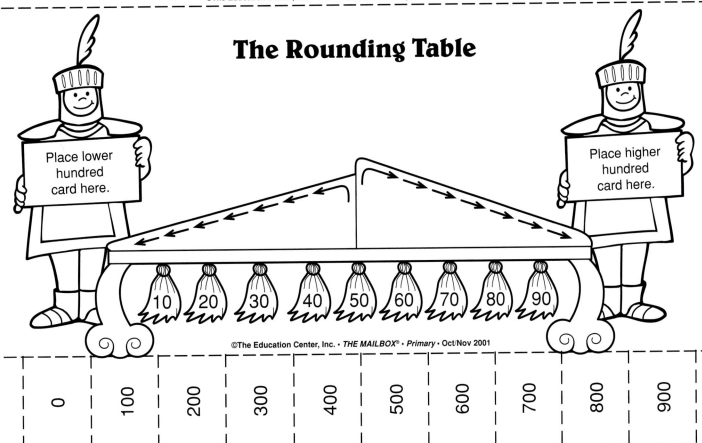

Place lower hundred card here.

Place higher hundred card here.

10 20 30 40 50 60 70 80 90

©The Education Center, Inc. • THE MAILBOX® • Primary • Oct/Nov 2001

0   100   200   300   400   500   600   700   800   900

Note to the teacher: Use "Nifty Number Shields" and "The Rounding Table" with "The Rounding Table" on page 209.

Hundred-Chart Investigation

Set your young sleuths hot on the trail of intriguing number patterns, mysteries, and challenges with these hundred-chart ideas!

Mystery Number

What does every math sleuth need? A number finder! Give each student a copy of a lens pattern on page 214 and a jumbo craft stick. Have the youngster cut along the outer edge of the pattern and then carefully cut out the inner rectangle (provide assistance as necessary). Instruct him to glue the lens to the craft stick as shown and then sign his name on the resulting handle. To present a case to be solved, give each student a hundred chart. Secretly choose a number between 1 and 100. Use the terms *greater than* and *less than* to identify the numbers immediately preceding and following the chosen number. Challenge students to use the clues and their number finders to locate the mystery number on their charts. Case solved!

adapted from an idea by Karen Saner—Grs. K–1
Burns Elementary
Burns, KS

Spin Off!

Count on students to track down large numbers with this partner game! Provide each twosome with a copy of the spinner on page 214, scissors, a paper clip, a hundred chart, a sheet of paper for keeping score, and a different-colored counter for each player. Have one player cut out the spinner. Explain that the goal of the game is to make the greatest numbers. To begin, one player uses a pencil and the paper clip to spin twice. He combines the numbers he got to make a two-digit number. (If the spinner lands on the star, he uses a number of his choice.) For example, if the spinner lands on 3 and 4, he may make either 34 or 43. The player places his counter in the corresponding square on the hundred chart. The second player takes a turn in a like manner. The player with the greater number earns one point. The players clear the chart. The game continues until one player earns five points and is declared the winner.

Sniff Sniff

Pattern Seekers

There's more to a hundred chart than meets the eye! Tell the class that a hundred chart has several horizontal, vertical, and diagonal patterns. Allow time for students to study a displayed hundred chart; then invite volunteers to share patterns they see. Next, give each student a booklet with construction paper covers and a desired number of pages formatted like the one shown. Instruct her to title the booklet "Detective [student's name]'s Math Notes." Throughout your hundred-chart unit, challenge students to find a variety of patterns. When a youngster discovers a pattern, have her illustrate it on a hundred chart and write about it in the provided space. No doubt students will be eager to share their discoveries, so be sure to provide time for a class debriefing!

1	2	3	4	5	6	7	8	9	10
11	12	13	14	15	16	17	18	19	20
21	22	23	24	25	26	27	28	29	30
31	32	33	34	35	36	37	38	39	40
41	42	43	44	45	46	47	48	49	50
51	52	53	54	55	56	57	58	59	60
61	62	63	64	65	66	67	68	69	70
71	72	73	74	75	76	77	78	79	80
81	82	83	84	85	86	87	88	89	90
91	92	93	94	95	96	97	98	99	100

Found: A diagonal pattern

Evidence: Start with 9. Move down diagonally.
For each number in that line, the digits add up to 9.

Letter-Perfect

Close inspection of a hundred chart reveals not only patterns but letters, too! In advance, copy a class supply of hundred charts plus one extra. On one copy, color the appropriate squares to form a selected letter. To begin, give each youngster a copy of an unmarked chart. Announce that you have discovered something special about the chart—a letter is concealed in it! To provide proof of your claim, verbally provide step-by-step directions for finding and marking each square needed to form the letter. For example, a direction for 63 might be the following: "Find 65. Color the number that is two less." If desired, provide additional hundred charts and challenge your youngsters to uncover other letters!

1	2	3	4	5	6	7	8	9	10
11	12	13	14	15	16	17	18	19	20
21	22	23	24	25	26	27	28	29	30
31	32	33	34	35	36	37	38	39	40
41	42	43	44	45	46	47	48	49	50
51	52	53	54	55	56	57	58	59	60
61	62	63	64	65	66	67	68	69	70
71	72	73	74	75	76	77	78	79	80
81	82	83	84	85	86	87	88	89	90
91	92	93	94	95	96	97	98	99	100

100th Day Riddles

If you have 47 and add 12, what do you get?

You get 59!

What better way to celebrate the 100th day of school than with a kid-pleasing hundred-chart activity? Read aloud *100 Days of School* by Trudy Harris, a collection of riddles that explores the concept of 100. Then provide each student with a hundred chart and a half sheet of paper. Secretly assign each student a different number from 1 to 100. Instruct the youngster to refer to the chart as he creates an addition or subtraction riddle about his number. Then have him write the riddle and its answer on his paper. Ask a volunteer to read his riddle aloud without revealing the answer. Then challenge his classmates to use their hundred charts to determine the answer. Invite the first student who correctly answers the riddle to share her riddle next. (If she has already shared it, have her call on another student.) Continue in a like manner until every riddle has been answered.

Missing!

Number sense helps crack this missing numbers case! Display a poster-sized 100-box grid. Program each of several grid boxes to begin creating a hundred chart. Cut a copy of a hundred chart into individual number cards. Remove the card for each number written on the grid and then place the cards in a container labeled "Evidence."

Tell students that although most of the numbers on the hundred chart have mysteriously disappeared, you have collected evidence that will help reconstruct the chart. Each day, ask a volunteer to remove a card and read it aloud. Ask her to find the corresponding grid box by counting back, counting forward, continuing a pattern, or using another appropriate strategy of her choice. When she identifies the correct box, have her tell the class her strategy and then write the number in the box. Invite a desired number of additional volunteers to contribute to the chart in a like manner. Repeat the process each day until the chart is complete.

Rosemary Camiolo—Grs. 1–2, Looping
Bells Elementary
Turnersville, NJ

Patterns

Use the lenses with "Mystery Number" on page 212.

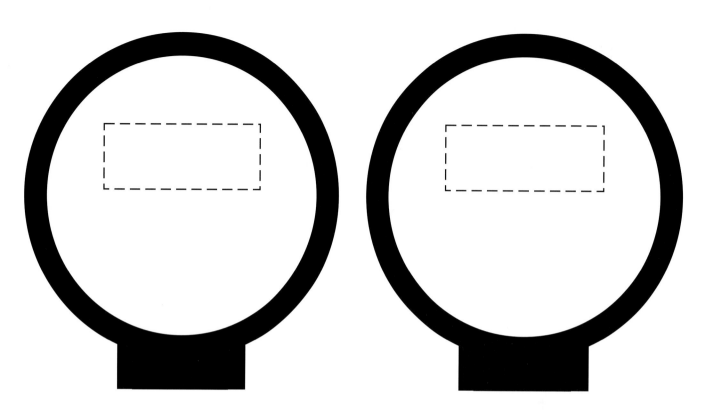

Use the spinner with "Spin Off!" on page 212.

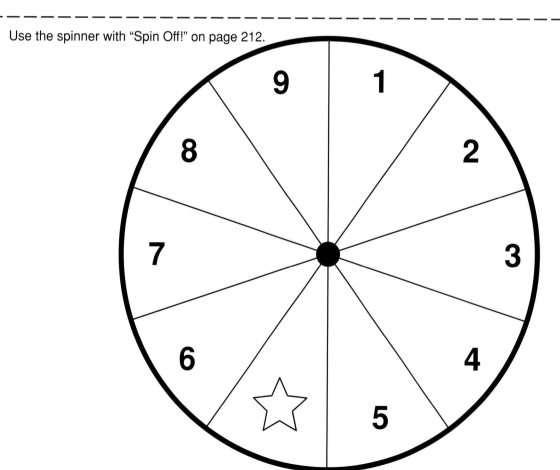

©2001 The Education Center, Inc. • *THE MAILBOX*® • *Primary* • Dec/Jan 2001–2

Made to Measure

Size up your youngsters' linear-measurement skills using the fresh and creative ideas in this collection!

How Big?

Fe! Fi! Fo! Fum! Set the stage for some giant-sized measuring with an oral reading of *Jack and the Beanstalk*! Then divide the class into six small groups. Provide each group with a length of bulletin board paper, construction paper scraps, markers or crayons, glue, and scissors. Ask the members of each group to use their supplies and imaginations to make a part of the giant's body. Ask two different groups to make one arm each and two different groups to make one leg each. Ask one group to make the giant's head and another to make his body.

When the projects are ready, assemble the giant. Invite students to talk about the giant's comical appearance. Next, help volunteers measure different parts of the giant's body. Write these measurements on the giant so that students can study and compare them. Invite students to suggest how they could collectively make a giant that is more uniform in size. No doubt students will agree that this time a giant-sized *measurement* project is in order!

Tami Bertini—Gr. 1
Gladbrook Elementary
Gladbrook, IA

Book of Measures

Oodles of opportunities for measuring are packed into this nifty booklet project! Give each child a construction paper booklet that holds five copies of page 219. Have each child write her name and "Book of Measures" on the front cover. Also have her complete the title of the first booklet page by writing "Our School" on the line provided. Next, take students on a guided tour of the school. Provide time for each child to measure and record in her booklet the length, width, and height of five or more items. For a fun follow-up, ask each child to state the measurements for the largest or smallest item she measured.

Instruct each child to complete the remaining pages of her booklet at home. To do this, she titles each page so that it describes the area, item, pet, or person she is measuring. Ask students to return their completed booklets to school on or before a designated date. When the booklets are returned, set aside time for students to share several of the measurements they've taken!

Melody Shaw
Carrollton, MS

For Good Measure

Sharpen measurement *and* writing skills with this partner activity. Pair students and confirm that each twosome has a ruler, a pencil, and a sheet of paper. Instruct each duo to measure the length of six classroom items of its own choosing. For each measured item, the pair composes a descriptive sentence that includes the gathered measurements. Next, have each pair exchange papers with another twosome, find each item described on the paper, and verify the measurements that were taken. Instruct students to star each verified sentence. Then, after a set amount of time, ask that the papers be returned to the students who wrote them. Students will enjoy choosing what they measure as well as confirming the measurements taken by their peers. Better plan to repeat this activity a few times for good measure!

Amy Emmons—Gr. 2
Enon Elementary
Franklinton, LA

Rodger and Chen

1. The purple and green tissue box on Ms. Emmons's desk is 4 inches wide and 5 inches tall.

2. The bright orange welcome sign on the classroom door is 10 inches long and 8 inches wide.

3.

A Royal Predicament

Rolf Myller's *How Big Is a Foot?* is a must for your measurement unit! In this delightful romp, a king decides to give the queen a bed for her birthday. Because beds have not yet been invented, no one is quite sure how large the bed should be. The king provides the answer—three feet by six feet. Read the story aloud, stopping when the apprentice learns the dimensions of the bed. Divide the class into small groups and give each group a length of bulletin board paper on which to design a quilt for the queen's bed. Ask each group to select an apprentice who will use the king's technique of using his own feet to measure the size of the group's quilt. Allow plenty of time for each group to measure, cut out, and decorate its quilt. Display the completed quilts so that the tops are level. Ask students to study the quilts and suggest why all the quilts are not the same size. Invite students to predict how their measurement experiences might play out in the story. Then read aloud the remainder of *How Big Is a Foot?* At the book's completion, students are sure to better understand why a standard system of measurement is essential!

Judy M. Christiansen
Harlan, IA

Community Planners

Merge math and social studies curricula when you challenge students to collectively construct a community named Measurementville! Post the name of the community on a bulletin board. Then have students craft construction paper components for the community that include buildings, homes, cars, streets, scenery, and people. Explain that each item must be measured and labeled accordingly before it can become a part of Measurementville. The final result is a picture-perfect review of linear measurement that provides a sense of community!

Gina Zimecki—Gr. 2
Bernice Young Elementary School
Burlington, NJ

On the Move

Students take their rulers on the road for this hands-on measurement activity! At each of several centers, provide five like items of varying sizes to be measured. Consider items such as books, pencils, tagboard strips, pipe cleaners, and so on. Assign a letter to each center and then number the items at each center from 1 to 5. During his assigned center time, a child heads to a center with his ruler, his pencil, and a recording sheet like the one shown. He measures the length of each item at the center, records his findings on his paper, and then moves on to another center. When he has measured each item in every center, he returns to his desk. If desired, store an answer key or two at your desk and invite students to use the keys to check the measurements they gathered. Now that's a measurement activity that brings students to their feet!

June Shaner—Gr. 2
Our Lady of Fatima School
Lakewood, CO

Name **Nick**

Measurement Centers

Center A	Center B
Pencils	Pipe Cleaners
1.	1.
2.	2.
3.	3.
4.	4.
5.	5.

Cuddly Calibrations

For this warm and fuzzy measurement activity, ask each child to bring to school a favorite stuffed toy. Be sure to have a few extra stuffed critters on hand. You will also need several tape measures. To begin, each child traces the outline of her critter onto a provided length of bulletin board paper and colors the resulting outline to resemble her cuddly companion. Next, she uses her ruler (and a tape measure when necessary) to measure her fuzzy friend. She labels her illustration with the measurements she gathers. Display the resulting posters in the hallway for everyone to see.

adapted from an idea by
Angie Lamb—Chapter 1
Rutledge Elementary School
Rutledge, TN

Spaghetti and Meatballs

Continue to whet your youngsters' appetites for measurement at this mouth-watering center! Cut ten meatball shapes from construction paper and label them in alphabetical order from *A* through *J*. Securely tape to the back of each cutout one end of a length of string (spaghetti). Vary the string lengths. To create an answer key, measure each string from the edge of the meatball to its unattached end. Trim the string to a desired measurement and record this measurement on the answer key.

Store the meatballs and spaghetti in a bowl or cooking pot. Place the bowl, a ruler, a yardstick, a supply of paper, and the answer key at a center. A student measures the spaghetti lengths and records his answers in alphabetical order on his paper. Then he uses the answer key to check his work. For added fun, place a recording of Tomie dePaola's *Strega Nona* at a different center for your youngsters' listening pleasure! Your students' interest in pasta is sure to grow!

Paula Beckerman
Arlington, TX

Sizing Up Animals' Tails!

24 inches	cheetah
30 inches	blue monkey
8 inches bobcat	
36 inches	lion

By the Tail

You can count on an enthusiastic response to this unique measurement activity! Copy page 220 onto construction paper. Cut the cards apart and place them in a container. Place the container of cards at a center along with two rolls of adding machine tape, a ruler, a yardstick, pencils, scissors, and markers or crayons. Inform students that each card is labeled with the name of an animal and the approximate length of its tail. Arrange for students to visit the center in pairs. A pair removes a card from the container and measures and cuts a length of adding machine tape that is the length of the animal's tail. Next, the duo writes on the paper the length of the tape and the name of the animal. Then the pair places the card in a discard pile.

As student pairs complete their work at the center, post their strips on a bulletin board so that a bar graph is created. After every student has completed the center with a partner, invite interested students to revisit the center to complete any remaining cards. When the graph is intact, pose a series of measurement-related questions for students to answer.

Karrie Jayne Johnson—Gr. 3
Joseph C. Caruso School
Keansburg, NJ

Measuring _____

Object	Length	Width	Height
1.			
2.			
3.			
4.			
5.			
6.			
7.			
8.			
9.			
10.			

©The Education Center, Inc. • THE MAILBOX® • Primary • April/May 2002

Note to the teacher: Use with "Book of Measures" on page 215.

Cards

Use with "By the Tail" on page 218.

lion		36 inches	sea otter		15 inches
bobcat		8 inches	gray wolf		24 inches
gray squirrel		10 inches	cheetah		24 inches
hamster		2 inches	Arctic hare		5 inches
red kangaroo		36 inches	gray fox		12 inches
giant anteater		35 inches	aardvark		24 inches
North American beaver		18 inches	coyote		16 inches
jaguar		30 inches	three-toed sloth		3 inches
llama		6 inches	blue monkey		30 inches
snow leopard		36 inches	raccoon		13 inches

©The Education Center, Inc. • THE MAILBOX® • Primary • April/May 2002

Bright Ideas for Making Math Real!

Sunglasses are not required, but they might be fun! Use this sunny collection of activities to reinforce math skills and shed light on ways math can be useful this summer!

Measure, Then Munch

Skills: capacity, problem solving

Here's a delicious recipe for reinforcing measurement and problem-solving skills! On a table at the front of the room, organize the items from the provided supply list. Then, on the board, write the recipe for Tricky Trail Mix.

First, have each child title his paper "Trail Mix" and rewrite the recipe to show an exact amount of each ingredient. Next, divide students into four groups. Have the members of each group compare their calculations and solve any inconsistencies in their recipe amounts. When a group has a correct recipe (see Answer Keys on page 312 to verify), it earns a turn at the supply table. Here all group members participate in making a batch of trail mix by measuring ingredients into a provided bag.

When each group has prepared a batch, hand out the paper napkins and invite group members to munch on the mix they made. Prompt students to think of additional opportunities for using their measurement skills.

adapted from an idea by Jill Waldrep—Gr. 3, Sanders Elementary, Austell, GA

Collecting Cool Info

Skills: collecting, graphing, and interpreting data

Create a thirst for data! Read aloud Stuart J. Murphy's *Lemonade for Sale.* In this math-linked literature selection, neighborhood kids use a bar graph to track lemonade sales for five days. At the conclusion of the story, help students name weekday data to collect. Suggestions include minutes spent reading, watching TV, or playing soccer; daily high or low outdoor temperatures; and math problems solved.

To complete a weekday data-collecting activity, each child selects a type of data and titles a copy of page 224 accordingly. He writes his name on the provided line and then he numbers the graph to reflect the amount of data he anticipates collecting. (If low numbers are expected, he writes numbers from 1 to 10. For higher data numbers, he writes numbers by tens from 10 to 100.) When the students' data-collecting exercise is complete, ask each child to interpret his results for the class.

For a fun finale, take a lemonade break with students and brainstorm a list of more data-collecting opportunities for summer. If desired, invite interested students to make data-collecting booklets by stapling copies of page 224 between construction paper covers.

Tricky Trail Mix

oat cereal = $\frac{1}{2}$ cup
sunflower kernels = 1 teaspoon
M&M's candies = 3 times the amount of sunflower kernels
raisins = $\frac{1}{2}$ the amount of oat cereal
honey-graham cereal = 3 times the amount of raisins
bite-size pretzels = $\frac{1}{3}$ the amount of honey-graham cereal

Supply List

4 gallon-size resealable plastic bags
measuring cups ($\frac{1}{2}$ c. and $\frac{1}{4}$ c.)
measuring spoon (1 tsp.)
class supply of paper napkins
6 bowls, each containing one of the following ingredients:
    4 c. honey-graham cereal
    3 c. oat cereal
    2 c. bite-size pretzels
    2 c. raisins
    $\frac{1}{2}$ c. M&M's candies
    $\frac{1}{4}$ c. sunflower kernels
(A small amount of each ingredient will be left over.)

Math on the Menu

Skills: adding and subtracting money

Provide several delicious servings of computation practice using student-made menus! Give each child three half sheets and two quarter sheets of writing paper. She titles the three half sheets "Breakfast," "Lunch," and "Dinner" and the two quarter sheets "Desserts" and "Drinks." On each paper, she lists three or more of her favorites from the named category and assigns a price to each that falls within a given range. To make her menu, she folds in half a 12" x 18" sheet of construction paper (to 9" x 12"). On the front cover, she writes the name of a personalized eatery and adds desired decorations. She glues the papers she prepared inside. Laminate the menus for durability, if desired.

To complete a menu-related activity, give each child a form like the one shown. Announce a time of day and a spending allowance that includes a count of bills and coins. Use a calculator to check each child's calculations or have students use calculators for this purpose. For added variety, have classmates trade menus before placing their orders. Students are sure to recognize the value of these skills!

Cynthia Mackel—Grs. 1–2

I had a whole watermelon slice.
I ate ⁵/₈ of it.
How much is left?

There is ³/₈ of the slice left.

Fair Shares

Skills: fractions, word problems

Pair fractions with food, and students are instantly interested! To begin, have each child fold in half a 9" x 12" sheet of drawing paper and trace a circle or rectangle template on the folded paper. Have him keep his paper folded and cut along the resulting outline. Instruct him to color one shape to resemble a favorite food and then color the second shape to match.

Next, have each child glue one cutout to the top half of a 9" x 12" sheet of light-colored construction paper. Also, give every student a sticky note labeled with a fraction. Below his glued drawing, a child writes a word problem about the food shown that includes the fraction he was given. To solve the problem, he turns his paper over and cuts the remaining shape into equal-sized pieces. Then, in a manner similar to the one shown, he glues the pieces on the top half of the paper and circles and writes the answer.

To follow up, challenge students to describe ways in which they benefit from their knowledge of fractions. Perhaps sharing a package of animal crackers will enhance their thinking.

Cynthia Mackel—Grs. 1–2
Rosemont Elementary School
Baltimore, MD

I Spy!

Skill: computation

This math game sharpens computation skills and shows students a great way to pass time during a road trip! Two or more can play. Each player needs a notepad and pencil. To begin play, say, "I spy," followed by two numbers, their locations, and a math operation. For example, "I spy a 2 on the board and a 7 on the calendar. Multiply!" The first player to solve the problem says, "Solved!" Ask for this student's answer. If the answer is correct, say, "Correct! Your turn." The winning player then spies the numbers for the next round of play. If the answer is incorrect, say, "Sorry, the answer is 14. Let's play again!" and begin a new round. Play a few rounds. When students are familiar with the game, divide them into small groups and have each group continue play on its own.

When game time is over, challenge students to name places where numbers can be spied during a trip. Answers may include highway signs, mile markers, exit signs, and license plates.

Suggest that students pack pencils and notepads for their next family outing and teach their families how to play this numbers game!

Deborah Cox—Grs. 1–2
Lost River Elementary
Bowling Green, KY

Shop Around

Skills: rounding, mental math

Students are sure to take a shine to this shopping center! Stock a corner of the classroom with clean and nonbreakable food packaging. Label each item with a purchase price. (To create an awareness of the value of money, use realistic prices.) Place a plastic shopping basket and a calculator at the center. Also, post a laminated sign that reads "Today's spending allowance is" and use a wipe-off marker to program the sign with a desired amount of money.

A shopper attempts to load the basket with items that come close to, but do not exceed, the posted amount. To do this, she rounds each purchase price and mentally calculates the total price of the items in the basket. When she is finished shopping, she uses the calculator to find the exact sum of her purchases and to determine whether she met her goal. To increase the difficulty of the center, provide coupons that can be used on select items.

Encourage students who accompany their parents on shopping trips to ring up estimation and mental math skills all summer long!

Wendy Borsari and Jennifer Steinman—Gr. 3
Hillcrest Heights Elementary
Prince George's County, MD

Data collected by _____

	Monday	Tuesday	Wednesday	Thursday	Friday

0

Monday   **Tuesday**   **Wednesday**   **Thursday**   **Friday**

©The Education Center, Inc. • THE MAILBOX® • Primary • June/July 2002

Note to the teacher: Use with "Collecting Cool Info" on page 221.

SCIENCE UNITS

Our "Moo-velous" Moon!

There's no "cowing" around—these one-of-a-kind activities are just what you need for an enlightening investigation of the moon!

ideas contributed by Stacie Stone Davis—Grs. 2–6 Gifted and Talented, Bloomfield Central School, Bloomfield, NY, and Monica Shiba—Gr. 1, Indian Trail School, Highland Park, IL

Cow on the Moon?

For an "udder-ly" fantastic start to your moon investigation, read aloud Chris Babcock's amusing picture book *No Moon, No Milk!* Sandwiched within this silly story are enough moon-related facts to pique your youngsters' interest in the earth's closest neighbor in space. List on a length of bulletin board paper the moon facts that are mentioned in the story. Add to the list other facts students already know about the moon. Then blast off into your moon studies. If desired, keep adding moon facts to the posted list throughout your moon investigation. "Moo-velous!"

Facts About the Moon

The moon has craters.

There isn't any usable water on the moon.

There is an American flag there!

Earth and Moon in Motion

Help students visualize how the earth and the moon travel together in space with this enactment. For every three students, label a set of three large cards with the words "Sun," "Earth," and "Moon." (Label an extra set of cards for a partial group of students.) Randomly distribute the cards and have each child illustrate on his card the celestial body named. Next, have students bring their cards to an open area. Select three volunteers who collectively hold a set of cards. Position the sun performer and explain that like the real sun, he will not move. Have the child acting as the earth revolve very slowly around the sun and then have the moon impostor revolve around the moving earth. Explain that while it takes the earth about 365 days to orbit the sun, it takes the moon only about 27 days to orbit the earth. Then have the remaining students form groups and enact the cycle.

Another Moon Move

Investigating the moon's rotation brings to light another fascinating fact! Have each child color and cut out a copy of the earth and moon patterns from page 232. First, have each student use her cutouts to demonstrate how the moon *revolves,* or circles, the earth (as learned in "Earth and Moon in Motion" on page 226). Next, explain that as the moon circles the earth, it also *rotates,* or spins, one time. To demonstrate this, have each child position the moon cutout so that the arrow points toward the earth cutout. Then have her slowly move the moon around the earth, making sure the arrow always points toward the earth. By watching the word *Moon,* a student sees that the moon cutout rotates one time each time it circles the earth. This also uncovers another fascinating moon fact—the same side of the moon always faces the earth!

Lunar Landscape

What is there to see on the moon? Lots and lots of gray! There are no plants and animals because there is no air or usable water. So what are those light and dark patches on the moon's surface? The darker areas are flat, low plains (which were once thought to be seas), and the lighter areas are highlands or mountains. Painting a realistic-looking moon is sure to help a student remember these important facts!

To make his moon painting, a student wads a plastic fold-top sandwich bag and uses it to apply gray tempera paint to cover a seven-inch square of black paper. When the paint dries, he traces a large circle onto the painted paper, cuts along the resulting outline, and then glues his moon cutout onto a 9" x 12" sheet of black construction paper. Then he cuts tiny star shapes from scrap paper and glues them to the project. As students complete their pictures, point out that the moon is always surrounded by the blackness of space because it has no atmosphere.

Gravity Guide

Since the moon's gravity has only one-sixth the pull of the earth's gravity, objects weigh less on the moon. This works out well for an astronaut whose special suit and backpack can weigh close to 180 pounds! On the moon, the same suit and backpack weigh only 30 pounds! To help students better understand this difference in gravity, have them complete the "moo-velous" math challenge on page 230. Whether students complete the activity individually, with a partner, or as a class, they're sure to remember that there's less gravity on the moon than on the earth!

Predicting the Phases

Predicting the moon's phases doesn't take magical powers, just observation. And this nifty booklet is guaranteed to sharpen observation skills! Give each student a copy of page 231 and two 2½" x 3" rectangles of construction paper. Have each child color the moons, using the provided color code. Next, have him cut along the bold lines and stack the resulting pages in sequential order. Staple each child's pages between his construction paper rectangles and provide time for him to decorate and personalize his booklet cover.

Review the moon's phases with the class. Remind students that *waxing* means "appears to be growing" and *waning* means "appears to be shrinking." Then challenge each child to watch the moon closely during the next couple of months and enter in his booklet the dates he observes the phases. If desired, incorporate a moon report into your daily morning routine. Students will look forward to sharing their moon observations with the class as well as their phase predictions.

A Lunar Eclipse

Bring a lunar eclipse into focus with this easy-to-prepare demonstration.

Materials needed:
2 plastic straws
box lid
4" Styrofoam® ball (for the earth)

1" Styrofoam ball (for the moon)
clay
desk lamp with a flexible neck

What to do:
Secure two small lumps of clay atop the box lid so they align. Poke one end of each plastic straw into the center of a different Styrofoam ball and then poke each straw into a different lump of clay so that the two balls align. Next, align the lamp with the larger ball as shown. Turn on the lamp and turn off all other lights.

Explanation:

The lamp represents the sun, and the larger and smaller balls represent the earth and the moon, respectively. When the sun, the earth, and the moon form a direct line with the earth in the middle, the earth's shadow darkens the moon and a lunar eclipse occurs. From the earth, the moon's surface appears orangey red because for a short amount of time the sunlight that reaches the moon is passing through the earth's atmosphere. A lunar eclipse can last for more than an hour.

Even though the earth passes between the sun and the moon about once a month, a lunar eclipse only occurs about once or twice a year. In order for a lunar eclipse to occur, the sun, the earth, and the moon must line up exactly and the moon must be full.

Man on the Moon!

On July 20, 1969, *Apollo* astronaut Neil Armstrong became the first man to set foot on the moon. By the end of 1972, five more Apollo crews had landed there. These six missions resulted in 12 American astronauts exploring and photographing the moon!

Use this mapping project to show students where each Apollo crew landed. Have each child color a copy of the moon map and related cutouts from page 232. Suggest that she color the map gray, coloring heaviest on the flat plains (which were once thought to be seas). Then have her color the small circles a contrasting color. Next, share the information provided on this page. After describing a mission, instruct each child to cut out the corresponding circle. Then have her glue the cutout on the moon map where the mission landed. (The numbered circles shown on the map correspond to the order of the moon landings.)

Last, have each child cut out her completed map and mount it on an eight-inch square of black paper. To extend the activity, staple seven pages of writing paper and a back cover to the child's project. Instruct each student to title one page for each Apollo mission shown on the map, plus one page for the *Apollo 13* mission. Challenge each child to write two or more facts about each mission, conducting additional research as needed.

Apollo Moon Landings (With Crews)			
Mission	Date of Landing	Time on the Moon	Fact
Apollo 11	7/20/69	22 hours	Neil Armstrong was the first astronaut to set foot on the moon.
Apollo 12	11/19/69	32 hours	The crew recovers instruments put on the moon in April of 1967. Because of these instruments, the effects of long-term exposure to the moon's environment can now be measured.
Apollo 14	2/5/71	34 hours	One famous moment is when commander Alan Shepard hits two golf balls on the moon!
Apollo 15	7/30/71	67 hours	This is the first Apollo crew to use a lunar rover for transportation.
Apollo 16	4/21/72	71 hours	This crew is the first to land in and explore a highlands area.
Apollo 17	12/11/72	75 hours	This is the longest (and the last) stay on the moon to date.

Hannah

A Moon Community

Planning and creating a moon community is an ideal way for students to show off their moon-related knowledge! First, have students recall facts they've learned that are critical to planning a moon community. List these facts on the board. Next, write a student-generated list of possible moon-based businesses. Guide the class in determining what each child (or student pair) will contribute to the community. Then provide a variety of arts-and-crafts supplies and set aside ample time for students to make and label their contributions. To create an eye-catching backdrop for the community, cover a bulletin board with black paper and sponge-paint a gray moonlike landscape on the paper. When the paint is dry, mount the students' projects for all to see!

Moon Pie® Treats and Moonlight Punch

Wrap up your moon studies with a just-for-fun finale! Serve students Moon Pie® marshmallow sandwiches and moonlight punch (equal amounts of pineapple juice and ginger ale). To add to the fun, read aloud *Jimmy Zangwow's Out-of-This-World Moon Pie Adventure* by Tony DiTerlizzi. Students will find the picture book wildly entertaining, yet they'll be eager to tell you that this story could *never* really happen!

Cow on the Moon?

Finish the Gravity Conversion Chart.
Remember: 1 moon pound = 6 Earth pounds

Gravity Conversion Chart										
Moon Pounds	1	2	3	4	5	6	7	8	9	10
Earth Pounds	6									

Complete the table. Use the Gravity Conversion Chart.

Moon Supply Checklist	Pounds on the earth	Pounds on the moon
water	42	
grass	18	
oxygen	60	
camera	3	
rope	3	
first-aid kit	6	
cowbell	6	
flag	6	
backpack	36	
space boots	12	
space helmet	18	
space suit	24	

Problem to solve:
Elsie is applying for the next Amoollo Moon Mission.
With her supplies, she may not weigh more than 100
moon pounds. Elsie weighs 360 Earth pounds. Can
Elsie go to the moon?

Write your answer in the answer box.
On the back of this paper, write how you solved the problem.

Answer Box

©The Education Center, Inc. • THE MAILBOX® • Primary • Oct/Nov 2001 • Key p. 312

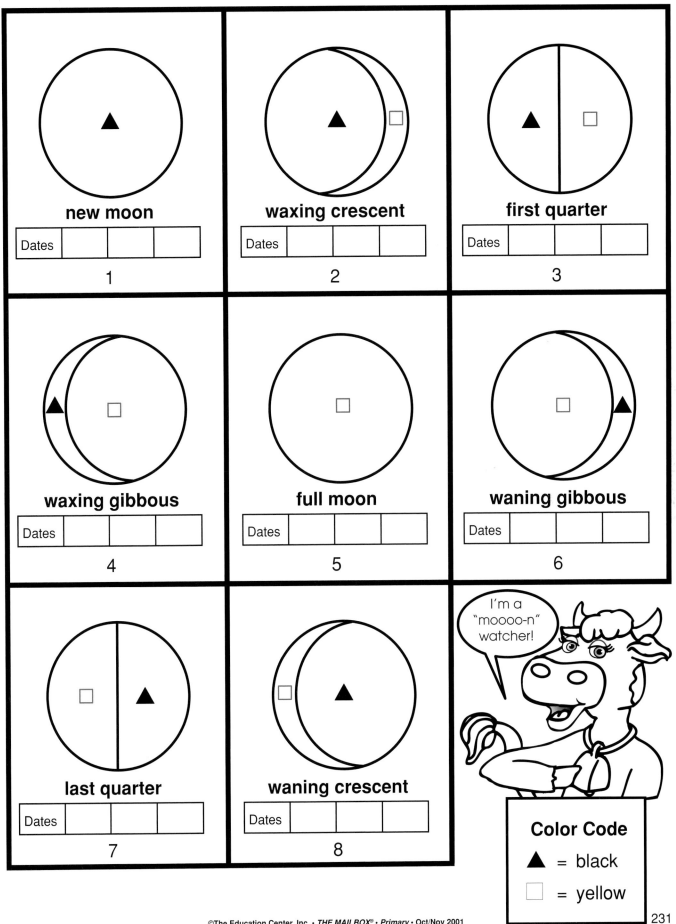

new moon

Dates

1

waxing crescent

Dates

2

first quarter

Dates

3

waxing gibbous

Dates

4

full moon

Dates

5

waning gibbous

Dates

6

last quarter

Dates

7

waning crescent

Dates

8

I'm a "moooo-n" watcher!

Color Code

▲ = black

☐ = yellow

©The Education Center, Inc. • THE MAILBOX® • Primary • Oct/Nov 2001

Patterns

Use with "Man on the Moon!" on page 229.

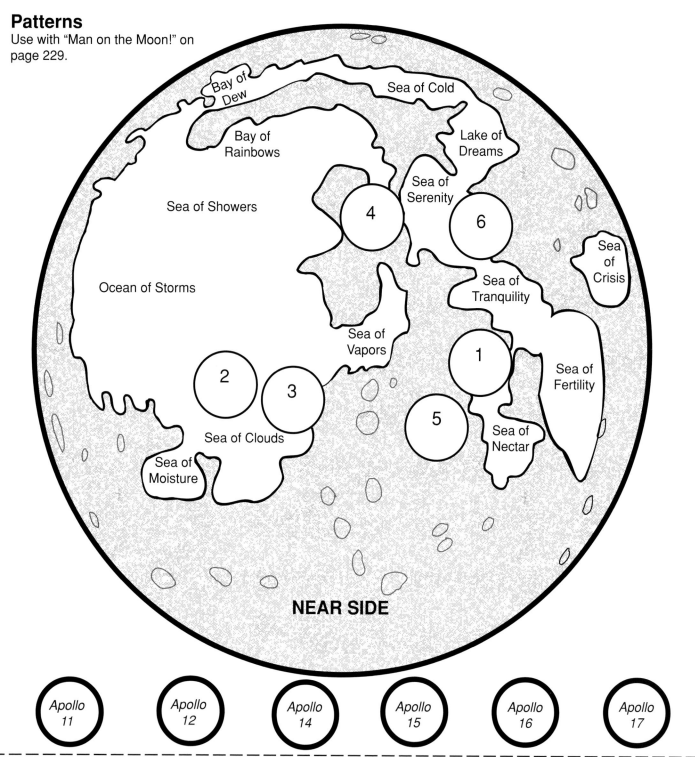

Bay of Dew

Sea of Cold

Bay of Rainbows

Lake of Dreams

Sea of Showers

Sea of Serenity

4

6

Ocean of Storms

Sea of Crisis

Sea of Tranquility

Sea of Vapors

1

Sea of Fertility

2

3

5

Sea of Clouds

Sea of Nectar

Sea of Moisture

NEAR SIDE

Apollo 11

Apollo 12

Apollo 14

Apollo 15

Apollo 16

Apollo 17

Use with "Another Moon Move" on page 227.

Earth

Moon

©The Education Center, Inc. • *THE MAILBOX®* • *Primary* • Oct/Nov 2001

Hear! Hear!
An Investigation of Sound

Keep students tuned in to sound with this collection of fun-to-use activities and reproducibles. In addition to being all ears, youngsters will be filled with good vibrations!

Sound Is All Around

What would the world be like without sound? It's hard to even imagine! Fine-tune your youngsters' awareness of sound with this small-group activity. In advance, cut out magazine pictures of different scenes, such as a city, grocery store, kitchen, freeway, and farm. Mount each picture on construction paper. Next, divide students into small groups. Give each group a picture, a sheet of chart paper, a marker, and five minutes to brainstorm a list of sounds that may be heard in the pictured setting. Then ask each group to share its list of sounds with the class and add to the list other sounds that are suggested. Display the group work on a bulletin board titled "Sound Is All Around!"

Ways I Count On Sound	Communication
	talking
	laughing
	ringing telephone
	footsteps
	running water
Danger Signals	**Enjoyment**
fire alarm	CDs
car horn	television
police siren	movies
scream	singing
thunder	radio

Counting On Sound

Sound—such as the buzz of an alarm clock, the ring of a doorbell, or the slam of a door—provides oodles of information. This activity strengthens students' awareness of different ways they count on sound. Have each student visually divide a sheet of drawing paper into fourths and label the sections of her paper with the title and headings shown. Explain that each heading describes one way in which people depend on sound. Then have each student list under each heading examples of how she relies on sound.

To extend the activity, reveal that animals count on sound, too. Then challenge each child to describe on the back of her paper ways in which sound informs animals.

233

Vibrating Matter

A riddle can help students discover (and remember!) that sound is made from vibrations! Ask the class, "What's made when something that takes up space and has weight vibrates?" To solve the riddle, give each child a three-inch-square sticky note. Instruct him to grasp one corner of the paper and use short, back-and-forth movements to quickly move the paper through the air. Students will see and hear firsthand that sound is the answer!

Sound Waves

Nurture an understanding of how sound travels with this enactment! First, explain that when an object vibrates, the air around the object is pushed outward in all directions. This pushed air pushes against air that is a little farther away from the object, which then pushes against more air, and so on. When pushed air enters the ear, the brain hears sound. This air motion between a vibrating object and an ear is called a *sound wave*.

To enact a sound wave, divide the class into small groups and have each group line up single file. Explain that the first child in each line is an ear. Then give each ear a bell. To start a sound wave, the child at the end of the line blows a puff of air on the neck of the person in front of her. When a child feels the air, she repeats the action. When an ear receives the pushed air, she rings her bell to signal that the sound wave has signaled the brain! Repeat the enactment, each time rotating the ear to the back of the line, until every youngster has enacted the ear. For a quick assessment, have each child describe on paper how sound travels. Challenge older students to also explain why covering one's ears makes sound more difficult to hear.

An Earful

Ears can't turn sound waves into sound single-handedly. To reveal what helps the ears make sound, have students complete the reproducible activity on page 236.

Sound Alert!

Students may be surprised to discover that even though they have excellent hearing, they do not hear all sounds. Humans have a range of hearing and so do dogs, bats, and many other types of animals. What does this mean? It means that a dog can hear sounds that a human cannot, and a human can hear sounds that a cat cannot. Use the reproducible on page 237 to further investigate this intriguing topic!

Tracking the Waves

Sound waves are amazing! Use these mini experiments to show students that sound waves can travel through air, water, and solids. Ask each child to write a sound-related observation at the conclusion of each activity. Then, when all three activities have been completed, invite students to use their observations to draw conclusions about sound. Refer to "This is why" to provide additional information about how sound travels.

Through air: Position students in two rows so that each child faces a partner in the opposite row. Have each pair choose a password that they will alternate whispering upon your signal. Give the signal. Every few seconds instruct each child who heard his partner's whisper to take one step backward. When several students are no longer stepping backward, stop the game.

Through water and a solid: Hold a sealed freezer bag of water parallel to a child's ear. Tap the opposite side of the water-filled bag. Then have the child press her ear against the bag. Repeat the motion. Repeat the process with each child.

Through a solid: Have each child gently tap or scratch the top of his desk. Then have him press one ear atop his desktop and repeat the motion.

This is why: Gases, liquids, and solids are all conductors of sound waves. However, the speed at which sound waves pass through the materials differs. Sound waves move from particle to particle. Because particles in solids are more tightly packed than particles in liquids and gases, sounds travel more quickly through solids. This means the sounds made from tapping or scratching a desk reach the ear more quickly (and sound louder) when the ear is pressed against the desktop. Sounds travel through liquids more quickly than gases because particles in liquids are more tightly packed than particles in gases.

Making Music

Wrap up your study of sound by making music! After all, without sound there would be no music! First, assist each child in placing a rubber band lengthwise on a flat ruler. Then, at each end of the ruler, have him slide a pencil beneath the rubber band as shown. Direct students to strum the raised band (between the pencils) and listen to the sound made. Next, have students slide the pencils closer together and strum the rubber band. Ask students if the sound produced is higher or lower (higher). Allow time for students to investigate the different sounds they can make using their specialized rulers. Lead students to conclude that they can make the sound higher and lower by adjusting the distance between the two pencils.

For a fun finale, divide students into small groups. Challenge the members of each group to create and later perform for their peers a musical presentation!

An Earful of Information

How much do you know about your ears? Touch one ear. What you feel is your <u>outer ear</u>. Its job is to guide sound <u>waves</u> inside your ear. These sound waves travel down a <u>canal</u>. The canal leads to your <u>eardrum</u>. When a sound wave hits your eardrum, your eardrum vibrates. This vibration makes three tiny bones vibrate in your <u>middle ear</u>. The vibrating bones make the liquid inside your <u>inner ear</u> ripple! And that sends <u>signals</u> to your <u>brain</u>. Your brain sorts the signals, and you hear sound!

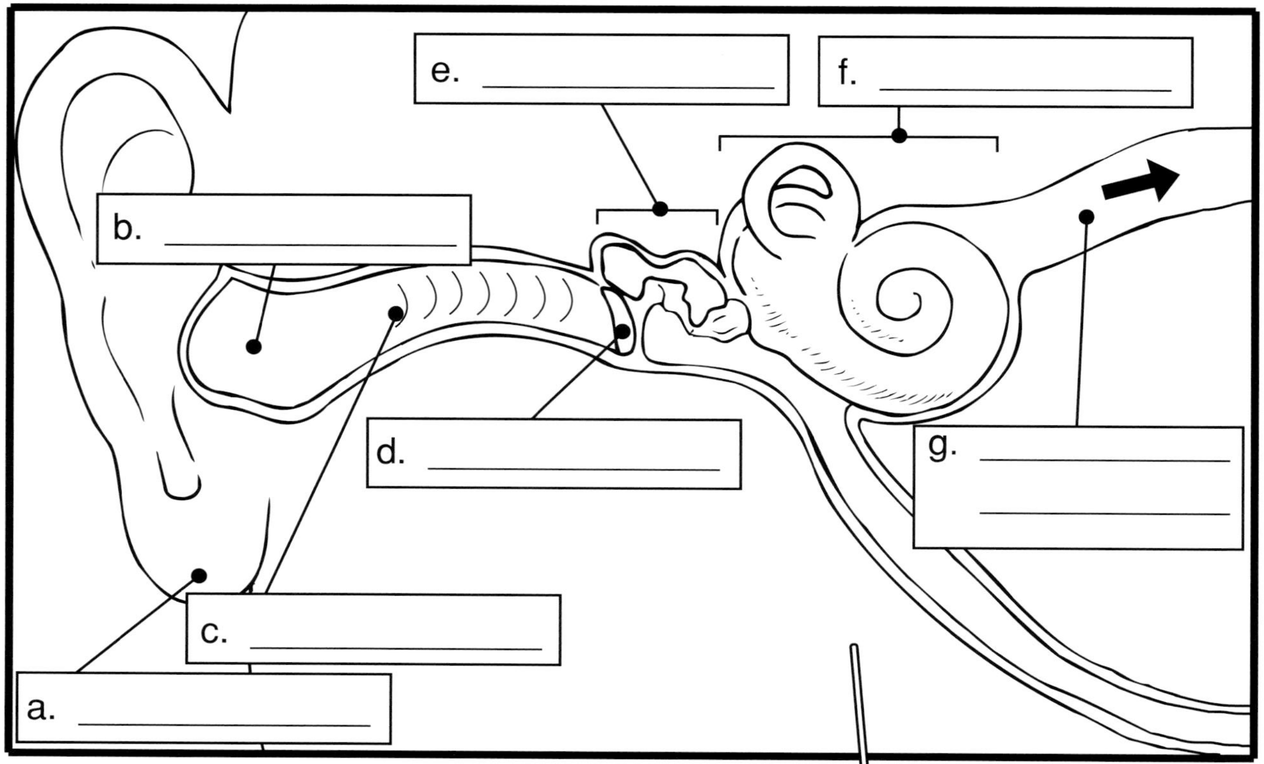

e. _____

f. _____

g. _____

b. _____

d. _____

c. _____

a. _____

1. Label the drawing.
Use the underlined words in the passage.

2. Complete the sentences.
One of my favorite sounds to hear is _____
I like this sound because _____
One of my least favorite sounds to hear is _____
I do not like this sound because _____

Bonus Box: On the back of this paper, write two tips for taking good care of your ears.

©The Education Center, Inc. • *THE MAILBOX*® • *Primary* • Dec/Jan 2001–2 • Key p. 312

Note to the teacher: Use with "An Earful" on page 234.

Sound Alert!

Did you know that you do not hear all sounds?
It's true! Humans only hear sounds within a certain *frequency,* or range.
The same is true for other animals!

Frequency is the number of sound waves that a vibration makes in one second!

Frequency Chart		
Animal	Lowest frequency heard	Highest frequency heard
bat	1000	120,000
cat	60	65,000
dog	15	50,000
dolphin	150	150,000
grasshopper	100	15,000
human	20	20,000
robin	250	21,000

Use the chart to answer the questions.
Remember! The slower the frequency, the lower the sound.

1. Which animal hears the lowest sounds? _____

2. Which animal hears the highest sounds? _____

3. Which animal hears lower sounds than a human? _____

4. Which animal hears the smallest range of sound? _____

5. Can a human hear sounds that a cat cannot? _____

6. Can a cat hear sounds that a human cannot? _____

7. The frequency of human speech is 100 to 400 vibrations per second.

   a. Which animal cannot hear any human speech? _____

   b. Which two animals hear only part of human speech? _____

8. Can a human hear more or less sounds than a robin? _____

Bonus Box: Which animal hears the largest range of sound? Write your answer on the back of this paper. Then explain how you got your answer.

©The Education Center, Inc. • THE MAILBOX® • Primary • Dec/Jan 2001–2 • Key p. 312

Note to the teacher: Use with "Sound Alert!" on page 234.

237

Open Wide!

An Inside Look at Animal Teeth

Incisors, canines, premolars, and molars—animals other than humans have them too! Use the kid-pleasing activities and reproducibles that follow to investigate some *very* impressive teeth!

contributions by Erin Harp, Lewisville, NC

"Tooth" or False?

Generate enthusiasm for a study of animal teeth with a just-for-fun "tooth" or false quiz. Have each child fold a sheet of writing paper in half lengthwise, write his name and date at the top of the folded paper, and number the paper from 1 to 6. Read aloud the six statements about animal teeth provided below. Instruct each child to draw a tooth if he thinks a statement is true and write "F" if he thinks it is false. Collect the completed papers. Tell students that during their study of animal teeth they will learn whether these statements are true or false. Promise to let them retake the quiz at the conclusion of the study (on the remaining halves of their papers). Your students will be all smiles!

"Tooth" or False Quiz
1. All animals grow two sets of teeth. *(F)*
2. Some animals have teeth that never stop growing. *(T)*
3. Animals must have teeth in order to eat. *(F)*
4. An elephant tusk is really a tooth. *(T)*
5. The larger the animal, the more teeth it has. *(F)*
6. Animals use their teeth only to eat. *(F)*

Take a Bite!

A knowledge of tooth terms is a must for investigating animal teeth. For a tasty review of the terms, serve each child two apple slices and a portion of popped corn. On the board list the four types of teeth (incisor, canine, premolar, and molar). Then, as students eat the snack you've provided, have them describe how these teeth help them eat. Lead students to conclude that incisors are for biting into food, canines are for biting and tearing food, and premolars and molars are for crushing and grinding food.

Explain that other animals have these kinds of teeth, too; however, their teeth may be specially adapted for their specific eating habits. For example, because a sheep eats only plants, it has very small incisors and canines and very large and flat premolars and molars (for grinding). A beaver, on the other hand, has four very large incisors for gnawing on trees and roots, premolars and molars for chewing, and no canines at all. Can the shape of an animal's teeth give you clues about its eating habits? You bet!

Tooth Tally

How many teeth do animals have? Unlike adult humans who can expect a set of 32 pearly whites, animal tooth counts greatly vary. An anteater has no teeth! It doesn't need them. An elephant has two curved incisors (tusks) plus a set of four molars. Each molar measures about one foot and will be replaced five times during the normal lifespan of an elephant. In contrast, a great white shark has row after row of teeth that grow continually. One great white may lose thousands of teeth in its lifetime, but it is never without teeth! Students are sure to enjoy tallying and graphing the tooth counts of the ten animals featured on page 241. Remind students that when an animal depends on its teeth for food, every tooth counts!

That's a Tooth?

Animal teeth are a variety of shapes and sizes; however, the size and shape of some teeth are a bit of a surprise! Students may not realize that the tusks of a walrus are actually extra long canine teeth. Or that an elephant's tusks are long, curved incisor teeth. The fang of a snake is another unique type of tooth. These super sharp teeth can be hollow and connected to poison-producing glands!

Turn a bulletin board into a museum of teeth. Post the title "Tooth Gallery." Nearby, furnish an assortment of books that include information about animals and their teeth. Invite each student to write and illustrate on provided paper an intriguing tooth-related fact. To avoid duplication, keep a running list of the animals whose teeth are featured at the display. Very interesting!

Now showcasing...
great white shark
gila monster
rattlesnake
tarantula
narwhal
walrus
crocodile
sawfish
snail
rhinoceros
piranha
baboon

Teeth as Tools

It's a fact that teeth and food go together! Humans and other animals use teeth to bite, tear, crunch, and grind food. Most animals in the wild must also catch their food, and for this their teeth come in very handy! Some animals have other uses for their teeth, too.

To introduce students to a few unique tasks for which animals use their teeth, give each child a copy of the booklet project on pages 242 and 243. First, ask each child to color and cut out the pictures on his copy of page 242. Next, instruct him to carefully read the descriptions on the booklet pages and glue the corresponding pictures in the boxes. When the pictures are in place, the student completes the booklet cover. Then he cuts out the booklet cover and pages, stacks the pages under the cover, and staples his booklet together. Be sure to remind students that even though animals have found additional uses for their teeth, human teeth are still to be used just for eating!

squirrel

I gnaw open nutshells with my front teeth.

A Daily Grind

Here's a dental problem that students should never face! Explain that rodents—such as chipmunks, squirrels, and beavers—have teeth that never stop growing. Most often the growth isn't a concern because a rodent's continual gnawing grinds down its teeth. However, if for some reason a rodent stopped gnawing, its teeth could grow and grow and grow until its jaw no longer worked properly.

Remind students of a rodent's ever-growing teeth and provide a fun review of basic facts with the "Busy Beaver" project on this page! Chomp, chomp!

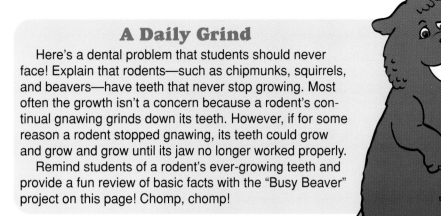

The Last Bite

You can count on students sinking their teeth into this culminating review of animal teeth! Instruct each child to write (and answer) a tooth-related question that she thinks will stump her classmates. When her question and answer are approved by you, she cuts out a tooth shape from a 9" x 12" sheet of white construction paper. She writes her question on one side of the cutout and its corresponding answer and her name on the opposite side. Then she drops the prepared cutout into a designated container.

To begin a review session, select a volunteer to remove a cutout from the tooth-filled container. Read the question aloud for students (other than the author) to answer. If the question is answered correctly, it is placed in a discard pile. If the question goes unanswered, it is returned to the container. Continue in the manner described for an allotted amount of time. Schedule a short review session on each of several days until all questions are correctly answered!

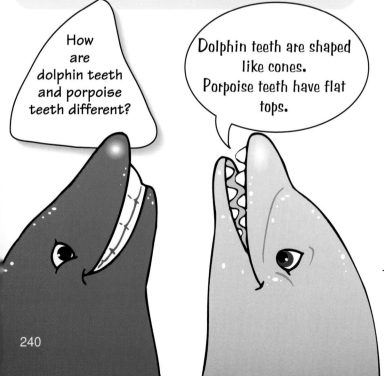

> How are dolphin teeth and porpoise teeth different?

> Dolphin teeth are shaped like cones. Porpoise teeth have flat tops.

Busy Beaver

Materials for one project:
$4^{1}/_{2}$" x 12" strip of brown construction paper
1" x 3" strip of black construction paper (for whiskers)
2" x 12" strip of white paper
glue
scissors
ruler
pencil
crayons or markers

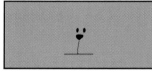

Step 2

Steps:

1. Gently fold the brown paper in half (to $4^{1}/_{2}$" x 6"). On the fold, make a $1^{1}/_{2}$-inch cut about one inch from the bottom of the paper.
2. Unfold the paper. Above the opening draw two eyes, a nose, and a line that connects the nose to the opening.
3. Keeping the drawing to the outside, roll the brown paper into a cylinder and glue the overlapping edges.
4. Position the seam at the back of the project and glue the top one inch of the cylinder closed.
5. When the glue dries, trim the top of the cylinder to resemble the shape of a beaver head.
6. Glue two ears (cut from scrap paper) and several whiskers (cut from black paper) in place.
7. Use a ruler and a pencil to draw a line down the center (lengthwise) of the white paper strip. Cut away the bottom corners of the strip. Write five challenging math facts on the left half of the strip. Write the inverse of each fact on the right half of the strip as shown.
8. Roll the paper strip from the top to the bottom, keeping the programming to the outside.
9. Poke the rolled paper inside the project and carefully thread the paper through the opening until a pair of math facts appears.
10. Each day "grow" a new pair of math facts and "grind off" (cut away) the old pair. On the fifth day, repeat Steps 7–9 to prepare another 2" x 12" strip of math review.

Step 4

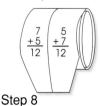

Step 8

Name_____

Tooth Tally

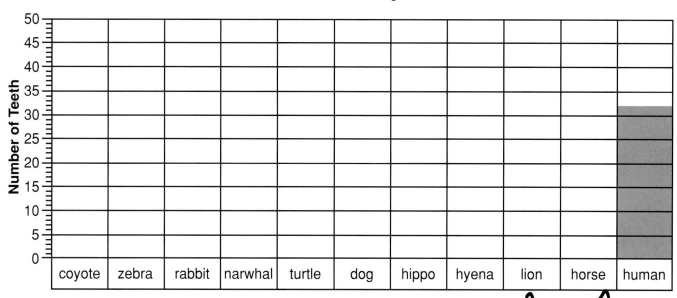

	coyote	zebra	rabbit	narwhal	turtle	dog	hippo	hyena	lion	horse	human

Number of Teeth (y-axis: 0, 5, 10, 15, 20, 25, 30, 35, 40, 45, 50)

Use the tally marks below.
On the graph show how many teeth each animal has.
Then use the graph to answer the questions.

1. How many animals on the graph have more teeth than a human? _____

2. Which animal on the graph has the most teeth? _____

3. How many animals on the graph have fewer than 20 teeth? _____

4. Which animal has the same number of teeth as a dog? _____

5. Which animal has the same number of teeth as a horse? _____

6. Does a hyena have more teeth or fewer teeth than a rabbit? _____

7. Which animal has more teeth: a lion or a rabbit? _____

8. Which animal has more teeth: a lion or a hippo? _____

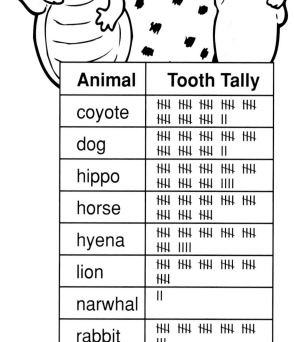

Animal	Tooth Tally
coyote	ЖЖ ЖЖ ЖЖ ЖЖ ЖЖ ЖЖ ЖЖ ЖЖ II
dog	ЖЖ ЖЖ ЖЖ ЖЖ ЖЖ ЖЖ ЖЖ ЖЖ II
hippo	ЖЖ ЖЖ ЖЖ ЖЖ ЖЖ ЖЖ ЖЖ ЖЖ IIII
horse	ЖЖ ЖЖ ЖЖ ЖЖ ЖЖ ЖЖ ЖЖ ЖЖ
hyena	ЖЖ ЖЖ ЖЖ ЖЖ ЖЖ ЖЖ IIII
lion	ЖЖ ЖЖ ЖЖ ЖЖ ЖЖ ЖЖ
narwhal	II
rabbit	ЖЖ ЖЖ ЖЖ ЖЖ ЖЖ III
turtle	
zebra	ЖЖ ЖЖ ЖЖ ЖЖ ЖЖ ЖЖ ЖЖ ЖЖ

Bonus Box: Do you think the number of teeth an animal has is related to its size? Write your answer on the back of this paper. Then write one or more sentences to explain your reasoning.

©The Education Center, Inc. • THE MAILBOX® • Primary • Feb/Mar 2002 • Key p. 313

Booklet Project

Name _____

**Teeth
as
Tools**

©2002 The Education Center, Inc.

I use my tusks to move fallen trees and dig for water.

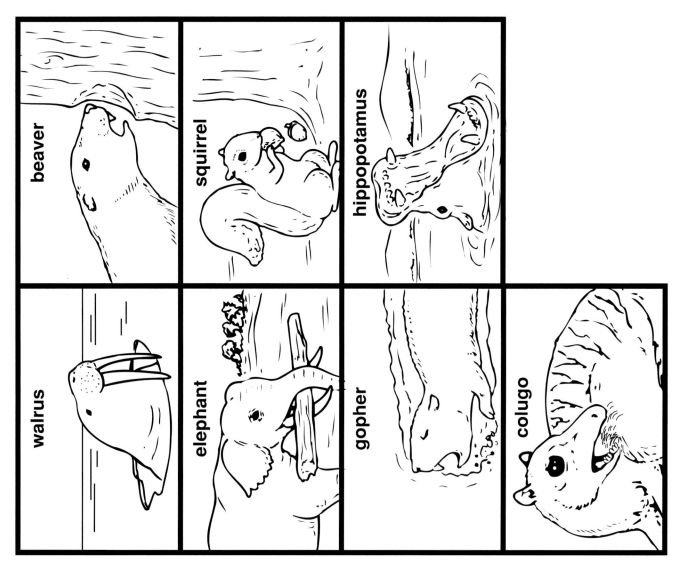

beaver

squirrel

hippopotamus

walrus

elephant

gopher

colugo

©The Education Center, Inc. • *THE MAILBOX*® • *Primary* • Feb/Mar 2002 • Key p. 312

Note to the teacher: Use with "Teeth as Tools" on page 239.

I use my tusks as hooks when I climb out of the water and onto ice.

My long front teeth help me dig underground tunnels.

My teeth are shaped like small combs. I use them for grooming!

I use my sharp front teeth to cut down trees!

I gnaw open nutshells with my front teeth.

I yawn and show off my sharp canine teeth to scare away a rival.

©The Education Center, Inc. • *THE MAILBOX®* • *Primary* • Feb/Mar 2002 • Key p. 312

Note to the teacher: Use with "Teeth as Tools" on page 239.

The Ocean
A Giant Web of Life

Make a splash with this unique underwater exploration of ocean life!

contributions by Monica Shiba—
Gr. 1, Indian Trail School, Highland Park, IL

The Blue Planet

Before diving into a study of ocean life, help students discover that oceans cover more than half (about 71%) of the earth. Have each child color a copy of the map on page 246 using the provided key. Then ask her to study the map and cast her vote for one of the following: there is more land than ocean, there is more ocean than land, there is an equal amount of land and ocean.

To learn the answer, pair students and give every twosome several blue and several green one-inch squares of paper. A pair sets aside one map and covers its remaining map with paper squares placed end to end. Students use blue squares to cover blue areas and green squares to cover green areas. When an area is both green and blue, they choose the most prevalent color. Collect extra paper squares. Students use their data to compare the earth's land and oceans (by counting each color of paper squares or matching unlike squares) and then each child completes her copy of page 246. No wonder Earth is called the blue planet!

Jo Massaro—Gr. 1
Howland Glen School
Warren, OH

Home to Many

Oceans teem with life! Reveal that the oceans of the world are home to zillions of living things that range in size from teeny tiny plants and animals called *plankton* to colossal blue whales. Have students name and describe plants and animals that live in the ocean. List their suggestions on two lengths of bulletin board paper, one titled "Plants" and the other "Animals." Keep the lists on display and add to them throughout your study. Tell students that because the earth's oceans are so massive, scientists continue to discover new forms of ocean life!

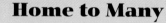

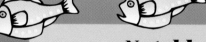

Notable Nonfiction

These fine nonfiction books are sure to create a wave of interest in oceans and ocean life!

What Makes an Ocean Wave?
Questions and Answers About Oceans and Ocean Life
Written by Melvin and Gilda Berger
Illustrated by John Rice

Exploring the Deep, Dark Sea
Written & illustrated by Gail Gibbons

Living in a World of Blue
Where Survival Means Blending In
Written by Tanya Lee Stone

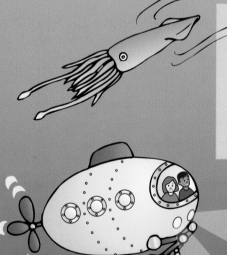

Under the Sea

What lies beneath the sea may surprise students! Introduce four ocean zones and a few critters that live in each one with this booklet activity. Give each child the following construction paper: 12" x 18" sheet of white and five 4" x 12" strips (two black, one brown, one dark blue, and one light blue). A student glues a black strip along the bottom of the white paper. She fashions an ocean floor from the brown paper and glues it on the black paper as shown. Directly above the black strip, she glues the second black strip, followed by the dark blue strip. She scallops the light blue strip and glues it above the dark blue one. Then she folds the project in half to 6" x 18", makes three cuts as shown, and titles the resulting booklet "Ocean Zones."

Make a class supply of page 247 and cut the papers along the dotted lines. To introduce an ocean zone, hand out the corresponding portion of page 247 and share the information from "Ocean Zones." Invite a student to integrate her handout into her work as she decorates the corresponding booklet flap with animals and then names and describes the ocean zone inside. (Clarify that some creatures, such as the squid, swim in more than one zone.) Now that's an in-depth look under the sea!

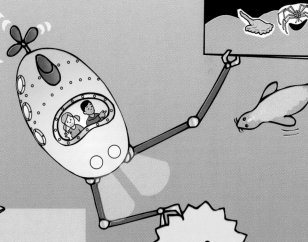

The Dark Zone

This part of the ocean is very dark. It is too deep for the sun to reach. The critters that live here are scary!

Ocean Zones

The Sunlight Zone: This is the shallowest zone and is home to almost 90 percent of all ocean life! It is the only zone fully lit by the sun. Plants and animals thrive here.

The Twilight Zone: Very little sunlight reaches this zone. No plants grow here. Some sea creatures living in this dark zone have special organs that glow in the dark.

The Dark Zone: This zone receives no sunlight and is pitch-dark. Ocean life is very scarce. Some animals living here are skillful hunters. Others are scavengers.

The Abyss: Very few animals live in this deep and dark zone. The water is extremely cold, and food is very scarce.

Finding Food

Investigate the ocean's food chain with this paper chain project! First, have each child trim an eight-inch yellow construction paper circle into a sun shape. Then have him use eight 1¹/₂" x 9" strips of blue construction paper to make a paper chain, using the final strip to connect the chain to the sun cutout. Explain that food links the plants and animals of the ocean. Ocean plants are fed by the sun. Certain ocean animals eat the plants. Other ocean animals eat smaller plant-eating animals and larger ocean animals eat them!

On the board, diagram a simple ocean food chain that features the sun, a plant, a plant eater, and two meat eaters. To complete his project, a student illustrates a similar ocean food chain on four 2" x 3" white paper rectangles and then glues his illustrations to his project to show the pattern of eating.

Toni DeToro—Gr. 3, Milwaukee, WI

A Saltwater System

Your budding oceanographers are sure to recognize that the ocean is a system. Remind students that within a system there is order. As a class talk about what happens when this order is disturbed. Ask students to name actions that cause disorder in the earth's oceans, such as oil spills, garbage dumping, and overfishing. Lead students to conclude that everyone must take responsibility for preserving the world's oceans and ocean life. To recap the value of oceans and the care they must be given, have each child complete the activity on page 248.

Ocean Life
Mapping skills

Oceans of the Earth

Color the map.
Use the map key.

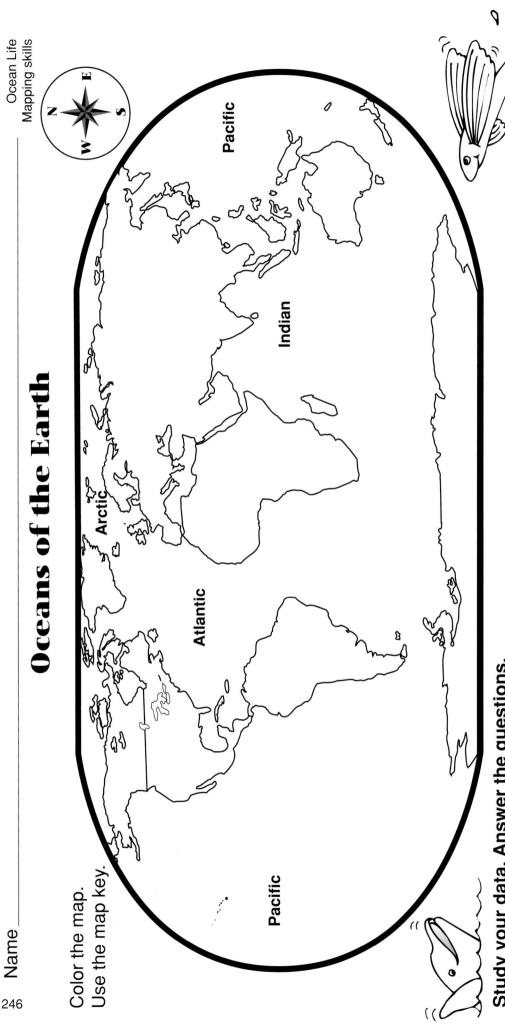

Map Key
land = green
water = blue

Pacific

Indian

Arctic

Atlantic

Pacific

Study your data. Answer the questions.

1. What have you learned about Earth? _____

2. Do you think "blue planet" is a good nickname for Earth? Why or why not? _____

Note to the teacher: Use with "The Blue Planet" on page 244.

The Sunlight Zone

plankton

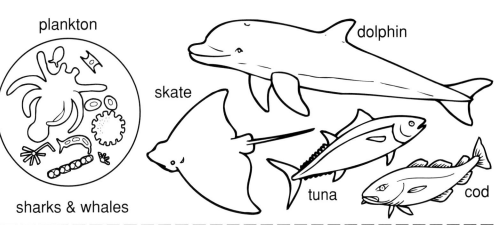

sharks & whales

dolphin

skate

tuna

cod

The Twilight Zone

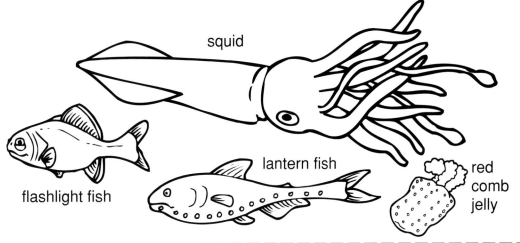

squid

flashlight fish

lantern fish

red comb jelly

The Dark Zone

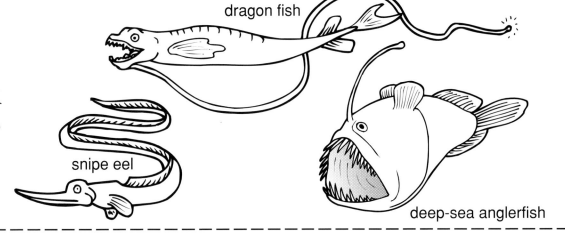

dragon fish

snipe eel

deep-sea anglerfish

The Abyss

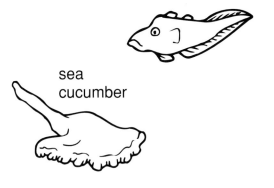

rattail

sea cucumber

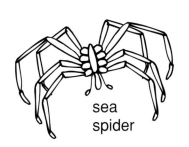

sea spider

©The Education Center, Inc. • THE MAILBOX® • Primary • June/July 2002

Name _____

Ocean Life
Conservation

Awesome Oceans

One word in each sentence is wrong.
Cross out the word that does not belong.
Find the correct word in the word bank.
Write it above the crossed out word.

1. Oceans heat the earth.

2. Fertilizer is helpful to oceans.

3. It is important to keep seawater polluted.

4. Oceans are a source of helpful wood.

5. Oceans provide pets for people who work.

6. Oceans supply candy to eat.

7. Never put sardines in the ocean.

8. The sun is boring to the ocean.

9. Reptiles must take better care of the oceans.

10. Oceans belong to nobody.

11. Oceans make fog to breathe.

12. Always dump garbage in the ocean.

Word Bank

seafood	clean	cool	jobs
everybody	oxygen	Never	People
medicine	harmful	important	chemicals

Bonus Box: On the back of this paper, list three reasons you think oceans are totally awesome!

©The Education Center, Inc. • THE MAILBOX® • Primary • June/July 2002 • Key p. 312

248   **Note to the teacher:** Use with "A Saltwater System" on page 245.

Reptiles Rule!

It may not be love at first sight, but reptiles have much more to offer than just their looks! Use this batch of activities, and students are sure to warm right up to these captivating, cold-blooded critters.

ideas by Starin Lewis, Kyrene School District, Tempe, AZ

The Fabulous Four

Begin your reptile study with an investigation of the four main groups of reptiles: crocodilians, snakes and lizards, turtles and tortoises, and tuataras. Gather books about reptiles, making sure photographs of each group are included. Also have students make field journals for the investigation. To do this, a child tightly crumples a 12" x 18" sheet of tan construction paper and then flattens the paper to give it a leatherlike appearance. Then she folds the paper in half (to 9" x 12"), titles the front cover "[student name]'s Reptile Journal," and staples five sheets of blank paper inside.

Tell students that reptiles can be divided into four groups. Use the information in "Types of Reptiles" and the resources you've gathered to introduce each reptile group. After each introduction, a child titles a journal page for the reptile group, lists one or more facts about the group, and then illustrates one group member. Have each child title her fifth journal page "Extinct" and illustrate on this page one reptile that no longer roams the earth. Urge students to add more illustrations to their journals by further investigating reptiles.

Types of Reptiles

Snakes and lizards make up the largest reptile group. These reptiles have long bodies. Many have large mouths and forked or notched tongues.

Turtles and tortoises are the only reptiles with shells. They do not have teeth! Tortoises live on land. Turtles live in or near water.

Crocodilians, such as alligators and crocodiles, are very large reptiles. They have long toothy snouts and powerful tails. Crocodilians live both in water and on land.

The tuatara looks somewhat like a lizard, but it is more closely related to its extinct dinosaur relatives. It is only found on islands near New Zealand!

Coil Up With a Reptile Book!

A chameleon's tongue can be as long as its body!

It's a Fact!

This eye-catching bulletin board inspires students to find fascinating facts about reptiles! Post the title and a cutout of a snake's head (pattern on page 253). Nearby provide several nonfiction books about reptiles and a supply of blank cards. When a student reads an intriguing reptile fact, he carefully copies it on a blank card. On the back of the card he writes the source and his name. Set aside time each day for students to share with the class the facts they've found. Then post the fact cards on the display so that the snake's body takes shape. By the time your reptile unit is winding down, the snake will be a record-breaking length!

249

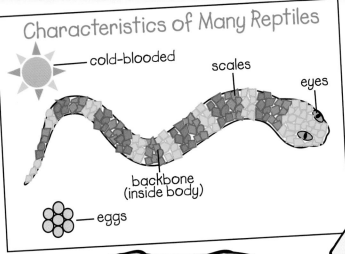

Characteristics of Many Reptiles

cold-blooded

scales

eyes

backbone
(inside body)

eggs

All in the Family

Students may wonder why scientists put animals that look so different in the reptile group! Here's a fun way to reveal traits that most reptiles share. First, make a copy of page 254, cut between the two patterns, and then copy each pattern onto a sheet of 9" x 12" paper so that you have one pattern for each child. Have each child title his paper "Characteristics of Many Reptiles." Then introduce the following characteristics:

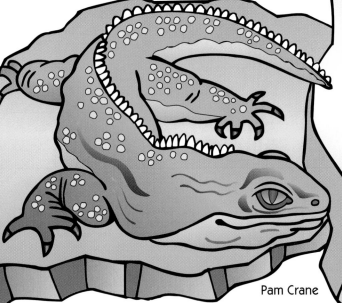

Pam Crane

Backbone: Ask each child to feel his backbone. Explain that like a human, a reptile has a bony skeleton that is supported by a backbone. Direct each child to sketch a backbone the length of his reptile and label it as shown.

Cold-blooded: Instruct each child to draw and color a sun near the top of his paper, write "cold-blooded" nearby, and draw a line that connects the two. Explain that reptiles cannot produce any body heat. This means to warm up, a reptile seeks sun. To cool down, it seeks shade.

Scales: All reptiles have scaly skin. The size and strength of scales vary. Give students access to construction paper scraps and glue. Instruct each child to cover his reptile's body with small, overlapping construction paper scales. Then have him label the scales.

Eyes: Most reptiles see well. The eyes of a reptile are set so that it can see into the distance. If a reptile wants to look at something close by, it uses muscles around its eyes to refocus its vision. Have each child color and label the eyes on his reptile.

Eggs: Most reptiles hatch from eggs. Ask each child to draw, color, and label a clutch of eggs near his reptile.

On the Move!

Because reptiles are different sizes and shapes, they move differently. Students will thoroughly enjoy trying out some reptile moves! Plan ahead for this activity by asking students to wear, on a specific school day, casual clothing for crawling around. On the day of the activity, spread out tumbling mats (or something similar) in an open area and have students get down on all fours. To begin, explain that tortoises move very slowly, typically taking just one step every two seconds. Help students practice this walk by clapping your hands together every two seconds. Next, tell students that because the four legs of a lizard are on the sides of its body, its feet are very far apart. This means the lizard has to bend its body from side to side to walk or run. Direct students to try out this movement for short distances, first walking slowly and then walking quickly.

Trying out snake moves comes next! First, have students lie on their bellies and try to move forward without using their arms and legs. Explain that some snakes use their scales and muscles to creep along the ground in this manner. Next, reveal that some snakes move by bunching up their bodies and then extending themselves forward. Have students try this method of movement. Also direct students to move like a wave atop the ground—another snake move. Last, challenge students to move like a sidewinder. This snake lifts its head and throws its body sideways! Then have your reptile copycats take a rest.

What's for Dinner?

What do reptiles eat? During this activity students discover that most reptiles eat other animals. In advance, copy each provided list (including the title) on individual index cards. For easy management, use a different color of pen or card for each reptile group. To begin, divide the class into four groups and give each group a set of cards. First, have each group discard from its card set any food not found in the reptiles' natural environment. Next, have each group sort its remaining cards by animals and plants. Ask each group to share its findings. Then explain that while most reptiles eat only meat, there are some lizards and turtles that eat mainly plants.

To further investigate reptile eating habits, have each group tape its word cards on a sheet of poster board. Display the posters, explaining that each is a sampling of foods eaten by the reptile group named. Help students identify which foods are shown on all four posters. To encourage additional thinking, share an observation and a related question. For example, you may say, "I notice that the tuatara doesn't have fish on its poster. Why might that be?" or "I wonder why insects are not shown on the poster for alligators and crocodiles." Now that's food for thought!

Snakes and Lizards	Alligators and Crocodiles
rats	birds
earthworms	ice cream
frogs	snails
popcorn	crabs
fish	peanut butter
birds	fish
pizza	frogs
bats	snakes
insects	turtles
spiders	wild hogs
plants	

Turtles and Tortoises	Tuatara
french fries	onion rings
fish	insects
insects	seabird eggs
frogs	birds
corn dogs	earthworms
snakes	chocolate cake
birds	snails
apple pie	waffles
plants	lizards
worms	frogs
snails	

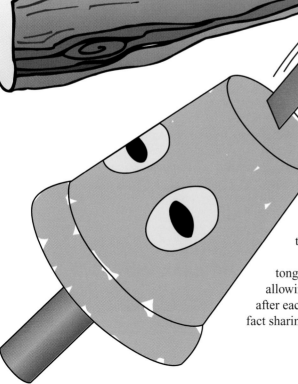

Amazing Tongues

Certain reptiles use their tongues in amazing ways! Some geckos use their tongues to clean off their eyes. A chameleon uses its amazingly long tongue to catch and taste unsuspecting insects. Encourage students to learn more about reptile tongues by pairing this puppet-making project with a fact-finding mission! To make his puppet, a child uses crayons or markers to color the sides and bottom of a Styrofoam cup green or brown and to draw and color two eyes as shown. Next, help each child poke the plastic end of a red or pink blowout party favor through the bottom of his decorated cup. Pull the favor through the cup until the paper portion is flush with the cup bottom.

Explain to students that they may operate their puppets whenever a tongue-related reptile fact is presented to the class. Share a few such facts, allowing students to blow on the party favor (unleashing the puppet's tongue) after each one. Challenge students to uncover more facts, and designate a time for fact sharing on each of several days!

251

A Perfect Home

Many reptiles make their homes in warm, tropical regions, but reptiles can be found all over the world, with the exception of the continent of Antarctica and frigid, polar waters. Remind students that wherever home is, it usually provides a reptile with safety, shelter, food, and a place to raise a family. Challenge each student to write and illustrate a four-fact report about a reptile's habitat. To do this, she chooses a specific reptile to research and gathers four facts about its habitat. Then, on a sheet of writing paper, she writes a title, an introductory sentence about her topic, her four facts, and a summary sentence. She mounts this paper near the bottom of a 12" x 18" sheet of manila paper. At the top of the paper she illustrates the reptile in its habitat.

To display her project, a child traces the triangular shape of a clothes hanger onto construction paper. She writes the title "Home, Sweet Home" on the shape and adds rooflike crayon details. She cuts out the shape and then tapes the resulting cutout and her illustrated report to the hanger so that a house shape results (see illustration). Display these eye-catching and informative mobiles for all to see!

Home, Sweet Home

Emerald Tree Boa

The Emerald Tree Boa is a big green snake. It lives in the trees of the rain forest. It eats birds and lizards that are found in trees. It is round on top and flat on the bottom. Its shape helps it coil around tree branches and not fall off! I hope I never see an Emerald Tree Boa!

written by Meg

Sea Turtle Life Cycle

Like all living things, reptiles have a life cycle. Most reptiles lay their eggs on land and leave them. This means newly born reptiles must survive on their own. Such is the case with the sea turtle.

To follow the life of a sea turtle, give each student a manila paper copy of page 255, a 9" x 12" sheet of brown construction paper, and a brad. A student colors the large circle brown, leaving the numbered sections uncolored. She cuts out the pieces. Then she sequences the events, numbers them, and glues them on the circle in the corresponding sections. Next, she traces the circle in the center of the brown paper. On the brown paper, protruding from the circle outline, she draws the head and four flippers of a sea turtle. She adds desired details with crayon before she carefully cuts out her drawing. To assemble the project, she aligns the circle atop the turtle and joins the cutouts with the brad as shown.

On the Defense!

Most animals need to find ways to protect themselves from natural enemies, and reptiles are no exception. Reptiles will play dead, hide, use camouflage, and even bluff their way out of risky situations! Use the reproducible activity on page 256 to introduce students to six reptiles that know how to defend themselves!

Circle sections:
6. A mother sea turtle returns to the beach where she was born.
1. A mother sea turtle lays her eggs. She returns to the sea.
A young turtle grows into an adult.
2. A baby sea turtle breaks free of its egg.
A baby turtle hides in seaweed, eats very tiny animals.
3. A baby turtle crosses the sand and enters the sea.

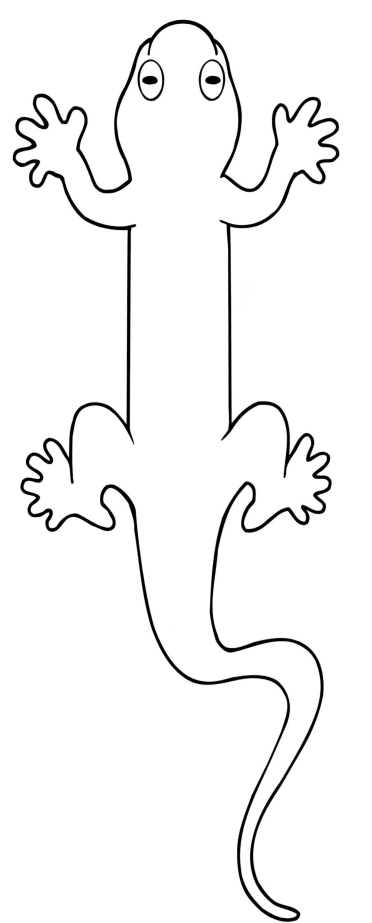

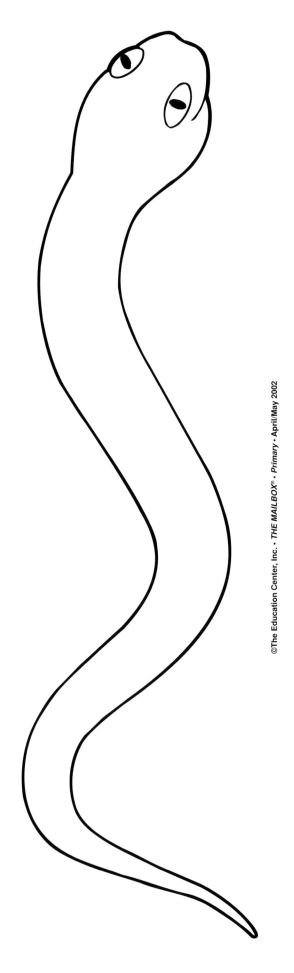

©The Education Center, Inc. • *THE MAILBOX*® • *Primary* • April/May 2002

©The Education Center, Inc. • *THE MAILBOX*® • *Primary* • April/May 2002

Note to the teacher: Use with "All in the Family" on page 250.

Life Cycle Project

Use with “Sea Turtle Life Cycle” on page 252.

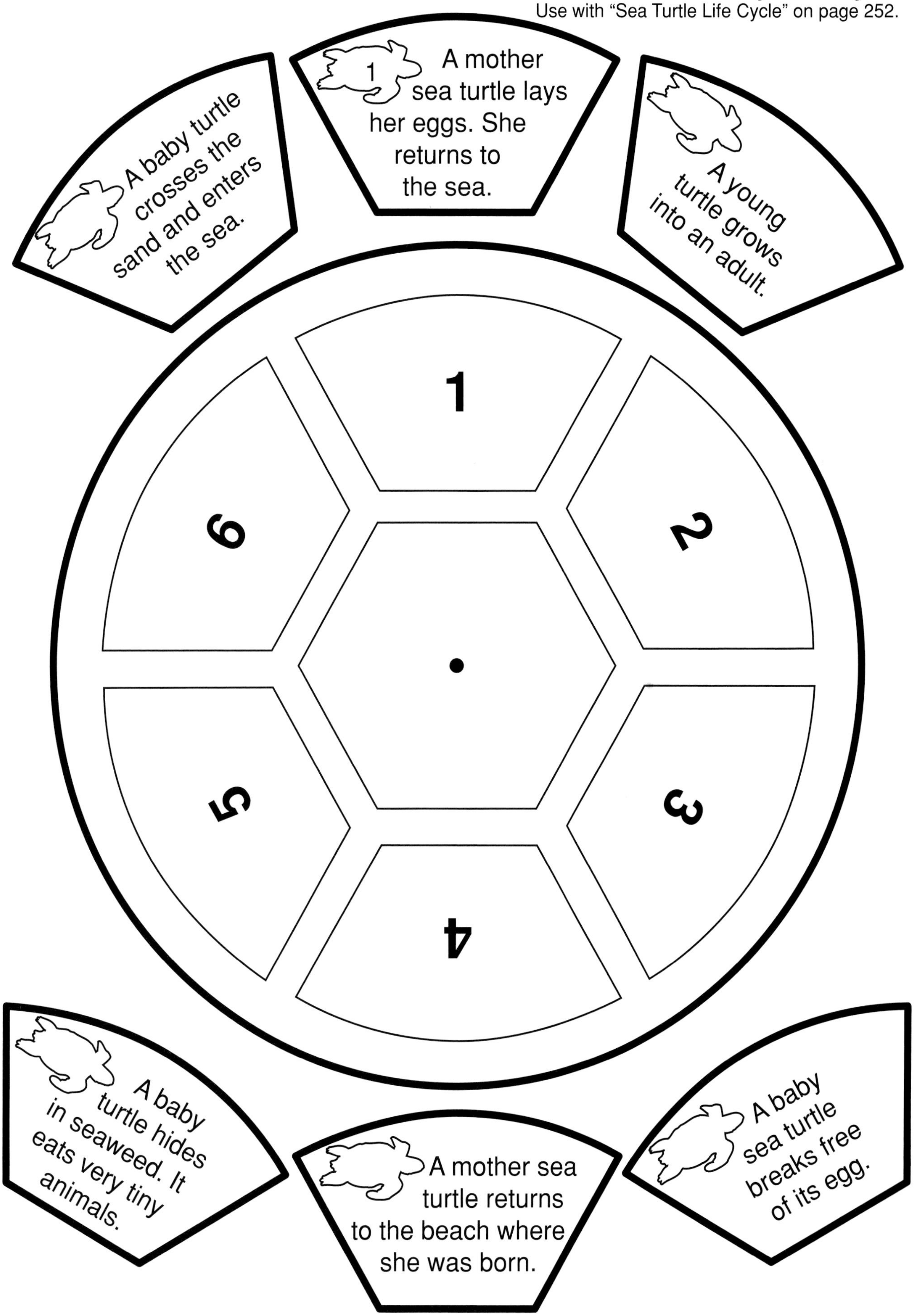
1 A mother sea turtle lays her eggs. She returns to the sea.
A young turtle grows into an adult.
A baby sea turtle breaks free of its egg.
A mother sea turtle returns to the beach where she was born.
A baby turtle hides in seaweed. It eats very tiny animals.
A baby turtle crosses the sand and enters the sea.
1
2
3
4
5
6

On the Defense!

Read each clue.
Color and cut out each picture.
Glue each picture beside the clue that describes it.

1.
My tough shell protects me.
It also camouflages me.
When I am frightened, I hide
inside my shell!

[ ]

2.
I am a bluffer.
I lie on my back, open my mouth,
and play dead until the danger is
gone.

[ ]

3.
I look like something I am not!
I have red, white, and black stripes.
I am left alone because I look like
a snake that is very poisonous!

[ ]

4.
My defense is camouflage.
My skin changes color.
I blend into my environment.
I turn green, yellow, red, or brown.

[ ]

5.
I am very big and powerful!
I have a large mouth and many teeth.
Other animals know to leave me
alone!

[ ]

6.
I really know how to bluff!
I raise the front of my body off the ground.
Then I open my mouth wide.
Then a big collar of skin stands out!

[ ]

©The Education Center, Inc. • THE MAILBOX® • Primary • April/May 2002 • Key p. 312

frilled lizard	tortoise	hognose snake	chameleon	crocodile	scarlet snake

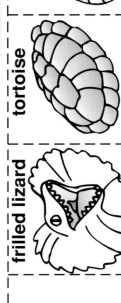

Note to the teacher: Use with "On the Defense!" on page 252.

Seasonal and Theme Units

'Tis the Season for…
Grandparents

Use these grand interdisciplinary ideas to celebrate grandparents and other grandfriends!

ideas contributed by Linda Masternak Justice

LITERATURE
Identifying Grandfriends

Begin your grandparent studies with an oral reading of Nancy Carlson's heartwarming book *Hooray for Grandparents' Day!* Youngsters who do not know their grandparents or do not have grandparents living close by will be especially comforted by the story. And all students will be encouraged to reach out to other grandfriends that they know. At the conclusion of the story, invite each child to tell the class about a special grandparent or grandfriend he has.

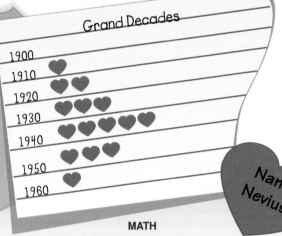

SCIENCE
Through the Years

Ask a youngster how her childhood differs from that of a grandparent or grandfriend, and she may have a few ideas. After completing this timeline project, she'll have several more ideas and a multitude of questions for her older relative or friend!

For easy management, ask a parent volunteer to prefold 4" x 18" paper strips into sixths. Each child needs two strips. To make her timeline, a child glues her two paper strips together by gluing the last section of strip 1 atop the first section of strip 2. Then she colors the illustrations on a copy of page 260 and cuts along the bold lines. She personalizes the title card and sets it aside. Next, she arranges the remaining cards in chronological order and glues them on her paper strip—one card per section. When the glue is dry, she folds forward the first section of the prepared strip, glues the title card to the blank surface, and accordion-folds her project. Challenge each student to learn more about the childhood of her grandparent or grandfriend by comparing her timeline data to the class graph (see "A Grand Graph").

MATH
A Grand Graph

Boost skip-counting, vocabulary, and graphing skills during this grand activity! Beginning with ten, have students count by tens to 90. Write the numbers on the board, leaving extra space between them. Explain that a period of ten years is called a *decade.* Next, add the number 19 to the front of each ten on the board and add "1900" to the front of the resulting line of numbers and "2000" to the end. Help students identify the decade in which they were born. Next, challenge students to find out the decade during which their grandparents or grandfriends were born. On a predetermined day, have students record their data on a graph like the one shown above. Help students interpret the data they've collected. Then keep the graph posted for use with "Through the Years."

LANGUAGE ARTS
From A to Z

Take an alphabetical approach to identifying cross-generational likes and a class ABC book is in the works! List the alphabet letters on the board. Ask students to name likes they share with their grandparents (grandfriends) and write their suggestions on the board alongside the corresponding letters.

To make a class book, write on the board the question and answer frame provided. Help each student select an alphabet letter that describes a like she shares with her grandparent or grandfriend. (When possible, have students select different letters or likes from the list.) Next, have each child copy and complete the provided frame on a 12" x 18" sheet of white construction paper and illustrate her work. Enlist your students' help in alphabetizing their completed projects. Then bind the pages into a class book titled "Grand Times."

Question and Answer Frame
Why is [alphabet letter] for [item from list]?
Because [student name] and [name of grandparent or grandfriend] love [item from list]!

Why is A for apple pie?

Because Diane and Grandpa Ray love apple pie!

Grandpa's Special Blend

SOCIAL STUDIES
Then and Now

No doubt students have heard older friends and relatives comment about the way in which prices have changed through the years. On the board write "candy bar," "postage stamp," and "movie ticket." Beside each item write its current price. Ask students why they believe that as children their grandparents or grandfriends paid less for these items. Encourage students to ask their older relatives and friends to talk with them about the changes they've seen in shopping prices. (For an enlightening look at shopping in the 1930s and 1940s, read aloud *Shopping in Grandma's Day* by Valerie Weber and Beverly Crawford.) Then give each child a copy of page 261 to complete. After students finish the activity, find out what surprised them the most about the changing prices of eggs. A brief discussion regarding supply and demand may be in order!

WRITING
Letters for the Future

Here's a first-class letter-writing idea that's sure to please! Ask each child to write a letter to his future grandchildren. Before students begin writing, review as a class several of the changes that have occurred since their grandparents and grandfriends were children. Suggest that students include in their letters the kinds of things they think their future grandchildren will enjoy knowing about them. Then give each student an envelope in which to store his letter. Encourage students to keep their letters safely stored until they themselves become grandparents!

September 21, 2001

To my grandchildren,
Today I am eight years old. I ride a big yellow bus to school. I use a pencil to a computer, too. shoes cost

259

Through the Years

by

_____

©2001 The Education Center, Inc.

1978

cellular telephone

1924

Pizza Puffs
Frozen Ice Treat

frozen food

1950

Buy Now   Pay Later
X02346600X112
J. J. Jones
4/2001

credit card

1946

:30

microwave oven

1940

Suntan Lotion

suntan lotion

1954

color television

1976

Disposable Diapers
Super Absorbent

disposable diapers

1959

car seat belt

1980

Fruity-O's

supermarket
checkout scanner

1930

sliced bread

1977

personal computer

Eggs by the Dozen

Use the egg data.
Graph the price of eggs for each year listed on the graph.

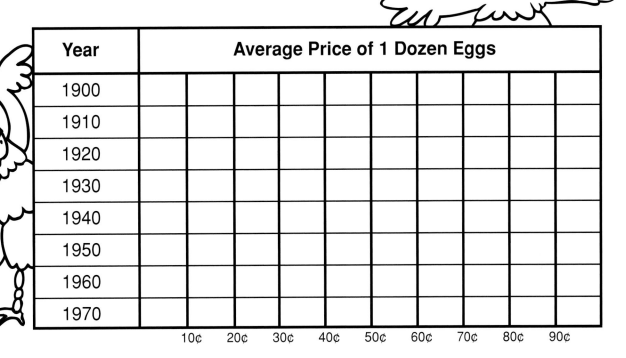

Year	Average Price of 1 Dozen Eggs									
1900										
1910										
1920										
1930										
1940										
1950										
1960										
1970										
	10¢	20¢	30¢	40¢	50¢	60¢	70¢	80¢	90¢	

Use the bar graph you made to answer the questions.

1. In what year did a dozen eggs cost the least? _____

2. In what year did a dozen eggs cost the most? _____

3. Did eggs get more expensive every year? _____

4. Why do you think eggs cost more in 1920 than in 1960? _____

_____

5. Do you think that today a dozen eggs cost more or less than in 1970? _____

   Why? _____

Bonus Box: On the back of this paper, write 2 things the price of eggs teaches you about the past.

Egg Data

Year	Average price per dozen
1900	21¢
1910	34¢
1920	68¢
1930	45¢
1940	33¢
1950	60¢
1960	57¢
1970	61¢

©The Education Center, Inc. • *THE MAILBOX*® • *Primary* • Aug/Sept 2001 • Key p. 313

'Tis the Season for... Leaves

Rake in heaps of learning fun with these leaf-related activities!

birch

vein

maple

chlorophyll

VOCABULARY
"Tree-mendous" Words

Investigate the leaves of deciduous trees as they take center stage this fall! To begin your study, tell students that *deciduous* describes trees that lose their leaves each autumn. Ask students to share their ideas about the meaning of *evergreen*. Explain that just as its name implies, this variety of tree does not lose its leaves seasonally and the leaves normally stay green. To further expand students' vocabularies, post a leafless, branched tree cutout on a bulletin board. Place a supply of colorful leaf cutouts nearby. Each time you introduce a leaf-related word, program a cutout accordingly and staple it to the tree. Students' understanding will grow with each leafy addition!

Foliage Facts

Leaves
- make food for plants
- give off oxygen
- can be used to make chewing gum
- make landscapes pretty
- help give shade
- are food for many animals

WRITING
The Important Thing

Why study leaves? Count on your students to have plenty of answers after they complete this writing project! Read aloud *The Important Book* by Margaret Wise Brown. Then tell students that just like the items featured in the book, leaves have several distinguishing characteristics. As students brainstorm the noteworthy traits of leaves, write their ideas on a sheet of chart paper. Share the facts shown or have students use provided resources to identify additional information.

When the list is complete, give each student a 4$^{1}/_{2}$" x 18" sheet of white construction paper. The youngster uses a ruler to draw a one-inch border along the edges of the paper and to divide the inner space into quarters. She uses the format shown to feature one or more ideas from the chart. Then she colors the border. A deepened appreciation for leaves is sure to result!

The Important Thing About Leaves
by Emily

The important thing about leaves is that they make food.

They start in buds. They grow and then change into colorful leaves. Finally, they fall to the ground.

But the important thing about leaves is that they make food.

MATH
Measure Up!

This reproducible activity will have youngsters scurrying to size up their estimation skills! Give each student a copy of page 264 and access to a supply of kidney beans, Unifix® cubes, and small paper clips. Read the directions on the reproducible with students. Explain that to measure, the paper clips and beans should be placed end to end and the cubes should be snapped together. All measurements should be made to the nearest whole unit. After each youngster completes his sheet, discuss as a class how a measurement that is made with one type of unit can be used to make a good estimate for another. If desired, collect a variety of fallen leaves to provide more estimation and measurement practice.

ART
Nature's Paintbrush

Add a splash of color to your classroom! Show students a green leaf (or a picture of one). Explain that the green, or chlorophyll, hides colors such as yellow or orange. In autumn, the chlorophyll begins to break down and the previously hidden colors are revealed. Maple leaves and other leaves that have a lot of sugar usually turn red. If there is not much sunlight though, they turn yellow or orange.

To bring some of the vivid fall colors inside, use the leaf pattern on page 265 to make several leaf-shaped templates. To make a pretty fall leaf, a student traces a template on a 9" x 12" sheet of orange or yellow paper. She uses a crayon to outline the tracing and draw veins. Next, she uses watercolor paints to embellish her tracing. After the paint dries, she cuts out her leaf. Suspend each student's colorful artwork from the ceiling. Looks like fall!

adapted from an idea by Karen Liere—Grs. 1–2
Cooper Elementary
Spokane, WA

POETRY WRITING
Leafy Poetry

What more fitting way to celebrate leaves than with haiku—a poetry form known for honoring nature! Review with the class the format of haiku (three lines with five, seven, and five syllables, respectively). Next, ask each student to visualize one or more fall leaves, keeping in mind the details explored in "A Close Look" on this page. To describe the image, have him draft a haiku on a sheet of writing paper. Encourage him to use precise words and phrases to help convey the image. When he is satisfied with his poem, give him a copy of the leaf pattern on page 265. Ask him to copy the poem onto the pattern. Next, instruct him to cut out the pattern and glue it onto a slightly larger piece of construction paper. Then have him trim the paper to leave a narrow border. Display students' work as desired to create a poetic tribute to fall foliage.

Danielle Conforti—Gr. 3, Old Mill School, Sea Girt, NJ

SCIENCE
A Close Look

Sharpen your young botanists' observation skills with this classification idea! Gather a variety of leaves. Tell students that the broad, flat part of a leaf is called a *blade*. Point out that leaves not only vary by the number of blades, but they also vary by size, edges, and vein patterns. Use the information shown to provide examples. Next, divide students into small groups and give each group several leaves. Have the students examine the leaves, sort them on provided paper as desired, and tape the leaves in place. Then invite each group to show the class its work and explain its sorting method. Now that's a nifty way to develop an "unbe-leaf-able" eye for details!

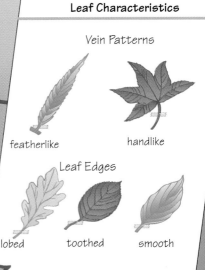

Leaf Characteristics

Vein Patterns

featherlike   handlike

Leaf Edges

lobed   toothed   smooth

263

Name _____

Measure Up!

Stripes and Patches are collecting leaves for their homes.
They want to be sure to use the best leaves.
Complete the charts to show how their leaves measure up.

Stripes		
Unit	**Estimate**	**Actual**
🖇		
🫘		
🧊		

Patches		
Unit	**Estimate**	**Actual**
🖇		
🫘		
🧊		

Bonus Box: Compare the actual measurements of the leaves that Stripes and Patches found. On the back of this sheet, write two sentences that tell what you notice.

©The Education Center, Inc. • THE MAILBOX® • Primary • Oct/Nov 2001 • Key p. 312

264   **Note to the teacher:** Use with "Measure Up!" on page 262.

by _____

'Tis the Season for... Candles

Candles play an important role in many holiday celebrations. Use the cross-curricular activities that follow to brighten the holiday investigations you're planning!

ideas by Vicki Dabrowka—Gr. 2, Concord Hill School, Chevy Chase, MD

PROBLEM SOLVING
Hanukkah Lights

Light up problem-solving skills with a menorah-based project! Give each child a copy of page 269 and ten candies. Explain that during the Jewish celebration of Hanukkah, a family participates in lighting a menorah like the one that is pictured. On each of the holiday's eight nights, the raised helper candle (called a *shamash*) is lit and used to light a candle for the current day of celebration and each previous day of celebration.

Challenge students to determine how many candles on a menorah are lit each night during Hanukkah and the total for all eight nights. To find out, a child uses candies to light the two candles for the first night of Hanukkah. In the provided box, he uses tally marks to record how many candles he lit; then he removes the manipulatives. He repeats the procedure for each of the other seven nights. Then he totals his tallies to answer the question. Invite students to munch on their candies as they complete the Bonus Box activity!

ART
Las Posadas Luminarias

In celebration of Las Posadas, have students create faux candles! Share with the class that in Spain, Mexico, and parts of the United States, a celebration called *Las Posadas* leads up to Christmas. During this time, outdoor candles called *luminarias* line the edges of streets and driveways, lighting the way for holiday visitors.

To create a glowing indoor holiday welcome, give each child a white paper lunch bag, two three-inch white paper circles, and two three-inch yellow tissue paper circles. A student trims the top two inches from her paper bag. Then she glues a yellow circle to the front and back of the bag (moving the bottom panel as needed). Next, she folds each white circle in half two times. She makes desired cuts in each folded paper, unfolds it, and glues it on a yellow circle. Last, she opens the bag to reveal a faux luminaria! Enlist your youngsters' help in displaying their artwork along the edges of the hallway that leads to their classroom door. To keep the luminarias stationary, place a small sealed plastic bag of sand or cat litter inside each project.

SOCIAL STUDIES
Crown of Candles

One of the darkest and longest winter nights in Sweden is brightened by candles! On December 13, candles are lit, sweet rolls and other goodies are eaten, and carols are sung in honor of St. Lucia, the patron saint of light. Traditionally on this day the oldest daughter dresses in a long white dress, red sash, and crown of candles, and serves her family breakfast. Communities and schools in Sweden often select someone to play Lucia in festivities. Other youngsters join the fun dressed as star boys and angels. St. Lucia Day in Sweden is the official start of the Christmas season.

After sharing this information with students, ask them to recall key words about the holiday. List the words on the board. Then set aside time for each child to make an informative crown of candles that is a serving tray for light snacks. (See the provided directions.) Tuck a few gingerbread cookies inside each completed project and suggest that each child share her cookies and her knowledge about St. Lucia Day with her family.

Crown of Candles Tray

Materials for one project:
2 white paper plates
green tempera paint
piece of sponge (for painting)
five 1½" x 5" strips of white
    construction paper
five 2" squares of yellow
    construction paper
scissors
glue
clear tape

Steps:
1. Cut the center from one paper plate and discard it. Invert the plate rim and the second paper plate. Sponge-paint the bottom of both plates green. Set aside to dry.
2. On each white paper strip, write a different word that describes St. Lucia Day. (Refer to the list from "Crown of Candles" as desired.) Write the words vertically. Leave a ½-inch margin at the top and bottom of each strip.
3. Cut a yellow flame from each yellow square. Glue each flame to a programmed strip.
4. When the plates are dry, align the edges. Keep the painted surfaces to the outside and the opening on top. Tape the plates together.
5. Use tape or glue to attach the five candles inside the plate opening.

WRITING
Christmas Candles

In today's Christmas ceremonies, candles are found most everywhere! Lighted candles adorn churches and homes, electric candles illuminate frosty windows, and colorful candle illustrations embellish greeting cards and holiday gift wrap. Prompt students to pen their thoughts about candles with this writing activity. Give each child a 5" x 8" sheet of writing paper on which to copy the title "A Candle." Challenge him to fill his entire paper with candle-related thoughts. Then have each child mount his completed work on a colorful 6" x 9" sheet of construction paper and glue a bright yellow flame to the top of his project. Showcase the lighted candles on a bulletin board titled "Glowing Thoughts."

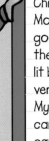

A Candle

A candle is a pretty Christmas decoration. Most candles smell good. I like to watch the wax melt. A candle is lit by fire so you must be very careful around it. My dog doesn't like candles very much. I like candles a lot.

Lighting the Kinara

Kwanzaa is a time for candles! On each of seven days, one or more colorful candles in the *kinara*, or candleholder, is lit in celebration of a different Kwanzaa principle. This activity increases understanding of the Kwanzaa principles and provides each child with a handy reference to use throughout the year!

To make a simple kinara with candles, each child folds a 9" x 12" sheet of white construction paper in half lengthwise and positions the fold at the top. He glues seven 1" x 3" strips of construction paper across the folded paper in the following order: three red, one black, three green. Then he glues a 1" x 12" strip of brown construction paper across the bottom of the project as shown.

Next, give each child a copy of page 270 and seven 1" x 2" strips of yellow paper. For each day of Kwanzaa, a child cuts out a yellow paper flame and glues it atop the correct color of candle. Then, following a class discussion of the corresponding Kwanzaa principle, he writes in his own words how he will practice this principle throughout the year. When all seven principles are addressed, he colors the artwork on his paper and cuts along the bold line. He glues this cutout inside his folded paper. For a finishing touch he writes "Kwanzaa" on the candle flames, one letter per flame. *Harambee!*

LITERATURE
A Glowing Bookshelf
Pick and choose from this luminous collection of literature!

Our Eight Nights of Hanukkah
Written by Michael J. Rosen

The Trees of the Dancing Goats
Written by Patricia Polacco

The Night of Las Posadas
Written by Tomie dePaola

The Christmas Candle
Written by Richard Paul Evans

An Early American Christmas
Written by Tomie dePaola

Seven Candles for Kwanzaa
Written by Andrea Davis Pinkney

Lighting the Menorah

Light the menorah for each night of Hanukkah.
Use tally marks to show how many candles you light.
Total the tally marks to answer the question.

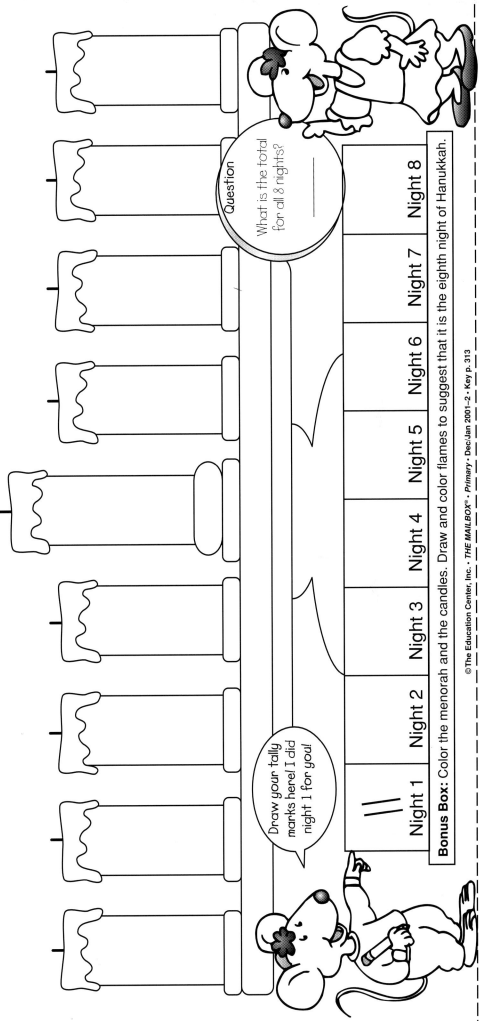

Draw your tally marks here! I did night 1 for you!

Question
What is the total for all 8 nights? _____

Night 1	Night 2	Night 3	Night 4	Night 5	Night 6	Night 7	Night 8

Bonus Box: Color the menorah and the candles. Draw and color flames to suggest that it is the eighth night of Hanukkah.

©The Education Center, Inc. • *THE MAILBOX*® • *Primary* • Dec/Jan 2001–2 • Key p. 313

Note to the teacher: Use with "Hanukkah Lights" on page 266. Each child needs ten wrapped candies.

Understanding Kwanzaa

Day	New Candle Lit	Principle	How I Will Practice This Principle
1		unity, joining together	
2		self-determination, being yourself	
3		working together, helping each other	
4		sharing	
5		having a goal or a purpose	
6		creating, being creative	
7		having faith, believing	

©The Education Center, Inc. • THE MAILBOX® • Primary • Dec./Jan 2001–2

Note to the teacher: Use with "Lighting the Kinara" on page 268.

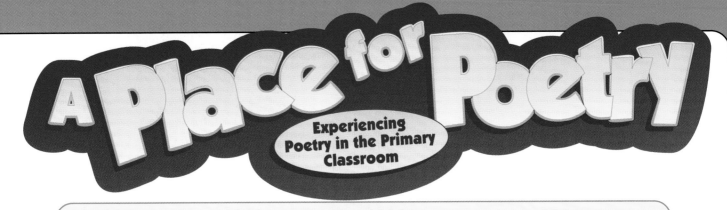

A Place for Poetry

Experiencing Poetry in the Primary Classroom

Soup's On!

The narrator of the poem on page 272 knows that a bowl of alphabet soup can be more than a delicious lunch. It can be a handy communication tool, too! Use the prereading activity below to kick off National Soup Month this January and introduce your students to soupy message possibilities. After students are familiar with the poem, use the second activity to serve up more message-sharing fun.

poem and activities by Geoff Mihalenko—Gr. 3, DeFino Central School, Marlboro, NJ

(Prereading Activity)

All Stirred Up!

Set the stage for "Soup's On!" with bowlfuls of word-building practice! Write a student-generated list of soup-related words on the chalkboard. Then pair students. Give each youngster a disposable bowl and spoon and two 11-inch strips of paper that you have marked into one-inch squares. Have the youngster write a soup-related word on one strip, using one square per letter. Instruct him to cut apart the programmed squares, drop them in his bowl, and mix them with the spoon.

Next, have each youngster trade his prepared soup bowl with his partner. Instruct him to remove the letters from his partner's bowl, arrange them to make a word, and then read the word aloud for his partner to verify. After each youngster successfully forms his partner's word, direct him to place the letters back in the bowl and return the bowl to its owner. Have each student empty his bowl and repeat the process with the second strip. Then tell the students that they will hear a poem about a youngster who also receives soup messages, only hers are in real soup! Ask the class to listen carefully to find out what messages the youngster finds.

Please send a postcard when you go on vacation.

Toad might say this because he never gets any mail. He would love to get a postcard!

Toad in *Frog and Toad Are Friends*

(Follow-Up Activity)

Soupy Storytime Messages

Whether they're in a soup bowl or on a notepad, the messages a person leaves can reveal a lot about her! Ask students to tell what they can conclude about the mom in the poem and why. Possible responses include that she is loving, supportive, and creative. Then have each student create her own soup-bowl message. To do so, give each youngster a soup-bowl and a soupspoon cutout similar to the ones shown. The student writes a chosen book title and character on the spoon. On the inside of the bowl, she writes a message that the character might leave. On the outside of the bowl, she writes why the character might leave the message. Ask each student to read her work aloud; then staple each student's bowl with her spoon on a bulletin board titled " 'Soup-er' Messages." What a satisfying way to enhance students' understanding of characters!

Soup's On!

Lunch is my very favorite time
Of each and every day.
I love to read the notes my mom
Creates and sends my way.

She makes me soup with noodles shaped
Just like the alphabet,
Then "stirs" a note to tell me things
She hopes I won't forget.

The soupy messages she sends
Float all around my spoon.
Sometimes she says, "I love you," or,
"Enjoy your afternoon."

Each day a different note appears.
And when I have a test,
She tells me, "I am proud of you—
You always do your best."

But today I'm disappointed,
And I sigh a quiet groan.
There is no message in my soup—
Mom served me minestrone.

by Geoff Mihalenko

©The Education Center, Inc. • THE MAILBOX® • Primary • Dec/Jan 2001–2

Note to the teacher: Give each student a copy of this poem to color. Then have her take it home and read it with her family members.

Enrich your celebration of Black History Month with the following kid-pleasing ideas.

❖ ❖ ❖ Famous Firsts Lotto ❖ ❖ ❖

Pique your students' interest in Black American firsts! Give each child a copy of page 274 and the picture cards from page 275. She also needs a quart-size resealable plastic bag for game storage. To prepare her gameboard, the child cuts out the cards and gameboard on page 274. She randomly glues the cards on the gameboard spaces. Then she cuts out the picture cards. As students work, cut out a set of picture cards and place them in a container.

To play, announce a type of game such as "Three (four) in a row" or "Four corners." Next, draw a picture card from your container and read the person's name aloud. The student finds her copy of the card and places it on her gameboard atop the person's famous first. Ask a volunteer to identify the corresponding famous first. Then have each child check the accuracy of her card placement and make any needed adjustment. Place your card in a discard pile and draw another card from the container. Continue play as described.

The first student to cover a winning set of game spaces exclaims "Famous firsts!" Visually confirm her win and then have her read aloud the matches. If desired, have the winner of the first game become the caller for the second game and so on until game time is over. Then have students store their games for play on another day. Before long your scholars will know these famous firsts by heart and they'll be ready to track down 12 more for a second edition of the game!

Colleen Majors—Gr. 2, Stephen Girard School, Philadelphia, PA

• • • • • • • Black American Firsts • • • • •

first doctor to perform successful heart operation	first black member of Supreme Court	first black scientist with federal monument	first black woman to earn pilot's license
first black to win Pulitzer Prize for poetry	first black woman to host a weekday talk show on national television	first black man to reach North Pole	first black man honored on postage stamp
first black woman on postage stamp	first black man to pitch in World Series game	first black woman in space	first black woman to win Olympic gold medal

Bessie Coleman

Mae C. Jemison

Thurgood Marshall

Gwendolyn Brooks

❖ ❖ ❖ All-Star Boxes ❖ ❖ ❖

Here's a perfect project for rookie researchers! Collect a class supply of empty cube-shaped tissue boxes and then cut blank white paper to fit the sides and tops of the boxes. Also display an assortment of children's books that contain biographical information about Black American achievers. After students have investigated the books you've gathered, ask each child to complete a copy of "Black American Achiever" from page 275. To do this, he names the Black American achiever he will research. Then he finds four interesting facts about the person, copies each fact on his paper, and writes where the facts were found.

When his research is approved for publication (by you), he copies each fact on a piece of precut paper. Then he decorates the papers and glues them to the sides of a tissue box. On another piece of precut paper he illustrates and labels the Black American he researched. He glues this paper to the top of his box. After each child shares his report with the class, exhibit the all-star boxes for further investigation.

Colleen Dabney, Williamsburg, VA

Aretha Franklin

Fact 1
Aretha started her singing career when she was 12 years old.

Fact 2
She is called the Queen of Soul.

Black American Firsts

first doctor to perform successful heart operation	first black woman in space	first black member of Supreme Court	first black woman to host a weekday talk show on national television
first black woman honored on postage stamp	first black man to reach North Pole	first black man to pitch in World Series game	first black to win Pulitzer Prize for poetry
first black woman to win Olympic gold medal	first black man honored on postage stamp	first black scientist with federal monument	first black woman to earn pilot's license

©The Education Center, Inc. • THE MAILBOX® • Primary • Feb/Mar 2002

Matthew Henson	Alice Coachman	Booker T. Washington	Oprah Winfrey
Mae C. Jemison	Thurgood Marshall	Bessie Coleman	Daniel Hale Williams
Satchel Paige	Gwendolyn Brooks	George Washington Carver	Harriet Tubman

©The Education Center, Inc. • THE MAILBOX® • Primary • Feb/Mar 2002

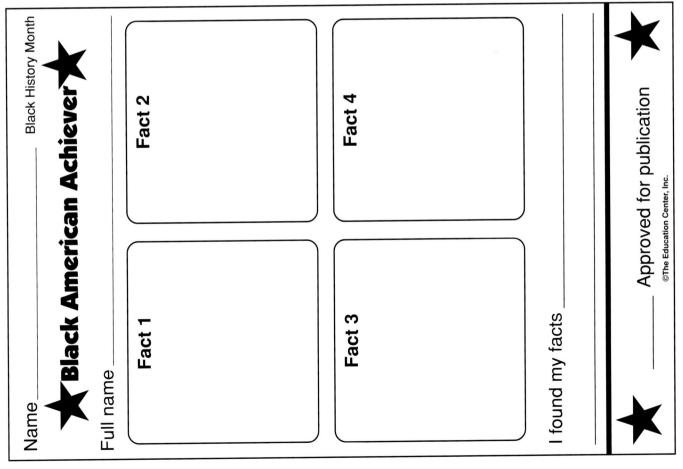

Black History Month

★ Black American Achiever ★

Name _____

Full name _____

Fact 1

Fact 2

Fact 3

Fact 4

I found my facts _____

Approved for publication

©The Education Center, Inc.

©The Education Center, Inc. • THE MAILBOX® • Primary • Feb/Mar 2002

Note to the teacher: Use the picture cards with "Famous Firsts Lotto" on page 273. Use the form with "All-Star Boxes" on page 273.

'Tis the Season for...
Groundhogs!

What's in the forecast? A cross-curricular investigation of groundhogs that's perfect for any type of weather!

contributions by Gail E. Gorske—Grs. 2–3, Roeper City and Country School, Bloomfield Hills, MI, and Monica Shiba—Gr. 1, Indian Trail School, Highland Park, IL

SCIENCE
A Curious Critter

A ten-pound bag of potatoes, a whistle, and a handful of clover are just what you need to introduce groundhogs! Blow the whistle and then show the class the clover and bag of potatoes. Invite students to tell what they know about the groundhog and speculate what the three props reveal about the furry forecaster. Write student-provided facts on a length of bulletin board paper along with facts from "The Groundhog Report" below. Lead students to conclude that a groundhog is about the size of the bag of potatoes, it eats clover, and it has a loud shrill cry that sounds like a whistle!

The Groundhog Report
- Groundhogs belong to the squirrel family.
- Groundhogs are also called woodchucks, marmots, and whistle pigs.
- A groundhog has mostly grayish brown fur, a bushy tail, and claws made for digging.
- An adult groundhog is about two feet in length from head to tail and usually weighs between five and 14 pounds.
- A groundhog eats green vegetation such as grass, clover, and alfalfa.
- Groundhogs live in underground burrows that may have more than one entrance.
- To communicate danger, a groundhog makes a piercing whistle sound.

COMPREHENSION
Dandy Dens

During this large-group game, students dig into facts and opinions about groundhogs! First, make three construction paper copies of the game cards on page 278 and label the cards with different facts and opinions. Cut out the cards and store them in a brown paper lunch sack. Explain that each winter a groundhog hibernates in a special grass-lined den that has just one entrance. On the board sketch a game trail like the one shown. Have each child illustrate a similar trail on blank paper and divide it into ten spaces. Then have him place a game marker in his den and label opposite sides of an index card "Fact" and "Opinion."

To begin play, remove a card from your "burrow" (the lunch sack), read it aloud, and place it in a discard pile. Each child displays his index card so that it shows what he thinks the sentence is—a fact or an opinion. Then reveal the correct answer. Players who answer correctly move their markers ahead one space. Continue play as described until several players have exited their burrows.

For continued skill review, have each child program a set of game cards for fact and opinion practice (or other desired skills). Provide brown paper lunch bags for card storage. Then provide time for students to play the games with their classmates.

Fact

MATH
Hibernating Hogs

What has a home in the ground and eats like a pig? A groundhog! Each year a groundhog fattens up before it *hibernates.* Its body uses the extra fat while it is sleeping. When the groundhog awakens in spring, the extra weight is gone! Use the reproducible on page 279 to weigh in youngsters' word-problem skills. As students explore the eating habits of an adorable groundhog named Gus, addition and subtraction skills are strengthened!

The Legend of Groundhog Day

CREATIVE WRITING
A Well-Known Woodchuck

Who's the world's renowned groundhog? Pennsylvania's Punxsutawney Phil, of course! Each year Phil's spring forecast is a worldwide media event. This year stage your own pre–Groundhog Day event! Collect one clean and empty soda can per student and provide a variety of arts-and-crafts supplies. Challenge each child to transform his can into a one-of-a-kind groundhog. Promote creativity by suggesting that students dress the woodchucks in shadow protection attire (if they're hoping for an early spring).

On the day of the event, have each student take his creation outdoors to an open area and determine if the groundhog sees its shadow. Then have the students return to the classroom with their groundhogs and generate front-page news! To do this, each child writes "The Groundhog Gazette" and "February 2, 2002" on a strip of blank paper. He glues this paper near the top of a full page of newspaper. Next, he pens a newsworthy article about the event on writing paper and illustrates the event on blank paper. He glues these papers to the newspaper project. When the glue is dry, he folds the project in half and presents the paper and his groundhog to his family on Groundhog Day!

SOCIAL STUDIES
Groundhog Day

To explain how Groundhog Day may have become an American custom, tell students the following information: In Germany long ago, on Candlemas Day (February 2), a farmer would watch for a hibernating badger to exit its burrow. The farmer believed that if the badger cast a shadow, then six more weeks of wintry weather would follow. If there were no shadow, spring would be early and crops could be planted. German farmers who settled in America continued this custom with local groundhogs. In time, February 2 became known as Groundhog Day!

Explain that today there is a legend associated with Groundhog Day that suggests a groundhog returns to its burrow because it has seen and become frightened by its shadow. Invite students to share their impressions of this tale. Then, for a fun follow-up, have each child pen her own thoughts about what happens on Groundhog Day. To do this, she writes her ideas on a 7" x 10" sheet of writing paper and mounts her writing on a 9" x 12" sheet of tan construction paper. Next, have her color a white construction paper copy of an enlarged version of the groundhog pattern on page 278, cut out the pattern, and glue the tab to the top back of the tan paper. To complete her project, she folds the tan paper in half by aligning the bottom edge with the top edge. She positions the groundhog's front legs over the folded paper to hold it in place and writes a desired title. Too cute!

The Groundhog Gazette
February 2, 2002

Groovy Greta Avoids Her Shadow

reported by Chester Reed

When Greta Groundhog exited her winter den, she wore a red cloak and king-size sunglasses. She carried a shiny umbrella. The crowd cheered. One child exclaimed, "I think Greta read <u>Little Red Riding Hood</u> this winter!" Whatever Greta did worked well. Even though the sun shone brightly, Greta did not see her shadow. Spring is on its way!

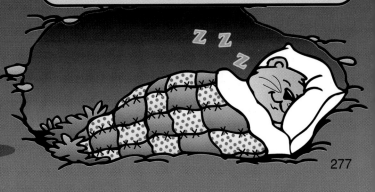

Game Cards and Pattern
Use the game cards with "Dandy Dens" on page 276.

Enlarge this pattern by 25 percent to use
with "Groundhog Day" on page 277.

tab

©The Education Center, Inc. • *THE MAILBOX*® • *Primary* • Feb/Mar 2002

Groundhog Grub

Add or subtract.
Write and solve each problem in the matching box below.

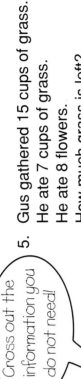

Cross out the information you do not need!

1. Gus whistled for 10 seconds.
   He ate 7 buttercups.
   Then he ate 6 more buttercups.
   How many buttercups did Gus eat?

2. Yesterday Gus gained 2 pounds.
   Today Gus weighs 11 pounds.
   Gus wants to gain 8 more pounds.
   How much does Gus want to weigh?

3. Gus ate 9 flowers.
   He took 2 bites of grass.
   Then he ate 4 more flowers.
   How many flowers did Gus eat?

4. Gus and Gill ate 19 flowers.
   Gus ate 7 flowers.
   Gill ate 12 flowers.
   How many more flowers did Gill eat than Gus?

5. Gus gathered 15 cups of grass.
   He ate 7 cups of grass.
   He ate 8 flowers.
   How much grass is left?

6. Gus ate for 18 minutes.
   Greta ate for 16 minutes.
   Gill ate for 12 minutes.
   How much longer did Greta eat than Gill?

7. Gus weighed 18 pounds last October.
   On February 2 he weighed 9 pounds.
   Gill weighed 10 pounds.
   How many pounds did Gus lose?

8. Gill weighs 10 pounds.
   Greta weighs 12 pounds.
   Gus weighs 14 pounds.
   How much do Gill and Greta weigh together?

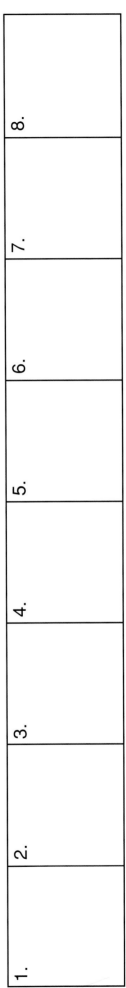

1.	2.	3.	4.
5.	6.	7.	8.

©The Education Center, Inc. • THE MAILBOX® • Primary • Feb/Mar 2002 • Key p. 313

Note to the teacher: Use with "Hibernating Hogs" on page 277.

Rodent Relatives

Help Greta read about other rodents!
Cut out the rodent names below.
Glue each name between the guide
words for that dictionary page.

Guide Word	Entry Word	Guide Word
plum		post
hammer		handle
gentle		germ
vinegar		vote
chin		choke
good		gorilla
gruff		gum
squid		stack
moon		mud
bear		bee
race		reach
potato		press

Bonus Box: Number the guide word pairs to
show the order that they would appear in a
dictionary. Write the numbers beside the chart.

©The Education Center, Inc. • THE MAILBOX® • Primary • Feb/Mar 2002 • Key p. 313

gerbil	guinea pig	hamster	rat	mouse	gopher
squirrel	chipmunk	porcupine	beaver	prairie dog	vole

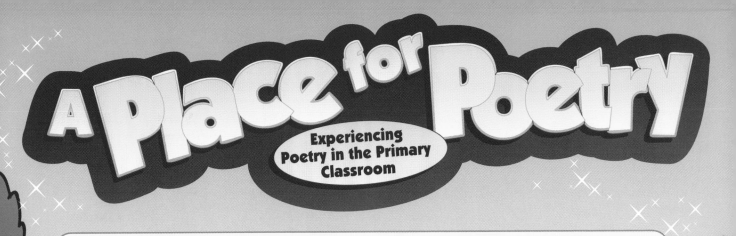

A Place for Poetry

Experiencing Poetry in the Primary Classroom

A Bug's Tale

This April, during Keep America Beautiful Month, motivate students to be more thoughtful about the environment. Prior to reading aloud the delightful poem on page 282, use the prereading activity from this page to clarify your students' understanding of the terms litter and litterbug. Then, after your youngsters are familiar with the poem, continue to promote environmental awareness with the provided follow-up activity.

poem by Geoff Mihalenko, Truman Elementary School, Sayreville, NJ

Prereading Activity

Who's a Litterbug?

By studying the behaviors of a litterbug, students can assess the earth-friendliness of their actions! Confirm with students that *litter* is trash that has not been placed in a trash receptacle, and clarify that *to litter* is to scatter trash. Next, write "litterbug" on the board. Lead students to agree that a *litterbug* is one who litters. Then write a student-suggested list of litterbug behaviors. As you write each behavior on the board, ask each child to draw a tally mark on a piece of scrap paper if he is occasionally guilty of the behavior described. When several behaviors are listed, have students privately assess how responsible they are for taking care of the environment. Then introduce "A Bug's Tale" from page 282. Explain that the poem is about a litterbug that doesn't realize the effect of its actions until it is almost too late!

Follow-Up Activity

Busy Bee Behaviors!

Here's a follow-up project that keeps students buzzing with earth-friendly behaviors! Give each child a 12" x 18" sheet of light blue construction paper, a copy of the poem on page 282, and a copy of the bee pattern on page 34. A child colors and cuts out his bee pattern. Next, he positions his blue paper horizontally and glues the cutout in one corner of the paper. He uses crayons to write on the paper (graffiti-style) earth-friendly behaviors he pledges to practice. Then he draws dotted lines to show the path of the very busy bee. Next, he folds the blue paper in half (to 9" x 12"), colors his copy of the poem, and glues the poem onto the front cover of the project. To complete his work, he signs and dates the back cover. Encourage each child to share the poem and his earth-friendly pledges with his family members.

A Bug's Tale

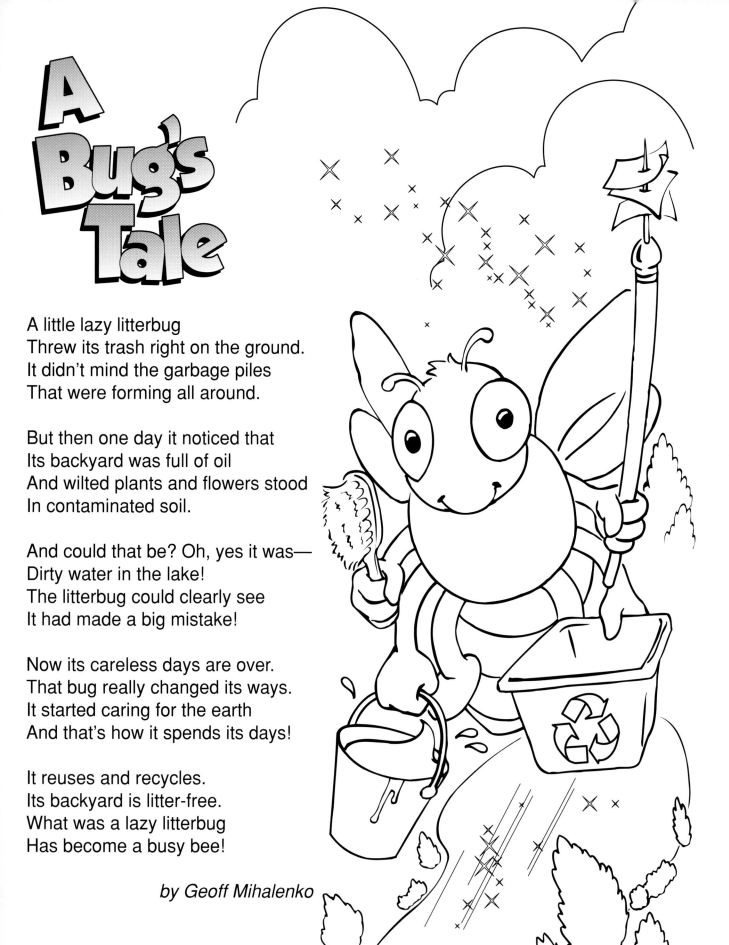

A little lazy litterbug
Threw its trash right on the ground.
It didn't mind the garbage piles
That were forming all around.

But then one day it noticed that
Its backyard was full of oil
And wilted plants and flowers stood
In contaminated soil.

And could that be? Oh, yes it was—
Dirty water in the lake!
The litterbug could clearly see
It had made a big mistake!

Now its careless days are over.
That bug really changed its ways.
It started caring for the earth
And that's how it spends its days!

It reuses and recycles.
Its backyard is litter-free.
What was a lazy litterbug
Has become a busy bee!

by Geoff Mihalenko

©The Education Center, Inc. • THE MAILBOX® • Primary • April/May 2002

Note to the teacher: Use the poem with "Busy Bee Behaviors!" on page 281. Or give each student a copy of the poem to color. Then have him take it home and read it with his family members.

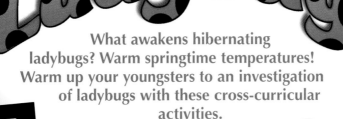

'Tis the Season for... Ladybugs

What awakens hibernating ladybugs? Warm springtime temperatures! Warm up your youngsters to an investigation of ladybugs with these cross-curricular activities.

What I Learned About Ladybugs

There are many different kinds of ladybugs.
A ladybug that is in danger might play dead.
A ladybug has a pair of wings and a pair of wing cases.
Some ladybugs hibernate.
Not all ladybugs are red with black spots.
Ladybugs eat harmful insects called aphids.

INVESTIGATION
Getting the Lowdown

Insect, beetle, and ladybird beetle—all three names are ladybug aliases! To launch your ladybug study, ask students what they know about ladybugs. Record their thoughts on a sheet of poster board titled "What We Think We Know." Then list questions your students have about ladybugs on a second sheet of poster board titled "What We Wonder." (For an eye-catching display idea, see page 29 of this issue.)

At the completion of the study, have each child title a sheet of writing paper "What I Learned About Ladybugs" and list facts he learned. Next, he mounts his paper on black construction paper, trims a strip of green construction paper to resemble grass, and glues the paper grass to the bottom of the project as shown. Then he uses a colorful stamp pad, his thumbprint, and a fine-tipped black marker to add desired ladybug details. Now that's getting the lowdown on ladybugs!

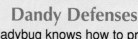

My Life by Lady Bug

MUSIC
Dandy Defenses

A ladybug knows how to protect itself from predators such as ants and birds. One way it does this is by lying on its back and playing dead. It can also ooze a liquid from its leg joints that tastes bad! This catchy tune reminds students that a ladybug can defend itself. Showcase the song on a decorated poster and encourage students to compose additional verses that teach about this amazing insect!

I'm a Little Ladybug
(sung to the tune of "I'm a Little Teapot")

I'm a little ladybug,
Round and hard.
I munch on aphids
In the backyard.

When I am afraid or
Danger is near,
I play dead
Until all is clear!

SCIENCE
That's Life!

For a ladybug, life is short! Use the provided information to present the four-stage development of a ladybug. Reveal that ladybugs born during the summer live only a few weeks. (Those born at the end of the summer live longer because they hibernate through the winter.) Then follow up by having each child make a metamorphosis booklet and leaf-shaped holder.

To begin, give each child a white construction paper copy of the cards and bug pattern on page 286, a green construction paper copy of the leaf pattern on the same page, and a 6" x 9" piece of green construction paper. To make her booklet holder, a child cuts out the leaf pattern. She applies glue to the back of the cutout, as shown, and then she attaches the cutout to the green paper rectangle. She trims around the cutout and sets the resulting holder aside. On her white paper copy she colors the artwork. She cuts out the bug, glues it onto the leaf-shaped holder she made, and adds desired details. Next, she cuts out the cards, stacks them in order behind the title card, and staples the left edge of the resulting booklet. Then she slides the booklet inside the holder. Encourage students to share their booklets and their knowledge about the ladybug with family and friends!

Ladybug Metamorphosis

Egg: A female lays bright yellow eggs where there are lots of aphids. After a few days the eggs turn white. They are ready to hatch!

Larva: A hungry larva about the size of a pinhead hatches from each egg. It eats 50 to 100 aphids a day. The growing larva outgrows its skin several times. When the larva is fully grown, it attaches itself to a plant. Then its skin splits open.

Pupa: The new soft skin of the pupa hardens. Inside the pupa an adult ladybug is forming.

Adult: A soft, pale ladybug pushes out of the pupa. Its body becomes more colorful as it dries. When the ladybug's wings are dry, it is ready to fly.

WRITING
Good Luck Bugs

It isn't clear why ladybugs are thought to bring good luck; however, for centuries people have believed that they do. For an entertaining writing assignment, have each child write and illustrate a tale about a ladybug encounter that results in good luck! Set aside time for students to share their stories; then bind the stories into a class book titled "The Good Luck Bugs."

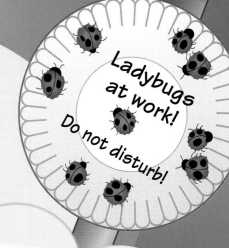

Ladybugs at work!
Do not disturb!

SOCIAL STUDIES
Aphid Eaters

It's no wonder that gardeners adore ladybugs. In just one summer an adult ladybug can eat up to 1,000 pesky aphids and produce hundreds of aphid-eating offspring! If possible, read aloud *What About Ladybugs?* by Celia Godkin. This beautifully illustrated picture book gives students an eye-opening look at the positive impact ladybugs can have on a garden. Then spotlight the earth-friendly work of ladybugs with a sign-making project. To make a sign, invert and flatten a white, nine-inch paper plate. Write a desired message on the bottom of the paper plate and then use a cotton ball to apply dots of red paint. When the paint dries, add ladybug details with a fine-tipped black marker. To weatherize the sign, laminate it. Encourage each child to display his ladybug sign in the yard or garden of a family member or friend.

MATH
Counting Spots

How many spots does a ladybug have? That depends on the type of ladybug it is! Some ladybugs have 2 spots, while others have 4, 7, 10, 14—even 22 spots! Keep your students' math skills sharp by posing daily ladybug problems for students to solve. For example, "If a ten-spot ladybug and a seven-spot ladybug are on a leaf together, how many spots (legs, antennae, body parts) are there in all?" *(17 spots)* or "If three 22-spot ladybugs join four two-spot ladybugs on a leaf, how many spots are there in all?" *(74)*

To add to the fun, have each child make a ladybug journal (see "Ladybug Log" on this page) in which to solve the daily math challenges.

Ladybug Log

Materials for one journal:
ten 4" x 5" pieces of white paper
4" x 5" piece of black construction paper
3" black construction paper circle
6" square of red or yellow construction paper
black construction paper scraps
2 small black pom-poms (for eyes)
black crayon or marker
brad
hole puncher
scissors
glue
access to a stapler

Steps:
1. Glue the black circle to the black rectangle. Glue in place two pom-pom eyes and two black paper antennae.
2. Hole-punch the top center of each white rectangle. Align these papers atop the black rectangle and then staple the top corners.
3. Fold the colorful paper in half and trim (see illustration). Unfold the paper and add desired spots. Cut along the fold line and overlap the top inside corners. Then poke the brad though the overlapped papers and through the notepad. Fasten.

Step 1

Step 3

READING
Ladybug Literature

These books about ladybugs are sure to hit the spot with students!

Bright Beetle
By Rick Chrustowski

Are You a Ladybug?
By Judy Allen and Tudor Humphries

Ladybug at Orchard Avenue
By Kathleen Weidner Zoehfeld

What About Ladybugs?
By Celia Godkin

The Ladybug and Other Insects
By Gallimard Jeunesse and Pascale de Bourgoing

Metamorphosis Project

Use with "That's Life!" on page 284.

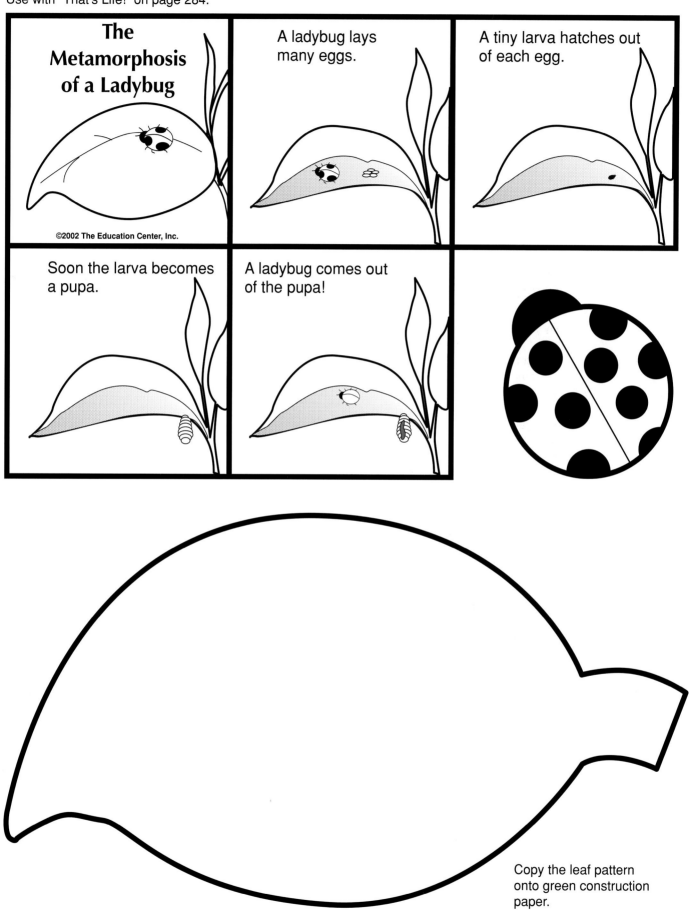

The Metamorphosis of a Ladybug

©2002 The Education Center, Inc.

A ladybug lays many eggs.

A tiny larva hatches out of each egg.

Soon the larva becomes a pupa.

A ladybug comes out of the pupa!

Copy the leaf pattern onto green construction paper.

©The Education Center, Inc. • THE MAILBOX® • Primary • April/May 2002

'Tis the Season for... SHELLS

Set the scene for summer with this cross-curricular collection of shell-related activities.

ideas contributed by Laura Wagner, Raleigh, NC

LITERATURE
The Scoop on Shells

Start students thinking about the science of shells with a carefully chosen literature selection. First, ask students what they already know about shells, guiding them to conclude that shells are important to many living things. Then read aloud an informative book that introduces a variety of shelled animals, such as *What Lives in a Shell?* by Kathleen Weidner Zoehfeld. Follow up by asking students to recall what they've learned about shells. List the facts on a length of bulletin board paper titled "Our Shell Discoveries." Plan to add facts to the poster throughout your study.

SCIENCE
Home, Sweet Home

A shell is a home that provides shelter and protection. Some shell homes are temporary, such as the eggshell that shelters and protects an unborn chick. Other shell homes are permanent. On the board, list animals that spend their lives inside shells. Invite students to share what they know about the animals. Next, have each child fold in half a 12" x 18" sheet of light-colored construction paper (to 9" x 12"), unfold the paper, and trace the fold line with a crayon. Then have her fold forward the top two inches of the paper, cut the resulting flap to make two equal-sized flaps, and label the flaps "Same" and "Different." A student illustrates a different animal from the list on each half of her paper. Then, under the flaps, she describes how the two animals shown are alike and different. Showcase the completed projects on a bulletin board titled "Shelling Out Comparisons."

MUSIC
Sing a Song of Shells

Pair shell facts with a familiar tune, and youngsters will be "clam-oring" to sing their shell knowledge!

Shell Serenade
(sung to the tune of "The Farmer in the Dell")

Some shells are beautiful.
Some shells are beautiful.
Heigh-ho, we all know
Some shells are beautiful.

A shell can be a home.
A shell can be a home.
Heigh-ho, we all know
A shell can be a home.

Additional verses:
Some shells are thick and hard.
Some shells are colorful.
A shell can be a shield.

A clam can open and close its shell. A turtle cannot.

Same

A turtle can move around a lot. A clam cannot.

287

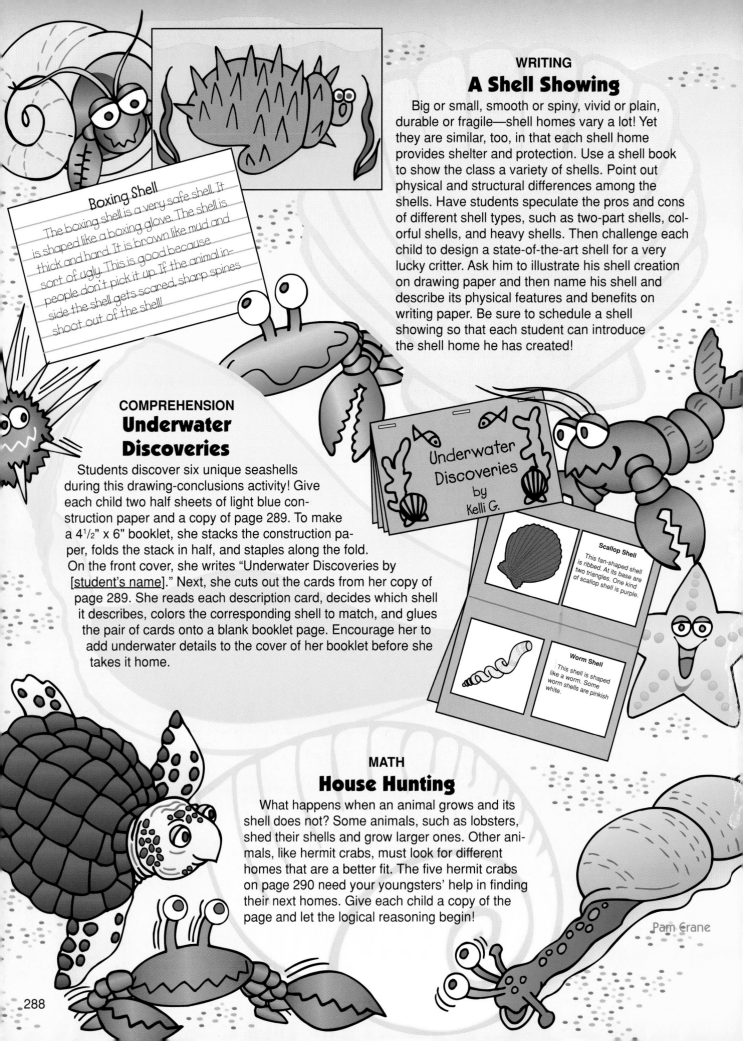

Boxing Shell

The boxing shell is a very safe shell. It is shaped like a boxing glove. The shell is thick and hard. It is brown like mud and sort of ugly. This is good because people don't pick it up. If the animal inside the shell gets scared, sharp spines shoot out of the shell!

WRITING
A Shell Showing

Big or small, smooth or spiny, vivid or plain, durable or fragile—shell homes vary a lot! Yet they are similar, too, in that each shell home provides shelter and protection. Use a shell book to show the class a variety of shells. Point out physical and structural differences among the shells. Have students speculate the pros and cons of different shell types, such as two-part shells, colorful shells, and heavy shells. Then challenge each child to design a state-of-the-art shell for a very lucky critter. Ask him to illustrate his shell creation on drawing paper and then name his shell and describe its physical features and benefits on writing paper. Be sure to schedule a shell showing so that each student can introduce the shell home he has created!

COMPREHENSION
Underwater Discoveries

Students discover six unique seashells during this drawing-conclusions activity! Give each child two half sheets of light blue construction paper and a copy of page 289. To make a 4½" x 6" booklet, she stacks the construction paper, folds the stack in half, and staples along the fold. On the front cover, she writes "Underwater Discoveries by [student's name]." Next, she cuts out the cards from her copy of page 289. She reads each description card, decides which shell it describes, colors the corresponding shell to match, and glues the pair of cards onto a blank booklet page. Encourage her to add underwater details to the cover of her booklet before she takes it home.

Underwater Discoveries by Kelli G.

Scallop Shell
This fan-shaped shell is ribbed. At its base are two triangles. One kind of scallop shell is purple.

Worm Shell
This shell is shaped like a worm. Some worm shells are pinkish white.

MATH
House Hunting

What happens when an animal grows and its shell does not? Some animals, such as lobsters, shed their shells and grow larger ones. Other animals, like hermit crabs, must look for different homes that are a better fit. The five hermit crabs on page 290 need your youngsters' help in finding their next homes. Give each child a copy of the page and let the logical reasoning begin!

Pam Crane

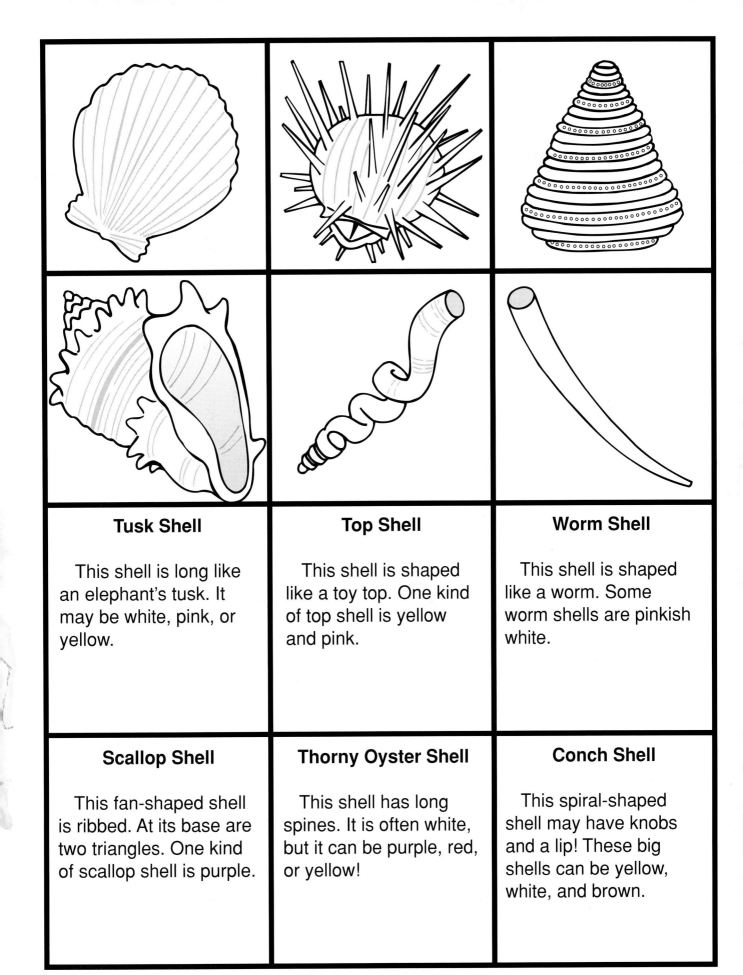

Tusk Shell

This shell is long like an elephant's tusk. It may be white, pink, or yellow.

Top Shell

This shell is shaped like a toy top. One kind of top shell is yellow and pink.

Worm Shell

This shell is shaped like a worm. Some worm shells are pinkish white.

Scallop Shell

This fan-shaped shell is ribbed. At its base are two triangles. One kind of scallop shell is purple.

Thorny Oyster Shell

This shell has long spines. It is often white, but it can be purple, red, or yellow!

Conch Shell

This spiral-shaped shell may have knobs and a lip! These big shells can be yellow, white, and brown.

©The Education Center, Inc. • THE MAILBOX® • Primary • June/July 2002 • Key p. 313

Note to the teacher: Use with "Underwater Discoveries" on page 288.

289

Name_____

House Hunting

Help each hermit crab find its new home.
Read the clues. Fill in the chart.
Draw a ✓ if the information is true.
Draw an X if the information is not true.

Pincher					
Crabby					
Hermie					
Crawler					
Sleepy					

Clues
• Crabby does not want spots on his shell.
• Hermie wants a smooth, round shell.
• Pincher wants a spotted shell.
• Crawler does not feel safe in a fan-shaped shell.
• Sleepy wants a shell with spines.

Study the chart.
Finish each sentence.

1. Pincher is moving into _____.

2. Crabby is moving into _____.

3. Hermie is moving into _____.

4. Crawler is moving into _____.

5. Sleepy is moving into _____.

©The Education Center, Inc. • *THE MAILBOX®* • *Primary* • June/July 2002 • Key p. 313

290   **Note to the teacher:** Use with "House Hunting" on page 288.

SOCIAL STUDIES
UNITS

Talk of the Town
An Exploration of

Hear ye! Hear ye! This collection of ideas transports students to colonial times and builds their understanding of communities in the process!

ideas contributed by Linda Masternak Justice, Kansas City, MO

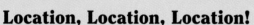

Location, Location, Location!

When the colonists arrived in North America, one of the first things they decided was where to establish their new community. They carefully considered the resources of various locations before selecting a site. Have your students follow suit and put their own decision-making skills to the test. First, tell the class that the selection of a community location was very important to the colonists. Encourage students to share their ideas about the reasons why, pointing out that the location directly influenced the colonists' lifestyle and livelihood. Then give each student a copy of page 295.

To complete her sheet, a student writes several advantages and disadvantages of living in each described location. Then she cuts two 9" x 12" sheets of white construction paper in half to 6" x 9". She glues each completed fact sheet on a separate piece of construction paper. She titles and illustrates the remaining construction paper to make a booklet cover. Then she stacks the cover atop the prepared sheets and staples the entire stack along the left edge. Finally, for each fact-filled page, she illustrates a corresponding scene on the facing page. At the completion of the project, invite students to tell the class which location(s) they prefer and why. Then poll the class to determine which location is tops among your students.

There was plenty of seafood to eat!

Gather Round!

Once colonists decided where to settle, they quickly set to work building their homesteads. Use this ongoing display idea to help your youngsters "build" their own colonial community. In advance, choose a type of location for the community or use the preferred location from the previous idea on this page. Cover the top portion of a large bulletin board with blue paper to represent the sky. Prepare the rest of the board to reflect the chosen location.

Tell students that many early colonists lived in one-room cabins that had shingled or thatched roofs. Every home had a fireplace that provided light and gave heat for warmth and cooking. Glass was expensive, so many families covered the window openings with oiled paper. Next, give each student a six-inch construction paper square. Instruct him to cut away the corners from one end of the square to make a house shape. Have him use construction paper, waxed paper, crayons, and glue to add desired details. Cluster students' houses on the prepared bulletin board and staple them in place.

After all of your youngsters' houses are displayed, have students share their thoughts about why the colonists grouped their homes. Lead the class to conclude that the closeness offered protection and enabled the colonists to share resources.

a Colonial Community

A Growing Community

Since there were no factories or large stores 400 years ago, it's no surprise that the colonists relied on their collective efforts and skills for needed resources. As tradespeople established businesses, the community grew dramatically. To expand the community your class created (see "Gather Round!" on page 292), duplicate the job descriptions on page 296. Cut the strips apart and then pair students. Give each twosome a strip, a 3" x 5" card, and a 4" x 6" rectangle cut from a brown paper lunch bag. On the card, the students summarize the assigned tradesperson's duties and how the person contributed to the community. To make a building for the corresponding business, the youngsters use crayons and construction paper scraps to add details to the brown paper rectangle. They include a sign that reflects the tradesperson's role. Then they flip the building over. The students place the card facedown on the building so that the bottom edges of the card and building are aligned. They tape the top of the card in place.

Help students reach a consensus about where to place the completed buildings in the community display; staple the top of each building to the board. Ask one student in each pair to read aloud her building's sign. Challenge the class to guess the community role of the corresponding tradesperson. Then have the student reveal the card and read it aloud to check the guesses. Later, arrange for volunteers to use arts-and-crafts materials to complete the display with additional scenery.

Laws of Selected Communities

- A poor man cannot have clothes that are as fancy as those of a rich man.

- Sledding is against the law.

- Every man must work on the town roads each month.

Fair Is Fair?

Every community needs laws to guide its citizens, and a colonial community is no exception! Point out that just as class rules help students know what to do, community laws help citizens know what to do. Share the laws listed on this page. Then encourage students to speculate about the reasons for the laws and how the laws might have impacted the community. On provided paper, have each student write a persuasive paragraph that tells whether he does or does not think a chosen law was fair and then sign his paper. Ask him to mount his work on a 9" x 12" sheet of manila paper, roll the paper, and then tie it with a length of ribbon. Collect students' resulting scrolls and place them in a basket.

To share students' opinions, give the news-related role of town crier an editorial twist. Each day of your study, select a desired number of scrolls and provide access to a small handbell. In turn, unroll each scroll and announce the owner's name. Then ask him to ring the bell and read his paragraph aloud. Now that's a newsworthy way to strengthen persuasive-writing skills!

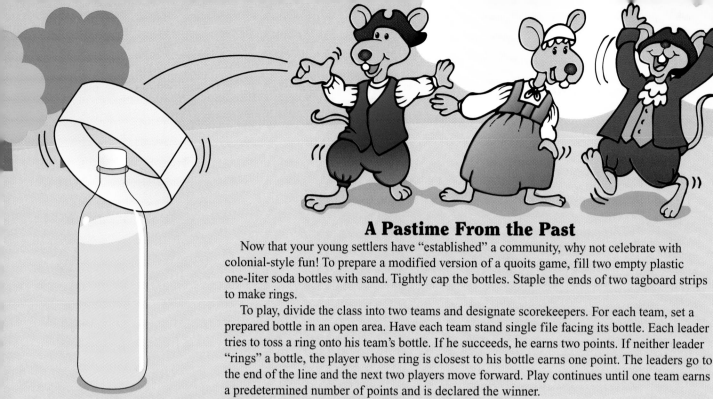

A Pastime From the Past

Now that your young settlers have "established" a community, why not celebrate with colonial-style fun! To prepare a modified version of a quoits game, fill two empty plastic one-liter soda bottles with sand. Tightly cap the bottles. Staple the ends of two tagboard strips to make rings.

To play, divide the class into two teams and designate scorekeepers. For each team, set a prepared bottle in an open area. Have each team stand single file facing its bottle. Each leader tries to toss a ring onto his team's bottle. If he succeeds, he earns two points. If neither leader "rings" a bottle, the player whose ring is closest to his bottle earns one point. The leaders go to the end of the line and the next two players move forward. Play continues until one team earns a predetermined number of points and is declared the winner.

Communities Then and Now

There's no place like home, or is there? Help students compare colonial communities with their own to determine the answer. Draw a T chart on a sheet of chart paper. Label the first column "Then" and second column "Now." Ask students to brainstorm characteristics of colonial communities. List the information in the first column. Then, for each characteristic, enlist students' help to write the comparable present-day information. Compare and contrast selected characteristics and the related basic needs or wants. Guide students to realize that even though the two communities look very different, they have underlying similarities.

Then	Now
A town crier spread the news in many towns.	People might get the news from newspaper, TV, radio, or the Internet.
People traveled by wagons, horses, and boats.	Transportation includes airplanes, trains, boats, and cars.
Young students used hornbooks.	Young students use books, computers, and other materials.

The Best of Both Communities

Put a creative spin on the theme of *Town Mouse Country Mouse* with this colonial and contemporary mouse mobile! Share selected colonial-themed resources to review what students know about the colonial community and to provide examples of clothing from that era. Then give each student two 3" x 5" cards. Have her title one card "Colonial." Ask her to write what she most likes about colonial communities and why. Instruct her to title the second card "Today" and complete it for her own community. Next, distribute the listed materials. Use the provided directions to guide each student in making a mouse mobile. Suspend students' completed projects from the ceiling to provide an eye-catching perspective on communities!

Mouse Mobile

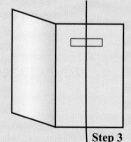

Step 3

Materials:
2 copies of the mouse pattern on page 296   crayons
9" x 12" sheet of construction paper   string
6" x 9" piece of yellow construction paper   tape
access to a hole puncher   glue
scissors

Directions:
1. Draw and color desired details on the patterns to make a colonial-style and a present-day mouse.
2. Fold the construction paper in half and glue a mouse on each side.
3. Unfold the paper. Tape a length of string to it as shown. Glue the paper closed.
4. Glue one prepared card in the center of the yellow paper. Cut around the card to make a cheese shape. Glue the second card on the other side.
5. Use a hole puncher to assemble the mobile as illustrated.

Location 1

This area is a forest. It has small streams. A lot of small animals live here. The land is rocky and the soil is very thin.

advantages: _____

_____

disadvantages: _____

_____

Location 2

This area is on the coast. It is a big fishing port. There are trees and rivers nearby. Some rivers are used for travel.

advantages: _____

_____

disadvantages: _____

_____

Location 3

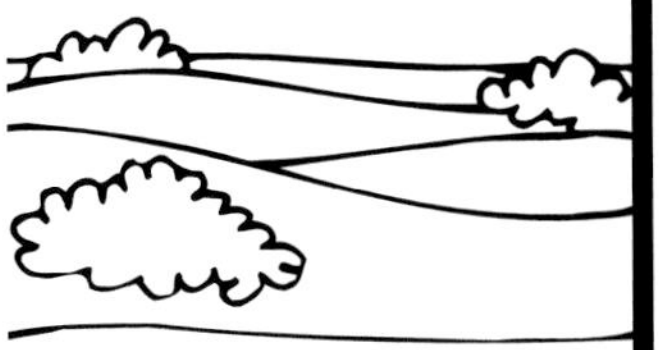

This area is inland. The climate isn't too hot or too cold. The soil is perfect for wheat, corn, and many other crops.

advantages: _____

_____

disadvantages: _____

_____

Patterns

Use the job descriptions with "A Growing Community" on page 293.

Apothecary **Job:** to supply medicines or herbs to sick people	**Milliner** **Job:** to mend and sew clothes
Cooper **Job:** to make barrels, buckets, and pails	**Wheelwright** **Job:** to make wheels for carriages and wagons
Blacksmith **Job:** to make iron tools and other items, such as horseshoes, pots, and nails	**Silversmith** **Job:** to use metals such as silver and gold to make spoons and candlesticks
Cobbler **Job:** to mend old shoes and make new shoes	**Cabinetmaker** **Job:** to make furniture, repair musical instruments, and make clock cases
Miller **Job:** to make cornmeal and flour by grinding corn and wheat	**Whitesmith** **Job:** to repair and make tin items, such as candleholders and foot warmers
Leatherworker **Job:** to make harnesses, saddles, and shoes from leather	**Clockmaker** **Job:** to make the insides of clocks
Basketmaker **Job:** to weave baskets	**Founder** **Job:** to melt together metals to create new metals
Brickmaker **Job:** to use clay and molds to make bricks	**Bookbinder** **Job:** to sew the pages of a book together and then fasten them to covers

Use the mouse with "The Best of Both Communities" on page 294.

©The Education Center, Inc. • THE MAILBOX® • Primary • Oct/Nov 2001

Zip Around the Zoo With Map Skills

Why not take this direct route to reinforcing your youngsters' map skills? After all, a zoo is the perfect place for map skills to come alive!

ideas by Laura Wagner, Raleigh, NC

Off to the Zoo!
Skill: purpose of maps

What's the best way to locate favorite exhibits at the zoo? By using a map! Help students draw the same conclusion with a quick and easy activity. First, write on the board a list of your youngsters' favorite zoo attractions. Next, ask students how they could find these attractions at a zoo they'd never visited before. Entertain all answers, eventually leading students to conclude that using a map is the most practical and timesaving approach. Post the list of zoo attractions for later use. Then invite students to describe times they or their families have relied on maps for directions.

A Bird's-Eye View
Skill: map point of view

A little bird can help students gain perspective on map point of view! In advance, suspend a colorful bird cutout above a table and display a map on the table. Tell the class that a bird and a map go hand in hand because a map shows an overhead view of a designated area. Prompt students to explain why a map showing a ground-level view would not be very helpful. Next, divide students into pairs. Ask each twosome to select a different entry from the class list of zoo attractions (see "Off to the Zoo!" on this page) and create a model for it. Provide assorted arts-and-crafts materials for this purpose. When the models are ready, remove the map from the table and assist students in assembling a tabletop zoo community. Challenge each child to draw a map of the zoo on provided paper— from the bird's view, of course!

The Key Is Key
Skill: map key

Reinforce that a map key is the key to reading a map! Make student copies of page 299. Cut away the map key on each copy and set it aside. Then give each child a map of Zippity Zoo. Ask students a few map-related questions, such as "What is on display at exhibit number 4?" and "Where is a good place to buy a hot dog?" Students will quickly surmise that a valuable part of their maps is missing! Then hand out the map keys. Proceed with a question-and-answer session, making sure every child has an opportunity to participate. Next, ask each student to color her map key and then color her map to match. Have her mount her work on a 9" x 12" sheet of construction paper. Collect the projects for later use with "Made to Measure" on page 298.

A Sense of Direction
Skill: cardinal directions

During this partner game, students discover that cardinal directions take them places! Give each child a copy of page 300 and an envelope for storing game pieces. A student colors the animal pictures and cuts along the bold lines. Then he writes his first and last initials on the back of his gameboard and each game piece.

To play, two students sit side by side. They stand a tagboard folder (or something similar) between them so that their gameboards are shielded from each other. Partner 1 places an animal cutout in a blank space on his gameboard. He tells Partner 2 which animal he selected, and Partner 2 lays the matching game piece on his gameboard in the square marked with a dot. To complete his turn, Partner 1 gives Partner 2 the cardinal directions for moving his game piece to the selected location. Next, Partner 2 takes a turn in a like manner. Play alternates between the players until each player has all eight animals placed on his gameboard. Then the partners compare their gameboards and assess their knowledge of cardinal directions!

Grids Are "Grrreat"!
Skill: map grid and coordinates

Students will agree that, when it comes to locating places on a map, grids are "grrreat"! To provide practice using a map grid, make a copy of page 300. White-out the black dot and compass rose on your copy and then label the rows with letters and the columns with numbers. (See the illustration.) Each child needs a copy of the resulting grid and his animal game pieces from "A Sense of Direction." For a large-group activity, have each child place his animals on his grid according to the map coordinates that you provide. When all eight animals are in place, check the students' work. Then have them clear their grids and prepare for another round of play. Repeat the activity as many times as desired, changing the locations of the animals each time.

For a partner activity, have students play a version of the partner game described in "A Sense of Direction." Instead of using cardinal directions to guide their partners, students must provide map coordinates.

Made to Measure
Skill: map scale

Make maps even more meaningful by introducing map scale. Remind students that a map represents an area that is much larger than the map itself. This means that places on a map will look smaller and appear closer together than they actually are. To demonstrate, give each child his map from "The Key Is Key" on page 297. Ask a volunteer to estimate the distance between the lion exhibit and the snake exhibit. Confirm that without a map scale there is no way to be sure. Then write on the board the map scale "1 inch = 1 mile" and have students use their rulers to determine the distance. Explain that even though the two exhibits look close together on the map, this map scale reveals that at the zoo the exhibits are about one mile apart! Continue to prompt your youngsters to find the distances between additional pairs of zoo attractions, using the provided scale.

In conclusion, remind students that a mapmaker must show accurate location and distance on the maps he makes. Then challenge your budding cartographers to create new maps of their tabletop zoo (from "A Bird's-Eye View" on page 297) that include map keys, map grids, and map scales! "Zoo-rific"!

Name _____

Zippity Zoo

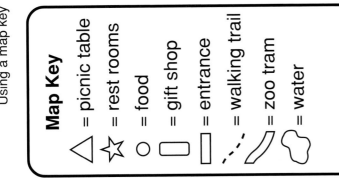

Map Key

△ = picnic table
☆ = rest rooms
○ = food
▭ = gift shop
▯ = entrance
⸝⸝ = walking trail
⟋⟍ = zoo tram
⬭ = water

○ = exhibits
1. chimpanzees
2. lions
3. snakes
4. polar bears
5. elephants
6. birds
7. insects
8. zebras

©The Education Center, Inc. • *THE MAILBOX*® • *Primary* • Dec/Jan 2001–2

Note to the teacher: Use with "The Key Is Key" on page 297 and "Made to Measure" on page 298.

299

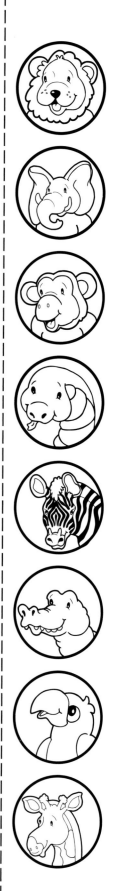

©The Education Center, Inc. • THE MAILBOX® • Primary • Dec/Jan 2001–2

Note to the teacher: Use with "A Sense of Direction" and "Grids Are 'Grrreat'!" on page 298.

TEACHER
RESOURCE IDEAS

WINDOWS ON LEARNING

Tips and Ideas for Student Portfolios

What's a proven way to get a clear view of your students' progress? By keeping portfolios! Use these practical suggestions to establish, manage, and celebrate collections of student work!

From Scrapbooks to Portfolios

Students' understanding of portfolios is sure to grow with this memorable introduction! Share with students a scrapbook from your childhood. Then, for each of several pages, ask students why they think the featured items are included. Lead the youngsters to conclude that each item reflects something significant about your childhood. Point out that collectively the items show how you changed as you grew older. Next, explain that throughout the year each student will compile a similar collection of keepsakes called a *portfolio*. The portfolio will celebrate the youngster's growth as a student by highlighting particular school accomplishments. And just like a scrapbook, it will undoubtedly become a treasured keepsake!

Kimberly Minafo
Pomona, NY

Go for the Goal!

Kick off a year of learning with portfolio-based goals! Display a large goalpost-shaped cutout on a bulletin board titled "Go for the Goal!" Prepare a number of football-shaped templates, each from a 9" x 12" sheet of tagboard. Give each student a quarter sheet of blank paper. Ask her to write an academic goal for the coming months. Then meet with students individually to discuss their goals as the class makes football-shaped folders to showcase their writing.

To make a folder, a youngster folds a 12" x 18" sheet of construction paper in half and traces a template on the fold as shown. The youngster carefully cuts along the tracing through both layers of paper. She writes her name on the front of the folder, draws lacing and stripes, and glues her teacher-approved goal inside. Staple each student's football to the board so that it can open. As you coach students in their learning, encourage them to keep their goals in mind and save any related work in their portfolios for later evaluation. Now that's an approach to learning that really scores!

Sue Lorey
Arlington Heights, IL

September 2001
My goal is to do a better job of explaining how I solve math problems.

Portfolio Pictures

A picture is worth a thousand words, so what better way to save student projects than with photos? Send a letter home to parents explaining that samples of student work will be collected throughout the year to document youngsters' learning. Further explain that some completed assignments do not lend themselves to easy storage, but that photos are great substitutes. Invite each family to donate one roll of a specified type of camera film to be used for this purpose. Their contributions will help make portfolio management a snap!

Tami Bertini—Gr. 1
Gladbrook Elementary
Gladbrook, IA

Pocket Organization

Plenty of storage space unfolds with this handy portfolio folder! To make a folder, fold the long side of a 22" x 28" sheet of poster board up approximately six inches. Firmly crease the fold and then staple the outer edges to form a pocket. Next, fold the poster board in thirds; then unfold. Label the three resulting pocket sections as desired (see the example). After each student personalizes the front of his folder, store the folders alphabetically in a plastic crate.

Darcy Brown
Elon College Elementary
Elon College, NC

Box Them Up!

Showcase creativity, accomplishments, and photos with these multipurpose portfolios! Give each student an unused pizza box. Ask her to use provided arts-and-crafts materials to decorate the box as desired. Next, have her label the front edge of it with her name. Photograph each student. Instruct her to mount the snapshot on the underside of the box lid and date it. Provide each youngster with separate subject folders to store in her box. Then stack the prepared boxes in a designated classroom location, making sure that the names are visible. When a youngster has work to add to her portfolio, ask her to retrieve her box and slip the work into the appropriate folders. At the end of the year, snap another photo of each student to mount beside the first one.

Rebecca Cobble—Gr. 3
McDonald Elementary
Mohawk, TN

A Clear Solution

If your students' portfolios are housed in three-ring notebooks, this tip is for you! To store a small or odd-shaped item, hole-punch the side of a gallon resealable plastic bag. Add self-sticking hole reinforcements for extra durability. Label the bag with the date and title of the corresponding assignment, secure the bag in the notebook, and then slip the item inside. There you have it—portfolio storage made clear and simple!

Colleen Fitzgerald
Crofton, MD

Choices That Stick!

Here's a colorful approach to portfolio organization! Display a key like the one shown. For each student, staple an open envelope to the inside of a manila folder. Place a supply of yellow and green circle stickers inside the envelope. As you grade assignments, mark each one that you would like added to a youngster's portfolio with a red circle sticker. Have the youngster store all of his graded work for the week in the prepared folder. Then, at the end of the week, he selects one assignment for his portfolio. He uses the stickers to code this assignment and any other uncoded work. The student adds the appropriate assignments to his portfolio and takes the green-coded assignments home.

Kimberly Minafo
Pomona, NY

Assignment Key

○ = teacher selected
○ = student selected
○ = take home

Blue-Ribbon Work

Honor jobs well done with this pride-boosting idea! For each student, arrange for a family member to view the youngster's portfolio at school. After each student shares the portfolio with his guest, have the family member select the assignment that he likes most and explain why. Provide him with a length of narrow blue ribbon and a blue circle sticker. Instruct him to fold the ribbon in half, place the folded part near the top of the chosen assignment, and then press the sticker atop it to hold the ribbon in place. The student returns the blue-ribbon work to his portfolio for a lasting reminder of the well-deserved praise. Outstanding!

Kimberly Minafo

Revealing Reflections

Teachers and students alike gain insight when youngsters' reflections become part of their portfolios! Stock an area near your students' portfolios with copies of the form on page 305. When a student chooses an assignment for her portfolio, she completes a copy and staples it to her work. Not only will the youngster learn to recognize her accomplishments, but you'll also know how she feels about her progress!

Linda Masternak Justice
Kansas City, MO

Portfolio Picnic

No ants or pesky flies at this picnic—just plenty of proud students and parents! At the end of the first grading period, schedule an indoor picnic to acquaint parents with your class portfolio process. Send home picnic-themed invitations. On the designated date, cover tables with red-and-white-checkered cloths. Set out cold drinks and picnic baskets stocked with pretzels or chips for refreshments. Invite students to sit with their parents at the tables or on provided picnic blankets. Have each child explain to his parent(s) how and why work is selected for his portfolio and then share the assignments it holds so far. This relaxed review of student work is bound to be a hit, so plan to schedule an end-of-the-year picnic too. Parents (and students!) will treasure the progress revealed by the completed portfolios!

Linda Masternak Justice

You are invited to a portfolio picnic!

Why: To celebrate our work

When: Friday at 1:00

Where: Ms. Justice's room

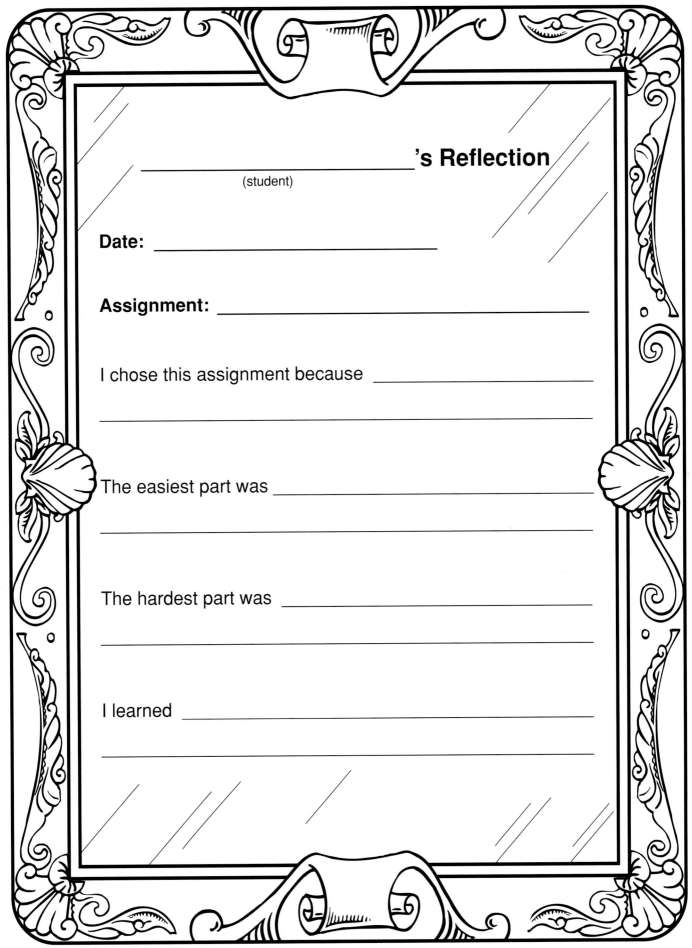

_____'s Reflection
(student)

Date: _____

Assignment: _____

I chose this assignment because _____

_____

The easiest part was _____

_____

The hardest part was _____

_____

I learned _____

_____

©The Education Center, Inc. • *THE MAILBOX®* • *Primary* • **Aug/Sept 2001**

Note to the teacher: Use with "Revealing Reflections" on page 304.

Six Super Suggestions for Using Parent Volunteers

Don't turn that page! Even if at this very moment you are without a single volunteer, these suggestions may be just what you need to entice parents into your classroom!

Web Site Work

Keeping up with your classroom Web site just got easier! Find out which students have Web-savvy parents. Then enlist qualified volunteers to digitally photograph classroom events, post digital photographs online, and assist you in maintaining and updating the site. You'll have happy parent helpers and a growing number of online visitors—and you can't beat that!

Peggy Bruno—Gr. 2, Squadron Line School, Simsbury, CT

Book Quests

If you've often wished for additional student books on a specific topic, try this! Recruit a parent (or two) who enjoys books and has easy access to the public library. About a week before you introduce a topic, ask the parent to check out from the local library student-appropriate books on the topic and bring them to school. Provide additional guidelines as needed. Preview the books and then make suitable titles available for classroom use. When it's time to return the books, ring the parent with your request.

Elizabeth Stalb—Gr. 1, St. Joseph School, Oradell, NJ

Once a Month

Here's an easy-to-manage approach to using parent helpers. Every month invite parents into the classroom to assist students with a theme- or season-related project. The extra help from parents allows students to engage in more complex activities. And the monthly invitation gives parents an ongoing opportunity to keep in touch with classroom events. Open your door to parents each month and positive parent relations are sure to follow!

Karen L. Bryson—Gr. 1, McKinley Elementary, Philadelphia, PA

Think Tank

What's the perfect undertaking for eager parent volunteers? Try a think tank, a place where parent volunteers assist small groups of students with special projects. Designate classroom space for the think tank and invite volunteers to decorate the area. Then enlist parent help as needed to assist students with enrichment projects, remedial activities, computer-related experiences, and other small-group endeavors. Parent volunteers and students are sure to think the world of this opportunity!

Janet Finley Landry—Gr. 3, Wren Hollow Elementary
Ballwin, MO

Celebrating With Centers

The next time you plan a learning celebration that requires students to rotate through a series of center activities, think parent helpers! Arrange for one parent volunteer to be at each center. Ask the helper to explain the provided activity to each new group of students and help the youngsters stay on task so they complete the activity in the allotted amount of time. Parents see first-hand how learning is being reinforced and you are free to move around the room. Now that's a perfect plan!

Nancy Lujan—Gr. 3, C. I. Waggoner Elementary School
Tempe, AZ

Writers' Workshop

Having the assistance of parent volunteers during writers' workshop is a dream come true! Recruit one or two volunteers per scheduled writing session. When a parent helper arrives, pair her with a child who is ready to have a conference about his writing. For best results, designate two writing elements on which you'd like the adult to focus during the individualized session. You'll quickly discover that meeting the needs of budding authors is easier when volunteers are involved!

Christine Schirmer—Gr. 1, Van Zant Elementary
Evesham Township, NJ

A High-Flying Skill Review

Take to the skies for a spectacular display of skill review! Pick and choose favorites from this carefully crafted collection of games and activities. Then watch in awe as young aviators perform breathtaking skill-related maneuvers.

Bid and Spell

For this inviting spelling review, compile a list of words for which all students are held accountable. Make student copies of the list. Also gather class-created books (and projects) from the past year. You need one per child. Organize the books into five groupings. Label each grouping for a different day of the school week. Also prepare a sign-up sheet for each grouping with the same number of spaces as group items.

To announce the five-day spelling auction, hand out student copies of the spelling list, show students the groupings of books, and explain that every child must bid and spell during one auction. Ask students to sign up for an auction day and study the provided word list.

To conduct an auction, introduce the day's participants and then present a book for bidding. Start the bidding at one word and end it at five. When the bidding is closed, announce a spelling word. Ask a child from the audience to repeat the word and say it in a sentence. Ask the winning bidder to spell the word. If his spelling is correct, select another word and repeat the spelling process as described, or award the student the book if he's fulfilled his bid. When a misspelling occurs, the next highest bidder spells to win. If there is not another bidder, set the book aside and reintroduce it later in the auction. Continue the auction until each of the day's participants wins a book!

Tammy Trouchon—Gr. 3
Meadowlark Elementary
Gillette, WY

In the Bag!

Skill review is in the bag when you take this approach! Label individual index cards with skill-reinforcing tasks (or questions) and program each card with a point value that reflects its difficulty level. To review skills, divide the class into small teams. Give each team a dry-erase board and marker and a paper towel (for erasing the board). Every team draws a card from the bag and completes the task or question on its board. In turn, each team shares its card and answer with the class. If a team is correct, award the team the points shown on its card and place the card in a discard pile. If a team is incorrect, return the card to the bag and award no points. Continue the game as described until one team earns a preset number of points or time runs out. Thank all teams for their efforts, and give the team with the most points an enthusiastic round of applause. Return the task cards to the bag for a future game and add new cards as desired.

Rhonda Fischer—Gr. 2
Cambridge Elementary School
Cambridge, MN

Canned Review

Try this canned approach to reviewing key concepts! Display a decorated container atop your desk and keep a fine-tipped marker and a supply of tongue depressors handy. Program one end of each of several individual depressors with large-group tasks that review key skills. Deposit the tongue depressors in the container so that the programmed ends poke out of the top. Each day a child removes from the container a tongue depressor with visible programming, reads the task aloud, and leads the class in completing it. Then he returns the depressor, placing the programmed end inside the container. When all the tasks have been completed, flip the tongue depressors and repeat the process. Add and remove programmed tongue depressors to reflect your students' current needs.

Anne E. South—Gr. 2
East Oro Public School, Orillia, Ontario, Canada

Sing "Mrs. South Had a Vowel."

Beginning with January, say the months of the year.

Skip-count by fives from 30 to 85.

Millionaire Wanna-Be

This takeoff of a popular television game show creates an uplifting skill review! Select a panel of contestants and use a basic math fact for the qualifying round. The child who is first to answer the qualifying fact becomes the first contestant. To begin play, ask the contestant a multiple-choice question. The contestant may single-handedly answer the question, or he may ask for assistance in one of the following ways: ask a classmate, poll the class, or narrow the field of answers to two. If he answers correctly, he earns $200,000. Five correct answers earns him millionaire status! If a child answers incorrectly, he returns to the audience and another qualifying round is completed. When every child on the selected panel has been a contestant, choose a new panel of youngsters or stop play for the day. A rich review of skills is guaranteed!

Phyllis Bowling
Hamilton, AL

Spin to Win

Put skill review into motion with this class game! Make a large tagboard spinner like the one shown that features different point amounts and a directive or two. To play, divide students into small teams, assign a recorder in each group, and give each recorder paper and pencil. Pose a question and allow 30 seconds for each team to discuss the question and write its answer on paper. Check each team's answer. A correct answer earns one spin for the team. Have each team keep a tally of its earned points. Continue play for as long as time permits. To conclude the game, have each team take a final spin without answering a question. Award double points for each final spin. Now that's putting a spin on skill review!

James W. Shafer—Gr. 3
Ramsey Elementary School
Monroeville, PA

Take one more turn!
100
300
400
700
200
500
600

Xs and Os

Playing this version of tic-tac-toe results in a fun skill review! Cut 18 six-inch squares from tagboard. Label nine of the squares "O" and nine "X." Laminate the resulting cards for durability. Use masking tape to create a tic-tac-toe grid on the floor.

To play, divide the class into an X team and an O team and have the teams sit on opposite sides of the grid. Ask review questions, alternating between the teams. Give each team 30 seconds to agree upon and state its answer. If a team's answer is correct, one player takes a team card and sits with the card in a strategically selected grid square. (If desired, have team members count off to determine order of play.) If an answer is incorrect, give the question to the opposing team. If the opposing team responds correctly, it makes its play and then play resumes with this team. If another incorrect answer is given, provide the correct answer before resuming play as described above. Play continues until one team wins the game (in which case the team members chant their team name three times in a row) or the game is a draw. Play as many games as time allows!

Rob Bauer
South Newton Elementary, Kentland, IN

The answer is the moon.

The Answer Is...

To give your next skill review a clever twist, provide the answers instead of the questions! Divide students into small groups. Number the groups and designate a recorder and a reporter in each one. On the board write "The answer is [the answer]." Challenge each group to generate questions for the provided answer. After several minutes, direct team recorders to put down their pencils. Ask Team 1's reporter to provide the first question. Then, in numerical order, invite each remaining reporter to share a question. Award one point for each correct question that is not a duplicate. Continue in this manner. When all questions have been shared, provide a different answer and begin a new round of play. To assure that every team has an opportunity to provide the first question of a round, play as many rounds as there are teams. Gather the first question of each round from the team having the same number.

Patricia B. Wright
Bloomington Elementary
Bloomington, TX

Breakfast for the Brain

Begin each day with a four-course brain booster! Have four different review questions on display when students arrive. For the first task of the day, have each child answer the questions on paper. Collect the papers at the same time each morning and then ask a different volunteer to answer each question. In a matter of minutes, your youngsters' brains are warmed up and ready for takeoff!

Robin Greene—Gr. 3
Mosheim Elementary, Mosheim, TN

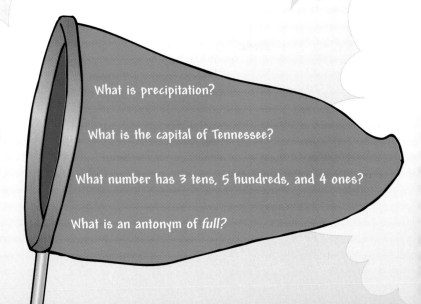

What is precipitation?

What is the capital of Tennessee?

What number has 3 tens, 5 hundreds, and 4 ones?

What is an antonym of *full*?

Page 72
1. the shamrock
2. the pot of gold
3. the rainbow and the harp
4. Answers will vary.
5. Answers will vary.
6. Larry will probably never need to give up his pot of gold because it is pictured on the smallest section of the spinner. This makes it the least likely object to be stopped on.

Bonus Box: Answers will vary. However, to increase the odds, the pot of gold must be shown on a larger section of the spinner.

Page 151
-ay	-ip	-ock	-ash
day	dip	dock	dash
hay	hip	hock	hash
lay	lip	lock	lash
ray	rip	rock	rash
clay	blip	block	clash
(flay)	clip	clock	flash
	flip	flock	
	ship	shock	

Page 154
Cowpoke Chitchat
Answers will vary. Each sentence must contain a subject and a predicate. Possible answers include the following:

Our campfire looks red at night.
A rattlesnake scares the cattle.
That silly cowpoke sings silly songs.
Charlie the cook eats marshmallows.
My old hat smells bad.
The wind feels cold.

Chili and Biscuits
1. (Charlie is the trail cook. He likes to make chili and biscuits.)
2. (His chili is hot. It is made with hot peppers.)
3. His biscuits are soft and fluffy.
4. Everyone knows when Charlie is cooking chili and biscuits.
5. The yummy smell travels for miles.
6. (Horses love the smell. Cowpokes love the smell.)
7. (What is that smell? Could it be chili and biscuits?)
8. (It's time to head back to camp. Charlie is cooking.)

Page 160
The rhyming pairs are as follows:

thud, mud	thump, bump
squeak, peek	laugh, giraffe
cock-a-doodle-doo, you	clatter, matter
bray, neigh	shout, out
quack, black	toot, boot
cluck, truck	bang, sang
rumble, mumble	hee-haw, saw
yell, well	ding-dong, long

Page 167
a.	4 quarters		k.	10 dimes	
b.	20 nickels		l.	2 half-dollars	
c.	5 dimes	2 quarters	m.	5 dimes	1 half-dollar
d.	50 pennies	10 nickels	n.	75 pennies	5 nickels
e.	4 nickels	8 dimes	o.	12 nickels	4 dimes
f.	30 pennies	7 dimes	p.	80 pennies	2 dimes
g.	50 pennies	2 quarters	q.	15 nickels	1 quarter
h.	50 pennies	1 half-dollar	r.	10 nickels	5 dimes
i.	5 nickels	3 quarters	s.	25 pennies	15 nickels
j.	10 nickels	1 half-dollar	t.	2 quarters	1 half-dollar

Bonus Box: Answers will vary. Each coin set must include three different kinds of coins and equal 100 cents.

Page 168
I like to count Aunt Dew's pennies.	My son thinks I don't understand Aunt Dew.	I look exactly like my father.	I want Aunt Dew to start a new life in her new home.
I no longer live in my own house.	My past is important to me.	I like to move to the music.	I am 100 years old.
I think Aunt Dew does not like me.	I play music for Aunt Dew.	I threw away some of Aunt Dew's things.	I hid some of Aunt Dew's things in the closet.

Bonus Box: Answers will vary. Responses may include that John is Michael's father and Ruth's husband. When John was young, his parents drowned in a boating accident. After John's parents died, Aunt Dew raised him. John loves Aunt Dew very much.

Page 173
1. Accept any two of the following: cyclone, twister, whirlwind
2. warm, funnel
3. Answers will vary but may include the following: Get inside and go to the lowest floor. Get in a cellar if possible. Do not open any windows. Do not stay in a car. Hide in a ditch if you are outside and cannot get inside.
4. Answers will vary.

Page 184
1. c
2. g
3. i
4. j
5. h
6. f
7. d
8. a

Bonus Box: Students should have copied sentences **b** and **e**. The rewritten sentences will vary but should include figurative or folksy language.

Page 195
Answers may vary. Possible answers are shown below.

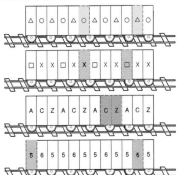

ANSWER KEYS

Page 200

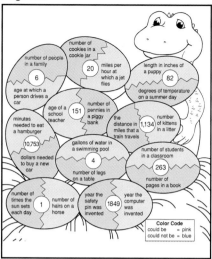

Bonus Box: Answers will vary.

Page 211

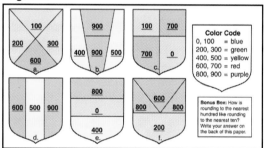

Bonus Box: Answers will vary. Students may respond that in both cases the number is rounded to the higher ten or hundred if the number being rounded is at least halfway between the tens or hundreds it falls between.

Page 221
Trail Mix

½ c. oat cereal	¼ c. raisins
1 tsp. sunflower kernels	¾ c. honey-graham cereal
3 tsp. M&M's candies	¼ c. pretzels

Page 230

Moon Pounds	1	2	3	4	5	6	7	8	9	10
Earth Pounds	6	12	18	24	30	36	42	48	54	60

Pounds on the earth	Pounds on the moon
42	7
18	3
60	10
3	½
3	½
6	1
6	1
6	1
36	6
12	2
18	3
24	4

Answer: Yes
Explanation: Student explanations will vary but should include the following information: Elsie would weigh 60 pounds on the moon. The total weight of her supplies equals 39 pounds. So with her gear, Elsie would weight 99 pounds.

Page 236
1. a. outer ear   e. middle ear
   b. canal   f. inner ear
   c. sound waves   g. signals to your brain
   d. eardrum
2. Answers will vary.

Bonus Box: Answers will vary. Possible answers include the following: Do not put objects in your ears. If a noise hurts your ears, cover them immediately. Avoid listening to loud music. Keep your ears clean.

Page 237
1. dog   6. yes
2. dolphin   7. a. bat
3. dog   b. dolphin, robin
4. grasshopper   8. less
5. yes

Bonus Box: The dolphin hears the largest range of sound. An explanation for how a student determines this must also be provided. Accept all reasonable explanations.

Pages 242 and 243
Order of answers will vary.
elephant: I use my tusks to move fallen trees and dig for water.
walrus: I use my tusks as hooks when I climb out of the water and onto ice.
gopher: My long front teeth help me dig underground tunnels.
colugo: My teeth are shaped like small combs. I use them for grooming!
beaver: I use my sharp front teeth to cut down trees!
squirrel: I gnaw open nutshells with my front teeth.
hippopotamus: I yawn and show off my sharp canine teeth to scare away a rival.

Page 248
1. Oceans <u>cool</u> the earth.
2. Fertilizer is <u>harmful</u> to oceans.
3. It is important to keep sea water <u>clean</u>.
4. Oceans are a source of helpful <u>medicine</u>.
5. Oceans provide <u>jobs</u> for people who work.
6. Oceans supply <u>seafood</u> to eat.
7. Never put <u>chemicals</u> in the ocean.
8. The sun is <u>important</u> to the ocean.
9. <u>People</u> must take better care of the oceans.
10. Oceans belong to <u>everybody</u>.
11. Oceans make <u>oxygen</u> to breathe.
12. <u>Never</u> dump garbage in the ocean.
Bonus Box: Answers will vary.

Page 256
1. tortoise
2. hognose snake
3. scarlet snake
4. chameleon
5. crocodile
6. frilled lizard

Page 264
Estimates will vary. The actual measurements are listed.
Stripes: 3 paper clips, approximately 5 kidney beans, 5 Unifix® cubes
Patches: 4 paper clips, approximately 7 kidney beans, 6 Unifix® cubes

Bonus Box: Answers will vary. Students might notice that Patches's leaf is longer than Stripes's leaf by one or two units. They might also notice that both leaves measure a greater number of beans and cubes than paper clips.

Page 241

Tooth Tally

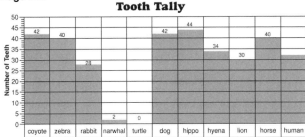

Bar graph showing Number of Teeth:
- coyote: 42
- zebra: 40
- rabbit: 28
- narwhal: 2
- turtle: 0
- dog: 42
- hippo: 44
- hyena: 34
- lion: 30
- horse: 40
- human: (32)

1. six
2. hippo
3. two
4. coyote
5. zebra
6. more teeth
7. lion
8. hippo

Bonus Box: Students should answer "no." Explanations will vary but must provide support that the number of teeth an animal has is not related to its size. For example, a student may explain that a lion is larger than a dog, yet a dog has the greater number of teeth.

Page 246

Answers will vary.
1. I have learned there are more oceans on Earth than there is land.
2. Yes. "Blue planet" is a good nickname for Earth because most of the planet is covered by oceans.

Page 255

1. A mother sea turtle lays her eggs. She returns to the sea.
2. A baby sea turtle breaks free of its egg.
3. A baby turtle crosses the sand and enters the sea.
4. A baby turtle hides in seaweed. It eats very tiny animals.
5. A young turtle grows into an adult.
6. A mother sea turtle returns to the beach where she was born.

Page 261

Year	Average Price of 1 Dozen Eggs
1900	
1910	
1920	
1930	
1940	
1950	
1960	
1970	

10¢ 20¢ 30¢ 40¢ 50¢ 60¢ 70¢ 80¢ 90¢

1. 1900
2. 1920
3. no
4. Answers will vary. Accept all reasonable responses.
5. Answers will vary. Accept all reasonable responses.

Bonus Box: Answers will vary. Accept all reasonable responses.

Page 269

44 times

II	III	IIII	THL	THL I	THL II	THL III	THL IIII
Night 1	Night 2	Night 3	Night 4	Night 5	Night 6	Night 7	Night 8

Page 279

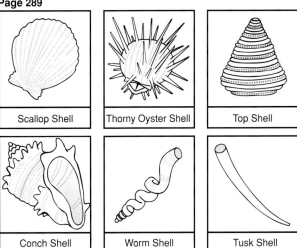

1. ~~Gus whistled for 10 seconds.~~
   He ate 7 buttercups.
   Then he ate 6 more buttercups.
   How many buttercups did Gus eat?

2. ~~Yesterday Gus gained 2 pounds.~~
   Today Gus weighs 11 pounds.
   Gus wants to gain 8 more pounds.
   How much does Gus want to weigh?

3. Gus ate 9 flowers.
   ~~He took 2 bites of grass.~~
   Then he ate 4 more flowers.
   How many flowers did Gus eat?

4. ~~Gus and Gill ate 19 flowers.~~
   Gus ate 7 flowers.
   Gill ate 12 flowers.
   How many more flowers did Gill eat than Gus?

5. Gus gathered 15 cups of grass.
   He ate 7 cups of grass.
   ~~He ate 8 flowers.~~
   How much grass is left?

6. ~~Gus ate for 18 minutes.~~
   Greta ate for 16 minutes.
   Gill ate for 12 minutes.
   How much longer did Greta eat than Gill?

7. Gus weighed 18 pounds last October.
   On February 2 he weighed 9 pounds.
   ~~Gus weighed 10 pounds.~~
   How many pounds did Gus lose?

8. Gill weighs 10 pounds.
   Greta weighs 12 pounds.
   ~~Gus weighs 14 pounds.~~
   How much do Gill and Greta weigh together?

Speech bubble: Cross out the information you do not need!

1.	2.	3.	4.	5.	6.	7.	8.
7 + 6 13 buttercups	11 + 8 19 pounds	9 + 4 13 flowers	12 − 7 5 flowers	15 − 7 8 cups	16 − 12 4 minutes	18 − 9 9 pounds	10 + 12 22 pounds

Page 280

Guide Word	Entry Word	Guide Word	Bonus Box
plum	porcupine	post	8
hammer	hamster	handle	6
gentle	gerbil	germ	3
vinegar	vole	vote	12
chin	chipmunk	choke	2
good	gopher	gorilla	4
gruff	guinea pig	gum	5
squid	squirrel	stack	11
moon	mouse	mud	7
bear	beaver	bee	1
race	rat	reach	10
potato	prairie dog	press	9

Page 289

Scallop Shell | Thorny Oyster Shell | Top Shell
Conch Shell | Worm Shell | Tusk Shell

Page 290

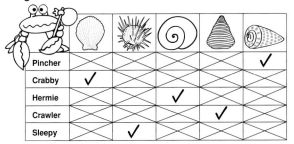

	(scallop)	(urchin)	(spiral)	(top)	(spotted)
Pincher					✓
Crabby	✓				
Hermie			✓		
Crawler				✓	
Sleepy		✓			

Wording of answers may vary.
1. the spotted shell
2. the fan-shaped shell
3. the round shell
4. the top-shaped shell
5. the shell with spines